W9-DGL-829

AFRICAN INDUSTRY IN DECLINE

African Industry in Decline

The Case of Textiles in Tanzania in the 1980s

Peter de Valk

Senior Lecturer in Development Economics
Institute of Social Studies
The Hague

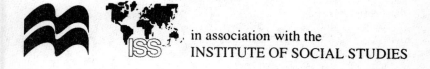

in association with the
INSTITUTE OF SOCIAL STUDIES

HD
9867
.T32
V338
1996

First published in Great Britain 1996 by
MACMILLAN PRESS LTD
Houndmills, Basingstoke, Hampshire RG21 6XS
and London
Companies and representatives
throughout the world

A catalogue record for this book is available
from the British Library.

ISBN 0–333–65445–5

First published in the United States of America 1996 by
ST. MARTIN'S PRESS, INC.,
Scholarly and Reference Division,
175 Fifth Avenue,
New York, N.Y. 10010

ISBN 0–312–16021–6

Library of Congress Cataloging-in-Publication Data
Valk, Peter de.
African industry in decline : the case of textiles in Tanzania in
the 1980s / Peter de Valk.
p.   cm.
Includes bibliographical references and index.
ISBN 0–312–16021–6 (cloth)
1. Textile industry—Tanzania.   2. Textile industry—Africa, Sub
-Saharan.   3. Tanzania—Economic conditions—1964–   4. Africa, Sub
-Saharan—Economic conditions.   5. Structural adjustment (Economic
policy)—Tanzania.   6. Structural adjustment (Economic policy)–
–Africa, Sub-Saharan.   I. Title.
HD9867.T32V338   1996
338.4'7677'009678—dc20   95–52538
                                                            CIP

10   9   8   7   6   5   4   3   2   1
05 04 03 02 01 00 99 98 97 96

Printed in Great Britain by
Ipswich Book Co. Ltd, Ipswich, Suffolk

Contents

List of Tables and Figures

Tables

Figures

1 Introduction

This study is motivated by the desire to understand the reasons for the slow and difficult process of industrial development in most of sub-Saharan Africa in the 1980s – a period of economic crisis and subsequent structural adjustment. Although mostly cast in economic language, the account of the process of industrialization in this book is both tragic and dramatic. While in the 1980s other parts of the developing world have taken major strides towards becoming industrialized countries, most African countries have stagnated and declined. In the late 1960s and most of the 1970s, state-led, import-substitution-based industrialization in Africa recorded impressive achievements in terms of growth of value-added, capital stock, and employment. Investments were financed by both high rates of domestic savings (initially) and large inflows of foreign aid. State participation in production was high but private sector firms also thrived in this period. But towards the end of the 1970s and continuing into the 1980s overcapacities developed and, with a lag, investment growth slowed down, with negative rates of growth of manufacturing value added recorded in the 1980s..Donor support first declined and later shifted from investment support to import support for production. Stabilization and structural adjustment policies came to dominate the macroeconomic policies of most African countries, exposing the weaknesses of many industrial sectors. Yet no coherent policies focusing explicitly on the industrial sector were included (Riddell 1990).

Even research on the impact of these adjustment policies on the industrial sector is largely missing, although more studies exist for the small-scale industrial sector (Pack 1988; de Valk and Mbelle 1990). Moreover, most research on developing countries tends to converge on the orientation of trade and industrial policies, generally joining the debate on export-oriented versus import-substitution strategies, to the neglect of the 'structural' factors that studies on developed countries focus on (Lall 1990:11). However, to really understand the problems of industrialization it is absolutely necessary to study the working of the economy not only at the level of macroeconomic and trade policies and their impact on the industrial sector as a whole, but also at the level where concrete decisions are made with regard to production characteristics (Helleiner 1990). Industrial development implies growth in the number and size of firms, their efficiency and productivity. Thus, the main actors are owners, managers and workers of firms, who work and decide in an

1

environment influenced by government, national and international conditions and institutions.

In recent debate on industrialization strategy the role of the state has been given much attention. The new orthodoxy, based on successful experiences in industrialization of East Asian countries, recognizes the fundamental role of the state and government administration in the development process of latecomers. However, both for an enhanced understanding of past experience as well as for a better appreciation of possible impacts of transferring successful policies from one continent to another, an analysis of the nature of the state and the functioning of government administration in the relevant countries is required.

It is interesting to note that though the question of 'the state versus the market' is debated quite heatedly in development literature, the equally important issue of 'the firm versus the market' has received much less attention. The internal structure of a firm can be viewed as a non-market form of organization which provides the necessary coordination and motivation not supplied by the market. Transaction costs determine which activities will take place inside the firm and which will be purchased on the market. The better the market functions, the lower the transaction costs, and the fewer the activities internalized by the firm. The recent innovation in production efficiency termed 'flexible specialization' (whereby firms react quickly to changing market conditions both on the input and output side aided by computerized production methods) can only be profitable under near-perfect market conditions (with efficient market institutions and fast and reliable market information). The extreme case is that of an ideal market in which firms are reduced to mere production functions (i.e. without any physical counterparts). In contrast with a flexible specialization situation, firms operating in the less perfect markets of developing countries attempt to bring more activities under their control by vertical integration, expanding their scope of action, and the formation of wider business groups. Market organization and firm organization are hence directly related. Similarly, innovations in market efficiency and production efficiency go hand in hand.

However, the distinction between market efficiency and production efficiency is not all that clear. From the point of view of one firm, the market has several dimensions (apart from the usual distinction between capital, labour, and product markets): there are its competitors, its suppliers of inputs, the buyers of its outputs, financial and legal servicing institutions including that of government support activities and socio-cultural institutions. The competitiveness of its competitors (efficiency and the degree of concentration) influence its profits negatively and drive it to greater efficiency, while the efficiency of provision of inputs and services positively affects it. This somewhat diffuse distinction between the individual actor and the aggregated outcome reflects the tense relation between the micro and the meso level.

A thorough understanding of interactions between production and domestic and international markets will lead to a better appreciation of what has happened under structural adjustment policies and of the type of difficulties involved in deriving policies and strategies based on successes under different market and production conditions. These differences combine to create conditions that allow firms to earn higher than 'normal' profits or to survive while being inefficient. A number of such differences are summarized below.[1] In the first place, despite the achievements of the 1970s, many developing countries (particularly those of sub-Saharan Africa) have small industrial sectors (the size of the industrial sector is often taken as the main indicator of economic development), concentrating on the production of final goods, often agricultural resource based, and dependent on imported industrial inputs with few linkages between domestic industries.

Second, given their population size and low income levels, even the demand for basic goods is relatively low in many countries, implying that a few medium-scale firms can supply the market, leading to conditions that facilitate oligopolistic behaviour.

Third, markets are underdeveloped and/or imperfect (compared to 'best practice' in developed countries). Formal capital markets are mostly lacking altogether; labour markets are fragmented spatially and by skill categories, and partially controlled by minimum and maximum (public sector) wage legislation. Exchange of goods and services is seriously impeded by poor communication and transport networks. Moreover, all markets are partially formal and partially informal with complex and often diffuse relationships between them.

Fourth, the industrial structure in developing countries is characterized by forms of ownership unlike those in developed countries. In the first place, for a variety of reasons (see section 2.2.7, below) the state participates in production on a large scale far beyond the level of intervention prescribed by orthodox economic theory. This gives rise to interdependencies between private and public sector firms with regard to pricing, supply of credit, allocation of foreign exchange, and donor support. Moreover, in both the public and the private sector, different forms of ownership exist: in the public sector, there are joint ventures, foreign management contracts, technical assistance schemes, fully government-owned and -managed companies; in the private sector there are subsidiaries of multinational firms, individual domestic firms, firms as part of domestic economic groups as defined by Leff (1978),[2] and firms owned by 'alien' entrepreneurs (Kilby 1983). Some of these categories overlap. Access to foreign exchange, technology, skills, finance, government, domestic and foreign markets, as well as export and investment behaviour differ among these groups.

Fifth, national and firm-level technological capability is weak, leading to technological dependency (Lall 1992). This results in a high share of imports in the supply of capital goods, low capability to adapt technology, and limited maintenance skills. Most technological change results from the imports of more recent vintages of capital goods, since indigenous technological change is almost completely lacking. Surprisingly, despite the low technological capacity and the abundant availability of unskilled and semi-skilled labour, there is a tendency towards adoption of capital intensive technology, especially by large scale, public firms (Perkins 1983, James 1989, Bagachwa 1992). Choice of sophisticated technology limits the capability to operate, adopt, maintain and repair such technology.[3]

Sixth, in some instances and by various means, forward vertical integration has included wholesale and retailing networks, adding further muscle to monopolistic arrangements forcing horizontal product differentiation onto the consumers.[4]

Further, balance of payments problems have made inputs scarce. Simultaneously, competitive imports are restricted through import licensing. This translates into low capacity utilization and undersupply of the final product market.

Finally, protection is high for final goods, and progressively lower for intermediate and capital goods. This, coupled with overvalued currency, leads to potentially high profit margins (or high inefficiencies) and favours capital intensive production and reliance on imported intermediate inputs.

In short, spatial monopolies, oligopolistic conditions, high protection levels both in terms of price and quantity, involuntary capacity under-utilization, and factors related to the structure of ownership, create an environment in which firms are able to survive despite inefficiencies caused by low technological capabilities. This pushes market prices upwards to the disadvantage of the consumer, fostering parallel market operations and the formation of larger economic groups.

The survival of firms is threatened when foreign exchange shortages become too severe to maintain productive capital and to achieve minimal levels of capacity utilization. Moreover, because of the adjustment policies that characterized the 1980s, firms which had been enjoying protection (of one form or another) suddenly needed to be able to compete with imports while prices of tradeable inputs were increasing relative to prices of their output.

With these differences in markets and production in mind, it will be clear that direct transfer of industrialization policies that were successful

in developed countries to developing countries will be far from straighfor-
ward. Policies for least developed countries derived from the flexible
specialization paradigm provide a case in point.

Thus, while the international textile market has become increasingly
competitive and flexible, the firms in the least developed countries remain
constrained by their poorly-functioning markets and hence attempt to
bring more of the economic environment under their control through vertical intergration. Under these conditions, even if the efficiency of the firms
is low, the market efficiency would be lower. With the advent of structural
adjustment policies, the efficiency of internationally competitive firms
operating in efficient domestic markets is let loose on the local economies
in the form of low-priced commodities of good quality. While this is a
boon for the consumers, the competitive imports do not improve the
efficiency of the local market but pass all of their competitive challenge on
to the domestic firms. In those countries where customs systems are
corrupt and/or inefficient, imports enter even more cheaply into the
domestic market. In order to survive, even with the very low labour costs
typical for least developed countries, firms have to be super-efficient.
Alas, most are not, having been bred and nurtured in inefficient markets
under protective conditions which allowed levels of industrialization
beyond the available managerial capability. Thus, the domestic market
will be lost and without a healthy domestic market share, the export
market is not easy to play. This, in very broad terms, explains the current
period of stagnation and de-industrialization in Africa.

THE APPROACH OF THE STUDY

What were the detailed reasons behind this stagnation and decline? Three
main avenues are explored to shed some light on this question: theory,
comparative experience, and detailed empirical research on a single case
study: textiles in Tanzania.

First, the theoretical investigation is both discouraging and challenging
since there is no single body of theory which exhaustively explains the performance of enterprises. Most theories of industrial performance are based
on developed country conditions. But, as summarized above, the development literature on industrialization stresses a number of differences with
developed countries. Appreciating these differences is also essential in
understanding the limitations of these theories. Given these differences, few
theories directly apply to the industries of developing countries. But an
overview of theory is helpful to extract useful elements that can be used as a

basis for an eclectic and more general theoretical framework, better adapted to the circumstances of developing countries. Based on this framework, the performance of manufacturing firms is analysed as the outcome of an interplay of factors at four distinct levels: at the international, macro-, meso-, and micro-levels. The international level comprises factors such as developments in technology and trade, international institutions, and policies of other countries. At the macro-level the main factors are macroeconomic policies and constraints, and the role of the state. At sectoral level industrial structure influences performance through factors such as the degree of competition, structure of ownership, marketing arrangements, and the regional structure of production. Micro-level factors consist of structural and behavioural characteristics of individual firms.

Second, empirically, a comparative perspective for the textile sector developed, with regard to technology, international trade institutions and world trade flows, and textile policies. Countries are compared on a technology ladder; their development path is defined in terms of textile trade, and the nature and scope of their policies. This provides classifications of African countries in terms of their industrial and technological development. This overview of experiences with and policies on the textile sector of selected countries in Europe, Asia, and Africa throws up interesting similarities and differences. Moreover, technical performance of Tanzanian enterprises is compared to that of leading firms in the rest of the world which are used as a benchmark for 'best practice'.

Third, the case study focuses on textile firms in Tanzania mainly discussing the period from 1980 to 1990. The comparative analysis shows that the particulars of Tanzania's experience are not unique in Africa. Although large differences in industrial performance exist among African countries, common trends with Tanzania emerge not only in countries comparable in terms of industrial development but also in the more successful countries.

The textile sector is an interesting sector to study. One could argue that if a country is not able to produce its own textiles, it has a problem with industrialization. Because of characteristics of technology and consumer preferences textile production is a common element in early import substitution strategies. In Tanzania, as in many other African countries, it is a rather large sector with both public and private ownership. The main input, cotton, is grown locally and partially exported. The output of textile firms can be exported at various stages of production; in the form of yarn, grey cloth and finished cloth. These may also be used as inputs to other local textile firms and producers of garments. Therefore, linkages exist with the world market at both input and output level as well as with agriculture, industry and consumers. Internationally, the textile sector is transforming itself from a standardized industry to become a high-tech industry. All these factors combine to make textiles a relevant sector to study in more detail as a case of industrial development.

The case study will reveal that, despite the general decline, performance of firms in Tanzania was highly dispersed. Particularly, private firms belonging to an economic group, with a high degree of vertical integration, were amongst the best performers, close to international standards. Also some public sector firms fared well, although many did not. Moreover, individual firms performed differently with regard to technological, organizational and financial management, and in terms of export achievements and investment efforts. Microeconomic explanations of these differences are found in factors related to technology, management, debt–equity ratios, supply of utilities and the structure of ownership. At the level of the sector, the degree of market control contributed to performance. Macroeconomic explanations are found in the specifics of trade policy and monetary policy: structurally, the persistent foreign exchange shortages, which have been the result of the inward looking approach to industrialization, were at the basis of the decline. Generous credit policies were used to keep many firms alive. Policies to redress the macroeconomic imbalances have aggravated the situation. Trade liberalization resulted in large inflows of cheaper commodities thus effectively reducing demand and exerting downwards pressure on prices, while the corresponding devaluations not only increased cost of production, but also dramatically increased the costs of servicing foreign loans and of replacement investments. Tight monetary policies have resulted in acute liquidity problems, while higher interest rates have increased cost of production without mobilizing domestic savings. The resulting supply squeeze points at the inflationary and contractionary consequences of this combination of policies, which is reinforced by the particular employment policies of parastatals.

The empirical evidence with regard to the various models of the firm found in economic literature tend to support behavioural explanations (in particular the Evolutionary Model of the Firm), coupled with elements of Principal-Agent theories and Transaction Cost Economics stressing the role of entrepreneurship, in interaction with structural characteristics of the firm and the economic environment, government policies, and the nature of the state. Sectoral factors (but not of the type stressed by the Structure-Conduct-Performance Model) play only a minor role. Three factors combine to limit the applicability of the Structure-Conduct-Performance Model: the predominance of micro- and macro-explanations of performance, the importance of structural factors related to the whole manufacturing sector rather than the textile subsector, and the influence of firm behaviour on sectoral structure.

By examining performance and its causes, this study provides insight into the scope and limitations of renewed industrial development in Africa. This development will entail, in the first place, revitalization of existing plants, higher degrees of capacity utilization, better management, higher quality, and, for some efficient firms, new investments. Macroeconomic policies need to be fine-tuned: targeted constraint relief to (potentially) efficient firms is required. Contrary to the dominant export-led-growth paradigm, the role of exports must be seen as to overcome the domestic constraints of limited markets and foreign exchange shortages. Only then, in the long term, will fully-fledged export-oriented development, integrated with local capabilities, become feasible. The findings of this study show further that, while it is widely assumed that African textile firms are inefficient, performance of Tanzania's textile firms ranges from fairly efficient (some firms are close to international standards) to very inefficient. Explanations of these differences suggest that the relationship between firms' characteristics, their micro- and macro-policy environment, and industrial performance need to be examined far more closely, both theoretically and empirically.

EXPLAINING PERFORMANCE

This book is about explaining performance of manufacturing firms. This formulation of the book's objective is deceptively simple. 'Industrial performance' is a rather complex concept and what constitutes 'explanation in social science' is not a simple question either. As the end of Chapter 2 will show, the resulting analytical framework will have to reflect these complexities. The remainder of this section summarizes some of the pertaining methodological issues with regard to industrial performance and explanation in social science. To begin with the former, performance is first of all a *relative* concept in three different ways:

(a) Performance is always in relation to an objective which means that it matters a great deal from which point of view performance is evaluated. For example, a firm can do very well in terms of its own objective, be it short term profit maximization or long term survival, without necessarily contributing to the national objective of expanding industrial exports.

(b) Performance towards an objective takes place in an environment in which active variables both affect the objective and restrict the possible ways in which to reach the objective.

(c) Standards are required for its evaluation, implying the need for a comparative perspective. These standards may originate from engineering data, 'best practice' firms, international data on cost structures, or on size and structure of the industrial sector.

Second, performance can be evaluated in terms of *statics* (for given structural parameters such as technology) or *dynamics* (with reference to changes in those parameters as they occur internationally).

Third, the issue of industrial performance can be addressed at *different levels* (firm, sector, nation) and the *scope of explanation* may vary. Thus, macroeconomic analysis often collapses all firms of the whole industrial sector into a set of equations describing production, income, savings, investment as if dealing with only one firm or a very limited number of sectors.[5] Neoclassical theories of the firm contrast with the more sectoral focus of the 'structure-conduct-performance' framework whereas 'New Industrial Economics' advances one more step on the latter by making 'structure' an endogenous concept of its theorizing. 'New Institutional Economics' expands the scope of its investigation even further in attempting to relate performance to an explanation of economic institutions such as markets and the firm.

Fourth, performance implicitly includes the *behaviour* (conduct) of human actors.[6]

The question of why people behave as they do constitutes the core issue of social science and leads again to questions related to the nature of explanation in social sciences. Explaining behaviour with regard to industrial performance, first of all, raises the set of questions related to the nature of explanations of behaviour and, second, the issue of the feasibility of partial analysis.

Starting with the first, behaviour can be classified in basically three different categories:

(a) rational behaviour as an outcome of a (sub-)conscious decision process to achieve desired objectives;
(b) programmed behaviour that can be characterized as following pre-determined patterns under certain circumstances (instincts, habits, traditions, routines, institutions); and
(c) non-explainable behaviour, that is not covered by (a) or (b).[7] Keynes' label of 'animal spirits' characterizing investment behaviour of entrepreneurs may serve as an example.

In real-life situations, behaviour will normally involve varying degrees of all three elements. The general assumption underlying social science explanation of behaviour is rationality. The debate within social science concerns not so much the rationality assumption *per se* but rather the type of rationality and the extent to which one type of rationality rather than another can explain the situation.

In most conventional economic theories, fully rational behaviour (complete information and knowledge and unlimited computational capacity) is assumed, often combined with rational expectations,[8] i.e. all individuals assume that all other individuals are also rational and each individual is only concerned with his/her own objectives (optimizing welfare) or, in other words, derives no benefit from changes in others' welfare that leave their own welfare unchanged.[9] In addition, most neo-classical theories of the firm apply the single actor model and consider only economic objectives. The assumption of full rationality and perfect information should be accompanied by another assumption which is essential for the model to work: perfect capacity to implement decisions. This introduces yet another element of remoteness from reality into the model.

In contrast, other theories discuss more disaggregated firm models, for example the Principal-Agent Theory, which separates managers and owners, or addresses organizational issues (such as the Organizational Theory of the Firm).

The assumption of full rationality is relaxed by the concept of 'bounded rationality' which acknowledges that information and computation include costs. Hence, bounded rationality can be understood as full rationality under constraints. A more fundamental definition of bounded rationality takes the existence of pervasive uncertainty or 'un-knowledge' as the essential element of boundedness (Lippman and McCall 1984; Wiseman 1991). Rather than defining rationality as a behavioural principle, Nelson and Winter (1982) in their Evolutionary Theory of the Firm focus on the decisions-making process and derive a form of sequential rationality. However, more disaggregated firm models consider 'procedural rationality' and the possibilities of conflict and conflict resolution as manifestations of bounded rationality.[10]

In much of the debate on rationality, the issue is not so much on the rationality assumption *per se* or even what type of rationality applies in a particular situation, but rather, the question of what is the subject of optimization or using concepts from welfare theory, what are the important variables in the utility function: 'company man', 'public man', 'bureaucratic man', 'economic man', 'engineering man', or 'family man' and their accompanying rationalities. In some cases different objectives of rationality overlap: a 'family man' may behave as a 'company man' within a particular incentive system. In a wider sense, this may be caused by socioeconomic, political and cultural institutions.

Thus questions arise about the role of institutions in facilitating 'collective' action in situations where individual interests prevail (non-cooperative games dominate). The most important of these is the state (in the widest sense), i.e. its apparatus and the prevailing ideology as it is expressed, interpreted, reproduced, and adjusted in the transfer of values in families, the educational system, and the wider society. The role of institutions in facilitating, shaping and conditioning behaviour has been stressed by the New Institutional Economics, thereby introducing elements of programmed behaviour into the analysis.

Analytical partiality can be either disciplinary or systemic. This study's systemic partiality is noted in the Introduction focusing on a subsystem of the wider national system, which, for purposes of analysis, is initially considered exogenous (but not necessarily constant). It analyses the ways in which exogenous changes in variables within the wider system may create effects in the subsystem that in turn have a second order impact on the wider system. However, the reverse does not hold: subsystem variables may affect the wider system, but do not generate a substantial second-order impact directed towards the original subsystem. For example, devaluation as a result of balance of payments problems will increase the costs of imported inputs used in textile production for the domestic market. This may lead to a lower effective domestic supply of textile products, which in turn might put marginally more pressure on the balance of payments and make devaluation marginally more desirable, but these second order effects are assumed small in relation to the initial devaluation.

Disciplinary partiality is another necessary ingredient of analysis (itself an instance of the bounded rationality of the author). But there are degrees of disciplinary partiality even within economic theory. There are a number of approaches to the theory of the firm and accompanying behavioural assessments. Lack of optimal performance (inefficiency) in one rational model requires for its explanation a wider rational model that can explain the inefficiency in the former as a rational outcome of the latter. What appears as unexplained (irrational) behaviour in a partial analysis may be rational in a more comprehensive analysis. Thus, neoclassical profit maximization theory of the firm is followed by profit maximization under constraint, structure-conduct-performance models, and models attempting to explain structure as well (New Industrial Economics). These in turn are followed by transaction cost models and models of organization and incentives using concepts like manager-owner conflict, principal-agent, incomplete contracts, monitoring costs, and so on.

Drawing together the various elements that have been discussed above, behaviour with respect to performance can be specified by (1) an actor (manager, owner, labourer, policy maker), (2) a behavioural rule (long- or

Table 1.1 Classification of firm models along several dimensions

Model / Theory	Actor(s)	Behaviour
Neoclassical Firm Model	Owner	Full rationality
Managerial Theory of the Firm: manager–owner conflict (Baumol, Marris)	Owners managers	Full individual rationality
Organizational Theory of the Firm: transaction cost approach (Coase, Williamson)	Owners	Bounded rationality
Oligopolistic models: game theory (Stiglitz, Schmalensee, Tirole)	Owner	Full rationality Strategic behaviour
Behavioural Theory of the Firm (Simon, Cyert, March),	Owners managers employees	Procedural rationality Conflict resolution Social rationality
Evolutionary Model of the Firm (Nelson and Winter, Leibenstein)	Owner employees	Sequentially bounded rationality routine creative strategic behaviour
Normative Theory of Public Sector Firms	Government	Full rationality
Political Market Theory of Public Sector Firms (Horn)	Managers civil servants employees	Individual rationality Bureaucratic rationality
Managerial Research Approach to Public Sector Firms (Nayar)	State managers civil servants employees	Individual rationality Social rationality

Table 1.1 continued

Auxiliary assumptions	Objective	Subject	Firm outcome
Perfect competition, information, implementation Rational expectations	Maximum profit	Firm	Maximum profit
Rational expectations, Perfect information Perfect implementation	Maximum income	Manager	Maximum growth Maximum sales Maximum profits
Limited information Limited computational power Limited implementation	Profit orientation	Firm	Maximum losses Maximum profits Long-term profit maximization
Rational expectations Uncooperative games with competitors	Market share Profit orientation	Firm	Minimum losses, Maximum profits Long-term profit maximization
—	Power Influence	Top managers	Survival Outcome of bargaining process
Limited information Limited search under uncertainty	Profit orientation	Firm	Survival Long-term profit maximization
Perfect information Perfect implementation	Maximizing employment Regional development Maximizing consumer surplus	Consumers Employees	Maximum output Maximum employment
Lack of accountability Many channels of influence Expanded objectives	Maximizing actors' income under constraints	Managers Civil servants Employees	Survival under maximum individual exploitation
Political economic and social factors influence performance	Mixture of objectives	Firm managers	Mixed outcomes

short-run maximization, satisfying, muddling through), (3) accompanying assumptions (full information, rational expectations), (4) an objective (income, profits, market share, exports, efficiency, welfare) combined with (5) a perspective (best practice, international developments), (6) an entity (individual, family, firm, sector, national economy), and a specification of choice limiting factors, i.e. (7) institutions (choice-constituting rules) and (8) conditions (including every type of circumstance). Table 1.1 provides an overview of theories of the firm along the lines of the above specifications.

STRUCTURE OF THE BOOK

Chapter 2 of the book develops a framework of analysis to be applied in the empirical chapters. It eclectically draws on various theories of the firm, macroeconomic issues, the role of the state, and the influence of international institutions. Both private and public sector theories of the firm are discussed. It establishes a linkage between trade-related efficiency concepts and micro-level performance. It discusses the relevance of micro-level analysis to understanding macro-policy impacts, and the need to understand the nature of the state when analysing the underlying rationale of past policy interventions and evaluating the margins of future policies.

The next two chapters develop the comparative perspective. Chapter 3 starts with an overview of textile technology and related innovations, and the role of the market therein. It constructs a textile technology ladder for countries with particular focus on Africa, from which four technology groups are derived for classifying African countries. Next, international trade developments are discussed, leading to a classification of countries based on textile trade. Chapter 4 discusses the experience of individual countries with regard to textile policies followed. Based on this, countries are compared with respect to these policies discussing the role of the state, the market, technology, intersectoral linkages, and foreign linkages.

The case study begins in Chapter 5 with a historical description of the political and economic development of Tanzania focusing on the manufacturing sector and with an analysis of the role of the state in Tanzania in industrialization. The debate between the World Bank and Tanzania on restructuring the public enterprise sector is summarized. Chapter 6 presents the data on the textile sector on various performance criteria such as profits, capacity utilization, and technical coefficients for factor inputs, and derives an index for technical performance in spinning and weaving by firm. Chapter 7 presents the data on macro-, sectoral, and micro-factors that influence performance. Survey results on macroeconomic constraints (as perceived by firm managers) are presented using simple statistical description. A narrative account supported by available statistical evidence is given on the issues of credit and foreign exchange constraints. The impacts of various macroeconomic policies on the price structure of a sample of firms are discussed and the effects of problems in the supply of utilities is estimated by firm. Indicators of concentration and of regional supply and demand, and a commonsense estimation of demand in relation to supply are developed. Because of its nature, the structure of ownership can only be presented descriptively. Finally, in Chapter 8 performance data are further developed into indices and aggregated into a total performance index. Technical performance of firms is measured using the 'best practice' approach which in turn is based on measurement of relative factor inputs and concepts related to production functions. Simple descriptive statistical techniques are used for calculation of total performance indices based on calculation of organizational performance, and measurement of financial, export and investment performance. The analysis of the impact of micro-factors on performance employs cross-section econometric estimation supported by qualitative analysis for the explanation of residual variance. This is backed up by a more descriptive account of factors constraining better performance. Macroeconomic influences on firm performance are estimated in a quantitative manner with the help of econometric time series analysis and supportive statistical evidence. Chapter 9 places the conclusions reached in the individual chapters within the theoretical framework.

Notes

1. This does not imply that no great differences between developing countries exist. See for example Kirkpatrick *et al.* (1984).
2. Leff defines an economic group as 'a multicompany firm which transacts in different markets but which does so under common entrepreneurial and financial control' (Leff 1978:663). For a more elaborate description of an 'economic group' the reader is advised to consult the reference given above. Its implications for public policy are discussed in Leff (1979).
3. See Bagachwa (1992) for a recent discussion of the issue of choice of technology in Tanzania.
4. This is related to so-called Hotelling Models. See Waterson (1989) for a full discussion of both vertical (for example by quality) and horizontal (for example by transport-cost-determined price differences) product differentiation.
5. Sectoral distinctions used are often based on whether the sector is producing consumer, intermediate or investment goods, or on whether the sector is exporting, import-substituting or non-traded.
6. Many authors use the term 'behaviour' ambiguously to refer to behaviour of functions, models, systems, sectors, firms, etc. as well as the behaviour of individuals. In this study, 'behaviour' will be used to refer to human actors either individually or collectively. When used differently, it will be specified.

7. This can take two forms: behaviour that is fundamentally non-explainable which raises the philosophical question of limits of knowledge and behaviour that is in practice non-explainable because (a) there are too many causes to deal with, or (b) no theories are yet available, or (c) it falls outside the particular theory being applied. The best theory can do in the face of non-explainable behaviour is to specify the limits of theoretical explanation.

8. Although not unrelated, this definition of rational expectations is different from the Rational Expectations Hypothesis (REH) in macroeconomic theory. The REH boils down to the fact that the effects of economic policy are limited because the important actors already take the effects of economic policy into account. Thus, a government aiming at an inflation rate of, say, 4 percent would induce economic actors to take the 4 percent inflation rate as their starting point for trying to improve their position (prices, wages) thus causing higher inflation. See Colander (1979) for a Keynesian response to the critique of the REH.

9. Maximization of utility as a choice rule turns rational behaviour into pro-grammed behaviour when objectively measurable variables are maximized. In fact any type of modelling of rational behaviour turns it very much into programmed behaviour. This gives rise to the paradoxical situation that when theory attempts to explain choice by specifying choice rules, behaviour becomes determinate and no choice exists. Where no choice exists, choice rules are a misnomer. To put it more mildly, choice is limited to the extent that choice rules can explain 'choice'. A statistical way of going around this problem would be to assert that people in fact have the option to behave rationally and that most people do so. At the aggregate level then it appears as if aggregate behaviour is explained by a certain choice rule to the extent that a certain proportion of people follow that rule (this ignores problems of aggregation and the relation of 'behaviour' of statistical aggregates to the behaviour of individuals). This is the old paradox of freedom and determi-nacy in another guise. We experience a certain degree of freedom, yet our reason is caught up in causality as the basic principle for understanding. In a discussion on explaining policies, the same paradox was recently cited by Bhagwati, who coined it the 'determinacy paradox' (1991:11). Behaviour is left partially unexplained when the choice rules are not sufficient to obtain definite and particular outcomes. Non-explainable behaviour of the first kind arises when individually weighted elements enter the utility function. The principle of utility maximization is a tautological statement when revealed preferences are called upon to save the principle: what in the end individuals have chosen to do maximizes their utility by definition.

10. See March (1978) for an overview of definitions of different types of rationality. Hargreaves Heap (1989) offer a more philosophical treatment of rationality in economics and identifies three basically different types of rationality: instrumental (neoclassical), procedural (behavioural) and expres-sive rationality. Instrumental rationality is equated to the neoclassical use of rationality (utility maximization); procedural rationality relates to the behav-ioural view of rationality; and expressive rationality is explained as an attempt of individuals to express their own way of making sense out of life and related values in action and choice of procedures. Expressive rationality can be under-stood as an attempt to come to grips with the paradox of determinacy and freedom embedded in the instrumental and procedural notions of rationality.

2 Micro- and Macro-Theoretical Explanations of Industrial Performance

2.1 INTRODUCTION

Micro–macro relations run two ways. Macroeconomic variables influence microeconomic conduct and performance while micro-outcomes through aggregation and interaction affect the main macroeconomic variables. Also, government–firm relations run two ways. Firms are affected by government policies and regulations while in their turn firms, organized in lobby groups or otherwise, attempt to influence government policies to their advantage. This chapter will provide a theoretical perspective that encompasses both macro- and micro-factors of an explanation of industrial performance as well as their interaction. The first part focuses on theories of the firm relevant to the issue of performance in 'least industrialized' countries. The second part develops the macroeconomic perspective and its relation with the micro-perspective. The third part will discuss the role of the state in industrial development. Many of the claims of the individual theories are complementary. In the last part, the theoretical framework will be developed, drawing eclectically on most theories reviewed and selecting those elements of these theories that can contribute to an explanation of performance.

2.2 THEORIES OF THE FIRM

The different theories of the firm explain firm performance on the basis of different aspects. They differ first on who decides about the major issues in the firm, how they decide, what they decide upon, and the firm level outcomes. Table 1.1, above, provides a schematic overview of theories of the firm with regard to these aspects. Second, they differ in their selection and weighting of the factors of the industrial environment that determine firm performance. Thus, principal–agent theories and behavioural theories focus on the internal functioning of the firm, the managerial theory on the top management in relation to owners and shareholders (i.e. the capital market) and the structure-conduct-performance approach on sectoral structure. The widest model is the managerial research approach, developed for public sector firms, which incorporates explanatory factors located in the 'polity' as well as in the 'society'. Third, theories differ with regard to their applicability to LDC conditions (as summarized in the first chapter). Their relevance and any required modifications will be indicated where appropriate. Finally, some theories are rather specific, while others are phrased more as research programmes indicating fields of explanation rather than concrete explanatory factors.

The discussion will start with the neoclassical theory of the firm focusing on measurement of technical performance rather than on the theory itself (as this is assumed to be widely known). Progressively more realistic models will be discussed, removing the restrictive assumptions of the neoclassical model. Models of oligopolistic competition will be described as developed under the umbrella of the structure-conduct-performance approach including the latest developments in industrial economics as captured in the new industrial organization. The single actor assumption of the neoclassical theory of the firm is dropped in managerial theories of the firm. Elements of new institutional economics as these apply to industrial economics will be discussed in the section on the organizational theory of the firm. One of the main pillars of the new institutional economics, namely transaction cost economics (along with its various offshoots) has fully entered the field of industrial organization. Many of its concepts can usefully be applied to other socio-economic fields. The behavioural theory of the firm constitutes the most radical deviation of the neoclassical model dropping simultaneously the assumption of full or bounded rationality (in the limited sense of constrained full rationality) and the single actor assumption. Next, a modern variant of behavioural theory, the evolutionary theory of the firm is summarized, emphasizing its focus on decision processes and the dynamic role of entrepreneurship. After this overview of theories of the private firm, literature on state owned enterprises (SOEs) will be reviewed. SOEs are alternatively named publicly owned enterprises (POEs), public sector enterprises (PSEs), or parastatals. These names can be used interchangeably.

2.2.1 Neoclassical theory of the firm: selected issues

The aim of this section is not to give a standard treatment of the neoclassical theory of the firm, but rather, to select some concepts in relation to performance that will be used to analyse the firms featured in the case study. The main assumptions of the neoclassical model are summarized in Table 1.1.

To understand the neoclassical approach to firm performance, it is important to realize that lack of optimal performance, i.e. the existence of inefficiencies, is a deviation from the orthodox neoclassical model of profit maximization under perfect competition. This can take two forms: perfect competition may be replaced by the assumption of conditions favourable to the existence of monopoly, monopolistic competition, or oligopolistic competition, leading to economic inefficiencies in consumption and distribution of income;[1] or, under either perfect or imperfect competition, inefficiencies in production may exist, the removal of which would lead to higher returns for the firm (see below).[2] In both cases, the optimal state of affairs is in fact taken as a yardstick against which actual performance is measured. Since the latter case concerns inefficiencies located in the firm, an introduction to production functions and related concepts becomes necessary.

Firm level efficiency analysis

When a firm is established it must choose its technology from what is currently available. Its choice will depend on the relative prices for capital and labour reflected in the iso-cost line p' (price line) in Figure 2.1. The efficiency production frontier shows the most efficient technology choice

Figure 2.1 Choice of technology and techniques, and inefficiency

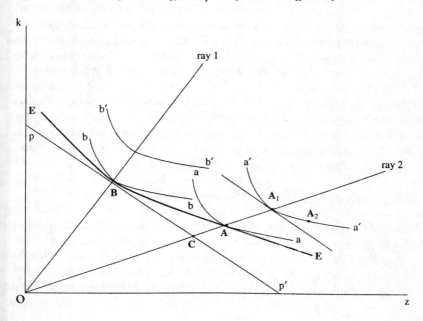

for varying amounts of capital (k) and labour (z) per unit output, for example, technology A or B. All points above the efficiency frontier use more capital and/or labour to produce the same output and are thus by this definition inefficient. With the relative prices for labour and capital given, the most efficient technology for a firm is where the iso-cost line is tangent to the efficiency production frontier. Thus, B is the optimal choice for newly acquired technology. The curve EE is the *ex ante* production function (isoquant).

After the choice has been made, some substitution between capital and labour may still be feasible for the chosen technology. This is called 'choice of techniques'. The corresponding most efficient factor combinations form the *ex post* production function. The curves aa and bb are examples of such *ex post* production functions. By definition the choice of technique functions never have greater possibility for substitution between labour and capital than the choice of technology function (since the technology function is the envelop of all choice of technique functions). The chosen technology can also be operated in a sub-optimal manner. The curves $a'a'$ and $b'b'$ show this possibility.

Thus, three different types of inefficiencies exist: (1) technical inefficiency: inefficient use of the chosen technology/technique, i.e. above the isoquant; (2) allocative (or price) inefficiency: when the firm is producing on the *ex ante* (b1) or *ex post* (b2) production function but not at the point where the price line is tangent to the isoquant. For example, at A_2 the actual point of production shows all three types of inefficiencies, A_1 reflects only (a) and (b2), while A reflects only (b1). The firm producing at B shows no technical or allocative inefficiency and is producing at a Pareto-optimum. The literature also distinguishes another measure of inefficiency, namely scale (in)efficiency. This will be discussed in the section on generalized Farell measures, below.

Discarding scale efficiency, total efficiency (*ex ante* or *ex post*) can be fully decomposed into technical and allocative efficiency. Referring to isoquant EE and point of production A_1 in Figure 2.1 (ignoring the curves aa, $a'a'$, bb, and $b'b'$), the relation between overall efficiency ($OE=OC/OA_1$), allocative efficiency ($AE=OC/OA$), and technical efficiency ($TE=OA/OA_1$) is given by $OE = AE\,TE$. This relation can be applied to both choice of technology as well as choice of techniques. These measures are usually identified with Farrell (1957) and are input based measures as opposed to output based measures. Input based measures define inefficiency in terms of the inputs that can be saved when producing one unit of output (lowering the iso-cost curve proportionally). Output based measures are defined in terms of the extra output that could be produced from the observed level of inputs (see also below).

Standardized best practice measures of inefficiency

The inefficient use of chosen technology/techniques implies less than optimal productivity of capital and/or labour. The optimal productivity for a given technique can be taken from engineering data or from what is called 'best practice' firms using a comparable technology. Since these firms may be located in different countries facing different factor price ratios, comparison of firms with their 'best practice' colleagues requires a transformation along the *ex post* production function to bring the firms on the same ray from the origin.

Total Factor Productivity (TFP) is defined as the distance from the origin to the best practice firm divided by the distance from the origin along the same ray to the transformed point on the (inefficient) *ex post* production function of the inefficient firm. Under the assumption of a linearly homogeneous production function (such as the Cobb-Douglas and CES production functions used later on), this amounts to comparing actual output to potential output with the same inputs or potential input use to actual input use for the same output.

Relative Total Factor Productivity (RTFP) is defined similarly as TFP but with reference to the 'best practice' plants rather than engineering data. When assessing managerial inefficiencies, 'best practice' comparisons giving better estimates as an engineering performance are feasible only in ideal circumstances, which cannot be found even in 'best practice' firms.

To derive an expression for relative total factor productivity for the case of a CES (constant elasticity of substitution) production function, consider two firms, A and B, of which B is the best practice firm. The CES production function for firm A is given as:

$$Q_A = C \cdot P_A \left[(1-\delta) L_A^{-\rho} + \delta K_A^{-\rho} \right]^{-1/\rho} \tag{2.1}$$

Here, δ is called the distribution parameter and ρ is related to the elasticity of substitution (σ) as $\rho = (1-\sigma)/\sigma$. C is a constant and P_A is the productivity parameter. Changing the subscript A into B gives the expression for the 'best practice' firm B. When firms A and B employ similar technologies but with possibly different choice of technique because of different factor price ratios, the RTFP measures the relative 'distance' between similar *ex post* production functions (i.e. between *aa* and *a'a'* in

Figure 2.1). To be able to measure this distance, the production function is essential to adjust for differences in factor intensity along the respective production functions of A and B.

The RTFP is obtained by deriving an expression for P_A divided by P_B:

$$RTFP = \frac{P_A}{P_B} = \frac{(Q/L)_A[(1-\delta)+\delta(K/L)_B^{-\rho}]^{-1/\rho}}{(Q/L)_B[(1-\delta)+\delta(K/L)_A^{-\rho}]^{-1/\rho}} \tag{2.2}$$

Production inefficiencies can be measured when data are available on output produced, and quantity of capital and labour used for normal operation of machines (i.e. when they are actually running). These inefficiencies are then different from other capacity reducing factors such as machine breakdown, interruptions in the supply of infrastructural inputs (water and electricity), lack of foreign exchange to purchase essential inputs and number of shifts. The RTFP thus offers an interesting opportunity to separate external from internal factors affecting efficiency.[3]

The advantages of assessing machine level technical inefficiencies are that this allows a separation of technical and economic issues at machine level and furthermore distinguishes inefficiencies arising from practices with regard to machine use when they are actually in operation from inefficiencies arising from under-utilization of plant level capacity. The intention is to incorporate this approach into the present analysis to the extent that the data permit this. Further details will be given when discussing elements of textile technology in Chapter 3 and in the empirical chapters.

By comparing firms with their 'best practice' counterparts employing similar technologies, the question of choice of technology is avoided. Actually, although it will be shown in Chapter 3 that a certain degree of choice of technology exists, the *ex ante* efficiency production frontier consist of only a few major technologies implying discontinuities in the elasticity of substitution. A well behaved *ex ante* production function as suggested in Figure 2.1 does not exist. Moreover, present structures of industrial sectors reflect choices with regard to technology made over a considerable period of time. To argue the rationality of such choice would require different research.

2.2.2 Theories of oligopolistic competition and their relevance to industrial performance

The condition of oligopoly, few firms and many buyers, together with otherwise unchanged neoclassical assumptions leads to the situation whereby the final outcome of one firm's decision with regard to output price (Bertrant competition) or quantity (Cournot competition) depends on the reactions of other firms in response to the former firm's decision. Oligopoly, in other words, becomes important when firm sizes are such that their individual decisions will affect the market conditions of other firms, forcing the latter to retaliate.

Theories of oligopolistic behaviour have constituted a growth pole in the field of industrial organization. The structure-conduct-performance approach (SCP) has been the dominant paradigm since the 1970s (Figure 2.2 provides a schematic overview). The causality runs from structure to conduct to performance. Performance covers a number of aspects: technical efficiency, allocative efficiency, profitability, technical progress, and growth. Profitability is ensured by a mark-up price, i.e. a mark-up over average costs. Essentially, this mark-up price is determined by the sectoral structure and the degree of collusive behaviour (see below). High profitability under static conditions could lead to technical and allocative inefficiency as under pure monopoly. However, competition under oligopoly can take the form of intensified search for technological change (Schumpeterian competition) and related product cycles (Vernon 1966). The innovative role of the entrepreneur is also stressed by the evolutionary model of the firm (to be discussed below), but without adopting the strict causality between structure and technological change of the SCP model. While many (textile) firms of developing countries provide instances of the tendency to reduced efficiency under conditions of higher potential profitabilty, internationally 'garments and textiles are showing signs of "de-maturing" with the advent of microelectronics-based production, data-processing, and communications systems' (Mody and Wheeler 1990:74), as discussed in detail in Chapter 3.

Conditions for oligopoly

Given the possibility of monopoly profits under oligopoly, other firms would be attracted to the industry, competition would increase and the mark-up margin would decrease. For oligopoly to persist, some conditions pertaining to its stability are necessary. The first, and perhaps the most obvious one, is when economies of scale (as discussed earlier in this chapter) are such that only a few firms of optimum size can operate in the market.

Although this condition can explain the number of firms in the market, it is not sufficient to explain stability for the individual firm when mark-up pricing is practised, since new entrants charging marginal cost prices would replace them. Indeed, the theory of contestable markets would claim this possibility as an argument in favour of the case that, even when the first condition for oligopoly applies, market prices do not deviate much from the perfect competition situation (Baumol, *et al.* 1982). Others (in fact the majority) argue that the degree of contestability is lowered by certain objective costs of entry and by strategic behaviour of incumbent firms: barriers to entry form the second condition for stability of oligopoly.

The strategic behaviour of incumbent firms towards each other forms the third condition of oligopoly: collusive behaviour either explicitly (as in cartels and collusions) or implicitly by evoking the assumption of rational expectations (i.e. a mark-up price is good for all and everyone acts as-if collusively). Models of price behaviour have been developed using the concepts of 'dominant firm price leadership', 'low-cost firm price leadership', and 'kinked demand curves' when firms do not follow a price rise of a rival but do follow a price reduction. Market arrangements may be developed and (tacitly or openly) agreed upon to maintain market shares and limit price competition: producer–distributor agreements and regionalization of markets can support the stability of the oligopolistic structure both between incumbent firms and towards potential entrants.

Quantity competition

Quantity competition can be more easily modelled than price competition, since under the assumption of a homogeneous good, price differences will lead to high demand fluctuations between firms.

For quantity competition, the mark-up price relative to average costs for an industrial sector is theoretically derived as:[4]

$$\frac{p-c}{p} = \Sigma \ s_i^2 (1 + a_i) / e \tag{2.3}$$

Thus, the performance of an industry, as measured by its mark-up price over costs, depends on three variables, two of which are structural variables: (1) the elasticity of demand (e) and (2) an index of the degree of concentration (Σs_i^2) called the Herfindahl Index, and one of which is a behavioural variable: (3) a measure of the degree of collusion between firms (a_i). This highlights the use of the name 'structure-conduct-performance' approach in industrial organization. Figure 2.2 gives a schematic version of composing elements of structure, conduct, and performance.

Measures of concentration of industrial structure

To assess the likelihood of the existence of oligopoly, concentration indices for market shares are used, the most useful of which are the Gini coefficient (GC) and the Herfindahl index or Herfindahl–Hirschman index (HI).

$$GC = (1 / T) \Sigma \ _{i=1}^{T} (T - 2i + 1)_{s_i} \tag{2.4}$$

Figure 2.2   The structure-conduct-performance paradigm

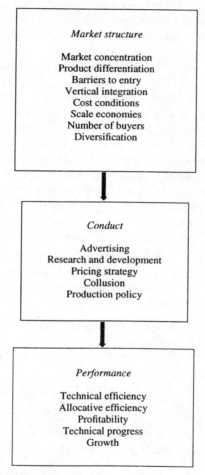

Source: Bonanno and Brandolini (1990).

The Gini coefficient is a relative index, expressing inequality in market shares compared to the case where all firms have equal shares. The Herfindahl–Hirschman index is an absolute index which depends on the number of firms in the sample. As shown in the previous section, the Herfindahl–Hirschman index has a direct economic interpretation in determining the mark-up for firms under oligopolistic conditions. In Chapter 7, where calculations are presented for capacity and production shares of Tanzanian firms, a relative version of the Herfindahl–Hirschman index is derived and compared to the Gini coefficient.

$$HI = \Sigma\,_{i=1}^{T}(s_i)^2 \qquad\qquad\qquad (2.5)$$

Inefficiency of oligopoly

As such, conditions of oligopoly do not lead to firm level inefficiencies of the type discussed earlier. The assumption of profit maximization under oligopoly and strategic behaviour towards potential entrants would dictate efficient production in terms of conversion of inputs into output. However, overcapacities may exist in order to enable firms to respond strategically. The major inefficiency of oligopoly is located with the consumers. If firms act under rational expectations they may behave as if they act collusively thereby charging higher than marginal cost prices or limiting total supply to the market to obtain higher prices. Apart from lowering the total output supplied, it also leads to a different distribution of surplus between producers and consumers.

New industrial organization

Starting with the work of Bain in the early 1950s, which culminated in his book on industrial organization (1968), the SCP approach has dominated the literature until the 1980s. Since then, the shortcomings of the SCP approach have received increased attention. It was recognized that market structure cannot be taken as exogenous to the theory and must be explained. Also, maximization of short run profits as a specification of conduct is seen as too deterministic in establishing the linkage between structure and performance. First of all, it could be argued that precisely the possibility of above-normal profits would allow firms to deviate from profit maximizing behaviour (such as 'limit pricing', management-owner conflict, and shirking, i.e. inefficient management behaviour). Second, rivalry between incumbent firms is largely ignored. Related to this is the observation that the SCP approach is basically static thereby focusing on equilibrium positions where rivalry is not acute. Finally, the assumption of symmetric information in the SCP approach has been considered unsatisfactory: information is a strategic instrument which in reality is asymmetric and differentiated.

Attempts to come to grips with the above shortcomings and limitations have been developed under what has been labelled 'new industrial organization' (Bonanno and Brandolini 1990). Barriers to entry, which previously were assumed to be determined by technology, consumer tastes and product characteristics, are now understood to be strongly influenced by strategic behaviour in the fields of investment in excess capacity and R & D, advertising, product differentiation, and contracts with customers.

The strategic use of product differentiation also influences entry conditions. With price competition, both vertical product differentiation (unambiguous ranking of consumer preference over one attribute, for example quality: when prices are the same only one product will be sold) and horizontal product differentiation (differentiated consumer preferences or tastes allow more than one product to be sold even if the price is the same) are likely to be practised (Sutton 1990). This means that strategic behaviour of incumbent firms towards each other (ensuring market shares by breaking up the market or market specialization) has consequences for conditions of entry as well.

Vertical structure has been largely ignored by the SCP approach. This may be understandable from a methodological point of view as without it the industrial sector can more easily be delineated. It is however a rather important issue with implications for entry conditions through horizontal product differentiation. Its treatment follows the approach of transaction cost economics and will be taken up in a separate section (2.2.4). Vertical integration is a typical feature of textile firms in Tanzania extending forward into distribution and retail while one firm has considered moving backward into cotton production. The reasons for this integration will be discussed in the case study.

Oligopolistic models and firm performance

The SCP model has drawn attention to characteristics of sectoral structure as determinants of performance. This study will calculate indices of concentration, discuss market structure in relation to production structure, and will show that, along with other factors to be considered (such as vertical and horizontal integration, product differentiation and foreign linkages), they are important aspects for understanding the ability of firms to secure their profitability.

2.2.3   Inside the firm: managerial, organizational and behavioural theories of the firm

The theories discussed above, dealing with the case of oligopoly, maintain the assumption of a single and rational actor (the firm). The following theories look inside the firm. The managerial theory and organizational theory maintain the rationality assumption, while the behavioural theory incorporates other assumptions like creativity, routines, and docility. The managerial theory of the firm focuses on the consequences of the separation between ownership and control, i.e. the fact that managers are important decision-making agents in the firm, with objective functions that do not necessarily coincide with that of the owners (particularly strong in the case of public enterprises). Specific models have been worked out for countries with a well developed capital market (Baumol 1959; Marris 1964). Williamson (1963) developed a model showing that, under imperfect competition with the possibility of above-normal profits, management preferences will absorb a share of these profits, leaving less at the disposal of the owners. In the form of reduced work effort (or management inabilities), these management preferences may lead to increased inefficiency.[5] The various performance indicators developed in the case study will be studied in relation to, amongst others, different forms of management.

2.2.4   Organizational theories of the firm

A major step forward in theorizing about the firm was taken with the increased acceptance during the late 1970s and the 1980s of the transaction cost approach for the explanation of a wide range of phenomena. Whereas Coase (1937) is usually identified as the originator of this brand of analysis, it was only with the work of Williamson (1975) that the transaction cost view of the firm gained ground. The transaction cost approach offers a particular mode of analysis and as such is not restricted to the economic discipline. Under the umbrella of the new institutional economics, transaction-cost-based explanations have entered many fields including law, political science, and rural development.[6]

To explain how transaction cost economizing works, assume that a business owner possesses the right technology to produce things. This owner can now enter the perfect labour market and buy labour hours, rent buildings per hour, cars and everything necessary on the (perfect) market. Suppose now that for one particular function, a worker requires some training. There are two possibilities. Either there is a market for such workers (in which case another example is required) or the worker needs skill training for the particular technology. This can be done by the worker or by the firm. In either case, the worker has become specific: a certain amount of costs have been sunk into him/her. The worker who incurred these costs is now dependent on the business owner for continued employment to recover the costs. If the business owner provided the training, the dependency is now with the latter. It is clear that this form of asset specificity calls for contractual arrangements, the terms of which will obviously depend on who is bearing such costs. The solution is to set up the contract before the costs are incurred. Thus, by contracting, what was a pure market transaction has become internalized: the firm comes into being by offering contractual employment. The particular skill that the worker required makes the trained person an example of what has been called 'asset specificity'. Given the assumption of limited use of this skill elsewhere, this skill asset has become specific. Asset specificity is defined as limitation to alternative use.

Other down-to-earth examples can be given. In regular firms, the costs of recruitment and on-the-job training can be reduced by offering employment contracts rather than by relying day-to-day on the market. Certain services not central to the production process, for example packing, could be left to the market or internalized. When the necessary packing equipment can only be used in the firm (by design, by costs of shipment, by costs of installation, etc.), asset specificity is present.[7]

Thus, explanations can be given for which transactions are better left to the market and which are internalized in the firm, thereby enhancing understanding of the size and nature of the firm. In the same vein, the issue of vertical integration can be better understood using a transaction cost approach. Moreover, development of managerial theories was spurred by the transaction costs approach, modelling the manager–owner conflict using principal–agent theory. Related is the notion that the manager–owner conflict is only one of the possible conflicts in the firm leading to more general principal–agent theories which incorporate notions of incomplete (and asymmetric) information and resulting behaviour in a theory of contracting. Together, these various strands of analysis form the theory of economic organizations (or the economic theory of organizations).[8]

Contracts governing transactions are necessarily unable to specify every routine and contingency. *Ex post* contract behaviour cannot be regulated *ex ante* (even with complete contracts) and given the assumption of opportunistic behaviour, the need for governance arises.[9] Transaction cost economics 'regards the business firm as a governance structure, rather than a production function' (Williamson 1989:136), whereas the ideal market is represented as the spot market and represents the extreme form of decentralization. Monitoring and incentive systems combine with issues of contracting in the principal–agent problem. The cost aspect of governance acts both as a limiting factor as well as a steering factor (minimization) for selecting different forms of organization, monitoring and incentive systems. It sets a constraint to firm size including the degree of vertical integration. It may be clear that the above description, as applied to firms, can easily be extended to incorporate institutions broadly defined. Governance structures then become specific institutions that regulate transactions (see also the section on theories of the state in this chapter).

Three major issues that have been put on the research agenda of the 'transaction cost economizing' approach in relation to the business firm follow quite naturally. The first relates to the question of what determines the functional size of firms: Which functions are left to market contracts and which are internalized? This in turn relates to firm boundaries (see below) and degree of vertical integration (see below). The second issue addresses the problem of separation between ownership and control (see below). How can the principal ensure, after some functions have been internalized, that the agents do what they have to do? The third issue concerns the broader question of which organizational form is best suited for what type and size of organization (see below). The latter two issues are directly relevant to performance while the former two will shed light on the observed degree of internalization of functions in relation to inefficiencies arising from underdeveloped markets. Thus, with regard to the case study, transaction costs form an important contribution to understanding the observed degree of integration in private firms facing imperfect markets for inputs and outputs. They can also be invoked to explain the observed ethnic compostion of top management of private firms.

Vertical integration

To discuss 'vertical integration' as an issue separate from the normal boundaries of the firm, it is necessary to have a view of what a 'normal' firm would look like. A high degree of vertical integration would mean high relative to that norm. Alternatively, the degree of vertical integration of a normal firm could be viewed as depending on the applicability of sets of circumstances typical to the particular industrial sector. In the latter case, explanations of firm boundaries and vertical integration coincide. Three such sets of circumstances are identified in Perry (1989): (1) technological economies, (2) transactional economies, and (3) market imperfections. To this one should add a fourth: (dis)economies of governance, which partly relate to management capacity. The cost and benefits of internalization of functions should be analyzed under the above headings.

Williamson (1989) underlines the preponderance of transaction costs minimization over production cost minimization with regard to vertical integration, since the market always produces at lower costs. With imperfect markets, not only market prices but also transaction costs are likely to increase. This connects Perry's transactional economies with market imperfections.

When it is assumed that normal firms have already absorbed all technological economies and have catered for transaction costs arising from normal market imperfections,[10] what remains to explain vertical integration is first, transactional economies and second, what is conventionally seen as market imperfections (such as conditions of oligopoly, monopoly or monopsony). In developing countries, other market imperfections exist such as unreliable supply and the variable quality of inputs, poorly developed markets for output (whether wholesale-retail networks for consumer goods or markets for intermediate goods). These would form additional reasons to internalize related functions. This suggests that firms belonging to an economic group and with a high degree of vertical integration would be the best performers. The case study will shed some light on this hypothesis.

Principal–agent theories

The earlier managerial theories of the firm focusing on the separation between ownership and control have become part of the broader organizational theory of the firm under the label principal–agent theories. Assuming opportunistic behaviour, incomplete contracts and information asymmetries (*ex ante* or *ex post* contracting) between principal and agents, adverse selection and moral hazard problems may arise and performance becomes a function of monitoring and control systems and related costs, as well as of incentives.[11] In incentive theory, the key problem for the principal is to obtain the highest level profit by designing contracts in such a way as to elicit the highest effort at least costs. The agent's problem is the opposite: how to obtain highest income at least effort. Principal–agent relations exist at different levels of the firm and one person can be agent in one role and principal in another. Firms are not only characterized by subcontracting along the lines of the firm's hierarchy but also by side-contracting and by collusive behaviour between agents. Dispute settlement will gain in importance as commitment to contract cannot be taken for granted. Monitoring systems become necessary as well as more general institutions (of the state) employed to maintain contract commitment.[12]

Various forms of discipline are acting on top managers to keep their behaviour within certain limits of the owners' objectives. These are (Holmstrom and Tirole 1989): (1) internal discipline, closely related to incentive systems and thus incentive theory which in turn is at the heart of principle-agent theory (Sappington 1991); (2) labour market discipline, i.e. managers need to perform in order to increase their market value (Fama 1980); (3) product market discipline: reduction of management slack through competition or, more subtly, through information about performance criteria in competitive (best practice) firms (this is the corollary of the argument of increased management slack under oligopolistic conditions; see Leibenstein 1976); and (4) capital market discipline, which relates to limiting take-over risks, as put forward by Marris (1964) and mentioned earlier under the managerial theory of the firm. Some of these types of discipline depend on the accuracy of assumptions about the sector and the functioning of the economic system at large. In developing countries, with less developed capital markets, a large state sector, and different macroeconomic and sectoral conditions, they will need some adaptation.

A much more limited set of factors applies to behaviour of agents below top management. The more remote agents are from strategic decision-making, the less their motivation derives from firm-level performance (capital and product market discipline) and the less firm-level performance is attributed to these agents, which attenuates the labour market discipline argument. There is, however, an internal labour market in large companies, inducing agents to follow various strategies to increase their value in that market and, through that, in the external labour market. Of the four factors mentioned above, only internal discipline remains viable for those agents who because of factors such as age, sex, race, skills, and health have few prospects for internal improvement.

Principal–agent theories provide an important basis for theories of state enterprises. The case study will show how the separation of ownership and management in the public sector has resulted in a self-defeating governance structure.

Forms of organization

Organizational design plays an important role in limiting agents' strategic behaviour. The appropriateness of an organization's design refers to a number of aspects such as the design of organizations for different functions and the design of functions within one organization. Mintzberg (1979) addresses both simultaneously and takes a positive approach to the issue of design in his attempt to explain observed forms and problems of organizations. He views coordination as the basic task of organizations and has related design of organizations to function and contingency factors such as age and size, technology, environment and power. He derives five structural configurations (idealized organizational forms) that 'represent a set of five forces that pull organizations in five different structural directions'(Mintzberg 1979:469). Each of these achieves the basic task of coordination in different ways. The five configurations are labelled (a) simple structure, (b) machine bureaucracy, (c) professional bureaucracy, (d) divisionalized form, and (e) adhocracy. Each of these configurations differs in its design characteristics and functioning and is more effective under different sets of contingency factors. Real life organizations are analysed within these dimensions in a dynamic sense: transitions occur and hybrid forms showing elements of more than one configuration exist while tensions cannot be completely solved by appropriate design. In his conclusions, he briefly contemplates the possibility of a sixth, 'missionary' configuration, ensuring coordination by socialization through indoctrination. Given the size (small to medium) and function (mass production) of firms analysed in this study, configurations that exert the strongest pull are the 'simple structure' and the 'machine bureaucracy' with the key coordination mechanism respectively direct supervision and the standardization of work. The latter mechanism was labelled 'procedural rationality' in the introduction of this chapter and is captured by the notion of 'routines' in the evolutionary model to be discussed in the next section.

Within the organizational theory of the firm, the organizational design problem is tackled differently, focusing on functions within firms rather than varying functions of organizations. It is also more rigorously backed up by various recent theoretical developments. Given its theoretical approach to a rather practical subject (coordinating opportunistic agents), it reflects a mixture of positive and normative (but at a rather abstract level) theory. Its focus on design problems with reference to particular functions within firms seems a natural contraction of focus given the subject area of organizations for market production of commodities. The following functions are distinguished: (a) flow of information, upwards for decision-making and monitoring, downwards for implementation and incentives and, depending on organizational form, laterally for coordination; (b) supervision structure; (c) incentive structure, related to internal promotion; (d) limiting side-contracting; and (e) task assignment, i.e. the right differentiation of jobs and the manner in which jobs are assigned to agents so as to maximize the benefits of comparative advantage for agents and to minimize their margins for opportunism.

Although it is clear that the above aspects are not independent of firm characteristics as elaborated by Mintzberg (1979), no systematic analysis is (yet) developed of how such internal functions relate to some less (compared to Mintzberg's approach) elaborated firm characteristics such as firm size and overall design, for example unitary form or divisional form

(U-form or M-form), and the related but wider issue of centralization versus decentralization. The firm type assumed in organizational theory is basically the 'simple structure'. The case study will show that private firms are more pragmatic with regard to their organizational structure. Public firms, inclusive of their wider control network, tend towards bureaucratic structures.

2.2.5 Behavioural and evolutionary theories of the firm

Behavioural theories of the firm go beyond the assumption of bounded rationality in the sense of maximization under constraints of time and cost of information. In addition to the problems arising from the design of an organization as stressed by Mintzberg, other elements impinging on full organizational rationality that have been included in the behavioural view are related to the consequences of conflict and power for organizational decision-making and related procedures of conflict resolution (March 1966, 1988). Moreover, Nelson and Winter (1982) acknowledge the sequential nature of decision-making in uncertain environments getting very close to Lindblom's concept of 'muddling through' (Lindblom and Cohen 1972).

Like Mintzberg, Simon sees coordination as the principal task of an organization: where markets do not coordinate, organizations will. Therefore, transaction costs are not considered to be the main explanatory variable for the existence of firms, although their relevance to explain firm boundaries is not denied. Moreover, he considers the organizational theory of the firm (identified with new institutional economics in the quotation below) as seriously incomplete: 'The attempts of new institutional economics to explain organizational behaviour solely in terms of agency, asymmetric information, transaction costs, opportunism, and other concepts drawn from neoclassical economics ignore key organizational mechanisms like authority, identification, and coordination, and hence are seriously incomplete'(Simon 1991:27).[13]

Behavioural theory acknowledges the relevance of incomplete contracts but maintains that *ex post* behaviour cannot be fully explained by strategic behaviour based on maximization of individual utility. There is some room for manoeuvre between the incompleteness of the contract, the type of *ex post* task assignment and monitoring possibilities. Not all commands can be specified to the letter. Rather than commands for specific behaviour, authority is used to transmit premises for decisions such as 'maximize sales' or 'increase quality'. Explanation is required of why people perform on the job towards organizational goals without step-by-step commands and excessive monitoring. Rewards are recognized as one reason, but observed reward structures are much simpler than required from an incentive theory point of view. Further explanation for behaviour is sought in organizational pride and loyalty.

To explain why people behave loyally and identify with organizational goals, the concept of 'docility' is introduced. In order to survive in a society (an evolutionary argument), human beings need to be socialized. 'Docility is used to inculcate individuals with organizational pride and loyalty' to work for organizational goals (ibid.:36).

The process of socialization or indoctrination is not considered to be the last level of explanation, since: 'the strength of organizational identifications will depend upon the extent to which a society uses the docility mechanism to inculcate them, and this appears to vary considerably from one society to another' (ibid.).[14] It follows that explanations for (lack of) performance could be found in the particulars of the process of socialization. These issues will be developed further when discussing the role of the state (later in this chapter).

Over the years, Leibenstein (1976, 1987) has developed a behavioural theory of the firm, detailing processes at individual level and organizational level that can explain both the existence of inefficiencies (X-inefficiency) as well as the fact that some level of efficiency is achieved. Drawing on, amongst others, Japanese management experiences, he employs concepts like loyalty, cooperative behaviour, and conventions (in addition to monitoring) to explain why the bottom line solution of the prisoner's dilemma of collective action is avoided. The worst case scenario of lowest performance would be produced by vertically uncooperative behaviour coupled with horizontally cooperative behaviour. The satisfying behaviour of actors is reflected in his notion of inert areas with regard to action or satisfaction: within certain limits, particular outcomes are acceptable. His main line of argument is that external pressures lead to internal pressures, which on their way downwards along the hierarchy are transformed, attenuated and blocked by different shades and degrees of non-optimizing behaviour of actors, thus leading to sub-optimal performance with regard to costs and revenue. Given the existence of inert areas, the equilibrium condition is labelled as a 'loose equilibrium' in contradistinction to the tight equilibrium of standard theory. Deviation from rationally maximizing behaviour is thus found in his use of conventions characterizing behaviour, in the existence of inert areas, and in the possibility of uncooperative behaviour of (groups of) actors at various levels.

Decision-making as a way of following conventions is also taken as an important deviation from rationality (called routines) in the evolutionary model of the firm developed by Nelson and Winter (1982). Routines are seen as the social 'genes', transmitted from one generation to the next, which are codes of behaviour to deal with uncertain environments. These routines, or Leibenstein's conventions, are the social-organizational counterparts of genes in genetics and evolution theory in general. These evolutionary models have a close link with new institutional economics in the sense that the concepts of routines and conventions approach the concept of institutions surrounding prisoner-dilemma type of situations.

Whereas theories of perfect competition are basically also survival-of-the-fittest models (concentrating however on its equilibrium conditions), Nelson and Winter focus on processes of change captured by Schumpeterian competition. Behaviour geared towards innovation and accompanying technological change explain the degree of concentration in industries (the reverse of the SCP approach where objective structural factors explain behaviour). Rationality is bounded and sequential and described by 'routines' to deal with the boundedness problem. Two kinds of routines are identified: those that deal with the normal operation of the firm, and those that are used for innovation and change called 'search routines'. Neither of these routines are mechanical but creative, and above all transferred in a subtle, yet powerful process of on-the-job 'socialization' in the organizational culture, very much in the sense of Polanyi's work on 'Personal Knowledge' (1962). Motivations like loyalty and identification with firm's goals become necessary for creative application of skills in both types of routines. Thus where new institutional economics is concerned with explaining existing institutions in a wide sense, the evolutionary models focus on processes of change of institutions within organizations. As will be shown in Chapter 3, the evolutionary model, with its focus on Schumpeterian competition, becomes very applicable for explaining international developments in the textile sector. The rather recent phenomenon of 'flexible specialization' combining elements of product and technology innovations has led to ever-shorter product cycles.[15] Moreover, because of its more realistic assumptions on the working of the firm in its environment and its emphasis on dynamic managerial–entrepreneurial behaviour (in particular technical capability) as determinant of performance, this model is positively referred to by industrial researchers such as Pack (1987), Leibenstein (1987), and Lall (1990). Although this study will not enter into detailed managerial research, it does address issues of technology, technological management, and other aspects of management in relation to performance.

2.2.6   State enterprises

The above survey of theories of the firm did not explicitly address the public–private divide with regard to firm ownership. Given the large share of state enterprises in textile production in many African countries including Tanzania, this section will discuss how the various concepts developed above apply to state enterprises. The section begins with defining state enterprises and a brief overview of both the normative and positive rationale for the establishment of state enterprises supported by some generalizations ('stylized facts') on the operation of state enterprises. From there, the extension of the above theories to state enterprises can be pursued.

After careful consideration, Jones, in the introduction to his study on Korean public enterprises, defines a public enterprise as: 'a productive entity which is owned and/or controlled by a public authority and which produces a marketed output' (1975:38). Output is defined as 'marketed' if sales cover more than half of current costs. This is the definition adopted here as well.

Although this definition seems to be a matter of fact, some caveats must be noted. It deliberately leaves out any reference to other sorts of 'outputs' related to general welfare such as employment, regional development and provision of goods that would otherwise not be forthcoming. Likewise, the distinction between private and public goods on the basis of excludability and rivalness is not explicitly invoked.[16]

Yet, evaluation of performance of public enterprises would have to be in relation to its stated objectives which may be more than just economically efficient provision of the marketed output in the sense of profit maximization. Objectives of state enterprises can be discussed in the normative and positive sense. In the normative sense, state enterpises should, broadly speaking, maximize national welfare.[17]

Positive theories would add some behavioural content to Jones' definition. As Bös argues with regard to ownership: 'from our point of view, the main difference is not ownership. The main difference is the multitude of political and economic determinants of public enterprise activities as compared to the mainly commercial determinants of the activities of private enterprises' (1985:13). He continues that first, state enterprises usually do not aim to maximize profits: instead they maximize managerial or political objectives and second, they face different constraints in markets, production, finance, and political environment.

A link with the organizational theory of the firm will be established when the public enterprise is understood as a firm in which the separation between ownership and control is great. The common mistake with reference to identifying principals and agents in the case of public enterprises is to take government as the principal owner (as done by Bös who assumes that there is somewhere a government that acts as the principal in maximizing social welfare) and boards or general managers as first-in-line agents (control). If, however, ownership (principals) is taken to refer to all individuals who are interested in maximizing social welfare through the firm's activities, i.e. the general public, control is almost non-existent and at best very remote through parliamentary action. Moreover, all *public servants* who have some leverage over the firm are now agents, interlinked by a rather complex web of opportunistic relationships. Within certain margins, the public enterprise obtains characteristics of a common pool resource: where it should be a 'private good owned by government', rivalry exists in the sense that agents' opportunistic behaviour reduces the value of the public enterprise and excludability is reduced because the benefits the public enterprise can offer to its agents are extended to a wider range of officials.

The crucial questions now become to what extent opportunistic behaviour is possible, how these opportunistic margins are determined and, assuming now a normative stand, how they can be reduced to salvage some of the normative functions of the public enterprise. Indeed, an empirical study by the World Bank identified three main factors that distinguished successful from unsuccessful public enterprises (Ayub and Hegstad 1986). These were: (a) the degree of competition to which the public enterprise was exposed, (b) the degree of financial autonomy and accountability under which they operate, and (c) the extent and manner in which managerial autonomy and accountability are ensured. Thus, both the functioning and the environment of public enterprises would have to resemble better the conditions prevailing for private enterprises. However, for explanations of the observed behaviour, a wider frame of reference is required, involving processes of socialization (as indicated by the behavioural theory of the firm) and, relatedly, the nature of the state (to be discussed later).[18]

Most normative theorizing about improving the performance of the state sector has located deficiencies in performance in inadequacies in the application of appropriate management and production techniques. Solutions, therefore, are phrased in terms of more (formal and/or practical) training and in more appropriate techniques. Of course, knowledge of this kind is a prerequisite for performance.

Either implicitly or explicitly, most positive theorizing about public enterprises has been conducted within the framework of either the managerial theory of the firm or the organizational theory of the firm. The focus has shifted to appropriate incentive structures, accountability and control systems, including more market-oriented solutions. Largely within the managerial approach, a vast literature has developed on the issue of choice of technology, which as observed, was not in line with the normative predictions. 'Economic man' was replaced by the 'engineering man' (Wells 1975), who was in turn replaced by the 'bureaucratic man' (James 1989). Whereas the 'engineering man' is defined as showing engineering biases to choice of technology, i.e. the latest and often most capital intensive, 'bureaucratic man' is an opportunistic maximizer given the structure of incentives in a bureaucratic environment. Depending on the assumptions on the specific circumstances, this can lead to capital intensive choice of technology, to maximizing output rather than profits, to restricting output in order to create scarcity, and to nepotism and patronage in general. Given the wide range of outcomes for the decisions of the 'bureaucratic man', specification of prevailing bureaucratic conditions is crucial to this explanation. Perkins (1983) adds new agents to the public enterprise by explaining the bureaucratic bias for high capital intensity in terms of shortcomings of the wider bureaucratic planning process *vis-à-vis* the preferences of aid-related financiers. Interestingly, Tanzania's most successful public sector textile firm employs labour intensive technology supplied by China.

Horn takes the organizational theory of the firm as an explicit point of departure:

> Relative performance [of state enterprises] is related to the characteristics of state ownership, such as diffuse and nontransferable ownership, the lack of a stock price to indicate performance, the organization's possible subjection to claims of the political process, and its insulation from the dissatisfaction of its residual claimants. (Horn 1988:42)

The term 'residual claimants' originates from the language of institutional economics and within that the 'property rights' literature.[19] It refers to the owners as the claimants of all residual net value (profits). Residual claimants also carry the losses. Horn identifies these claimants with the general public or the voters.

Following the logic of a political market theory, legislators (politicians) exchange support from constituents for delivery of services and commodities by administrators (managers). Administrators are seen as agents for the legislators who aim at reducing agency costs. Mechanisms reducing agency costs of delivery (constraining agency's opportunism) are competition on the output market, internal and external job and career competition, and participation of the relevant constituency in governance of the delivery systems. Administrators' attitudes toward risk in relation to decision-making are somewhat paradoxical. While very risky (and eventually faulty) decisions can be taken by the administration, assignment of individual responsibility for such risky decisions proves very difficult in practice. Thus where the administration cannot be said to be risk-averse, administrators are. This is made possible by various processes internal to the bureaucracy and expressed in judgements such as 'lack of accountability and responsibility'.[20] Using the terminology of the Leibenstein model (described above), as applied to state enterprises, legislators can be interpreted as an element of the external environment adding pressure on the firm.

Although it can be argued that state enterprises are at least partially a response of legislators to satisfy demands of their various constituencies thereby explaining the establishment and continued existence of public enterprises despite their assumed inefficiencies in production, Horn's model is not able to explain in detail the causes of such inefficiencies. A more behavioural view of the public enterprise, identifying the various agents involved in management, production and control as *de facto* residual claimants of surplus, and the government (or the general public) at large as *de facto* residual claimant of losses is not developed. Leibenstein's 'inside-the-firm' model can make up for these deficiencies in Horn's model.

This last aspect is taken up by Nayar (1990) in his study of Indian public sector enterprises in what he calls the managerial research approach (MR approach). Public enterprises are seen to perform a role in the two fundamental functions of the state: accumulation and legitimation. The key assumption of the MR approach is that public and private firms that operate under similar conditions may vary in the degree to which they exhibit certain behavioural traits, but not in kind. This leads to the importance of the environment in which public firms operate so that performance (as in the SCP approach) is shaped by the following sequence:

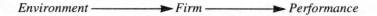

Environment ⎯⎯⎯⎯⎯▶ Firm ⎯⎯⎯⎯⎯▶ Performance

The environment is subdivided into the economy (nature of industry, structure of market), the polity (nature of the state, public policy, operational intervention, political parties, interest groups) and the society (level of development, social culture, cultural ethos). The firm is characterized by the nature of the firm (age, size, mission, importance to the country), the nature of management (professionalism, motivation, organizational culture), and management strategies (in production, distribution, and labour relations). The schematic presentation in Figure 2.3 can easily be compared to Figure 2.2, which presents the causational scheme for the SCP approach. Figure 2.2 elaborates the box labelled 'Economy' in

Figure 2.3. Thus, the MR approach adds new spheres of explanation of performance to the firm's environment. The 'Polity' sphere has been stressed by the political market theory, whereas the 'Society' sphere comes closest to aspects of the behavioural theory of the firm. Polity and society together can be analysed within a broader concept of the state, as in fact Nayar himself argues by stressing the legitimation aspect of the state (1990).

The MR approach to state owned enterprises appears to be the most mature one: it also corresponds better to the development theorist view of the state and its role in industrialization (discussed later in this chapter).[21] However, the economic aspects need to be developed along the lines identified in the survey above.

Figure 2.3   The managerial research approach

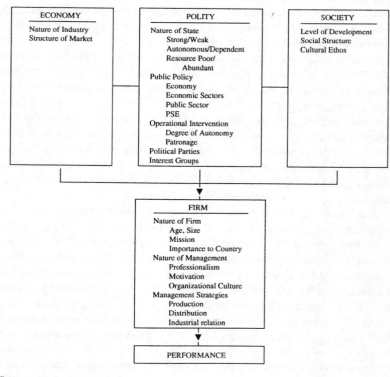

Source: Nayar (1990).

2.3   MACROECONOMIC ASPECTS OF INDUSTRIAL PERFORMANCE

Because the macroeconomic conditions of developed countries are relatively more stable than those in developing countries, the importance of macroeconomic factors for understanding firm performance may not be highly visible. As a result, recent research on industrial development has focused on firm-level structural factors (Lall 1990). However, even for developed countries macro-factors cannot be ignored. Movements in the exchange rate and the interest rate, protective policies (see Chapter 3 on protection in developed countries in the textile sector), and government spending all have important consequences for the industrial sector.

This applies *a fortiori* to developing countries, where the macroeconomic policy environment of the 1980s has been very unstable and unpredictable; and, has been characterized by structural adjustment policies involving large devaluations, liberalization, restrictions in domestic credit, rising interest rates, and some degree of privatization. These changes have been accompanied by inflation that, under the circumstances, has been modest (see chapters 4 and 6). Although these policies were directed at containing demand (stabilization) and increasing domestically produced supply (structural adjustment), many of the measures taken simultaneously affected both the supply and the demand side. They relaxed some constraints on the input side and lowered relative wage costs, but they have had (and continue to have) serious consequences for enterprises by increasing production costs in a variety of ways while at the same time exerting downward pressure on prices and on demand for their products. Capacity utilization, which would be expected to increase as a result of the improved input supply, has not been very responsive and in most cases profitability has suffered.

Two broad sets of circumstances have led to this disappointing outcome. First, firms could not adjust easily. In the decade before structural adjustment, their performance gradually declined in an environment of generally depressing economic conditions. During this period external constraints were translated into internal constraints. Lack of inputs led to low capacity utilization, low or negative profits, lack of finance for replacement, and the neglect of repairs and maintenance, to say nothing of innovation. Eventually, working capital shortages nearly brought some firms to a standstill. This implied that firms could only produce when production is prefinanced by an outside agent, for example a purchaser or the government.

Management and worker morale sank and the general conditions of scarcity prevailing in the wider economy pushed incomes downwards, leading to processes of 'de-socialization' with regard to the firm and resulting in a production culture favourable to high inefficiency and corruption. All this was exacerbated by poor physical infrastructural services, such as water and electricity supply and transport systems. Thus, at the beginning of the structural adjustment programmes, most firms were in the worst state of their history, poorly suited for market-led adjustment. Within this general picture, individual differences existed between firms which, because of characteristics such as ownership, management and other factors, reacted differently to the adverse circumstances.

Second, structural adjustment policies were inappropriate, especially under the circumstances described above.[22] The large devaluations increased the cost of essential imports (inputs, spares and replacement capital) as well as the local equivalent costs of servicing foreign loans. Any savings for replacement of old machinery (depreciation) were proportionally reduced. With respect to firms' current accounts, only those firms that exported more than they imported were net beneficiaries. These were very few indeed. Deterioration of quality under adverse production conditions of whatever origin had reduced quality below the minimum requirements for exports. Tight monetary policies leading to higher interest rates and quantity restrictions on credits respectively, increased cost of production and foreclosed the opportunity to recover from low levels of production. Moreover, economy-wide illiquidity caused transaction friction, leading to decline in turnover and reduced efficiency and general economic activity. On the input side, liberalization could not be utilized. On the output side, however, competition increased from imported final goods (including, for the textile sector, enormous quantities of second-hand clothing) which reached the local market at low cost because of dumping and underdeclaration at customs (UNIDO 1989a; Chapter 3).

Again, as in the pre-structural adjustment period, firms reacted differently to these adjustment policies as they enjoyed different forms of access to technology, management, finance, foreign exchange and export markets; which resulted in a differentiated impact on various cost categories and different rates of profitability and capacity utilization. Performance indicators that were directly affected by such macroeconomic changes are discussed below (section 2.3.3).

2.3.1   Structural adjustment programmes and the firm

To what extent do structural adjustment programmes live up to a development strategy? And what, if any, is the underlying view on industrial adjustment? Reflecting on the process of negotiation between countries and IMF, Stiles concluded that IMF's decision making with regard to conditionality can be best understood as a process of 'bargaining and compromise among IMF staff and between the Fund and borrowing countries' (1990:959), along the lines of what he calls a neo-functionalist explanation of decision making. On the other hand, Khan, *et al.* (1990) have found that comparably simple theoretical models form the basis of not only IMF but also World Bank decisions and Mosley and Toye (1988) show that a typical package of measures has developed in relation to stabilization and structural adjustment programmes. Therefore, Stiles' bargaining and compromise process must be understood to be confined to a rather limited range of options.

The novelty of structural adjustment programmes of the 1980s has been due to the efforts of the World Bank to link its financial support to far-reaching supply side intervention over and above the more conventional demand side oriented stabilization measures by the IMF, with the aim of deregulating or liberalizing the economy away from state intervention towards clearer market orientation. Rodrik (1990) notes a 'consensus regarding policy reforms that developing countries must undertake on their path to recovery from the debt crisis': first stabilization by fiscal restraint and devaluation, and, with stabilization progressing, followed increasingly by structural adjustment through policies directed at trade liberalization, price deregulation in industry and agriculture, financial liberalization, and privatization. The model of the behaviour of economic agents on which these interventions were based was primarily one of responsiveness to market signals without much regard to historically formed inefficiencies, rigidities, and constraints (some of which were the outcome of the structural adjustment package itself).[23]

Less consensus exists over the questions of the desired pace, sequence and scope of interventions. Experience has shown that the shock treatment approach produces dramatic results leading to political instability and economic uncertainty.[24] This has led Rodrik (1990) to argue for sustainability, implying a reduced scope of intervention, permitting economic agents to base their decisions on more informed guesses regarding the future, important especially for investment decisions. In this context, Mosley and Toye (1988) distinguishing between policy choice, tightness (how stringent are the policies) and sequencing (the feasible order of implementation), have stressed the political nature of these measures as they involve substantial relocation of power within both the government of the recipient country and the dominant economic groups, and require the administrative capability to coordinate these changes in a non-conflicting manner.

Apart from the existence of internal differences in the World Bank view (as explained by the neo-functionalist view), changes have taken place over time. In 1989, even the World Bank itself noted that 'it would be naive to pretend that African firms can be transformed overnight into effective competitors on the world market' (1989a:187). By that time, the World Bank had already moved into supporting subsectoral rehabilitation programmes (Mosley and Toye 1988). These programmes are based on firm by firm assessments. Also, a re-appreciation of the role of the state in economic development has taken place, based on Korea's success in state-led export oriented development.[25] Finally, during the 1980s the role of export-led industrialization has been increasingly stressed (World Bank 1987a).

What then, has been the underlying view of the firm in the design of World Bank policies? No clear answer to that question exists, not only because decision making in large institutions such as IMF and World Bank is neo-functionalist (a fact that perhaps becomes most explicit in differences between theoretical models of adjustment and the more pragmatic subsectoral interventions), but also because the position of the World Bank has changed over time.

For example, the role of entrepreneurs, a typical feature of the behavioural theory of the firm, has been stressed in the well known World Bank publication on sub-Saharan Africa, *From Crisis to Sustainable Growth* (World Bank 1989b). However, in all of this, the ability of firms to react and adjust is vital. Firms are to adjust first to more competitive conditions in order to increase efficiency, and second to changing relative prices by reorienting from the domestic market to the export market. A different version of this argument can be cast in sectoral terms, including the possibility that a sector adjusts by shedding inefficient firms. While in practice both types of adjustment take place, dominance of the latter would lead to a substantial reduction in industrial capacity, which had been so painfully developed over the previous decades. It can be argued that it was precisely the latter outcome of the 'shock treatment' version of structural adjustment that gave way to the more pragmatic view addressing constraints to higher efficiency and improved access to external markets.

2.3.2 The microeconomic underpinning of macroeconomic policy

Above it has been argued that performance may differ greatly between firms. However, macroeconomic models and theories operate at a high level of aggregation, often supplying interesting insights. Firms are normally represented by one or a few industrial sectors which are assumed to behave rather simplistically, supplying demand at costs (including capital costs as in the neoclassical model) or at mark-up prices (as in Kaleckian or oligopolistic models), investing at rates determined by investment possibilities and interest rates (determined by monetary factors) or by own savings (using its mark-up surplus). Keynesian type, short run, multi-sector input-output models assume idle capacity and fixed coefficients, while if these models are closed by relating value-added categories to final demand categories, sector-wise behavioural functions are assumed for investment, consumer demand, and export performance (Bulmer-Thomas 1982). In more aggregated short term models, supply elasticities are assumed for the tradeable and non-tradeable sector with regard to relative prices for tradeables and non-tradeables (D. Lai 1989a). Long term models of economic growth are usually even more aggregated: collapsing (as in the Harrod-Domar model) the whole productive sector into a fixed coefficient production function (of capital) to derive (knife-edge) equilibrium conditions for stable growth; or (as in Feldman and Raj-Sen models) differentiating between consumer, intermediate and capital good producing sectors in order to establish different growth paths with different allocation of investment over these sectors; or (as in Solow's model) assuming one production function with factor substitution and technical progress to arrive at different conditions for economic growth (the 'golden age' growth path).

In contrast to these highly aggregated macroeconomic models stand the 'inside the firm' theories of the firm and their 'between firms' counterparts (SCP) which disaggregate sector and firm to understand firm performance. Is it then true that microeconomic performance is irrelevant for macroeconomic performance? Few economists will say so. And in fact, recent advances have been made in the field of microeconomic foundations of macroeconomic theory (including firm behaviour), but concrete models that can form the basis of policy formulation are still lacking (Fischer 1988).

In particular with regard to the firm, there is an increasing recognition that the study of economic organizations should supply a better linkage between macro-, and micro-economics (Stiglitz 1991b).

In a more pragmatic vein, Porter in his book *The Competitive Advantage of Nations* argues that macroeconomic measures aiming at establishing more competitive conditions at a general level such as depreciation of the real exchange rate cannot explain success in international competition. In his words, 'seeking to explain "competitiveness" at the national level, then, is to answer the wrong question. What we must understand instead is the determinants of productivity and the rate of productivity growth. To find answers, we must focus not on the economy as a whole but on *specific industries and industry segments'* (1990:9, italics in the original). His analysis stresses the role of the competitive process underlying the process of upgrading national productivity which he describes as 'the outcome of the thousands of struggles for competitive advantage against foreign rivals ...' (ibid.:9), while '... government's proper role is to push and challenge its industry to advance, not to provide "help" so industry can avoid it' (ibid.:30). However, his observations are based on the experience of industrialized countries (including some NICs), and need significant modification when dealing with problems of industrialization in least developing countries, which are struggling to compete in much more standardized industrial products.

More attuned to the conditions of developing countries, Lall addresses both firm-level and national technological capabilities, as well as their relationship. Technological capability is defined as 'the entire complex of human skills (entrepreneurial, managerial and technical) needed to set up and operate industries efficiently over time' (1990:17).[26] This definition can refer to a plant, firm, industry, or a country. After identifying many factors influencing firm-level capability, he derives a simplified analytical framework for comparing successfully industrializing countries (both 'old' and 'new' NICs). The following elements are singled out for this comparison: (a) rate of growth of physical capital, (b) human capital, (technological effort and policies), (c) trade and competition policies, and (d) macroeconomic environment (ibid.:30). The last factor relates to the openness of the economy and related competition and incentives. The role of institutions is considered vital to the functioning of the industrial economy but are left out because of difficulties in quantification. Thus, the overall explanatory dominance of the degree of competition, argued by Porter, is considerably reduced (albeit not eliminated in the least) by considering additional factors which influence firm-level capability (or performance).

A very concrete example of the importance of specific micro-behaviour with respect to macroeconomic policy is supplied by Blinder (1989) who raises the possibility that credit rationing can be both contractionary and inflationary by allowing for the possibility that 'credit-rationed firms might be forced to curtail production due to a shortage of working capital'. One could add here that under certain conditions applicable to the economy at large and the particular sector, this may even lead to pressures to increase the output price. Thus, one of the popular elements of conditionality to curtail inflation can in fact lead to opposite results which can only be understood by the impact it has on firm behaviour. This implies that when credit supply is targeted to those firms for which it is an-effective constraint, the result would be deflationary by increasing supply. In some cases, illiquidity in the economy is so severe that firms without sufficient working capital cannot produce; even using consumer credit in the form of advance payments for orders. The possibility of supply multipliers would even strengthen the deflationary impact (Barro and Grossman 1974). For example, supply multipliers can exist when the constrained output of one firm is an intermediate input of a downstream firm, or when firms are constrained in supplying low income consumer goods to farmers engaged in commercial production. The relevance of this possibility will be discussed in the case study.

In short, despite the usefulness of these macroeconomic theories, the question is warranted to what extent detailed insight in the working of firms would complement macroeconomic analysis. More concretely, some macroeconomic concepts such as sectoral price elasticities of supply have no microeconomic basis. For example, increasing the relative prices of tradeables relative to non-tradeables is assumed to induce production switching (a switch from supplying the domestic market to supplying the foreign market) and expenditure switching (using more domestic inputs and less imported inputs). The use of overall (sectoral) supply elasticities for exports is only a rough approximation of the sum of individual supply elasticities because of the non-linearity of the concept itself. It fails to capture irregularities arising from individual firm behaviour: some firms are able to respond up to a certain level of exports, some may not be able to export at all, while others may even be forced to close down production altogether. Still others may be able to invest in additional capacity. No single indicator can capture all these processes.

Other macroeconomic concepts such as net sectoral profits (and thus net sectoral investment) are pseudo-concepts, because of the difficulties of relating these sectoral outcomes to other sectoral variables in such a way that the firm-level relations between these variables are fairly represented by their sectoral representations. For instance, a falling sectoral rate of profit may be the result of more entrants into the sector, increasing competition, reducing the monopoly profits and increasing output. It may also be caused by lower rates of profits achieved by the new entrants due to their 'infant' problems. In either case, the sectoral relation between profits and output cannot be modelled as if the sector acts as a large single firm. Only by disaggregating the sector into firms can the relation between sectoral profits and sectoral output be understood. When policies are designed to influence firm behaviour on the basis of these macro-sectoral concepts, they automatically become pseudo-policies in the literal sense of the word.

Thus, to answer important questions concerning the future of the industrial sector in the context of national development such as 'whether it is advisable for the sector to invest, rehabilitate, train, commercialize, liberalize, or privatize, whether and how an export orientation should be adopted, and what should be the role of the state with regard to policy interventions aiming at industrial development', a firm level approach has to be adopted both to supply empirical information about behaviour of firms and to design appropriate policy interventions (such as practised by UNIDO and increasingly recognized by the World Bank).

2.3.3 Performance indicators affected by macroeconomic conditions

In this chapter it has been noted that where conditions exist that would allow for super-normal profits, production inefficiencies may develop that capture part of these extra profits. Such conditions could take the form of protection, spatial monopolies, and economic rents under scarcity. However, such inefficiencies do not invariably develop under these conditions and additional causes, such as those discussed in the various theories of the firm, are necessary for a full explanation. Thus, reversing the conditions that facilitated development of inefficiencies would not necessarily and automatically make inefficient firms efficient. Some may resist through lobbying for favourable treatment and some may fold, leaving a few that may (partially) adjust. In addition, capacity utilization and investment are directly constrained by the supply of credit and/or foreign exchange. These constraints originate in macroeconomic structure and policy. Other external problems include inefficiencies of public utilities and transport. Separate measurement of these various sources of total inefficiency would be required to understand the causes of inefficiency.

From the macroeconomic point of view, three important performance indicators are discussed below. These are: capacity utilization, investment, and exports. All three indicators can be used at firm-level and are easily aggregated to the sectoral level (and, for exports and investment, to the national level). They are however not independent. Capacity utilization and cost efficiency are important determinants of the profitability of firms. A firm's investment efforts largely derive from profitability, whereas exports both indicate successful management and contribute to the relaxing of foreign exchange constraints, leading to increased capacity utilization.

Additional performance indicators for public enterprises are based on their stated goals, such as their contribution to employment, regional development, and the legitimation of the state in general. These goals of public enterprises will not be systematically evaluated, although in passing, reference will be made to them in the case study.

With regard to *capacity utilization*, the total installed capacity can be understood to be reduced to a certain level of attainable capacity by production inefficiencies which can be measured by the 'best practice' method. Any residual underutilization of capacity could then be attributed by external supply or demand constraints, the priority of which may change over time. For example, liberalization may turn a supply constraint into a demand constraint (especially for textiles with high levels of second-hand clothing imports), or at least reduce the supply constraint relative to effective demand. Different products may be affected differently. For example, traditional clothing (Khanga, Kitenge, and black cloth), uniforms, blankets and sheets, and so on, are less likely to be affected by second-hand imports although cheap (new) imports may still result in substantial competition.

Investment is determined by investment opportunities, and by access to finance and foreign exchange. In the case of investment aiming at vertical integration, investment may be either defensive or aggressive. For example, investments may be made in order to protect the quality of output in relation to export potential or to reap the advantages of market control. Much backward integration appears to be defensive, whereas forward integration into wholesale and retail distribution can be either, i.e. breaking the excessive control by retailers/wholesalers over producers or capturing their control over consumers. Some investments (including horizontal investment) may replace productive capacity elsewhere, which in turn may be characterized by asset specificity or not (in the latter case it finds deployment elsewhere). At present, in many African countries, rehabilitation investment is more important than expansionary investment although the border between the two is not always clear. The need for rehabilitation has its roots in the general lack of performance of firms and without tackling this, rehabilitation as such may be short lived (Pack 1987).

Access to finance is a complex issue. Sources of finance can be internal or external. Internally, the profitability of the firm is an important direct determinant of available finance capital, but in the case of economic groups (see section 2.3), finance may be found outside the firm but within the group. In the absence of financial markets, external finance can be obtained from a wider (ethnic) group, from domestic private or public commercial banks, from government (through participation), from foreign commercial banks, or from actors in the aid circuit. Private and public differences with regard to access to these sources exist. Profitability of the firm undertaking the investment and of the investment itself influence access. Since many investments have a large foreign exchange component, access to foreign finance is especially important. This places extra emphasis on the role of foreign aid when other foreign linkages (through ownership or otherwise) are weak. The role of the public sector as a vehicle for accumulation could be evaluated. Experience, however, has been that investments have been financed from the surplus of other sectors while profits generated have been small or even negative. The investments of individual firms or subsectors could be compared to the national or industrial sector average, to other countries, to the past (using time series) or to firms in the same sector. Dis-investment under adverse conditions (see section 3.1) has been widespread, given the need for large rehabilitation programmes (UNIDO 1989a).

Export capability depends heavily on quality. Without a minimum level of quality there is no point in considering other factors. This is the static, short term view. Quality is the outcome of a dynamic, ongoing process within which various factors play a role. In many countries, including most African countries, the dominant industrialization strategy has been that of import substitution (Meier 1989, Riddell 1990a). But the production inefficiencies that could develop behind tariff walls have led not only to trade inefficiencies but even to a form of product differentiation in which lower quality goods are produced specifically for domestic consumers. Eventually, failure in pursuing import substitution to its logical end, i.e. export competitiveness, and other (internal and external) causes of technical inefficiencies, have meant that much of the existing machinery had lost its capacity to produce export quality. The long march back, towards trade efficiency through both technical and production efficiency, involving all factors of production, will have to incorporate a concerted effort on all fronts; much along the lines of UNIDO's approach (discussed in section 3.4), in combination with carefully administered changes in the macroeconomic environment. Simultaneously, market contacts will have to be developed supplying information about quality, design, technological change, quantities and destination (see chapters 3 and 4).

In terms of internal linkages, the textile sector consists of a long value chain with a number of intermediate tradeable outputs. Export capability in terms of quality is determined by the technical efficiency of individual links in the whole chain: from raw cotton to finished garments. Lack of quality in one stage directly affects the next. Thus, as quality problems increase along the chain, export capability declines. It is therefore expected that in times of technical decline exports will concentrate on earlier and earlier stages of the chain, i.e. from garments back to processed cloth, then to grey cloth, yarn, and finally cotton.

Of course, as with the other indicators, the export capability and actual performance of individual firms differ. In many countries, particular export incentive systems developed during the period of foreign exchange shortages, and more recently, large devaluations have reversed the bias from production for the domestic market to production for the export market. The few firms able to benefit from these changes tended to have some form of foreign linkage.

2.3.3.1 Trade-related efficiency indicators

Trade efficiency is normally measured by nominal and effective rates of protection (*NRP* and *ERP*) and by domestic resource costs (*DRC*), while changes in comparative advantage are monitored with the help of the real exchange rate. The *ERP* gives an indication of extra incentives (through the net effect of tariffs on output and inputs) a domestic producer is given as compared with world market colleagues. The *DRC* measures the actual costs (opportunity costs, i.e. using shadow prices) to a country of producing the output rather than importing it. When $DRC>1$, it is more profitable to import, if $DRC<1$ it is more profitable to produce domestically and a value of $DRC=1$ implies indifference. *DRC*s are essentially short term indicators based on actual performance and therefore do not take into account potential improvements in efficiency. When market prices for factors of production are equal to opportunity costs (as in the case of 'perfect' markets), actual domestic prices are equal to world prices plus tariffs, and rents are zero (i.e. profits only consist of a normal return to capital), $DRC - 1 = ERP$ or $DRC = ERP +1$. When furthermore, the tariff structure is uniform $ERP = NRP$ (Meier 1989); the real exchange rate is defined in different ways depending on its particular application (Dornbusch and Helmers 1988). Changes in the real relative value of currency between a country and its trading partners (world) with respect to a base year (b) is determined by the relative nominal rate of exchange and inflation on each side as measured by p_d and p_w. Thus the real exchange rate $E_r = (E_n^t/E_n^b).(P_w/P_d)$. To measure changes in the competitive position of industries that produce internationally traded goods, the domestic wage index (WI') can be substituted for the domestic price level to obtain: $E_r = (E_n^t E_n^b).(P_w/WI')$. Indicating the base year *DRC* by DRC^b, the relation between *DRC* and the real exchange rate can be shown as:

$$DRC = DRC^b \frac{e_n^t e_n^b}{e_r} = DRC^b \frac{WI'}{infl_f'} \tag{2.6}$$

The real exchange rate and the DRC are inversely proportional: a higher real exchange rate index relative to the nominal exchange rate index increase firms' efficiency from the national perspective, other things remaining equal. Equation 2.6 shows that this can only happen when the wage index decreases relative to foreign inflation, as an indication of lower domestic resource costs (remember the assumed relation between the wage bill in the base year and opportunity costs; when this assumption is relaxed the possibility of lowering the base year wage bill by more efficient labour use is another possibility).

Combining the relations between *ERP*, *DRC* and e_r, an expression is derived that is valid only under the particular assumptions shown above:[27]

$$ERP = DRC^b \cdot \left(\frac{e_n^t e_n^b}{e_r}\right) - 1 \tag{2.7}$$

2.3.3.2 *Inefficiency, the effective rate of protection (ERP) and domestic resource costs (DRC)*

What is the relation between these measures and the microeconomic (in)efficiency measures such as RTFP and X-efficiency (discussed earlier)? Assume the usual case of a two factor (labour and capital), homogeneous production function *aa* in a situation without any tariffs (see Figure 2.4). Unlike Figure 2.1, here output is expressed in the value of one unit, i.e. pO while the vertical and horizontal axes measure quantity of capital per value of unit output, K/O, and quantity of labour per value of unit output, L/O. Consider the imposition of tariff, t_O, on output raising the domestic price of output from p_O^0 to $p_O^t = (1 + t_o) p_o^0$ leaving all other prices unaffected. This price rise is reflected in the graph by a downwards movement of the production function to *bb* (less factors per unit of output). With the assumption of unaltered prices for labour and capital, the most efficient point of production shifts downwards along a ray from the origin *A* to *B*. If profits were zero (only normal return to capital measured by capital costs) before the imposition of tariff and the firm uses the same quantities of capital and labour per quantity of output, K_q and L_q, the full impact of the tariff is captured by profits, $t_o p_o^0$ (which, when understood as economic rent, is considered a transfer payment in the terminology of economic cost benefit analysis with accounting ratio equal to zero).

While before tariff imposition, firms on or below *aa* were efficient with respectively *DRC=1* and *DRC < 1*, after tariff imposition DRC-efficient firms should be on or below *bb*. Firms on *bb* have an ERP equal to *AB/AO*,

Figure 2.4   Efficiency, ERP and DRC

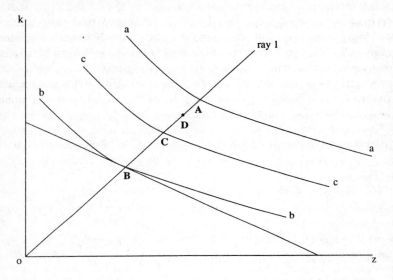

X-efficiency equal to *BO/BO=1* (or X-inefficiency equal to zero), and a DRC equal to *BO/BO=1*. Only when all extra revenue dissipates into inefficiency through the firm's employment of larger quantities (and thus equivalently higher opportunity costs which by assumption are equal to the market price) of labour and capital, will *DRC=AO/BO=1+AB/BO=1+ERP*. X-inefficiency is then equal to *AB/AO=ERP*. In the intermediate case, for example at *D*, X-inefficiency is equal to *DB/BO*, while DRC equals *DO/BO* so that X-inefficiency is equal to *DRC-1*.

The two-factor representation is rather limited as it can only interpret consequences of tariffs on capital but not on intermediate inputs. When output is defined as net of intermediate inputs, Figure 2.5 can still be used. Tariffs on intermediate inputs that enter into fixed proportions (quantities) in production decrease the potential economic rent (profit). Input tariffs decrease the value of output, implying on upward movement of the production function to, say, *cc*, defining the margin that will be allocated to a mix between increased profits and inefficiency as the area between *aa* and *cc*. Inefficiencies increase through higher labour and capital costs per unit of output, as shown by a movement of the actual point of production from *cc* to *aa*, but also by inefficient input use which would shift the whole curve *cc* upwards. Since the definitions of both ERP and DRC take actual input use as reference point, the relationship between DRC and ERP, shown above, is unaffected by inefficiencies.

However, X-efficiency relates actual use of inputs to best practice input use. Thus, with inefficient input use, the simple relation between DRC and X-efficiency breaks down. This shows up in the mathematical behaviour of these measures. The X-inefficiency increases monotonously from zero with higher than best practice input use. The ERP and DRC both approach infinity for very small values of world value added and switch to minus infinity at the point where world value added becomes negative. Very high or very low values of DRC and ERP are difficult to interpret economically. The ERP and DRC are therefore not suitable as performance indeces since there is no linear relation between their value and the degree of inefficiency.

For example, use of labour could be increased without incurring losses by moving from *B* horizontally until *aa* is intersected. This would affect both allocative efficiency and technical efficiency. Moving along a ray from the origin (constant labour to capital ratio) would affect only technical efficiency. In both cases the DRC would increase. However DRCs cannot discriminate between these two cases. Tariffs on capital goods would change the slope of the iso-cost line so that under allocative efficiency the point of production chosen would shift to the right. Without substitution, as in the case of fixed coefficient production functions, tariffs on capital goods will just increase the costs of production as in the case of intermediate inputs. The DRC thus measures actual inefficiency from the national point of view and the ERP measures the maximum inefficiency possible without incurring losses from the perspective of the firm.

When the DRC is taken as a measure to evaluate firm level performance from its individual point of view and its ability to cope with liberalization of trade, it supplies aggregate information on inefficiency. To understand how a firm could adjust to a more competitive environment, the general causes and specific sources of inefficiency should be analysed including the time it would take to remove them. The DRC as a measure of static (in)efficiency is, like cost-benefit analysis in general, open to the criticism that it ignores dynamic interpretations of comparative advantage. However, even so, it still provides important information on firm performance that, while it must be interpreted with care, certainly should not be ignored.[28]

Increased output prices and input costs are not necessarily due to inefficiencies of the firm. Within the SCP approach and the organizational theory of the firm, it was seen that prices can be higher than under perfect competition when conditions of oligopoly prevail. This can be caused by horizontal product differentiation and/or vertical integration especially forwards into wholesale and retail.

Extra costs are incurred by firms in LDCs as compared to world market colleagues as a result of general difficulties of doing business in an environment where transport and telecommunications are poor, where the supply of public utilities is frequently interrupted, and where bureaucratic procedures cumbersome. Monitoring costs are normally higher and labour efficiency is lower. Thus, a best practice production function based on countries with similar conditions would generally be above *aa*, *bb*, or *cc* (as the case may be), with part of the increased margins obtained from protection going to higher capital and labour costs and part to other costs not covered by this representation. The latter could be treated as intermediate inputs reducing the value of net output. Such extra costs in LDCs arise from what could be labelled 'infant industrialization', although even mature firms would have to face these costs.

2.3.4 The state and industrial development

In behavioural theories of the firm, the state is seen as one of the actors involved in a process of socialization to the norms and values of productive society (capitalist or socialist). Theories of public enterprises highlight the role of the state in commodity production. The macroeconomic perspective stresses the role of the state in policy making. Ensuring a socially acceptable distribution of income can be seen as a fourth role. Together these roles can be captured by the three basic and related concepts of legitimation, accumulation and distribution. Opinions regarding the desirable extent of state involvement in these three functions differ greatly. While over the years the major contrast has been between ultra-neoclassicals at one end of the spectrum and Marxist writers on the other (if they ever were on speaking terms), within conventional economics the debate was conducted more between neoclassical and (neo-) Keynesian economists. With respect to the latter, the debate was limited on one hand to the extent of intervention in regulation of markets and participation in production to obtain full employment of resources (accumulation), in particular with regard to employment of labour and on the other to differences of opinion on the distribution of income (i.e. as an outcome of the economic process or as determined from outside by the balance of power between classes possibly influenced by government's distributive measures). The aspect of legitimation was seldom addressed within conventional economics, but has been a cornerstone in Marxist reasoning.

In development economics, this discussion acquired an extra dimension in the attempts of newly independent countries to speed up economic development by development planning, often implying regulation of markets and participation of the state in production. Main contributions centre around distribution and accumulation. In recent years, the debate on the role of the state has intensified in response to both the apparent failure of many developing countries to industrialize along the lines of import substitution and the success of some in export oriented industrialization and the role of the state therein. The current wave of structural adjustment policies generally aiming at deregulation and a withdrawal of the state to its 'proper' place, and the accompanying neoclassical solutions to the development problem, has been interpreted to imply a crisis in development economics in the sense that it can no longer claim a status separate from mainstream economics. Ironically, the success of the NICs, the fiscal and economic crises of many developing countries in the 1970s and early 1980s and the problems associated with structural adjustment programmes, all have increasingly drawn attention to processes of legitimization.

One outcome of this has been the concern with social dimensions of adjustment, resulting mainly in large reports and theoretical treatises. Another has been the development of a combined neoclassical/new institutional view of the state in poor developing countries labelled 'the predatory state' (Lal 1987, 1989b; Ostrom 1988). Development economics, forced to acknowledge many shortcomings of the naive 'benevolent state' concept implied in much normative planning theory and actual planning practice, is reformulating the role of the state by recognizing limitations in administrative and political capabilities and possibilities of state failure; and developing a better appreciation of market forces without losing sight of market failures (Colclough and Manor 1991; Killick 1990; Shapiro and Taylor 1990). They maintain their view that extensive state involvement is required, albeit acting more through the market than against the market. Their position is strengthened by comparative studies on success stories (NICs) and rather inconclusive evidence on the role and performance of state enterprises per se (Gereffi and Wyman 1990; Nayar 1990).

Within these debates the state has been conceptualized differently. Without attempting fully accurate definitions here, it is advantageous to distinguish between: (a) the state apparatus (policy, jurisdiction, legislation, services and administration, production), (b) those running the state apparatus (state agents), (c) those commanding the state apparatus (at the top of the state hierarchy, the state elite), (d) the state as a fabric of institutions (the mosaic of organizations, institutions, norms and values), and (e) the nation state (all its citizens within its geographical boundaries). Two of the most common uses are a very wide definition of the state including all elements (a) to (e), and a more narrow definition identifying the state with government, combining (a), (b) and (c).

Below, the currently fashionable concept of the 'predator' state will be contrasted with evidence on the role of the state in successfully industrializing countries and on the limitations of structural adjustment policies in least developed countries, leading to a reformulation of the development theorist' view.

The neoclassical attack: the predator state and its new institutionalist claws

To understand the predator model of the state, the new institutionalist view of the ideal state should first be made explicit.[29] This view is based on pluralistic democratic models such as that of the United States: the state elite is kept accountable for the performance of its tasks by the political market, which is optimized in a pluralist democracy. State agents below the state elite act in accordance with the principal–agent model, with the state elite acting as managers and the voters as stockholders (as residual claimants exercising their bottom line property rights). Assumed opportunistic behaviour of all agents and voters (the utility maximizing individuals of neoclassical economics) leads to Pareto-optimality. Deviations from optimality can be discussed in terms of incomplete contracts, incomplete information and strategic behaviour. The main task of the state is in the legitimization sphere of ensuring that cooperative solutions obtain in prisoner's dilemma-type situations by supplying the by-rules to the game through legislation and socialization (state as fabric of institutions), and through providing goods and services that show characteristics of public goods. Accumulation and distribution is best left to market forces. This system is seen to minimize transaction costs as compared to other forms of organizing the nation state.[30]

The predator state comes into shape when the link between voters and state elite becomes remote. To develop his case of the predator state, Ostrom (1988) draws on similarities between Lenin's view of establishing state power, Copeland's famous book *The Game of Nations* describing CIA efforts to stabilize the Egyptian regime after the British involvement, and Hobbes' theory of sovereignty and the related concept of the 'leviathan'. Lal's account of the predatory state, which will be described in more detail below, spells out for the specific case of developing countries for the historical period preceding structural adjustment; in it, Tanzania has earned the dubious merit of special attention (1987). The separation between voters and state elite leads to state autonomy and a state elite is no longer controlled or held accountable. Legitimation and control become acute problems. Legitimation is achieved through distribution and transfers, which create entitlements for vested interests groups and lead to specific property rights. Opportunistic behaviour on the part of both the state elite and state agents in general, and the need for control and legitimation explain the overextension of the state apparatus (as in the neo-Marxist concept of the overdeveloped state resulting from a different mode of explanation).[31] In the first instance, overextension leads to the development of a new relationship between the private and the state sector characterized by rent-seeking behaviour (labelled by Bhagwati (1982) as DUP activities: directly unproductive profit-seeking activities) and simultaneously to diminishing control through the 'exit' option offered by the parallel market and within the state apparatus through increased shirking and corruption by state agents. These are at the basis of the fiscal crisis leading to various efforts of financing the crisis (Lal 1987). When finance is sought in excessive taxation of agricultural surplus 'the state will have a fiscal, foreign exchange and domestic output crisis. The predator will have a problem of surviving as it has virtually destroyed its prey!' (Lal 1989b:296). The loss of control and the resulting inability to finance the various entitlements and eventually even to maintain its own apparatus 'leads to the unexpected and very un-Marxist withering away of the state' although it has rarely reached its full denouement (Lal 1987:283).

Liberalization, when adopted, is interpreted as a way for the predator, after comparing the cost and benefit of liberalizing against not liberalizing, to regain control. This usually takes the form of a half-hearted attempt at some degree of tax reform, monetary contraction and export promotion. According to Lal, liberalization programmes fail because 'without a commitment to reducing unviable levels of entitlements, the liberalization attempts have tended to worsen the fiscal situation'. Thus, 'prior establishment of fiscal control through a reduction of unsustainable public expenditure commitments' is essential for success. The political problem that remains however becomes clear as follows:

Given the government's own rate of discount (which may be much higher than that of society), even if the resulting purely technocratic economic welfare integral is positive, policy makers may still be reluctant to undertake the reforms if they feel uncertain about their ability to survive the political pressure during the transition (ibid. 1987:285). Although Lal does not state explicitly that a more pluralistic political system would prevent the development of predatory states, it is implicit in the neoclassical view of the ideal political system.

Thus, the nature of the state and the extent of its intervention is seen as the major impediment to industrialization and development in general. It is used to explain inappropriate policies, such as the general failure of import substitution; the failure of the state apparatus itself, including public enterprises; and a general loss of control of the state leading to fiscal and other crises, and to parallel economies. However, the neoclassical political economy does not provide sufficient historical, cultural, and indeed political–economic understanding of its own subject area based as it is on an extension of neoclassical economics.[32] A more comprehensive view is even more urgent considering the recent use of conditionality to incorporate demands on the state itself (Doornbos 1991). The potential for ethnic and regional conflicts that may erupt with imprudent interventions is clearly demonstrated in Africa, Europe, and elsewhere.

Diverse evidence

Rather mixed empirical evidence however, comes forward on such issues as privatization, public enterprise performance, the nature of the state and the extent of its interventions in economic policy, distribution and production.[33] A recent comparison of Asian and Latin American NICs on these points showed that not only have they followed different strategic routes towards industrialization but they also exhibit rather diverse characteristics in these areas (Gereffi and Wyman 1990). All countries starting from an primary export economy shift to primary import substitution, but while the East Asian countries then became oriented toward primary EOI, the Latin American countries continued their import substitution with secondary ISI. More recently, as they approach the structure of industrialized countries, the two groups are converging toward an economy with further deepening of both export and import substituting activities.

When explaining the particular patterns of development, Gereffi and Wyman show that at the national, institutional and the organizational level, the state plays an important role in shaping the conditions within which the lower level operates. State-owned enterprises feature prominently in the last two phases of industrialization, especially in the Latin American countries. Moreover, the countries differ in size, culture, and resource endowment. Furthermore, in contrast with what the predator-state view would consider beneficial, the state played a major role in production, through direct and indirect (services and infrastructure) participation, policy making, and actual subsidization of export and import substituting industries.

In the two other domains, legitimation and distribution, fundamental differences among these countries make simple judgements impossible.

Thus, in the words of Ellison and Gereffi (1990): 'The patterns and strategies of industrial development in Latin American and East Asian NICs defy easy description, let alone explanation' (ibid.:397). However, 'the role of the state emerged as a key factor ... in terms of the state's capacity to select and implement successful development strategies' (ibid.:399). On the other hand, Evans (1990) expresses doubts about reproducibility of the East Asian experience arguing that in the case of weak states 'the imperfect market may well be better than the imperfect state' (Evans 1990:48). These arguments come surprisingly close to arguments about the role of the state in import substitution. What then are relatively weak states supposed to do if neither EOI nor ISI is a feasible option?

The development theorist's defence: reformulating the role of the state

Development theorists have argued first that state failure has indeed effectively undermined the naive notion of a purely benevolent state. Naive as this notion may be, modern behavioural theories of organizations have made clear that more is required to explain the workings of the state apparatus than just the assumption of opportunistic maximization of individuals in the neoclassical political economy.

Second however, the old arguments for state involvement in development, and particularly industrialization, cannot be ruled out by pointing at ways in which state involvement can degenerate. In this context, Gerschenkron's work is frequently cited to demonstrate that effective state intervention is required to overcome substantial disparities in industrial development (see Gerschenkron 1962). Furthermore, many problems associated with the overdeveloped state have arisen partly from the fact that the favourable international conditions (including attitudes of donor countries and international private banks) have led to optimistic state expansion which *ex post* can be judged to have been over-optimistic. Thus the neoclassical reaction to reduce the role of the state to its bare minimum has been labelled as 'a reaction too far' (Killick 1990).

Third, not only the recent successes of the NICs but also some modest and partial successes in implementation of structural adjustment policies in poorer countries have relied strongly on market intervention by states (Shapiro and Taylor 1990). And where failures have been recorded, some of these may be attributed to market failures (in particular the capital market), or to inadequate or inefficient intervention by the state (Streeten 1987). In this context, Chakravarty (1991:14) argues that 'the set of presuppositions which equated a "market system" with "capitalism" and "socialism" with "central planning" needs critical reexamination'. He further comments that 'the role of political institutions and political ideologies cannot be overlooked in any analysis of development planning' (ibid.:16). Implicitly addressing new institutionalist conceptions of the political market theory, he adds that 'a simple extension of the tools used by economists, such as self-interested maximizing behaviour by ruling groups, is by itself insufficient to explain the problems which arise' (ibid.:16).

Fourth, the predator state and the benevolent state can be seen as extremes on a continuum along which real states can be located according to differences in internal structures and external ties. As described by Evans (1989), these two dimensions are captured by the composite concept of 'embedded autonomy', which 'joins well-developed, bureaucratic internal organization with dense public-private ties' (ibid.:581). Evans call states with this characteristic 'developmental states' and notes Japan, South Korea, and Taiwan as examples. Along this continuum, relationships between business and government are not only different from those in advanced western countries, but also different from each other. This will prevent 'dominant policy advice emerging from the economics profession and international institutions, such as the IMF and World Bank, treats the Third World as an undifferentiated whole' (Hamilton 1989:1529).

Thus, the more differentiated view of states draws attention to capacities and internal organization of the state apparatus itself, and its relationships with the wider society. More pragmatically, Evans (1989:583) comments that 'this differentiated view of states suggests that policy should be two pronged, aiming at increasing the selectivity of tasks undertaken by the state apparatus but devoting equal attention to reforms that will help reconstruct state apparatuses themselves'. This selectivity implies a process of mutual adjustment of capacities of the state apparatus with its social connectedness. In many cases where states have overextended themselves, this may involve increased human capacity building coupled with improved incentive systems in the public sector, but will definitely imply increased reliance of state intervention on market forces (Shapiro and Taylor 1990; Killick 1990). With regard to the latter, Killick (1990) comes to four main conclusions: (a) the way in which the public sector goes about its task is more important than its absolute size; (b) to the extent that policy interventions are necessary, it is better that they should work with, or through, market forces than against them; (c) policy advice derived from mainstream economic theory should be approached with caution because of its value biasses, frequent lack of consensus, particular limitations of the neoclassical school, and its contextual bias towards conditions in the advanced economies of the west; and (d) the politics of policy reform should be explicitly addressed.

It remains to be seen how recent donor-advise will work in practice in African states. The pervasive poverty of these countries, the very low salaries of otherwise highly trained civil servants, dependencies between and mutual encroachment of private and public spheres, and, indeed, weak accountability structures make guided adjustment to conditions implied by embedded autonomy not only a very long term project, but also raises the question of who in the system can perform such a task. Moreover, the manner in which first world concepts of state and government will take shape in practice is likely to be influenced by the more fundamental conditions of these countries such as their poverty, dualism, dependency, cultural differences, colonial experience (as the first contact with 'modern' government) and the dominance of ethnic minorities in trade and industries. Hyden (1982) has attempted to capture some of these aspects in his concept of 'the economy of affection' which is used to bring out the importance of the different basis of decision making (family, clan) in Africa as compared to the individualistic approach of mainstream political science and economics. Legitimation of the state under such circumstances in order to establish a modern state capable of steering accumulation with a socially acceptable distribution of income is one of the main problems of African nation states. Providing education and health services, and establishing state enterprises, can be understood as both an answer to objective needs (developmental state) and an outcome of the state's fundamental need for legitimation.[34] The conflict, thus, has been less an economic one between distribution and growth but rather a more fundamental political-economic one between legitimation versus accumulation. Where and when this has led to overextension and subsequent state failure, states cannot be labelled with the superficial and a-historical concept 'predatory' which disqualifies the struggle of the people in African countries, including many of their leaders, to overcome problems of colonialism and underdevelopment. The latter is the realm where the real contradictions shape the outcomes.

Interestingly, many of the failures of government are also identified in developed countries, with a better separation of the political and administrative spheres. For example Self (1985), after reviewing four broad theoretical approaches to modern government: *in casu*, public choice theory (criticized for its narrow assumptions and extreme approach and in which the concept of the predatory state has its origin), pluralism, corporatism, and bureaucratic theories. He comes to the following conclusions about government (as distinct from the political sphere):

(1)   Governments are inadequately responsive to both the goals of political leaders and the needs of disadvantaged groups. They are too responsive to the demands of strong private interests that they have helped to entrench.

(2)   Political parties have inadequate leverage in the face of pluralist and corporatist influences, both within and outside government.

(3)   Bureaucracies have become in various degrees ineffective and irresponsible or too beholden to powerful interests. The articulation and application of distinctive public interests and of a public service ethos has become eroded.

(4)   The capacity of governments to cope effectively with the many problems of modern societies has been weakened, by the failings of both political consensus and bureaucratic organization and ethos.

Thus, even if third world states do become close copies of first world models, quite similar problems remain. Surely, it is partly a matter of degree. Many of these problems apply *a fortiori* to many least developed countries. However, once blame has been laid on certain aspects of the state, one must still identify ways, means, and most importantly, actors; detailed insight is required in the historical development and present working of the state. States are not states but processes. Interactions occur between socioeconomic conditions, values and cultures of the society, established and emerging interests, and modern and traditional forms of government (Kunz 1991). The greatest problem therefore, facing economic and political liberalization is 'how to elevate the various practices which embody a tradition of constitutionalism but which are themselves occluded within the ethnic segments of civil society, onto a pan-social sphere, to make them operational at state level' (ibid.:235). But, in the words of Evans (1989:584), 'the task of constructing a credible comparative political economy of the Third World is just beginning. Trying to move it forward is likely to be onerous and frustrating, but such efforts are crucial if we are ever to discover how Third World states might become less part of the problem and more part of the solution'.

One conclusion is immediately clear: any simplistic labelling of 'the' state, reveals more about the 'state of mind' of the speaker than about the nature of the state. At the same time, in all countries at various levels and in relation to various aspects of the state, processes involving institutions and civil servants *can* be identified which can, to a certain extent, be explained by opportunistic behaviour under conditions that facilitate a divergence of interest between the individual civil servant and the general public. But these explanations should be augmented by an analysis of the environmental factors that are creating conditions of an overextended state in relation to: its resources and capacities, poverty, and to the general weakening of legitimation, accumulation and distribution functions. But this analysis must also explain the simultaneous developmental processes which over time and perhaps with fluctuations have contributed to accumulation, distribution and legitimation. Thus, rather than adhering to one single theory, a pluralistic approach to theories of the state is likely to be more fruitful.

It is equally important to explain the extent to which things do work or do not work. Market oriented theories explain markets positively (why they work) but are biased to explain only state failures. When industrial performance is measured by the extent of inefficiency, the yardstick of full efficiency and whatever efficiency is achieved require no explanation. However, when, under conditions of market failure, the state enters the picture, the correct framework of comparison is not a fully-efficient state intervention but an intervention that is an improvement over the case of market failure. In that light, the achievements of even poorly performing states and rather inefficient public ventures acquire new credibility.

This does not imply that state interventions always remain superior where the market has failed. There is no need for a 'sticky' state intervention concept. Conditions change and each solution generates its own contradictions. The degree of accumulation achieved by state intervention during one particular historical period can form a basis for a period where market principles can and even should be given more room. State directed efforts can be progressively directed to new fields of market failure where intervention is required.

2.3.5 The analytical approach

The focus of this chapter has shifted from the neoclassical theory of the firm, successively to the SCP approach, organizational theories of the firm, behavioural views, the MR approach, and finally to macroeconomic determinants of firm performance as captured in the most general way by the nested hierarchy scheme. As the chapter developed, not only were more explanatory factors added, but the concept of performance itself became differentiated, involving the individual view (of the firm) and the national view of performance.

Whereas there is little ideological debate on the functioning of private firms, what should be seen as the national interests and therefore as the final yardstick for performance, continues to be controversial. Thus where neoclassical theory assumes a given distribution of assets and income, an unproblematic relation between the short and the long run, and optimum allocation of resources under free markets, structuralists would argue that distribution of income, achievement of long run comparative advantage, and optimum allocation of resources requires state intervention.

The evidence reviewed and cited resulted in a pragmatic mix of both schools. On one hand the role of the state in development (however defined) is essential, but on the other, opinions from different camps seem to some extent to be approaching one another on the issue of the emphasis required to bring about a convergence of private and national interests. Debate has shifted from direct toward indirect control of the behaviour of micro-actors, i.e. from direct state intervention to state intervention through the market. However, despite this convergence of opinions, differences in emphasis remain.

Research focus and approach

Within such a broadly defined field, one's research focus must be narrowed to a considerable extent to be able to make a contribution at all. The focus here is on measuring and explaining the performance of firms in one particular sector from a micro-, meso-, macro- and international perspective. Excluded as direct research questions are issues pertaining to the performance of other sectors, income distribution, quality of life, and political dynamics, although these may be called upon as explanatory elements. The world level is represented by world market developments in the textile sector and by its institutional aspects in the form of the World Bank, IMF, donor countries, GATT and the Multi-Fibre Arrangement (MFA). The macro-level encompasses national institutions and policies, whereas the meso-level defines the major economic actors and their interaction, with government agencies as the major actor in policy formulation and implementation. The micro-level is formed by the individual firms and their diverging characteristics.

The final outcome of the interaction between these levels (performance) is mediated through the firm and its characteristics. The structure-conduct-performance approach (see Figure 2.2) stresses structural elements of the market and supply characteristics to explain performance which have been insufficiently detailed by the managerial research scheme (see Figure 2.3). In addition, the new industrial organization theory explains elements of structure as outcomes of strategic conduct.

The firm in the managerial research approach is described by different characteristics such as age, size, type of management, and management strategy. Ownership is omitted as the approach concerns only state owned enterprises. When dealing with a mixture of private and public firms, ownership obviously matters. Moreover, even for state owned enterprises ownership forms may be different. All of these factors influence performance. The organizational theory of the firm explains vertical integration as a rational attempt to minimize transaction costs but, together with horizontal differentiation, vertical integration can also be understood as strategic conduct in the style of new industrial organization theory. The organizational theory together with the wider new institutionalist explanations of, in particular, state owned enterprises, draw attention to opportunism and its consequences for performance. On the other hand, behavioural and evolutionary theories analyse the internal structure of the firm in relation to performance in more detail, and together with the managerial research approach emphasize socialization as a countervailing force against opportunism.

Explanation of performance will proceed along two lines. First, international developments in the textile sector will provide the comparative perspective. Chapter 3 reviews developments in technology and trade at world level. Chapter 4 describes the experience of selected countries from Europe, Asia, and Africa in the textile sector in terms of macroeconomic and sectoral policies, output growth, and export success. Second, against this background, the performance of Tanzanian textile firms will be analysed.

The overall analytic framework: schematic presentation

The main line of argument will run as follows (see Figure 2.5):

(a)   Mega-, macro-, meso- and micro-factors combine to have their impact on the textile industry (boxes 13 to 9).

(b)   Because of the particular structure of the textile industry (its constituting institutions, the firms), analysis will show that this impact is differentiated with regard to the structural characteristics of firms (indicated by the grid at the bottom of box 9).

(c)   Firm-level responses to these impacts will be varied not only as the result of the different impacts that firms experience, but also as a consequence of different behavioural characteristics of the firms (boxes 6 and 4, the grids at the bottom reflect the different behavioural characteristics and the differentiated outcomes).

(d)   Taken together and interacting with other sectors, firm-level responses contribute to macroeconomic outcomes with respect to: short and long term macroeconomic policy targets relating to output, prices, employment and consumer demand; demand for imports and therefore for foreign exchange; supply of foreign exchange through export earnings, revenue for the government, demand for money, investment and growth (box 1).

(e) These macroeconomic outcomes will not necessarily be consistent with the desired policy targets for which the macroeconomic policy was designed. When such inconsistencies are recognized at the level of the various institutions that interact to produce macroeconomic policy (government agencies, party, IMF/World Bank and donors), interpretations of these inconsistencies may lead to adjustments in the macroeconomic policies which then start a new cycle at the level of microeconomic responses (boxes 2, 7, 10 and 11).

(f) Given the fact that different institutions involved in the making of macroeconomic policies may have different theoretical frameworks (box 7) for interpreting these inconsistencies and, in addition, may have different agendas and different constraints with regard to macroeconomic policy targets, the outcome of the process of macro-economic policy making (box 10) is not easily predictable.

(g) The international institutes in box 2 influence policy making at the level of perceptions (box 2), theoretical interpretation (box 7), and policy processes (box 10).

(h) The world market represents foreign linkages and the comparative perspective. Linkages with the world market have an impact on the industrial sector and firms therein (box 9), giving rise to different firm behaviour (box 6), and providing a comparative perspective with regard to performance and future possibilities (box 4).

(i) The whole diagram is embedded in the state in the widest sense of the word, including economic institutions, private–public relations, processes of socialization, and the provision of social services. Boxes 12 and 13 are open to the outside of the diagram to show that they (very) partially overlap.

(j) Relations between various levels of explanation are assumed to be predominantly from higher to lower levels (nested hierachy). However, the relation between the meso-, and micro-level is recipro-cal as new industrial economics has asserted. Moreover, relations between the micro-, and meso-level and the macro-level cannot be ignored, although the precise macro-outcomes of these linkages are determined in interaction with other sectors.

Differentiation of structure and behaviour

Differentiation of structural and behavioural factors of actors and institu-tions refers to firms, government, economic institutions, the state, and international institutions.

(a) *Firms:* The following structural characteristics are found important determinants of the direct impact of economic policies on

Figure 2.5   Interaction micro-, meso-, macro- and mega-levels

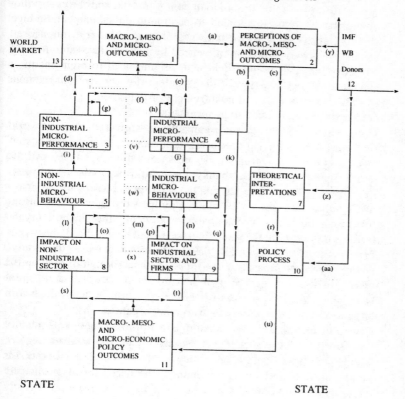

Notes: in addition to what has been explained in points (a) to (f) in the main text above:

– The causal flow is from box 1 to 2, 7, 10, 11, 9, 6 and 4 back to 1. Alternatively, one could start at 2, 7, 10, or 11 through the cycle.
– Linkage (f) runs both ways.
– Linkages (c) and (l) and boxes 2, 7, and 10 indicate the political nature of policy processes and decisions.
– The non-industrial sector remains underdeveloped in this diagram since the focus is on manufacturing industries in general and the textile industry in particular.
– However, linkages (f) and (m) indicate interactions between industry and other sectors both at the level of impacts and at the level of responses.
– Linkages (g), (h), (o) and (p) refer to linkages within sectors. A more detailed diagram would show these more explicitly.
– Linkage (q) indicates the impact of behavioural variables on the impact variables.
– All boxes and linkages deserve a full analysis. The present study leaves boxes 8, 5, and 3 of the main causal cycle together with their linkages underdeveloped.

enterprises: technology, age, location, export share (which is fixed in the short run for some firms), loan commitments, and the proportion of imported inputs. Responses to economic policy impacts, which already vary because of the above factors, are further differentiated by firm behaviour which is influenced by factors such as ownership structure (i.e. private/multinational, private with foreign linkages, private/local, public), type of management (i.e. foreign management of public enterprise, local management of public enterprise, holding corporation) and relation to government.

(b) *Government:* Government organizations surround the industrial sector with rules and procedures, opportunities and constraints. A large number of government organizations have linkages with the textile sector: commercial banks, the central bank, the Ministry of Industry and Trade, internal and external trade boards, the Ministry of Finance, the National Planning Commission, special institutions for the public sector, Parliament and political parties. These organizations do not share the same interest in, and views about, the manufacturing sector in general or the textile sector. Some of them have power over allocation of scarce inputs such as foreign exchange and credit. Others can decide over investment or labour management issues. In short, the success or failure of a firm is determined to a large extent by its relation to government organizations.

(c) *Economic institutions:* The economic institutions that have gradually developed in the Tanzanian economy create the environment in which the firms operate. The emergence of parallel markets for inputs, outputs and foreign exchange, the necessity of cultivating relations with government, and the possibility of corrupt practices in the absence of strict government control, have enabled private firms to survive and have caused public firms to run into even greater losses.

(d) *State:* The paradox of the simultaneous existence of excessive bureaucratic interference and the softness of the Tanzanian state underlies much of the observed behaviour of managers in both public and private firms. Resolution of this paradox requires a deeper analysis of the Tanzanian state. Such analysis will also shed some light on the tenuous relationship Tanzania entertains with the IMF and World Bank, which have presented themselves as the main force behind the introduction of policy reforms.

(e) *International institutions:* International institutions play a key role in determining development policies through project assistance, import support programmes, conditional financing, and rehabilitation programmes. As of late, much of this influence goes beyond supplying expertise and finance, and even beyond economic conditionality towards political conditionality. This has been characterized by Doornbos (1991) as 'state formation under supervision'. The IMF and the World Bank do not promote identical types of policies. Within the World Bank, different views exist on the degree to which markets may solve all the problems. This becomes apparent when analysing their rehabilitation programmes, which show the World Bank's shift towards more intervention. It is not fully clear whether this shift over time has constituted a deliberate policy or reflects a 'learning by doing' approach.

Measurement of and data on performance indicators

Measurement of performance will start from the bottom up and from the top down. At the shop floor level, technical X-inefficiencies of production will be estimated using the best practice approach detailed in section 2.2.2. These inefficiencies effectively reduce the attainable capacity of firms. Data are available for one year only (1988). From the macro-side, overall under-utilization of capacity is partly explained by these X-inefficiencies, while the remainder (attainable capacity under X-inefficiency) is assumed to have its causes in constraints that arise from financial and economic management of firms under conditions set by macroeconomic variables which themselves are outcomes of particular macroeconomic policies. Time series data on capacity utilization are available from 1973 to 1989 for public sector firms, and from 1980 to 1989 for private firms.

Other performance indicators such as profits, output, exports and investment will be reported for the period 1973 to 1989 for public enterprises and from 1980 to 1989 for private firms. Export data are scanty and restricted to a few private and public sector firms. Data on large investments are available over the years, although private sector data are incomplete.

Explanation of performance

The explanation of performance will start with explaining technical inefficiency caused by micro factors and of inefficiencies caused by constraints that have their origin in macroeconomic variables. Firm characteristics such as ownership, management, age of machinery, foreign linkages, loan structure, and export performance, together with sectoral characteristics and the macroeconomic context, will form the basic set of explanatory variables. Thus, the explanation of capacity utilization is at the core of this analysis. For the public sector, where long time series are available, an econometric estimation will be made of its capacity utilization in relation to a set of macroeconomic and sectoral variables.

Thereafter, profits will be analysed. The profits of public sector enterprises, like capacity utilization, will be related to a set of macroeconomic and sectoral variables. For the sector as a whole, time series data on profits are incomplete (for the private sector these are available for 1985–88). Moreover, data on the profits of private sector firms are not only notoriously unreliable but also suffer from definitional problems. Rigorous quantitative analysis is infeasible. Instead, trends in these data are qualitatively and tentatively analysed in relation to the microeconomic and sectoral variables identified above, and to macroeconomic developments.

Also, the available data on exports and (dis)investment will be related to firm characteristics and macroeconomic policies. Public sector exports have been insignificant and restricted to one or two firms. Private sector exports are restricted to a few firms as well. Moreover, different mechanisms and reasons for exporting exist. This makes comparison between firms difficult and may affect the significance of the results although certain general conclusions can be drawn.

Similarly, investment data over the years are incomplete. However, a detailed survey of rehabilitation requirements is available which shows investments likely to occur in the next few years, but more importantly gives an indication of the amount of disinvestment that has taken place over the preceding years. Together, these data give another indication of performance that can be related to micro-, meso-, and macro-characteristics.

At various points in time management perceptions on constraints have been recorded, which will be presented in order of importance. Evidence on the applicability of these constraints is analysed and contrasted with management views and the results obtained from the foregoing performance analysis.

At various points in the argument, reference has been made to different aspects of the state. Thus, the analysis would be incomplete without an account of the Tanzanian state and its relations to industrial development.

Notes

1. Economic inefficiencies refer here to sub-optimality of consumption and distribution as compared to the case of neoclassical perfect competition in all markets.

2. A third deviation of the neoclassical model of the firm occurs when the firm is no longer understood in terms of a single actor/decision-maker but as an organizational form involving many actors with objectives that may differ from the owners' objective of maximizing profits. This will be discussed in the section on institutional economics (section 2.5) and on the organizational theory of the firm (section 2.6).

3. In his comparative study on textile firms in Kenya and the Philippines, Pack (1987) takes one step further by analysing the underlying factors that contribute to the measured RTFP. Equation (2.8) shows the decomposition of RTFP into management (P^M), labour (P^L) and other (P^{Oth}) sources of inefficiencies.

$$RTFP = \Pi i^{P_A^i} = P_A^L \cdot P_A^M \cdot P_A^{Oth} \qquad (2.8)$$

4. See Sawyer (1985) for the derivation of this result.

5. Other, more long-term, rational specifications of managerial behaviour are possible, for example, by assuming that managers want to maximize their market value or want to maximize their discounted expected consumption (more in line with modern consumer theory: permanent income hypothesis or life-cycle theory). Literature discussing these possibilities can be found in Holmstrom and Tirole (1989).

6. By expanding the notion of transaction to include non-monetary transactions and the wider interests of exchanging parties, it has come very close to the traditional political economy approach. However, whereas the political economy approach is critical and therefore directly and explicitly normative, new institutional economics takes the interests for the given in a positivist sense. As such, it contains strong implicit ideological elements.

7. Categories of asset specificity relate to: (1) site, (2) physical asset (inputs), (3) human asset, (4) dedicated asset (capital), and (5) brand name capital (Williamson 1989).

8. Some of the above elements were already discussed under the heading 'New Industrial Organization'. This may appear slightly confusing, but new industrial organization (i.e. explaining firm behaviour and performance in relation to sectoral structure) is concerned with the consequences of new theories of economic organizations (firm behaviour and performance as explained by factors inside the firm). Some issues, such as incomplete and asymmetric information, feature both within as well as between firms. Furthermore, the issues of vertical integration and of centralization versus decentralization are really on the interface, relating to both characteristics of the firm and elements of industrial structure. Because of this and the declining relevance of the pure SCP approach, the two fields of analysis seem to be merging, with conduct and performance analysed in relation to both structure and internal functioning.

9. While this is normally perceived as governance of principals over agents (owners over workers), a contract has two sides both of which are opportunistic. Governance is required by the agents over their principals as well. That this issue is ignored in the literature on transaction costs economics is

typical for its ideological underpinning. The omission is however not essential to the theory. In fact, all kinds of governance structures on behalf of agents exist (labour unions, labour law).

10.   In the extreme case of 'ideal' markets for everything, no firms would have to exist and everything would be left to the market. This is a fundamental contradiction of the neoclassical theory of the firm. Its assumptions explain away the very firm it wants to describe. Certain governance structures (i.e. nonmarket structures) are necessary ingredients of a firm.

11.   Adverse selection occurs when information asymmetries exist between principal and agent before entering into the contract. The principal may select agents with higher propensity to moral hazard (opportunism).

12.   A special, but relevant case of incomplete contracts occurs when principals have better information before contracting about working conditions. Commitment of agents to such contracts may be considerably reduced. This could lead to lowered effort, non-renewal or breaking of contract, and reduced work pride or loyalty to and identification with the firm (these latter factors will be discussed under the behavioral theory of the firm).

13.   While this may be true for the organizational theory of the firm, it is unfair to accuse the new institutional economists of a lack of consideration for the role of the wider institutional setting. In their explanations of markets and other outcomes of 'collective action' they focus very much on explanations referring to institutional conditions and institutional developments including those of the wider society. See for example Nabli and Nugent (1989) and Ostrom, Feeny and Picht (1988).

14.   It is interesting that the behaviouralists, with their analysis of processes of socialization, come very close to what marxists would refer to as a process of indoctrination leading to the reproduction of the dominant ideology. This parallel is similar to the use of opportunism as an explanatory concept by the new institutional economists which brings them very close to political economy analysis. The crucial difference between, on the one hand, the political economists and marxists and on the other, behaviouralists and new institutionalists, is not located in the differences of opinion about recognition of certain types of behaviour or the role of socialization to make society tick, but in the critical character of the former. The latter claim a positive point of view, and if anything, use their results in an applied, uncritical sense to the status quo, thereby reinforcing it. This would make these latter theories part of the process of socialization. Critical analysis of this process interfere with it.

15.   See Vernon (1966) for a discussion of product cycles in international trade and related investment patterns. Businesspeople in textiles use the concept of product cycle in a slightly different sense, relating to various market stages of new products internal to the firm's marketing strategy: i.e. first experimentation on the domestic market, then full scale on the domestic market followed by internationalization (see Chapter 4 for more detail).

16.   Excludability of a good refers to the feasibility to exclude consumers from using the good, which makes it possible to charge a price. Rivalry (with as its counterpart jointness of use) means that the consumption of a good by one person detracts from the possibility for others to consume that good. Goods that have both properties of excludability and rivalry are 'pure private

goods'; goods with only excludability are referred to as 'toll goods'; those with only rivalry are called 'common-pool resources'; and goods that show neither excludability nor rivalry are 'pure public goods'. While this characterization has been formulated using dichotomies, the four cases can also be interpreted as extreme cases on sliding scales with intermediate cases in-between the extremes. Further extension of these concepts would include the possibility of negative and positive effects (externalities) of consumption and indirect effects of consumption.

17. See Bös (1985) and Gillis *et al.* (1987) for an overview of the various normative objectives of public enterprises.

18. For example, Sobhan (1979) explains the growth of public enterprise as a consequence of the interaction between the circumstances under which the post-colonial state was created and the balance of social forces in the state. Similarly, performance of public enterprises is seen as dependent on the resolution of contradictions between contending forces within the regime over the nature of the state. He notes the possibility of, for example, a regime where the role of public enterprises is in fundamental contention and surplus is used for party building and improving the lifestyles of the bureaucracy, which may lead to labour unrest and deterioration of morale and performance. Conflicts within the state bureaucracy may arise between public enterprise executives and permanent civil servants about control of state enterprises. Shortages may be artificially created to increase prices or to capture benefits through control over distribution. He does not mention the case of a populist regime which uses public enterprise as an instrument for legitimation by supplying employment, high wages and low prices thereby eroding the profitability of public enterprise by price controls. This possibility can coexist with other forces acting on the public enterprise, turning them into something like a common pool resource.

19. For a discussion on 'property rights' in relation to transaction costs and inefficiency, see De Alessi (1983). Alessi's article also provides an example of the tautological character of the rationality assumption in relation to the neoclassical theory of the firm. By rephrasing the model to include more constraints to, and more arguments in the utility function, the neoclassical model is preserved by definition of its own logic.

20. Outside the field of institutional economics, the work of Schaffer has concentrated on these issues. His work may be classified as a critical and normative political economy approach, critical with normative intentions. For a more elaborate statement on these issues, see Schaffer (1984), and for a case study of some of these processes de Valk and Sibanda (1986).

21 The term 'managerial research approach' seems to be unfortunate as it suggests a close relation to the managerial theory of the firm. A better name would be the 'environmental approach'.

22. See Taylor (1988) for a comparative study of stabilization experiences for a sample of 18 countries including the following African countries: Egypt, Ghana, Côte d'Ivoire, Kenya, Sudan, and Tanzania. While these basically macroeconomic studies do not go into much detail for the industrial sector, Taylor concludes that 'a fair assessment would say that the outcomes of orthodox packages ranged from moderately successful to disastrous' (1988:147).

23. See Stein (1992) for a critical discussion of the consequences of the structural adjustment strategy of IMF and World Bank with regard to its consequences for industrialization in Africa.

24. See Chapter 4 for a sample of country experiences with particular reference to the textile sector.

25. As explained in Chapter 4 of the 1987 *World Development Report* (World Bank 1987a), this role is not seen in direct participation with regard to the production of private goods. The report provides a series of examples where state production has failed and privatization has been successfully undertaken.

26. This definition comes close to the one adopted in this study (see Chapter 10).

27. See de Valk (1992) for more details.

28. That efficient firms have a *DRC* < 1, should definitely not be taken to mean that all firms with *DRC* > 1 should be closed down. Rather (and to a certain limit), this should be taken as a first step in identifying firms that are likely to experience problems of adjustment and should be assisted in that process.

29. See Srinivasan (1985) for a more complete discussion and overview of different contributions to neoclassical political economy. For a more critical treatment, the reader is referred to Evans (1989); what has been called here neoclassical political economy, he has labelled neo-utilitarian description of the state.

30. However, when both the political and economic market show market failure rooted in the concentration of the same power, these market failures may reinforce each other and the optimum solution clearly does not obtain. Also the interests of minority groups will not be properly represented on the political market.

31. See Othman (1980) for a comprehensive treatment of the post-colonial state, the overdeveloped state and related concepts. For the whole development of the debate see the journals *Review of African Political Economy* and *New Left Review*, particularly the issues of the 1970s.

32. Ostrom in particular misses the opportunity to apply his concepts to processes rather than to states (as a set of static conditions). Such processes can be found in all societies. Both accounts can be classified as a-historical, a-cultural, ethnocentric, first world views of third world countries.

33. See Milner (1990) for a recent overview of theory and evidence related to Export Promotion Strategies, including the role of state intervention and a number of country case studies. Jenkins (1991) offers an explanation of differences in industrialization performance between Asian and Latin American countries based on differences in effectiveness of policies rather than economic policies *per se*. This is further explained by 'the degree of autonomy enjoyed by the state ... in terms of the contrasting historically determined class structures of the two regions' (ibid.:201). His analysis is generally supportive of Gereffi and Wyman (1990), quoted in the main text. See Heald (1990) and Killick and Commander (1988) for an overview of the issues on privatization in developing countries. Grosh (1990) provides an interesting application to Kenya.

34. De Valk (1990) applies these ideas to the policy of decentralization of development planning.

3 The Textile Sector in International Perspective

3.1 INTRODUCTION

This chapter sets the background against which the experience of the textile sector in Asian and African countries (in Chapter 4), and that of Tanzania (in Chapters 5 to 8) can be appreciated. The type of technology (vintage, modernization, scale, integration), imports and exports of different textile products (UNIDO model) and textile policies pursued in Tanzania and other African countries will be compared to developed and other developing countries.

During the last three decades the interplay of technological change, management techniques, labour market characteristics and consumer tastes in the textile sector have altered the comparative advantages of nations. Moreover, governments of both developed and less developed countries have reacted to these sectoral developments with particular textile policies in the wider macroeconomic setting.[1]

In many countries manufacturing developed around the textile sector because it supplies a basic need: the domestic market is substantial and compared to other sectors rather homogeneous. With standardized technology and, in many cases, a local supply of its main raw material (cotton), it has been one of the sectors in which import substitution has been most successful. Even today the textile sector continues to play a leading role in the industrial development of many developing countries. Technology has been gradually changing: in the 1970s major innovations took place both in spinning and weaving technologies, while in the 1980s and the 1990s the microelectronic revolution has progressively affected textile technology in all stages, in particular weaving and finishing. It is envisaged that the sewing of garments will remain a rather labour-intensive process in the near future.

The changes in technology of the 1970s reflected the industrial environment of industrialized countries in terms of factor costs, availability of skilled labour and sophisticated management, and allowed the industrialized countries to regain their comparative advantage, especially in the production of high-quality textiles. The introduction of microelectronics in the 1980s and the 1990s has allowed for a highly flexible technology, which, combined with sophisticated management techniques such as 'quick response' and medium to high consumer tastes (fashion), has further reinforced the comparative advantage of industrialized countries in the high-quality, fashion-sensitive textile and garment market. Timely delivery to the fashion market has become a more important 'cost' factor than cost of production. Therefore, those parts of the production process that are sensitive to the fashion requirements of the main consumer market require a less remote location. Especially for more labour-intensive processes such as garmenting the mediterranean low-wage countries became attractive locations for foreign investment.

Broadly speaking, while in the 1960s and the 1970s a process of locational deconcentration shifted textile production to low-wage countries (with market niches for high-quality textile products remaining with the high-wage countries), towards the end of the 1970s and the 1980s this trend came to a halt. The end of the 1980s and the beginning of the 1990s saw a reversal, with the locational concentration shifting closer to the main fashion markets, towards higher and high wage developing countries. This has led to changes in international trade flows.[2]

The present chapter introduces sector-specific information on four main issues: textile technology, industrial organization, world market developments for different textile products and policy interventions in international trade with regard to the textile sector. The purpose of this introduction is also fourfold. First, the presentation of some basic facts about textile manufacturing processes (section 3.2) will provide a better appreciation of the economic analysis in the present and following chapters. Second, together with technological progress, the changes in industrial organization (section 3.3) that have occurred in the textile sectors of developed countries have enabled firms of these countries to regain competitiveness in particular market segments. A clear understanding of these changes is essential to appreciate the policies pursued by developed countries discussed in Chapter 4 and the opportunities and constraints in textile development of both successful and less successful developing countries. Third, both technological progress and corresponding changes in industrial organization have led to new developments in international trade (section 3.4), halting the decline of market shares of developed countries and adding 'time of delivery' and 'flexibility of production' to the list of factors determining comparative advantage with regard to the main markets of Europe and the USA. Fourth, these new developments in international trade take place in the international institutional environment (section 3.5) regulating textile trade such as GATT, MFA and the Lomé Convention. While it may be argued that these institutions are designed to protect developed countries' markets, it is shown that least developed countries can and do benefit from some aspects of the operation of these institutions. Chapter 4 concentrates on the policies and performance of selected European, Asian and African countries.

3.2   TECHNOLOGY

This section will first give a brief overview of technical processes applied in textiles and clothing manufacturing and the major technical innovations that have taken place (section 3.2.1). Second, global data on technological innovation and diffusion with particular reference to African countries are supplied, leading to a classification of African countries with regard to technology (section 3.2.2). Third, some aspects of technology supply are discussed (section 3.2.3).

3.2.1   Technical processes and innovations in the cotton textile sector[3]

This section briefly reviews the major technical processes applied in the manufacturing of cotton textiles and garments. Traditional techniques that are still in use in many parts of Africa are not discussed because of their rather insignificant contribution to output in Tanzania.[4] No space is devoted here to man-made fibres because the overwhelming majority of African textile firms, including those in Tanzania, process cotton fibres. With cotton widely grown in various parts of Africa, cotton textiles have an advantage over man-made-fibre-based textiles in terms of availability and transport costs of their main raw material.

From cotton to cotton lint

Raw cotton comes from the seed ball of the cotton plant, a perennial plant or bush. Cotton plants require a stable, high temperature and a stable, relatively low humidity. They grow in almost all tropical and some subtropical areas, roughly between 37° north and 37° south of the equator. Raw cotton consists of cotton fibre and seed. Many varieties have been developed to suit different environments and climates. The most important distinction is staple length, i.e. the length of the elementary cotton fibres in the cotton seed ball. There is long, medium and short staple cotton, with long staple cotton classified as the highest quality because the finest yarn can only be spun from long staple cotton. Yarn quality is determined by the quality of the fibre used (see section above) and by the lack of impurities in and evenness of the thread. The high quality cotton grown in Tanzania, (AR grade) has a fibre length of 3 to 4 centimetres. Other factors that are important for cotton quality are the elasticity of the fibre (important to reduce wrinkling), the colour (the whiter it is the easier to apply colours, the pull strength of the fibre (important for the strength of the yarn), the shininess of the fibre (this indicates the fineness of the fibre) and the fineness (fine fibres are stronger than coarse fibres and can be used to spin finer yarn). After picking, the price of cotton is also determined by purity, since pieces of stems, leaves and seed boxes, sand, immature or dead cotton cause so-called 'neps' in the yarn (little parts of the yarn that are slightly thicker than the rest). Immature and dead cotton fibres are difficult to process and do not easily accept dyes.

The cotton balls are further processed in ginneries where the seeds are separated from the fibres, after which cotton lint is obtained. Seeds are pressed for production of vegetable oil while the remainder, called the seed cake, can be used for animal feed. Cotton lint is compressed into cotton bales to form the agricultural 'raw' material input into the first stage of textile manufacturing, i.e. spinning. Already at the stage of cotton lint, the choice exists to export or to process locally or, as is more common, a combination of the two.

Textile manufacturing (spinning, weaving, processing) and garmenting

Textile manufacturing consists of three main processes, i.e. spinning weaving and finishing. Each of these, in particular spinning and finishing, consists of a number of subprocesses. Integrated textile mills exist, which vary in size from medium to large scale, and where all these processes take place within one establishment. This degree of integration is not technologically required, since these processes can also be carried out in separate mills on either a large or small scale. Garment manufacturing can be part of an integrated mill but is often carried out separately, since economies of scale are not very significant.

Spinning subprocesses

The various spinning subprocesses are summarized opposite in the sequence in which they are carried out. Different machines exist for each of these subprocesses. In practice different degrees of automation exist in terms of transport, quality control, yarn-break monitoring, and repair, although fully automatic spinning plants do exist. Despite the use of different machines for each stage, it is clear that spinning constitutes an integrated process that cannot be divided economically over different firms.

Machine	Process
Bale breaker	Loosening of the cotton lint bales, mixing cotton lint from different bales to obtain a more homogeneous quality, preliminary cleaning
Hopperfeeder	Further mixing and cleaning
Opener	Loosening of the fibres, cleaning, initial formation of the 'lap', consisting of a continuous loosely composed blanket of fibres about one centimetre thick
Scutcher	Further cleaning, final formation of the lap, flattening and smoothening of the lap
Carding machine	Aligning of fibres, further cleaning, formation of the lont (sliver), a thick, round, loosely composed string of fibres
Draw frame	Stretching of the lont and further combing for better fibre alignment
Flyer or speedframe	Roving, i.e. forming of rough yarn by further stretching and twisting; this process can be repeated to obtain successively finer rough yarn
Fine-spinning machine	Further stretching and twisting to form the final yarn on the *ring-spindles* or using *open-end* spinning technology.

Automation in spinning has progressed so that fully automated spinning plants process cotton from the opening subprocess to fine-spinning. Roving technology has improved to the extent that only a single roving stage is required, thus decreasing through-put time. Future improvements in the processes prior to roving may eliminate roving altogether (Laidlaw 1990). The latest major development in the fine spinning process is *open-end spinning* (O-E spindles). Rough yarn is decomposed into individual fibres after which they are directly put together into the final yarn using mechanical (*rotor*), pneumatic (*air jet*) or electrostatic processes. Yarn can be exported and/or used for further processing into fabric. Yarn can be dyed before weaving which is more economical in terms of input use than when fabric is dyed after weaving.

Weaving subprocesses

Apart from weaving, fabric can be produced from fibres through techniques such as knitting-weaving and by assembling different layers of fibres directly together using mechanical, aerodynamic, hydrodynamic or thermodynamic technology (non-woven fabric). Since these techniques are of minor importance relative to traditional weaving techniques, and since no such techniques were found in Tanzania, only weaving will be discussed here.

The weaving technique starts with setting up the warp, a series of parallel yarn threads suspended in a frame. Between these threads, at perpendicular angles with the warp, another thread is inserted, the weft, usually by means of a shuttle. In the most simple form of weaving the weft alternatively passes over and under the successive warp threads, but other patterns are equally feasible. The warp is wound around a large coil with a width equal to the final width of the fabric. This coil is continuously unwound as the weaving progresses. Each time a new line of weft is inserted, a reed moves along each warp thread and presses the newly woven thread against the already formed fabric. The whole weaving machine is called a loom. Technology in use varies from hand looms to fully automatic looms.

The warp must be kept under tension and is exposed to some stress because of the reed action. To strengthen the warp, it is washed in water with an additive (sized) – often starch (in Tanzania experiments took place with cassava flour) – which after weaving has to be removed again.

The main processes are thus warp preparation, weft preparation and the weaving itself according to specified patterns (colours and the relative weft/warp pattern). The weaving is laborious, and major innovations have concentrated on automating the monitoring and repair of warp and weft breakages, monitoring and adjusting weft and warp tension, changing the weaving patterns and developing better ways to insert the weft.

Different technologies are classified by the way the weft is inserted – hand looms (not discussed here), shuttle looms, – and shuttleless looms – and by the number of different fabrics that can be woven simultaneously on one loom (single shed looms, the most common, and multished looms, a recent innovation).

The shuttle employed in the shuttle loom is a (generally wooden) projectile that contains a coil of weft yarn. It is mechanically launched between the warp from one side of the warp frame and back again, leaving the weft behind. The shuttle cannot contain a large coil of weft, and must be changed often. Automation has concentrated on improved weft insertion (for example the unifill system, which automatically fills a battery of about six shuttles from which empty shuttles are automatically replaced).

Because shuttle systems are noisy, slow, energy consuming, and fragile, shuttleless looms have been developed whereby the weft can be unwound continuously from very large coils. Shuttleless looms include projectile looms, rapier looms, airjet and waterjet looms:

– Projectile looms use a relatively light projectile with pegs or grips that grab the weft straight from the large coil and pull it across the warp.

Several projectiles can be operated simultaneously, thus increasing speed and versatility with regard to different colours.

- Rapier looms use bars that reach across the warp to pull the weft through the warp.
- Airjet and waterjet looms use respectively air and water pulses to guide the weft through the warp.

Projectile looms (manufactured by Sulzer) have been in existence longest and enjoy great popularity. Airjet looms have recently gained considerable ground.

Automation using microelectronic hard- and software can also considerably reduce loom conversion time (when different loom settings are required for a new run of fabric) and thus allow for more flexibility. It is at the weaving stage (and later stages) rather than spinning where technology has to be flexible to be able to respond quickly ('quick response') to changing market demands for rather short runs of throughput ('flexible specialization') of high quality (fashion market or market 'niches'). Section 4.3 provides more details.

After washing the starch from the fabric, the so-called 'grey cloth' can be exported and/or used for further domestic processing.

Processing subprocesses

Processing consists of washing, bleaching, dying and printing as well as all other activities that aim to ameliorate the final product quality and appearance. Mostly, these processes are applied to the grey cloth but some can also be applied to yarn directly (for example dying) and even to fibres. Figure 3.1 shows the processing routes for white and coloured fabrics in the Friendship Textile Mill, Tanzania. This is a basic process. A full list of all possibilities (more than 30 such as fire protection, water resistance, no-iron, etc.) is unnecessary here. Each subprocess has its own machinery.

The standard processing stage can be broken down into four subprocesses:

- preparation, including all activities until colouring,
- dying, whereby the whole fabric is submerged in paint,
- printing, whereby the paint is usually applied on one side of the fabric by means of a stamp, and
- finishing, which consists of fixing the paint, removing the paint reactives, chemical finishing, washing and drying and pressing.

Figure 3.1　Simple processing routes for white and coloured fabrics

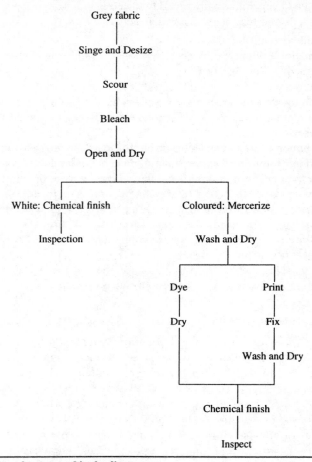

Explanation of terms used in the diagram:

Singing	the burning off of small, extruding pieces of fibre from the fabric to smoothen it;
Desizing	removing the starch by passing it through an enzyme solution;
Scouring	washing with caustic soda to clean the fabric of fats before dying or printing;
Bleaching	lightening the fabric by applying chemicals, for example hydrogen peroxide;
Mercerizing	washing in a solution of natriumhydroxide with the fabric under tension to obtain a shiny fabric that can withstand washing; this is only possible for long staple cotton such as grown in Tanzania and Egypt;
Chemical finishing	giving the fabric its final appearance by hardening (with starch) or softening.

Source: Friendship Textile Mill, own data, 1988.

The finishing stage is the most import intensive stage for countries such as Tanzania that must import dyes and chemicals. It is also the most water-intensive stage because energy requirements of generating steam, boiling and drying are considerable.

Automation in finishing technology is undergoing a major breakthrough with the application of microelectronics. The current market possibilities and requirements arising from flexible specialization have gone hand in hand with the development of Computer Aided Techniques (CAT) consisting of computer-aided design (CAD), computer-aided engraving (CAE), computer-aided colouring (CAC) and an automated 'colour kitchen'. This has the important advantages of permitting experimentation from initial design to market testing, quality control, replicability (whereby information on the relevant parameters can be communicated all over the world), flexibility and efficiency. In addition, it is estimated that the chemical load waste water can be reduced by more than 50 percent, thereby making the new technology attractive from an environmental point of view.

Knitting subprocesses

Here knitting consists of a single process only involving the knitting machine itself although technologies do vary from hand knitting to fully automated knitting of garments. Knitting allows for rather complex colour patterns. However, the bulk of knitting in Tanzania consists of white T-shirts for the export market.

Garment making subprocesses

Garmenting involves three sets of activities:

- pre-assembly, when the garments are designed, patterns made and individual components (such as sleeves, pockets, front and back panels) cut from cloth,
- assembly, when the components are sewn together into a finished garment, and
- finishing, when the garment is pressed, packaged and dispatched.

Automation possibilities are greatest in the pre-assembly stage with the help of CAD and computer numerical control (CNC) cutters which allow for cloth savings of up to 15 percent. There are fewer possibilities for automation in assembly. Most common are microelectronic-based control units added to a conventional sewing machine. Two other computer-aided applications are an expensive automated machine to perform high volume, specialized tasks such as collar stitching, and a cheaper, more flexible sewing machine that can learn specific, repetitive, sequential tasks from the sewing operator which it then can repeat at much higher speed. Diffusion of these last two innovations is limited but each has contributed to the regaining the competitiveness of (especially) European firms. Technological research continues into more fully computer-aided manufacturing (CAM) applications in apparel manufacturing. In its *Global Report 1989/90*, UNIDO estimates that 'within the next ten years, most of the apparel-manufacturing process is expected to be automated' (UNIDO 1989b:219). However, as far as developing countries are concerned, Hoffman points out that: 'rather than facing rapid erosion of competitive advantage in one of their most important sectors, assembly automation at the moment is in fact a barely visible phenomenon. At least in terms of shifting trading patterns, assembly automation is unlikely to cause developing countries any significant worry in the short term' (Hoffman 1989:88).[5] Conventional sewing machines will remain the rule for the near future for most tasks.

3.2.2 Characteristics of technology supply

Important questions for developing countries with regard to technology choice and technological change are (a) whether such choices exist, (b) whether technological change can be expected in more appropriate technologies in terms of factor use, skill requirements etc. and (c) whether there are any scale requirements for the most efficient use of available technology.

According to a thorough study on textile technology by Boon, 'for textile and apparel production a rather wide technology and supply variety is available from which an appropriate choice of technology for the urban industrial sector in developing countries can potentially be made' (Boon, 1981:470). For both spinning and weaving this choice is available because both the most recent technology as well as the more conventional technology are being produced, each with different degrees of automation.

Second-hand technology appears to be a feasible option (Pack 1985).[6] Presently, at times of high investment in new technology, second-hand machines of the conventional type are widely available without necessarily being old in the sense of requiring costly maintenance and repair efforts.[7] This combines with the fact that conventional technology is still a viable option as discussed above. Producers of textile technology do not look upon second-hand technology as a source of competition and are quite willing to supply maintenance services to the purchasers of second-hand machines (Boon 1981:265).

Choices related to the purchase of technologies, such as choice of supplier, choice of technology and choice of age of equipment, are influenced by type of ownership (James 1989), by source of finance (related but not identical to ownership), by product characteristics in relation to market orientation and by macroeconomic variables such as level and structure of protection and interest rates. Foreign aid is an important source of finance for public sector enterprises (Burch 1987),[8] some of which are established with the explicit aim to export and others to produce for the local market. Local private firms often rely on own finance in combination with supplier arrangements. Some employ second-hand technology of an old vintage to produce for the low income, low quality market. Others aim at exports with more advanced technology. Private firms with foreign linkages in one form or another make choices influenced by their mother company. These issues will be elaborated upon when the case of Tanzania is discussed.

Technological change is both geoconditioned, i.e. responding to supply conditions of the areas where technological research and development takes place (industrialized countries), and market induced, i.e. responding to demand and marketing conditions such as new requirements arising from high quality, fashionable consumer demand (flexible specialization) and 'quick response' marketing systems (see section 3.3).

Boon comments that technological change in spinning, weaving, processing and apparel manufacturing will lead to new technologies which 'may prove to be superior in almost every sense' and which 'may affect present comparative production realities and therefore First World textile and apparel production may remain, or become again, economically feasible' (Boon 1981:471). At present, however, new textile technologies do not dominate the older ones in developing countries. Referring to the comparison of the most modern technologies and currently available conventional technologies for both spinning and weaving shows that the former have higher production costs at market prices for the factors of production; the discrepancy would be greater at shadow prices (Pack 1987:3).

However, aspects of markets, organization and management combine with technology to reduce the choice of technology for certain products to the most recent ones (Hoffman 1989).[9] But new technology is also market induced, so where markets remain in more standardized commodities, these can be serviced by conventional technologies. This means that international trade in textiles and apparel remains an important possibility for developing countries.

Developing countries could benefit from more appropriate technologies than those currently available. According to Boon (1981:244), given their different production constraints and endowments, developing countries apply different criteria with regard to machine choice as compared to developed countries. They focus more on (a) capital costs (price of machinery), (b) credit facilities, (c) skill requirements. and (d) homogeneity of technology at the firm level, whereas developed countries give priority to factors such as (a) labour costs, (b) machine design: universality, flexibility, productivity, and durability, and (c) quality of output.

However, little effort is directed at developing such technology for developing countries and where such products have been developed, they have met with little commercial success (Boon 1981:212).

With regard to the question of scale, the nature of the technical processes of spinning, weaving and apparel manufacturing are such that scale (total installed capacity) can be altered simply by increasing or reducing the number of machines employed in the process. In this sense, scale is not embodied in the technology. Large variations in plant size are therefore possible and in fact are realized. For example, the textile/clothing sector in many Asian countries consists of a mixture of small, medium and large scale firms (UNIDO 1988). Korea, one of the most successful countries in textiles and apparel development, is a good example (Khan 1985). The highly successful textile industry in Prato (Italy) also shows the viability of small and medium scale of production (Bhalla and Stevens 1984; see also Mazzonis, Colombo and Lanzavecchia 1983).[10]

Thus, it can be concluded that considerable choice exists both with regard to new and second-hand technology but that little R&D effort has been undertaken to develop technology specifically appropriate to Third World conditions, while considerable choice exists *vis-à-vis* the scale of production.[11]

Technological change in the Third World is induced by conditions imposed by market orientation rather than by relative factor endowments. Old equipment and outdated technologies are still in use to meet low quality, low income consumer demand, while more recent equipment with current technologies is employed for standardized, medium to high quality world demand and new equipment and the latest technologies are required for high quality, fashion sensitive demand, especially in weaving and colouring processes.

3.2.3　Technological innovation and diffusion

Technological change in the processing chain from cotton to garments comes in various forms:[12]

Activities that were once carried out by hand are now done by a machine. This is direct, labour-replacing technological change. All forms of automation of existing processes are in fact labour replacing. Examples include automatic factory floor transport of the intermediate product between different machines, aspects of computer-aided technology (when previous CA designs are reproduced), automatic setting of weaving looms and automatic colouring.

Existing machines for particular subprocesses are replaced by more efficient ones as in the case of O-E spinning and shuttleless looms. This can be called indirect labour replacing technological change in the sense that it leads to higher labour productivity which, under constrained demand conditions (or per unit output), leads to lower employment.

Activities that previously were not carried out by any combination of machines and labour are made possible by new machines. In essence, this implies an improved or new product. Higher quality new designs made possible by new technologies fall in this category. Demand interactions will occur between the old and new products. In some instances, this change may be partial replacement of inferior products, in others it may add to a product range (strictly speaking, improved products should be treated as new products). Whether or not this is labour replacing in the absolute sense in terms of its effects on employment is difficult to say as, in the case of improved products, it depends on the technology of both the inferior product and the improved product, and, in the case of new products, the concept of labour and/or capital saving does not really apply even if employment effects are created by demand substitution effects.

Many new machines embody a combination of all three types of technological change. For example, a modern shuttleless loom produces higher quality cloth, requires less labour per loom (because of automatic setting, monitoring, fine adjustment of settings, and repair of thread breakages) and has a much higher throughput per machine. In addition, many new machines, apart from their labour replacing impact, require a different type of labour (including management) which is often a mixture of both more as well as less skilled labour, or just differently skilled labour. These changes may be called skill replacing technological change, sometimes requiring a retooling of existing labour in service or through short training courses, sometimes replacing existing labour with other labour.

The two following subsections will supply evidence on the distribution and diffusion of textile technology and discuss the source of new technologies in relation to their characteristics.

Installed capacity and technological modernization by country

Available indicators for spinning and weaving technology by African countries and world regions are detailed in tables A.1, A.2 (in the

Appendix) and 3.1. Table 3.1 shows that 52.1 and 58.4 percent out of total
world spinning and weaving capacity are located in Asia, compared to
26.9 and 21.5 percent in Europe, 10.9 and 7.7 percent in North America,
5.6 and 7.3 percent in South America, while only 5 percent is located in
Africa. From 1975 to 1987/88 major restructuring took place in this
period, especially in favour of Asian countries. The main losers are
Europe and (in particular) North America. South America has maintained
its share while Africa has gained a great deal in terms of its own installed
capacities, but its small base inflates the percentage change. Relative to the
rest of the world, its share has remained very small. In addition, the higher
share of more efficient spinning and weaving installations in Europe,
North America and some Asian countries makes these figures look more
dramatic than they would be in terms of production capacity.

Further evidence shows that Korea and Taiwan have the highest number
of spindles and looms per inhabitant, with Korea slightly ahead of Taiwan
but both about 2.5 times the number of the third highest, Japan (calculated
from UNIDO 1990b). Significant is that two Mediterranean countries,
Egypt and Turkey, score fourth and fifth for spinning and fifth and sixth
for weaving. Also countries close to the US market such as Mexico and
Argentina score quite high on both indicators. In Asia, Thailand is the
leading the non-NIC.

With regard to spindles per inhabitant in African countries (see Table
A.1), the top ten countries are (in descending order) Egypt, Swaziland,
South Africa, Sudan, Morocco, Tanzania, Zimbabwe, Botswana, Algeria
and Tunisia. They include most North African countries and the countries

*Table 3.1   Regional distribution of installed capacity in spinning (number of
spindles) and weaving (number of looms) in 1975 as percentage of world total*

Region	Spinning			Weaving		
	1975	1987	% change	1975	1988	% change
Africa	3.2	4.5	+40.6	3.3	5.2	+57.6
Asia	44.0	52.1	+18.4	48.1	58.4	+21.4
Europe	32.1	26.9	−16.2	28.9	21.5	−25.6
North America	15.1	10.9	−27.8	12.3	7.7	−37.4
South America	5.5	5.6	+1.8	7.4	7.3	−1.4

Source: Calculated from UNIDO (1990b) with data for 1975 from Boon (1981).

with strong linkages with South Africa. Quite surprisingly, Tanzania is number six in this list, far ahead of countries like Côte d'Ivoire, Kenya and Nigeria. For comparison, note that Turkey is 43 percent higher, while countries like Taiwan and Korea are almost 250 percent higher.

The top ten countries for weaving looms per inhabitant in Africa (see Appendix, Table A.2) are (in descending order) Egypt, Libya, Tunisia, Algeria, Benin, Ghana, Morocco, Côte d'Ivoire, Zimbabwe and Tanzania. Noteworthy again is the dominant presence of North African countries and Ghana and Tanzania. Again for comparison, note that Egypt, with the highest score in Africa, is at the same level as Thailand, while Taiwan's and Korea's weaving capacity per inhabitant is higher than that of Egypt by about 250 percent.

Columns nine and ten of Tables A.1 and A.2 show indicators of the state of technology and technological change for spinning and weaving.[13]

With the help of these indicators, the following classification of African countries has been defined for spinning or weaving technologies:[14] group one (39 and 33 percent for spinning or weaving) consist of unsuccessful countries, without any technological change and mostly small in size; group two (33 and 33 percent for spinning or weaving) comprises the 'struggling' countries, partially modernizing and/or little or no technological change; the countries in group three (17 and 16 percent for spinning or weaving) are progressing, partially modernized with high technological change; and group four (11 and 16 percent for spinning or weaving) consists of successful countries with medium to highly modern technology and high technological change. The first two columns of Table 3.4 show the distribution of African countries over these groups. Since technology and trade are very much interlinked, the discussion of these results will have to be preceded by a discussion of changes in international trade and corresponding changes in industrial organization.

3.3 CHANGES IN INDUSTRIAL ORGANIZATION

After the rather dramatic changes in hard technology (O-E spinning and shuttleless weaving) beginning in the late 1970s, the 1980s have seen a major breakthrough in the application of microelectronics to the textile-clothing manufacturing complex. It is estimated that in the 1990s this process will lead to further systematic integration of the production process, providing much more flexibility, standardization of product specifications and a further shortening of the production sequence (Hoffman 1989:80).

These technological innovations have been accompanied by (a) new market characteristics, (b) innovations in management practices, and (c) changing production relations.[15] Technological change, quick-response marketing, and production taken together have led to changing world trade patterns which will be discussed in section 4.4.

New market characteristics

Flexible technology has facilitated flexible specialization which has allowed producers to become more sensitive to changing consumer demands and retailers to further induce such consumer demands.[16] In a market already characterized by fashion, this has led to even higher consumer demand for fashionable garments. In addition, further product differentiation has become possible which has led to market fragmentation (market 'niches').

At the same time, standardized product specifications and increased international communication have internationalized fashion markets. Fashions spread more quickly throughout the world, while flexible technology allows them to be adjusted to the particular characteristics of the local market.

At the retail level, the strategy with regard to risk in relation to fashion is to keep low stocks for fashionable products with larger stocks for more conventional items (Nijhuis 1990:32). This strategy implies that for high fashion garments relatively small, repeat orders are made depending on the success of the particular item. These repeat orders must have the same (high) level of quality, with exactly matching specifications and should be delivered quickly in order not to miss the market wave. Microelectronic applications in quality control and standardization allow for these demands, while management practices are adjusting to them.

Quick Response (QR) management practices

The major change from the point of view of management with regard to fashion in contrast with conventional demand is that production time becomes as essential as production cost. Additional requirements facing the producers are quality, flexibility and standardization. More detailed QR management requirements included:[17]

1.   quality standards leading to the integration of quality control over the whole chain, from machine producers and cotton growers to garmenting and finally retailing, including all subprocesses;
2.   reliable production processes to avoid downtimes and rejects;
3.   versatile machines and processes, to allow for quick responses to changing demands (shorter runs with more repeat orders lead to

longer downtimes, often accounting for more than 70 percent of total through-put time), allowing inventories to be kept low;

4. ease of operation to eliminate the need to train or retrain workers (thus adding to versatility);

5. speed of production to reduce throughput time;

6. standardized communication between machines and managers to allow for international exchange; and

7. minimal environmental impact to avoid increasingly high producer costs.

Production and trade relations

The market demands that textile-clothing producers develop better control over the whole textile-clothing system and achieve faster market penetration. The industry has developed a number of communication and information systems in different parts of the pipeline, such as point of sale (POS) scanning for immediate market feedback, electronic data exchange (EDI) speeding up information exchange, the universal product code (UPC) facilitating communication and the standardization of custom procedures with the help of carton labelling (CL) (Nijhuis 1990:32).

A further development is found in improved service systems such as FASLINK between fibre producers and textile companies, TALC. (Textile/Apparel Linkage Council), SAFLINK between sundry suppliers and apparel producers and VICS. (voluntary inter-company standards) between apparel firms and retailers. Machine producers no longer claim to support a single machine but a system, while 'software and service around the product becomes more important than the machine itself' (Hutti 1990:39).

Moreover, various textile industrialists stress the importance of mutual trust between producers in the various parts of the system (Nijhuis 1990; Laidlaw 1990; Hutti 1990). Because time is increasingly crucial for 'catching the wave' of the market, reliability of timing and quality of supply have come to be of utmost importance. Business must be conducted under conditions of mutual trust and penalties for breaking promises are high. Under these circumstances, transaction costs may be high.

In addition, alliances between producers in the textile-clothing chain and outsiders such as large chemical companies (manmade fibre producers and firms producing new products for finishing) and machine manufacturers speed up production responses to rapidly changing market demands (UNIDO 1987; Winsemius 1990).

Finally, international competition has increased to the extent that firms can no longer afford to delay selling new products internationally. Thus the product cycle for new products is shortened by eliminating the national expansion phase. New products are marketed simultaneously both nationally and internationally.

Thus, developments in technology, management and markets have led to a new competitive balance whereby the ailing textile-clothing industries of developed countries have gained new dynamism, particularly in the high quality, high fashion end of the market.

In many industrialized countries, the restructuring of the textile-clothing industry has been achieved through substantial government involvement expressed in various national textile restructuring plans which began as attempts to deal with low cost competition but which in the context of subsequent developments in technology and markets have contributed to regaining competitiveness. Textile policies have consisted, on one hand, of increased protection expressed in trade policies, for example the Multi-Fibre Agreement, discussed below (section 4.5) and on the other of industrial structural adjustment policies, involving sectoral and firm level state intervention. These textile-clothing adjustment policies for developed countries have been described in detail in de la Torre (1984) and are summarized in Chapter 4.

The irony is that the success of these policies materialized at the same time that structural adjustment policies for developing countries stressed liberalization without any attention to structural adjustment for the manufacturing sector in general and the textile-clothing sector in particular. Scope for such policies still exists. Although one part of the market may be captured by advanced countries, less fashionable, more standardized products remain in demand and even within the fashion branch itself standardized components of fashion items can be separately produced in large lots so that different production and trade conditions apply. Chapter 4 will elaborate further on textile policies in selected individual countries.

3.4   WORLD TEXTILE AND APPAREL TRADE DEVELOPMENTS

World consumption of finished textile goods declined during the first half of the 1970s, recovered slowly until 1983 and faster from 1984 onwards (Coker (1990). Substantial increases were recorded especially in the years 1986 and 1987. Consumption in both developed and developing countries increased. While undoubtedly increases in population and income underlie these developments in developing countries (with high income elasticities of demand for clothing at their lower level of income), the large increases in final consumption of developed countries seem to indicate a shift in consumption patterns towards clothing. This has resulted in the highest-ever levels of final consumption per head in almost all regions of the developed world, and in China and East and South East Asia.

World trade in textile and clothing (measured in current prices) more than doubled every five years from 1965 to 1980 (UNIDO 1987). In the 1980s this trend abruptly came to a halt. Although in absolute terms value of exports increased by 11 percent annually over the whole period, when inflation is taken into account there was an increase in real terms of about 3.7 percent over the period 1965 to 1980 and in the last five year period of 4.8 percent.[18] Simultaneously the structure of trade has changed significantly. Developed market economies (DMEs)[19] have lost their dominant share in exports while steadily increasing their import shares, with the result that they became net importers by 1975. Data from the International Textile Manufacturing Federation (ITMF) show that for the period 1985 to 1989 exports (measured in volume) from Western Europe and the USA have increased again and those of Japan have declined during the same period (Table 3.2). This is confirmed by Coker (1990) using FAO data. Despite these absolute increases in exports, shares declined. Self-sufficiency,[20] which for the EC countries as a group had increased during the first half of the 1980s, decreased from 1984 onwards to about 77 percent while for the USA self-sufficiency declined steadily to the same level.

Advanced textile exporters (ATEs)[21] have increased their share in this expanding trade especially in the 1960s and early 1970s. Data from ITMF (Table 3.2)[22] reveal that, of these countries, Brazil has shown a rather

Table 3.2   Exports of textile and clothing (thousand tons) by ITMF member countries, 1981–89

Country/Region	1980	1981	1982	1983	1984	1985	1986	1987	1988	1989
Brazil	235	278	212	299	262	310	255	269	296	303
Japan	600	653	605	651	646	631	612	549	451	440
Korea	667	771	724	798	848	896	989	1090	1552	1324
Taiwan	568	656	603	649	745	904	1002	1070	1122	1181
Turkey	119	131	137	156	183	232	262	327	362	389
USA	598	461	319	317	320	310	356	415	475	523
West. Europe	295	299	292	303	328	349	344	357	382	402
Total ITMF	5832	6033	5631	6038	6374	6918	7116	7532	8310	8507

Source: International Textile Manufacturers Federation, Zurich.

fluctuating export performance (in volume terms) during the 1980s without much overall increase. Clothing exports suffered in the period 1984-7, but recovered in the two last years. Korea's exports increased steadily until 1988, but declined suddenly in 1989 for yarn, textile fabrics and apparel. Taiwan, not covered by the data in the tables shown, has more than doubled its total textile export volume during the 1980s.

In the 1980s the expansionary role of the ATEs was taken over by the group of other developing economies (ODEs),[23] which became net exporters somewhere between 1975 and 1980. The ODEs are a widely divergent group of countries within which many Asian countries like Thailand, Malaysia and Indonesia and some African countries like Morocco, Tunisia and Mauritius are particularly successful. Turkey should be mentioned as a specially successful case, more than tripling its exports in the 1980s (Table 3.2).

Centrally planned economies (CPEs) roughly maintained their low share in exports while slightly decreasing their import share. As a group, the CPEs are roughly in trade balance throughout the period.

These overall changes do not reveal changes that occurred in the sectoral composition of trade and changes that occurred within the identified groups of countries. As was shown above, the textile-clothing sector is vertically composed of basically three tradable subsectors (yarn, textiles and apparel) with rather different characteristics. Horizontally, the chief distinction that can be drawn is between synthetic and natural fibres and fabrics. Composition of exports and imports with regard to these sectoral distinctions will be discussed in section 3.4.1 using the same country groupings. Due to the focus of this study, section 3.4.2 will highlight subsectoral trade developments of the African countries within the group of ODEs.

3.4.1 Composition of textile and apparel trade by subsectors for major groups of countries

Subsectoral trade patterns reflect the success or failure of (groups of) developing countries to adopt technologies inherent to those subsectors. In this context, the success of developing countries (ATEs and/or ODEs) is at the expense of DMEs. The particular conditions of a country play an important role. For example, countries may enter the textile-clothing trade by developing their forward linkages from cotton exports to yarn exports, textile exports and finally apparel exports, thus progressively adding downstream value to their exports. Or, they may move backwards from apparel production to textiles and yarn, deepening their import substitution or export content. Differences may exist depending on the stage of industrialization of a particular country. For example, backward linking may be more or less likely for synthetic than for natural fibre-based production. UNIDO (1987) supplies some preliminary evidence on these issues.

(a) On the export side, the DMEs have seen a gradual increase in their share of clothing while the other categories show a more cyclical behaviour. Synthetic yarn reached a peak in 1970 and declined thereafter. Synthetic fabrics reached their peak in 1975. The share of natural fabrics declined drastically after the first period, to remain roughly stable until 1985. On the import side, the DME share of clothing almost doubled over the whole period. Together with knitwear the DMEs account for nearly 70 percent of the total import bill in 1985. Natural fabrics declined from a substantial 22.9 percent to only 9.6 percent.

(b) The export composition of ATEs reveals an increasing share of clothing and knitwear (from 63.0 percent in 1965 to 76.5 percent in 1985) and of synthetic fabrics. This shift was at the expense of natural fabrics, which declined from a share of 26.4 percent to 6.2 percent. On the import side, a declining share of natural fabrics can be noted, with synthetic yarn and fabrics experiencing a peak in 1970. Noteworthy as well is that the share of clothing and knitwear imports increased in the early 1980s to 32.1 percent in 1985.

(c) For ODEs, there is an impressive shift from exports of natural fabrics (57.0 percent in 1965 and 13.4 percent in 1985) to exports of clothing and knitwear (24.8 percent in 1965 to 68.0 percent in 1985). With regard to ODE imports, the major change is a shift from natural fabrics (42.2 percent in 1965 to 15.0 percent in 1985) to synthetic yarn and fabrics (23.1 percent in 1965 to 50.3 percent in 1985). Most of this shift occurred between 1970 and 1975.

Summarizing, clothing and knitwear export shares have gone up for all groups of countries but most dramatically for the ODEs. Exports shares of synthetic fabrics have increased for DMEs and ATEs with an increasing import share of synthetic yarn and fabrics for ODEs. Both export and import shares for natural fabrics have declined for DMEs, ATEs and ODEs alike.

This suggests for the ODEs that they have progressively been able to integrate lower stages of textile production (i.e. yarn and fabrics) with the higher stage (clothing). A more elaborate scheme of the development process of ODEs over time with regard to the textile-clothing sector by UNIDO (1987:13) identifies four stages:

I.   an 'infant industry' phase, characterized by net imports of both clothing and textiles but with declining trends;

II.   an 'export promotion cum import substitution' phase, during which the overall trade deficit of the textile and clothing complex is increasingly reduced by growing net-exports of clothing and advancing substitution of textile imports;

III.   a 'clothing-led growth' phase, in which textile import substitution is terminated, though typically at a modest net-trade deficit of textile goods. Exports of clothing continue to expand, but the surplus of net-clothing exports is insufficient to compensate the persisting deficit of textile trade;

IV.   a 'surplus phase', in which either (a) exports of clothing are larger than imports of textiles, and/or (b) textile exports are larger than textile imports.

Based on this model of development, UNIDO has traced the development of a number of countries. See Table 3.3.

This suggested sequence of 'stages of growth' for the textile-clothing sector is broadly supported by the way the various countries have been classified. Only few countries (Brazil, Mexico and Pakistan) contradict the suggested growth model, and they do so only between stages IVa and IVb. Whether this is a sign of success, with the apparel subsector requiring more textile inputs than the domestic textile subsector can deliver, or whether it is due to supply problems in the textile subsector is not obvious. The UNIDO 'stages of growth' model does not go into sufficient detail to classify such developments.

The UNIDO growth model is quite explicit on how textile industrialization proceeds. The progressive movement from import substitution to export promotion takes place in textiles and clothing alike but clothing is supposed to export from phase II onwards with textiles adjusting to the expanding requirements of the clothing sector.[24] Almost until the very end clothing remains the dynamic sector. Only in phase IVb are net textile exports supposed to take place. All the countries selected for the classification, apart from Singapore, have been successful in reaching phase IVa or IVb. As such, it can be seen as a model of success. Whether or not less successful and/or unsuccessful countries digress from this growth path of success and where such countries would be classified cannot be assessed. The following section fits African countries into the classification.

Table 3.3 Changes in the global textile system

	1962	1965	1970	1975	1980–1985
PHASE I	Colombia, Greece, Indonesia, Malaysia, Morocco, Philippines, Singapore, Sri Lanka, Thailand, Tunisia, Turkey	Colombia, Greece, Indonesia, Malaysia, Morocco, Philippines, Singapore, Sri Lanka, Thailand, Tunisia, Turkey	Indonesia, Malaysia, Thailand, Philippines, Tunisia	Indonesia	
PHASE II	Korea		Greece, Morocco, Singapore, Sri Lanka	Malaysia, Philippines	Singapore
PHASE III	Spain, Yugoslavia	Spain, Yugoslavia	Mexico, Yugoslavia	Sri Lanka, Thailand, Tunisia	
PHASE IVa	Hong Kong	Hong Kong, India, Korea, Mexico	Hong Kong, Korea	Brazil, Hong Kong, Pakistan, Mexico, Morocco, Yugoslavia	Tunisia, Brazil, Hong Kong, Korea, Indonesia, Malaysia, Mexico, Morocco, Philippines, Thailand, Sri Lanka
PHASE IVb	Brazil, Mexico, Portugal, India, Pakistan	Brazil, Mexico, Portugal, India, Pakistan	Portugal, India, Colombia, Pakistan, Spain, Turkey	Colombia, Greece, India	Korea, Mexico, Portugal, Spain, Turkey

Note: For Brazil, Pakistan and Yugoslavia the complete trajectory has not been given in the source, while India and Mexico have been inserted twice in the columns for years 1965 and 1975 respectively, which is possible.

Source: UNIDO, 1987.

3.4.2   Subsectoral trade developments of African countries

Applying the UNIDO classification to African countries gives the following results (see Table 3.4):[25] Of the 34 countries classified, 29 countries (85 percent) fall in group I, no countries in groups II and III, while 5 countries are placed in group IV.

Of these last five, Morocco and Tunisia were already reported in the UNIDO classification. Table 3.4 shows that they have invested in advanced textile technology and are medium to large in size. Egypt, Madagascar and Mauritius are new entrants. Success of these countries is not based on forward processing of cotton since Morocco, Tunisia and Mauritius are in fact large cotton and yarn importers.

Madagascar appears to be a 'misfit' with respect to the UNIDO development model. It has a relatively modest surplus in textile trade and exports no clothing. Madagascar has achieved trade surplus in textiles first and may move into clothing later. However, it has done so with a rather small textile sector employing outdated technologies. Its textile-clothing sector is its largest manufacturing sector (Appendix, Table A.3). While it has expanded its manufacturing sector in the 1970s, it recorded negative growth rates of manufacturing value-added (MVA) in the 1980s (Riddell 1990a). Madagascar's manufacturing experience does not seem to be a success, although relatively speaking its textile-clothing sector appears most developed.

Egypt is clearly a genuine 'class four' case with its textile import/export ratio far below unity and declining and with its exports of clothing increasing between 1984 and 1987. Its trade position also corresponds with its size position, i.e. large, although its textile technology is rather outdated. The experience of Egypt (and to a less extent of Madagascar) shows that substantial exports are possible without the most recent textile technology.

Mauritius has a highly export-oriented garment sector with a small textile sector (Table 4.7) and consequently high textile import/export ratios. Like Madagascar, Mauritius' development seems at odds with the UNIDO sequence as it appears to be based on exports of garments, perhaps later developing backwardly into textiles. As one of the few exceptions in Africa, Mauritius has been expanding its manufacturing sector (Riddell 1990a) and has reached a significant share of MVA in GDP (Appendix, Table A.3). Also its manufacturing exports have increased rapidly in relation to total exports. From these data Mauritius is presented as a success. This success is partly attributable to a foreign investment drive by Asian textile-clothing manufacturers as a result of the impact on

Asian countries of the quota system under the Multi-Fibre Agreement (see section 3.5.2 and World Bank 1989a:111). The case of Mauritius is discussed in more detail in Chapter 4, section 4.4.1.

The first trade group, comprising the remainder of African countries, includes relatively more successful countries such as Côte d'Ivoire, SACU and Zimbabwe as well as unsuccessful countries. Clearly, for the purpose of comparison between African countries, UNIDO's phase one needs to be differentiated further. Within trade group one countries, a further division

Table 3.4   *Classification of African countries as textile producers*

Country	Technology Group		Size[a]		Trade group[b]	
	spinning	*weaving*	*spinning*	*weaving*	*UNIDO*	*This study*
Algeria[c]	2	4	M	M	1	1a
Angola	2	2	S	S	1	1a
Benin	1	1	S	S	1	1a
Botswana	3	4	M	S		
Burkina Faso	1	1	S	S	1	1b
Cameroon	1	2	S	S	1	1b
Chad	1	1	S	S		
Congo	1	1	S	S	1	1a
Côte d'Ivoire	3	3	M	M	1	1c
C. African R.	1	1	S	S	1	1a
Egypt	2	2	L	L	4b	
Ethiopia[c]	3,	2	S	S,	1	1b
Gabon					1	1a
Ghana	1	1	S	M	1	1a
Guinea	2	2	S	S	1	1a
Kenya[c]	2	3	S	S	1	1b
Libya	1	2	S	L	1	1a
Madagascar	2	2	S	S	4b	
Malawi	2	2	S	S	1	1c
Mali	1	1	S	S	1	1b
Mauritius	4	4	S	S	4a	
Morocco	4	4	M	M	4b	
Mozambique	2	1	S	S	1	
Niger	1	1	S	S	1	
Nigeria	3	3	S	S	1	1b
Rwanda					1	1a
Senegal[c]	2	3	S	S	1	1b
Somalia	1	2	S	S	1	1a
South Africa[d]	3	4	L	S	1	1c
Sudan	1	1	L	S	1	1b

Table 3.4 continued

Country	Technology Group		Size[a]		Trade group[b]	
	spinning	*weaving*	*spinning*	*weaving*	*UNIDO*	*This study*
Swaziland[c]	2	4	L	S		
Togo	2	1	S	S	1	1a
Tunisia	4	3	M	L	4a	
Uganda	1	2	S	S		
Tanzania	2	2	M	M	1	1c
Zaire	1	1	S	S	1	1a
Zambia[c]	4	2	S	S	1	1a
Zimbabwe	3	3	M	M	1	1c

Notes:
(a) Textile producing capacity per caput.
(b) The trade classification is obtained by applying the UNIDO classification. However, for some countries the result needs further qualification.
(c) These countries show mixed results between the combined first two and the combined last two technology groups.
(d) In UN trade data, South Africa has been grouped together with Botswana, Lesotho and Swaziland in the Southern African Custom Union (SACU). Therefore the trade grouping of South Africa is the combined SACU position.
Source: Derived from tables A.1, A.2 and 3.3.

can be made between countries that do not export at all (Ia), countries that either export textiles or clothing (Ib) and countries that export both (Ic).

Countries in group (1c) are: Côte d'Ivoire, Malawi, SACU, Tanzania and Zimbabwe. Of these countries, only SACU and Zimbabwe show declining trends of their import/export ratios. Further information presented in Table A.3 shows that Zimbabwe is amongst the more industrialized countries in Africa. Its textile sector is of medium size, employing quite advanced technology. Despite its current problems, Zimbabwe's future in manufacturing is cautiously and conditionally estimated to be promising (Riddell 1990b). The same judgement seems to apply to the future of textile-clothing sector. The case of Zimbabwe is discussed in more detail in Chapter 4, section 5.4.2. Especially SACU shows a rather balanced development between textiles and clothing, roughly in line with the UNIDO development model. In addition its technology is rather recent.

Côte d'Ivoire, Malawi and Tanzania are in fact increasing their ratios, indicating stagnation and decline of what had appeared to be a promising development away from cotton to textile and apparel exports. This is confirmed by the poor growth performance of MVA of these countries (negative for Côte d'Ivoire (–0.4) and Tanzania (–4.5) and only 2.7 for Malawi during 1979–1986, Riddell 1990a) while the share of manufactured in total exports is rather low for Côte d'Ivoire (Appendix, Table A.3) and Tanzania which had declined to 8.0 percent in 1986 (United Republic of Tanzania 1988).[26] Of these three countries Malawi appears to be the least troubled. Thus the ordering of the countries in group (1c) is SACU, followed by Zimbabwe, and then at some distance Malawi, Côte d'Ivoire and Tanzania.

There are eight countries in group (Ib): Burkina Faso, Cameroon, Ethiopia, Kenya, Mali, Niger, Senegal and Sudan. Apart from Ethiopia, all have some textile exports but no clothing exports. Five are at the lowest level of technology (Burkina Faso, Cameroon, Mali, Niger and Sudan) while Kenya and Senegal are at intermediate levels. Five export large quantities of cotton. All countries have small textile sectors with the exception of the yarn sector of Sudan, which is large. Thus, it appears that textile export is a more feasible undertaking for these countries than apparel export. Yet the level of textile exports is low to very low when compared to their textile imports.

The rather poor performance of Cameroon is somewhat surprising. Riddell (1990a) reports that it is the fastest growing country in Africa in terms of MVA.[27] However the poor performance of its textile-clothing sector is confirmed by Karmiloff (1990). In addition, Cameroon's exports are increasingly dominated by oil exports (ibid.).

Kenya has acquired an image of success. Indeed, Kenya was amongst the fastest growing African economies in the 1970s with MVA growing at 10.8 percent, but this fell in the 1980s to 4.9 percent. Its textile-clothing sector is on the small side with a 12 percent share in total MVA (Appendix, Table A.3). Sharpley and Lewis confirm Kenya's poor performance when they comment that if the present (dis)incentive system is not changed in favour of exports, Kenya's manufacturing industry will 'remain a drain on, not a contributor to, the possibilities for economic growth' (Sharpley and Lewis 1990:241). Kenya's case is further discussed in Chapter 4, section 4.4.3.

Senegal maintained modest growth rates of MVA from 1963 to 1986 while gradually expanding its share of manufacturing exports in total exports (Appendix, Table A.3). However its textile-clothing industry is rather small (Table 3.4 and Appendix, Table A.3). As De Bandt observes, the Senegalese textile industry has suffered badly from imports of second-hand clothing and, referring to structural adjustment in the 1980s in general, that 'without exception, attacks from diverse sources have rapidly become excessive and, in most cases, unbearable' (De Bandt 1989:47, my translation).

Sudan, Mali, Niger and Burkina Faso all have much higher import/export ratios than Cameroon, Kenya and Senegal, smaller capacities (with the exception of Sudan's spinning capacity), and lower levels of technology (Table 3.4). They have shown poor growth performance of MVA although Mali and Sudan are slightly better than the rest. Finally, Ethiopia is the only country in this group that exports apparel, although its textile capacity is small and its manufacturing exports are a very small fraction of total exports (Table A.3). Its growth performance in terms of MVA was quite reasonable (Riddell 1990a) considering the political and social turmoil it has experienced during the 1980s. Based on the above considerations, the ordering of group (1b) countries is as follows: Cameroon, Kenya and Senegal followed by Ethiopia and Mali and the group consisting of Sudan, Burkina Faso and Niger.

Finally, the fifteen countries in group (Ia) have reported no exports at all. Discussing each of these countries individually goes beyond the scope of this chapter. Included in this group are oil exporting countries like Algeria, Libya and Nigeria (which are cotton and yarn importers) and Zambia, which still suffers from the aftermath of the 'Dutch disease' syndrome caused by heavy dependence on copper exports and accompanying problems of diversification (Meijer 1990). All the remaining countries operate at low levels of textile technology, have small yarn and weaving sectors, and are cotton growers (either export or do not import cotton). They exhibit varying growth performances in terms of MVA and other indicators used. As an example of this group, Ghana is discussed more fully in Chapter 4, section 4.4.4.

This classification does not present a conclusive logical ordering of countries with regard to development of the textile sector. Madagascar would be more appropriately grouped with SACU, Zimbabwe and to a lesser extent Malawi, while Côte d'Ivoire and Tanzania have more in common with Cameroon, Kenya and Senegal. The group consisting of Mali, Ethiopia, Sudan, Burkina Faso and Niger cannot be clearly distinguished from group (1a) excluding the oil exporting countries (Algeria, Libya and Nigeria) and Zambia (which is a special case because of the role that copper has played in its industrial development). A more complete analysis would require a more comprehensive view of the manufacturing sector within the whole economy in combination with aspects of economic policy and possibilities for trade including issues of location and foreign linkages. For Mauritius, Zimbabwe, Kenya and Ghana, this will be done in the next chapter. Tanzania is the focus of the case material presented in this study.

In summary, of the few African countries that have successfully entered international trade in the textile-clothing sector, none were sub-Saharan

African countries. Only Madagascar and the southern African countries SACU, Zimbabwe, and to a lesser extent Malawi show potential for further textile-clothing development.

Most sub-Saharan African countries have achieved little textile-clothing development and export little. Where exports are reported, these tend to be textiles rather than clothing. Côte d'Ivoire, Cameroon, Ethiopia, Kenya, Mali, Senegal and Tanzania have had some success in building up their textile industry by supplying their domestic markets, but not very efficiently.

Most sub-Saharan African countries grow cotton and have attempted some degree of forward linking into textiles and apparel. The apparel sector (directly) and the textile sector (indirectly) of these and other sub-Saharan African countries are threatened by second-hand clothing imports.

The above considerations show that the UNIDO classification needs further elaboration at the lower end of the scale, and more importantly, that the development sequence implied by UNIDO is not applicable to many of these countries, including some of the more successful ones. Some countries show more potential as textile (yarn and fabric) exporters, but countries such as Mauritius have moved very rapidly into a clothing trade surplus without achieving anything close to trade balance in textiles; instead, they accumulated deficits with the increasing success of their clothing sector. Many African countries are cotton exporters, and those that do not export often grow cotton for domestic processing. In sum, it appears that most of the possible development trajectories are included.

3.5 INTERNATIONAL INSTITUTIONS AND TEXTILE TRADE

This section provides the institutional background in relation to the textile-clothing trade against which African export potential can be viewed. It raises important issues pertaining to relevant trading institutions and arrangements, in particular the Multi-Fibre Arrangement (MFA), and the prospects of least developed countries wishing to trade within the existing institutional framework – issues such as the role of non-tariff barriers to trade, the relation of IMF conditionality and trade arrangements and finally the potential benefits of the MFA for least developed developing countries (LDDCs).

3.5.1 Institutional framework and textile trade

World trade in general and the textile-clothing trade in particular are regulated and facilitated by a large number of institutions and arrangements.

First, markets and trade interests of individual countries are organized in trade blocks, regional and economic interest groups such as the African, Caribbean and Pacific (ACP) countries, the Economic Commission for Africa (ECA), the European Economic Community (EEC), the group of seventy seven (G-77) developing countries, the Organization of Economic Cooperation and Development (OECD), the Organization of Petroleum Exporting Countries (OPEC) and others. The interests of such blocks and of individual countries can diverge depending on the issue.

Second, trade is regulated by several institutional arrangements, of which the General Agreement on Tariffs and Trade (GATT) is the most important. GATT aims at stimulating world trade by removing tariff distortions. Under GATT, developing countries can obtain (and lose) special and differentiated (S&D) treatment which allows them to deviate from agreements on tariffs and other protective measures and to obtain preferential market access to developed countries under the Generalized System of Preferences (GSP). Within the context of preferential access and with particular relevance to African countries, the EEC scheme called 'the Lomé Convention' provides preferential access to 66 ACP countries, mainly in manufactured products. Under the auspices of GATT and particularly important for textile and clothing trade is the Multi-Fibre Arrangement (MFA) which is designed to protect textile-clothing industries of developed countries against imports of lower wage countries by a system of import quotas. The institutional side of MFA will be discussed in more detail in section 3.5.2 while its impact on trade will be discussed in the section 3.5.3 on non-tariff barriers to trade.

The developing countries, which viewed GATT as 'the rich men's club', organized themselves in 1964 under the auspices of the UN as the United Nations Conference on Trade and Development (UNCTAD) which has become a permanent institution. Its success has been limited because developed countries have been unwilling to cooperate (Mark and Weston 1989). However UNCTAD did produce the 1988 Global system of Trade Preferences (GSTP) Agreement, designed to regulate and stimulate South-South Trade (SST).

In the last decade, the IMF and the World Bank have strengthened their role in enforcing liberalization of trade regimes in developing countries by imposing conditionalities in balance of payments support and structural adjustment loans.[28] Thus they can be viewed as institutions that impinge on the S&D status of developing countries and the GSP largely outside the framework of GATT. It has been argued that IMF/WB interventions should be better linked to GATT negotiations so that liberalizing developing countries would obtain credit by better access to the markets of developed countries[29] which increasingly resort to non-tariff barriers to trade (see section 3.5.3).

Third, sectoral (producer) organizations exist that can express mutual interests to the outside world and/or smoothen the production and trade processes within the sector such as the International Textile and Clothing Bureau (ITCB), the International Textile Manufacturers Federation (ITMF) and those institutions discussed in section 4.3(c) which are more concerned with microprocesses of production and trade.

The ITCB, set up only in 1985, is an intergovernmental advisory institution whose main function is to provide technical assistance for developing countries in textile negotiations in order to reduce the barriers to their textile exports. In the Uruguay Round it has favoured a quick transition (six years) to normal GATT rules, with existing quotas to be increased by 6 percent in 1991 and by some higher percentage thereafter. It is clear that only textile and clothing exporting countries affected by the MFA are interested in membership, which in 1991 consisted of 22 countries.[30]

The ITMF is a private organization supported by similar national organizations within its fifteen member countries: the OECD countries and NICs such as Brazil, Korea, Taiwan and Turkey. It exchanges information on market developments, production management and technology. Its mixed composition makes it unsuitable as a lobby group in global trade negotiations. No African countries are member of this organization.

3.5.2   Multi-Fibre Arrangement

The first MFA was concluded under the auspices of GATT in 1973 as the result of pressures by the US and Europe to protect their textile and clothing industries against cheap imports. Since then three more agreements have been reached, with MFA IV covering the period 1986 to 1991. As summarized by Dao, 'The Arrangement is a derogation from the free trade principle of GATT. It permits the developed countries to deviate from the basic GATT rules of non-discrimination and elimination of QRs, and allows them to impose quotas on products from so-called 'low cost countries'' (Dao 1989:84). Importing countries may seek an agreement with exporting countries with regard to export restraints when real risks of market disruption exists. When no agreement is reached, the importing country is free to impose unilateral restrictions. Exporting countries are given some special provisions such as (a) a minimum 6 percent growth rate for items under restraint, (b) the condition that importers should enable exporting countries to utilize their quota efficiently and (c) special treatment for new entrants, small suppliers and exporters of cotton textiles (Dao 1989).

While the stated objectives of the MFA are to expand trade, reduce trade barriers and progressively liberalize world trade in textile products, it is clear that it is the outcome of trade protectionism by developed countries.

However the MFA does not affect very small exporting developing countries, including most African countries. Within the EEC, imports of such countries are monitored until they reach a certain level after which negotiations on restrictions are initiated. In this way, an export market is reserved for least developed countries that would otherwise be absorbed by more successful textile exporters. The World Bank reports that this helps to explain the high investment rates in Mauritius' textile-clothing sector by Asian investors (World Bank 1989a:111). As the examples of Kenya (Ikiara 1989), Nigeria (Oyejide 1989) and Tanzania (Lipumba 1989) show, manufactured exports are often supply constrained and countries are struggling to find the right economic policies to increase manufactured exports under IMF imposed liberalization. It is thus not surprising to find that most less developed countries are not interested in GATT rounds apart from the GSP (Kahler and Odell 1989). Their interest is not served by removing or expanding quota but by maintaining them.

Following the (latest) Uruguay Round of GATT, which time the MFA had not yet been discussed (because the negotiations broke down on the conflict between EC and USA on agricultural subsidies) Finnerty summarized: 'The EC and all the main textile negotiating groups in the Uruguay Round seem to agree that, following the termination of MFA IV in 1991, there will need to be a lengthy transitional period during which an MFA regime will be gradually phased out and parallel moves made to strengthen GATT rules in the interest of fair trade' (Finnerty 1991a:21). This has been confirmed by the actual outcome when the GATT negotiations were concluded at the end of 1993. This rather moderate attitude towards abolishment of MFA can be explained by the fact that the lifting of quotas and a return to fair trade would bring about fiercer price competition between countries, possibly at the expense of the higher wage Asian countries and in favour of the lower cost countries, including African countries. Thus the international investment process would be directed by cost of production rather than market access as under MFA. Also within the EC, countries such as Spain, Portugal, Greece and Italy fear low cost competition under fair trade (see also the discussion on the case of Spain in section 5.2.2).[31]

3.5.3 Non-tariff barriers to trade

While GATT has achieved a steady reduction of tariffs, non-tariff barrier protection has been increasing substantially in terms of incidence, type and impact, thus undermining the principle objective of GATT (Laird and Yeats 1990).

A detailed classification of non-tariff barriers has been given by Laird and Yeats (1990) who distinguish three types of measures: the first two operate both on quantity and prices of imports and the third only on quantity. Type I measures are defined as having a trade distorting intent for imports. These include (*Ia*) quantitatively operating measures such as import quotas, licensing practices, voluntary export restraints (VERs) and (*Ib*) domestic content regulations and measures operating on prices/costs such as countervailing charges (or duties) when imports are assumed to be subsidized by the exporting country, antidumping duties, orderly market agreements (OMAs) and international commodity agreements. Type II measures are defined as having a secondary trade restrictive intent of which (*IIa*) communication and advertisement restrictions operate quantitatively while (*IIb*) measures such as regulations on health, safety and packaging and customs procedures operate on prices/costs. Type III measures are defined as spill-over effects on trade and comprise a wide-ranging list of policies and practices that have a predominantly quantitative impact on imports, for example structural and regional policies, variations in depreciation methods and various externalities of government subsidies to industry.

The MFA would fall under measures of type *Ia*, while the rules of origin imposed by EC under the Lomé Convention[32] have also been cited as a type *Ia* non-tariff barrier to trade (McQueen 1990). Textile trade has definitely been affected by type *II* and *III* as well, for example, by the extensive structural textile policies pursued by many developed countries (de la Torre 1984) which has enabled many firms to restructure toward the high fashion, high quality market discussed in previous sections.

As reported by Laird and Yeats (1990), within the manufacturing sector, the incidence[33] of non-trade barrier measures has increased most rapidly between 1966 and 1986, while starting from the second highest base in 1966: by 82 percent for textiles and clothing as compared to 77 percent for ferrous metals (SITC 67), 52 percent for chemicals (SITC 5), 26 percent for non-electric machinery (SITC 71), 57 percent for electric machinery (SITC 72), and 55 percent for transport equipment (SITC 73).

This picture is confirmed when this index takes account of the value of transactions. Sampson shows that from 1981 to 1986 this index further increased for textile yarn and fabrics, from 18.6 to 21.2, while decreasing for clothing from 40.2 to 38.9 (Sampson 1989).

A study of the impact of trade liberalization on imports into developed countries estimated that the removal of non-tariff barriers would have a greater impact than would tariff barriers on imports from developing countries (Laird and Nogues 1989). For the three African countries included in the sample, the increases in total exports (1983) to developed countries for removal of respectively tariffs and non-tariff barriers were estimated as: Côte d'Ivoire 2.7 percent and 2.9 percent, Morocco 7.1 percent and 14.0 percent and Nigeria .02 percent and .01 percent. The rather low figures for Côte d'Ivoire and especially for Nigeria and the higher figures for Morocco reflect their export composition in relation to the structure of tariffs and non-tariff barriers. Morocco, as was discussed earlier has substantial exports of clothing and textiles.

In contrast, the MFA quota and especially the ACP status under the Lomé convention have had quite positive impacts on less advanced textile-clothing exporters (Khanna 1989; McQueen and Stevens 1989). MFA quotas reserve market access for such countries which, in the absence of quota, they would be unable to obtain because of competition from more advanced producers. In addition, foreign investment is spurred by the existence of under-utilized quotas while price competition is restricted, implying a certain amount of economic rents arising from the quantity restrictions. This is corroborated by the fact that, within countries, a trade in quotas has developed. *A fortiori*, the conclusions on foreign investment apply to the duty-free access that ACP countries have been given to EC markets, restricted only by rules of origin.

In short, non-tariff barriers to trade have become more important than tariff barriers. Although the low share of exports of many African countries in high NTB-incidence categories of trade leaves these countries largely unaffected, with a policy towards expanding manufacturing exports, these barriers will gain considerable importance in both positive and negative terms and especially in the textile-clothing sector. The case studies discussed in Chapter 4 will throw more light on these issues.

3.6 CONCLUSIONS

The last two decades have witnessed the emergence of a new trade pattern in a major segment of the textile-clothing sector. Industrialized countries have resumed leadership and developing countries closer to the main industrial markets have started to play an increasingly important role. This has been the result of a combination of government support, technological change, a new product mix and the niche marketing strategy pursued by developed countries.

Consequently, a large part of the market has been effectively closed to less advanced producers, not only because comparative cost advantages between low and high labour cost countries have declined but also because of requirements of quality management, production speed and market responsiveness based on detailed market information.

Increasingly, the remaining export option for less advanced textile producers has become the market for more conventional, slower moving products as well as less processed intermediate textile products.

Furthermore, while technological development has been relatively high in some African countries, especially those in northern and southern Africa, most other African countries are technologically stagnant with rather small installed capacities (per caput) in both spinning and weaving.

Third, in combination with this and again with the exception of northern and southern African countries, little success has been achieved in textile exports. Most countries are in UNIDO group (1), the 'infant' stage while most of these are in group 1a, showing no exports at all in either textiles or clothing.

Fourth, international trade institutions in the textile-clothing sector are designed to protect and promote developed countries' producers. This is further enhanced by pervasive non-tariff barriers to trade.

Fifth, because of this, a market has been reserved for small exporters because the quantity restrictions imposed under the Multi-Fibre Agreement do not (yet) apply. Especially, the position of ACP countries under the Lomé convention offers good possibilities for export expansion, although other non-tariff barriers may be more difficult to overcome.

Sixth, a rather wide range of technological choice exists both in terms of scale of production as well as in capital labour ratios. Because of dynamic innovation, a large supply of second-hand machinery should be available.

Finally, the development path suggested by the UNIDO classification does not appear to be the route that African countries follow. Instead, the available evidence suggests other routes, namely (a) backward linking from clothing exports into textile exports, (b) self-sufficiency in both clothing and textiles with some exports followed by decline, (c) initially only cotton exports with progressive forward linking into textiles and apparel and (d) success in clothing leading to increasing textile imports. From this it appears that no particular *a priori* development path can be identified. The model of development implied in UNIDO's classification is based on the experience of successful Asian countries. It does not (and perhaps was not intended to) apply to countries facing other historical conditions, particularly those of structural adjustment and the decline of the manufacturing and the textile-clothing sectors, and conditions arising from very low income per capita and rather fragile manufacturing sectors. The question is whether one *should* look for a single, standardized development model at all

Can and should group (I) countries climb the technological ladder that exists in textile-clothing manufacturing? To what extent will they be able to increase their exports in the conventional and advanced textile markets? Which development path should they choose and which macro and sectoral policies and firm level measures would stimulate such developments? The next chapter will focus on these questions with a more detailed discussion on the textile policies that have been pursued by both developed and developing countries and by reviewing the experience of the textile-clothing sector in selected African countries in the wider economic context.

Notes

1. This study will not identify which of these factors has taken the leading role in this dynamic process. The role of demand and supply factors is interlinked as high labour costs relate both to high consumer income (taste for fashion) and to labour saving technological change, which in its turn leads to higher labour productivity.

2. Mody and Wheeler (1990) conclude that in the future, both highly industrialized countries and very low wage countries will have a comparative advantage in textile and garments: the high wage countries to the extent that 'robotting' is appropriate to their endowments (high technological capability and high wage) and the low wage countries for their wage cost advantages. Countries between these two extremes will find it increasingly harder to compete.

3. This section is based on own observations and the following references: van Gorp and Hombergen (1972), UNIDO (1989a), Leijdekkers (1990).

4. For an interesting and colourful description of traditional technologies in Africa the reader is referred to Picton and Mack (1989).

5. However, especially for low-income developing countries with a textile sector oriented to produce for the domestic market, a major threat for apparel manufacturing has come from second-hand clothing imports.

6. As Pack puts it: 'the analysis presented suggests that, at factor prices relevant for many poor countries, the choice of used equipment would be optimal' (Pack 1985:178). But he adds that other factors such as availability

of skilled labour for higher maintenance requirements, transport costs, licensing fees and other costs should be considered before reaching a final conclusion.

7. According to Cooper and Kaplinsky (1985:131), a market for second-hand equipment exists when the maximum price that purchasers are willing to pay is higher than the price at which potential sellers want to sell. In case only factor (a) would be operational, the seller's price would reflect the economic value of the machine under the circumstances prevailing in the seller's country. This maximum price is the point of indifference between new and old machinery, while the first price is determined by the above three factors. The assumption is that the rate of interest and the rate of profit should be higher in the purchaser's country than the seller's country. The authors raise a number of potential objections to this and other assumptions made in the argument and show in their case study on jute processing equipment in Kenya that considerable risks are attached to the use of second-hand machinery. Nevertheless, as Boon has reported, 'trade in used textile machinery is quite significant' (Boon 1981:265).

8. One of Burch's conclusions is that 'it can be postulated that the aid policies of most donor countries have been framed in ways which accord top priority to the needs of domestic interests within the donor country ... reacted to the need to expand or maintain export markets for the output of developed centres at times of increased competition and depressed trading conditions' (Burch 1987:341).

9. As Hoffman comments: 'other factors and trends have emerged which are now of equal if not more importance than technological factors in determining international competitiveness in the textile-clothing sector and the pattern of North–South trade. There have been fundamental changes in the structure and nature of the market for both intermediate products (yarn and textiles) and final products (garments)' (Hoffman 1989:75). He adds: 'These non-technology induced changes have already had a significant impact on the relative competitiveness of different firms and countries in the OECD and are just now starting to affect developing country trading patterns' (ibid.).

10. This example shows that decentralized production in weaving is possible as far as technology is concerned. Spinning technology shows the same characteristic with regard to scale. Thus both spinning and weaving take place in firms of varying size, from very small to large integrated mills. For a complete understanding of the success of the Prato experience other factors have to be considered as well, especially the organization of production between firms, technological change and technological support and its historical development. For example, few integrated mills exist: 'more common are the firms who control only one section of the process and sub-contract to other phases, thus decentralising specific types of production' (Bhalla, *et al.* 1984:108). A variety of supply linkages between firms exist. Also, technology is of all vintages, with both small and large firms employing increasingly more new technologies as their size increases. In addition, technological modernization of old machines is very common but only made possible by very skilled labour organized in specialized firms, while the textile processing tradition dates back to the twelfth century.

11. For processing and especially dying and printing the menu of technological choice is quite broad. Small scale as well as medium to large scale technologies exist.

12.. The definitions that follow deviate from the conventional ones as formulated by J. R. Hicks, *The Theory of Wages* (Macmillan, London, 1932) and quoted by Södersten (1980). Hicks defines labour-saving technical progress as increasing the marginal productivity of capital more than the marginal productivity of labour. Capital-saving technical progress increases the marginal productivity of labour more than the marginal productivity of capital while neutral technical progress increases both in the same proportion. The point made here is with regard to employment of labour: when a demand constraint exists, increases in the marginal productivity of one factor (capital), with other things being equal and assuming maximizing efficiency of factor use, will lead to absolute decline in the use of the other factor (labour).

13. To obtain an indicator for the state of technology in spinning, columns (5) and (6) have been added. For weaving a similar indicator was constructed by adding columns (7) and (8). As indicator of technological change in spinning (some measure of the share of O-E spindles in total spinning capacity), the highest value of columns [(2),(6)] and the value of column (7) have been combined as follows: [(2),(6)] + 0.2 · (7) *OVER* 1.2 As indicator of technological change in weaving (some measure of the share of shuttleless looms in total weaving capacity), the highest value of columns [(2),(8)] and the value of column (5) have been combined as follows: [(2),(8)] + 0.1·(5) *OVER* 1.19 The weight of 0.2 given to column (6) in spinning is based on the consideration that the year 1988 is one tenth of the period covered by column (2) but since it is the most recent year a 100% mark-up has been added to obtain the weight of 0.2. The weight of 0.1 for column (8) in weaving is based on the extra consideration that column (5) is expressed in money spent on looms; shuttleless looms are considerably costlier than shuttle looms so implicitly the extra weight (as for spindles) has already been introduced.

14. For spinning the following classes were defined:

Size:	small	0–10
	medium	10–20
	large	20–100
	very large	100
Modernity:	low	0–25
	medium	125–50
	high	50–100
Technological change:	no	0–1
	low	1–3
	medium	3–6
	high	6–20
very high	20–100	

For weaving the following classes were defined:

Size:	small	0–2
	medium	2–5
	large	5–15

	very large	15
Modernity:	low	0–25
	medium	25–50
	high	50–100
Technological change:	no	0–4
	low	4–8
	medium	8–20
	high	20–50
	very high	50–100

15. Together, these developments are labelled 'Quick Response'.
16. If consumer demand is led into high fashion items by advertisements etc., the quick response strategy can be interpreted as a competition device that enables efficient high technology retailers and producers to remain in business. This contrasts with the view that technological change is demand driven in the ordinary sense that consumer demand is directly at the basis of technological change. It also contrasts with the view that technological change is purely supply driven, i.e. responding to changing factor prices. From a narrow, sectoral point of view, the present technological change in the textile sector can be characterized as market driven, a mixture between technological change driven by induced demand changes and technological change driven by supply characteristics that are partly determined by the product characteristics and partly by changing factor prices. From a wider point of view, however, it could be argued that product innovation in the textile-clothing sector has only been possible because of technological innovation in other sectors which is basically supply determined. In other words, whether this new development is demand driven or supply driven is not obvious.
17. A director of a textile producing firm has listed these seven points as what he calls 'the seven virtues of Q.R. Textile Processing' (Laidlaw 1990:35).
18. This growth figure partly reflects world inflation over the period. Between 1965 and 1980, the world deflator for trade in manufactured products moved from 0.31 to 1.00, implying an inflation of 47 percent over a five year period or 8 percent annually. In the period from 1980 to 1985, world prices actually declined by 14 percent, or 3 percent annually. In addition, intra-DME exports between DMEs accounted for more than three quarters of total DMEs exports of textiles and clothing (UNIDO 1987:3).
19. Those countries that are classified by the World Bank as 'upper middle-income'.
20. Self-sufficiency is defined as domestic mill consumption of fibres over final domestic fibre consumption.
21. These are Hong Kong, Korea, Brazil, Mexico, and Yugoslavia. Taiwan should have been included but UN data do not treat Taiwan separately from China.
22. These and other data were kindly supplied to me by Mr. P. Munkholt, economist with the International Textile Manufacturers Federation.
23. All countries not covered by DMEs and ATEs.
24. When the textile sector expands to supply the requirements for an expanding export sector this can no longer be called pure import substitution, which is

defined as domestic production substituting for imports for domestic demand. It is rather a form of export deepening.

25. Trade data were obtained from United Nations (1989 and 1990). The picture is distorted by imports of second-hand clothing, which are quite substantial. For example, Angola, Benin, Ghana, Niger and Zaire report imports of respectively 9569, 8333, 6136, 2138 and 3233 tons with a trade price ranging between 500 and 3000 US$. However the US trade value of second-hand clothing is a very poor indicator of its importance. With roughly 5 metres of fabric per kg, 2 metres of fabric per garment and a price of US$ 15 per new garment, this would amount to an imports equivalent of new clothing of respectively respectively 6, 11, 10, 33 and 16 times the figures for imports of new apparel for the same countries. Thus from the point of view of measuring the degree of import substitution of the textile and apparel sectors of the various countries, the level of second-hand clothing imports is a very important parameter. Reporting of second-hand clothing (under fibre imports) is rather incidental. Many more countries in fact import second-hand clothing than has been reported. For the present purposes it implies that the classification needs to be adjusted such that more countries would fall in group (I). Thus where doubt exists, countries are adjusted downwards.

26. The difference between this and Table A.7, where it was put at 16.9 percent, perhaps can be attributed to re-exports of fuel.

27. This may be an error as elsewhere in the book the growth rate for 1975–1984 is quoted as 5.0 percent (Riddell 1990:113).

28. For a critical discussion of economic liberalization see Clive (1989); Meier and Steel (1989) provide a large collection of papers with particular reference to sub-Saharan Africa more favourable to the IMF/WB position.

29. See Whalley (1989:8,16).

30. These countries were: Argentina, Bangladesh, Brazil, China, Colombia, Costa Rica, Egypt, El Salvador, Hong Kong, India, Indonesia, Jamaica, South Korea, Macau, Maldives, Mexico, Pakistan, Peru, Sri Lanka, Turkey, Uruguay and Yugoslavia. Surprisingly, some successful Asian countries such as Thailand, Philippines and Malaysia, are not represented.

Table 3.5   Second-hand clothing imports and new imports equivalent

Country	Second-hand imports (tons)	Equivalent value (new) (US$ 000s)	New apparel imports (US$ 000s)
Angola	9 569	358 838	55 747
Benin	8 333	312 488	27 302
Ghana	6 136	230 100	22 725
Niger	2 138	80 175	2 427
Zaire	3 233	121 238	7 388

Source: United Nations International Trade Statistics, 1987; own calculations.

31. See also the discussion of textile policies in Spain in Chapter 4.
32. The purpose of rules of origin is to exclude redirection of exports by quota-restricted countries to non-restricted countries. However 'these rules go beyond that which could be reasonably expected to simply prevent trade deflection, and in fact they act to protect 'sensitive' industries in the EC from competition from preference receiving countries' (McQueen 1990:25).
33. As measured by the number of transactions affected by NTBs.

4 Policy and Performance: The Textile Sector of Selected Countries

4.1 INTRODUCTION

Large disparities in economic performance exist not only between the groups of developed countries, newly industrializing countries, and other developing countries but also between the individual countries within these groups. Some of these differences are reflected in the widely varying degree of success in textile/clothing production in the various countries. However, the previous chapter has shown that a one to one relationship between general economic development and performance in the textile sector cannot be assumed. These differences can only be understood in relation to historical processes of (under)development within a broad international context. The analysis presented in this chapter is more modest in scope. It will survey different policies affecting the textile/clothing sector in selected countries with the aim of obtaining insight into the successes and problems of textile development and into the type, scope and effects of intervention by governments in developed and 'open' economies, in successful export-oriented developing countries and in inward-looking African countries. Lessons can be learned from the comprehensive textile plans of developed countries, the export orientation of the Asian countries, and the adjustment experience of the African countries. Moreover, this overview will apply the UNIDO classification (discussed in Chapter 3) to African countries. Finally, it shows that Tanzania's experience is not unique, and that it has lessons for other countries in the early phases of textile development.

Therefore, first, the policy experience of some selected European countries (section 4.2) and Asian countries (section 4.3) will be discussed in rather general terms. Second, a small number of African countries will be discussed in more detail (section 4.4). For the latter countries, in addition to a discussion of policies and their effects at sectoral level, attention will be given to structural adjustment policies in relation to industrial development and to firm-level problems and constraints (depending on availability of information). Third, policies pursued by the three groups of countries will be compared and related to their particular stage of development and

118

elements of firm strategies will be reviewed, setting the stage for the detailed case study of Tanzania (section 4.5).

4.2 TEXTILE POLICIES IN DEVELOPED COUNTRIES

This section will first establish the fact that substantial government intervention has taken place in the textile/clothing sector in many developed countries (section 4.2.1). Second, it will summarize the diverse nature, scope and effectiveness of such interventions at a general level and briefly review the Belgian and Spanish experiences. The former has implemented a rather elaborate structural adjustment plan, while the latter is interesting because of Spain's preparations to enter the then European Common Market (section 4.2.2).

4.2.1 Nature of state intervention in developed countries

State intervention in industrialized countries came about under increasing threats of employment losses in the textile/clothing industries because competitive production in developing countries led to a loss of export and domestic markets. This occurred in a world environment of general international imbalances, oil shocks and with many countries plagued by balance of payments difficulties. Employment in the textile and clothing sectors in EC member countries continuously declined from the 1970s to the 1980s (EC 1988, 1990, 1991).

Although these developments did not occur in all countries simultaneously and in the same depth, a general picture of state intervention can be described. As the crisis in industrialized countries deepened in the 1970s, governments first sought to protect their textile/clothing industries by both providing subsidies to protect jobs and through trade protection.

When the costs of job protection became unsustainable in the late 1970s, efforts towards industrial restructuring began. At the beginning of the 1980s governments moved towards what has been called the 'neoliberal' approach (de la Torre 1984:224), which in essence means maintaining a certain degree of protection while stimulating employment in sectors with higher comparative advantage.

With regard to the subsequent developments in the 1980s, the discussion in Chapter 2 has shown that surviving textile/clothing firms in developed countries have become more competitive, with the markets in which they compete more under their control. Their practice of subcontracting labour-intensive processes to lower wage countries closer to the domestic market enhances their competitive position. Simultaneously, however, trade protection continues to play an important role.

Therefore, de la Torre's forecast, implicit in his observation that 'the evolution of public policy towards the industry has come nearly full circle' (ibid.:225) to a phase of market-led adjustment has not fully materialized. A recent EC report on textile and clothing comments that with the internal market integration and stronger ties with neighbouring regions 'the tougher competition will force all industries to adapt faster than in recent years and is the reason why government action is needed to create the most favourable environment in which industries can do so' (EC 1991:1).

4.2.2   Overview of particular measures of state intervention in developed countries

The general sequence of events as summarized in the section above has not been followed equally and with the same intensity by all countries. Germany, for example, hardly interfered at all, Japan and USA only much later, while Italy has relied more strongly than other EC countries on state investment, and France was quicker in realizing that technological improvement should lie at the basis of recovery.

In addition, the role of the European Community *vis à vis* its member countries has been to put pressure on governments to limit interventions which would lead to competitive distortions within the Common Market while at the same time advocating measures to protect the market from outside competition (UNIDO 1987).

Despite this, as Table 4.1 shows, a rather extensive collection of measures has been applied with regard to different policy objectives directed at the various levels of industry. They range from policies to improve the functioning of markets for general industrial development (upper left corner) which from a liberal perspective would be considered to be the normal role of the state, to protective measures (moving downwards) with more specificity with respect to region or sector (moving right). Tariff barriers to trade and the Multi-Fibre Arrangement would fall in the lower right corner. In fact, most of these measures (apart from market-led adjustments and tariffs) could also be classified as type I, II and III measures in the scheme of non-tariff barriers to trade discussed in section 3.5.3.

At the end of this chapter a modified version of this scheme will be presented as a classification of policies that have affected (rather than

Table 4.1   Classification of public-assistance measures to textile/clothing industry of developed countries

Policy objectives	Policy orientation		
	General promotion of industrial development	*Regional development*	*Sector-specific development*
Improve the functioning of markets	Competition and anti-trust policies Regulatory environment National investments in infrastructure	Improve infrastructure and other basic services Remove or reduce cost disadvantages	Sponsor the collection and dissemination of information Promote joint industry research and productivity centres
Influence resource allocation	Incentives for industrial research and development Accelerated depreciation allowances Labour training schemes	Investment grants and concessions Fiscal advantages Mobility and training grants	Subsidies and special grants for research and development Government procurement schemes Defence spending
Industrial restructuring and modernization	General merger policy Investment and dividend tax policy Early retirement and shorter working week Retraining and relocation grants	Added incentives for relocation facilities Exemptions from crisis measures applicable elsewhere	State ownership and rationalization Capacity-reduction schemes Promotion of mergers and takeovers
Relief from competitive pressures	Employment subsidies Investment grants tied to employment maintenance Competitive devaluation	Income-maintenance schemes Support for continuing wage differentials	Trade protection Creation of crisis cartels Wage and employment freezes

Source: de la Torre (1984:7).

assisted) industrial development in developing countries. It will have to include other policies as well such as those aiming at correcting major macroeconomic imbalances, liberalization and export promotion policies.

Before moving to a discussion of textile/clothing sector oriented policies in developing countries, some details will be presented of structural adjustment plans implemented by Belgium and Spain, because although the reasons for structural adjustment in these countries may be different from those in developing countries (industrial decline and loss of employment caused by market penetration of Asian countries for Belgium and other long standing EC member countries and the incorporation into the Common Market for Spain), lessons may be learned by developing countries from the specific details of these plans.

The Belgian Textile Plan[1]

Since the middle ages, Flanders (the Dutch-speaking region in Belgium) has been an important textile centre. Today, Belgium is an important textile technology exporter. The first Belgian government intervention in the textile/clothing sector came about in 1975 as a response to pressure from manufacturers through an existing tripartite body (government, industry and labour unions). It consisted of direct subsidies to ailing firms aiming at maintaining employment. Early efforts at restructuring were included in the 'safeguard plan' in 1977.

The last and most integrated textile plan implemented in Belgium (in 1981), the 'Claes plan', was the outcome of quite intensive negotiations with the Commission of the European Community. Negotiations began in 1978 in reaction to the 'safeguard plan' and continued into the 1980s even after the first year of implementation of the 'Claes plan' (de la Torre 1984). As the plan's objectives were to restore the competitiveness of Belgian firms, at least within the European Community, and to stabilize employment in the sector, the Commission was keen to see that no competition-distorting elements were incorporated.

Four key features of the plan (Ramboer 1985) were: first, the establishment of a three-tier institutional framework responsible for plan implementation. A new tripartite institution was created to approve requests for assistance by firms in line with the plan's criteria and to implement the auxiliary service component of the plan. After approval, requests were to be submitted to a public holding company for ratification. This company was also the government's instrument for financial participation in assisted firms. Finally, in cases of disagreement between these two institutions, the Ministries of Finance and Economic Affairs played the role of arbitrators.

Thus a system of checks and balances was provided involving all actors in the sector.

Second, measures were adopted aiming at financial and technological restructuring in order to reduce overcapacity, overhead and variable costs, and to increase productivity. Companies could be granted support if:

- they were viable at the time of submission of the request or within three years thereafter;
- the project submitted for assistance would not result in additional capacity;
- the company would contribute 30 percent or more to the financing, the financial sector 25 percent (at subsidized interest rates), and government no more than 45 percent which was to be repaid within 15 years; from mid-1984 onwards, under pressure from the EC, companies would have to finance projects entirely by themselves;
- government would participate through a public holding company which purchased non-voting stocks to an amount equal to its financial participation.

Third, a system of assistance to auxiliary services in industry was set up to improve industry's capacity to react innovatively to market developments by concentrating subsidies in the three areas: creativity and promotion, research and development, and training. Collective action in these areas between small and medium scale producers was stimulated. This section of the textile plan, which did not come into force until 1983, was to be terminated in 1987 but instead was extended to 1991 since the objective of a Belgian 'Quick Response' industry had not been achieved. To complement efforts in this field, a research institution was formed by industry and trade unions in 1987.

Finally, a system of social services was put in place to ease the movement of labour out of the sector. This system was phased out in 1985.

Thus, partly through the intervention by the European Commission, a plan evolved that concentrated on restructuring potentially strong firms, limiting creation of additional capacity, and leaving aside those firms and subsectors that were already competitive, while ensuring firm-level commitment by obliging firms to share the financial implications while phasing out government involvement. The Belgian case shows how quick response strategies and the newly emerging comparative advantage of Belgian (and European) firms discussed in Chapter 4 have been made possible by intensive government intervention. Also, it appears that the rather 'soft' Belgian state was forced by the European Commission to act 'hard'.

The Belgian textile plan has been judged a success. Before 1984 about 190 textile companies (representing 42 percent of sector employment) took advantage of the financial scheme and more than 500 participated after 1984. It has contributed to stabilizing production in the early 1980s and even to modest growth in the late 1980s. The year 1989 saw a recovery of the garment sector which continued into 1990. In this sector the number of large scale (100 employees) enterprises declined continuously from 179 in 1973 to 66 in 1988, whereas very small producers increased from 1986 onwards. Exports continued to decline in the early 1980s but started to increase in 1988 in volume terms and in 1989 also in value terms (by more than 15 percent). Creativity in fashion design and aggressive marketing have improved and many Belgian firms have moved into the high quality market.

However, problems such as the low value of the US dollar, increased imports from low cost countries and fierce competition from high quality clothing imports from Germany and Italy still remain. The profitability of firms in both sectors is reported to be below the plan's objective of a real return of 5 percent. The increasingly smaller average size of firms in the clothing sector will be a problem when capital intensive innovations will have to be adopted to remain competitive.

Finally, developing countries should note Belgium's increasing interest in using East German firms for outward processing of textiles and the strong linkages exist between North African countries for garment manufacturing. Interest to other developing countries.

Spanish Textile Plans[2]

Spain is a medium-wage country in the process of reaching full equivalent status within the EC. Its competitive challenges originate from other EC countries gaining better access to Spain's market and from the special trading arrangements that the EC has with developing countries.

Between 1960 and 1985, ten textile plans have been implemented in Spain. Within this 25-year period three main phases can be identified. During the first phase, from 1960 to 1967, the Spanish government was concerned with modernizing, rationalizing and increasing textile/clothing capacity, mainly by offering preferential credit to producers. In contrast, during the second period, from 1968 to 1980, the emphasis was on consolidating the industry with restrictive rules for new investment (until 1974), closing non-viable plants and softening the impact with compensation schemes for dismissed employees. With the beginning of the 1980s, economic recession and preparation for entry into the European Common

Market necessitated new investment and a general upgrading of productive capacities to improve competitiveness, productivity, flexibility and the share of higher value-added items in output, and to improve the managerial, productive and financial structures of textile/clothing firms.

In some respects, Spain's textile and clothing industries in the early 1980s reflected some of the problems familiar to African developing countries. They were rather inward looking, producing mainly for the domestic market behind high tariff barriers. Less than five percent of Spain's output was exported, and imports accounted for 10 percent of consumption. Commercial structures for both domestic and export marketing were poorly developed. As a result, Spanish textiles and clothing were generally neither of high quality, nor cheap and mass-oriented, and Spanish firms were largely noncompetitive.

Employment in both textiles and clothing was declining especially throughout the early 1980s, although it stabilized somewhat in the latter half.

In order to deal with these problems and to ease Spain's entry into the EC, the government introduced the 'Conversion Plan' in 1981 with the following aims:

(a)   to increase productivity by 60 percent, to 83 percent of the EC average;

(b)   to reduce unemployment;

(c)   to ensure that half of the industry's plant was less than five years old by 1987 by providing financial facilities for capital investment;

(d)   growth in foreign trade to an export/import ratio of 3.5:1.0 and;

(e)   updating and systematizing statistics for the whole sector.

As in Belgium, the measures adopted were fiscal and financial incentives for investment in new plant and for developing activities aiming at improvements in design, fashion, quality and marketing, and social security assistance enabling firms to better cope with seasonal fluctuations and the reduction of their labour force.

However, between 1981 and 1986, only 683 companies obtained approval for 976 programmes, far short of the goal of 2000 firms, and insufficient progress was made in the area of fashion, marketing, product standardization, training of personnel and development and dissemination of information. Participating firms have shown significant increases in productivity (more than 60 percent) and exports (more than 370 percent) while their employment declined more slowly than in the rest of the sector. The low participation rate was due to the caution with which many small and medium size firms approached new technologies and their distaste for the fiscal clarity demanded upon participation. In addition, interest rates were rather high during the period, thus forming an obstacle for investment lending.

In 1985, a more systematic plan, called the 'Intangibles Plan', was initiated particularly for the promotion of design and fashion to run until 1987. Under the plan assistance was given to (a) develop promotional infrastructure, (b) develop creativity in design and fashion and (c) promote exports. In addition the plan created training centres for industry and the Centre of Promotion of Design and Fashion, an advisory institution channeling applications for support from firms to government for support and advising on government policy with regard to the promotion of design and fashion.

From Table 4.2 it can be observed that investments increased during the eighties although more in textiles than in clothing which declined in 1989. This trend is corroborated by data on textile machinery imports. Both textile and clothing imports expanded faster than textile and clothing exports, increasing the deficit in textile trade. In addition, the average size of clothing firms declined between 1980 and 1985.

In sum, despite the 'Conversion Plan' and the 'Intangibles Plan', the Spanish textile and clothing industry is likely to face difficult times as trade barriers are increasingly dismantled with its accession into the EC in 1986.

Table 4.2   Selected statistics for textile and clothing sectors in Spain

	1980	1985	1986	1987	1988	1989
Average employment per textile firm	34	34	37	36	36	35
Average employment per clothing firm	42	36	35	35	35	34
Investments in textile sector*	12.4	34.2	41.9	51.7	51.8	46.3
Investments in clothing sector*	7.6	9.8	10.3	11.4	9.9	9.3
Textile exports*	–	–	–	–	105.2	113.3
Textile imports*	–	–	–	–	120.4	159.7
Clothing exports*	–	–	–	–	67.3	62.3
Clothing imports*	–	–	–	–	79.1	123.0
Textile machinery imports*	–	10.4	20.7	25.6	25.6	23.2

Note: *In billions of pesetas.
Source: Compiled from various tables in Fitzpatrick and Montague (1990).

Because of its difficulties in penetrating the high quality export market, it will have to compete in more standardized goods with the low cost countries which have access to the EC market under the Multi-Fibre Arrangement. Pressures from Spain, Italy, Portugal and Greece will form an obstacle to EC's intentions to bring the textile/clothing trade within GATT.

4.3   TEXTILE POLICIES IN ASIAN COUNTRIES

The general economic setting for Asian countries is even more dynamic. It is characterized by the struggle for foreign investment and MFA quotas, the search for market outlets and cheap labour, the shifting comparative advantages between Asian countries, existing American and European producers' and trading firms' relations with Asian countries, the approaching incorporation of Hong Kong by China and the expanding role of China itself in textile/clothing production.

Within this general economic environment many differences exist between individual Asian countries. There are countries that have successfully industrialized (the four NICs), very large countries such as China and India which have combined a very large domestic market with a rather inward-oriented industrialization strategy and a large group of countries that have opted for an export strategy, facilitating foreign investment while attempting to integrate the expanding clothing sector backwards into the textile sector.

For the purpose of comparison with African countries and to evaluate present possibilities and constraints in development of textile/clothing production and exports, policy experience of the latter group of countries including the 'new NICs' and the 'aspiring NICs' will be more revealing than that of the 'old NICs'. In terms of Table 3.4, countries such as Indonesia, Malaysia, the Philippines, Singapore, Sri Lanka and Thailand only recently started their journey from phase I towards phase IV of textile/clothing development while countries such as Bangladesh, Brunei, Cambodia and Vietnam have not entered the stage as yet. Because of the scope of this study only three countries will be discussed in more detail, one from the group of more successful countries (Thailand) and two of the group of most recent starters within Asia (Bangladesh and Sri Lanka).

4.3.1   Textile/clothing policies and performance in Thailand: trailing the four tigers[3]

Thailand has been very successful in expanding its textile and clothing production and exports. Employment in the sector accounts for about

30 percent of the total manufacturing workforce and it is the biggest foreign exchange earner (14.5 percent of total export earnings in 1988, followed by its traditional export rice with 8.6 percent). Self-sufficient in clothing before 1975, it attained overall trade balance in textiles and clothing in the latter half of the 1970s as a result of fast growing clothing exports which increased from 8.8 percent of total production in 1975 to 44.5 percent in 1989. Initially, until 1985, the textile sector kept pace with the continuing expansion of the clothing sector but in 1987 the figures indicate a bottleneck in further expansion of the textile sector leading to a subsectoral trade deficit of nearly 50 percent of textile exports.

Behind this success are international factors such as the appreciation of the currencies of Japan and the NICs in the 1980s and the working of the MFA, inducing textile and clothing producers to search for lower cost countries with unused quotas. Internal factors are the relatively low wage costs, macroeconomic stability as indicated by low inflation and high real growth (Table 4.3), clear investment and export oriented policies and an open policy towards foreign investment.

Table A.4 (Appendix) shows that Thailand's wage costs in spinning and weaving were amongst the lowest in the world in 1980, but have been rising steadily throughout the 1980s with one of the highest wage increases in 1989/90, indicating that Thailand is moving out of a period

Table 4.3   Selected statistics for textile and clothing sectors in Thailand

	1975	1980	1985	1987	1989
Real GDP growth (%)	–	–	3.5	8.4	12.3
Consumer price inflation (%)	–	–	2.4	2.5	5.8
Employment in textiles (×1000)	79	106	133	154	195
Employment in clothing (×1000)	326	385	431	547	700
Textile exports (m. Baht)	973	5 131	9 142	12 853	–
Clothing exports (m. Baht)	1 044	4 913	14 734	36 307	–
Textile imports (m. Baht)	3 317	5 950	10 157	18 094	–
Clothing imports (m. Baht)	48	26	35	100	–
Volume of clothing production (m. pieces)	470	709	950	1 323	1 884
Clothing exports as % of production	8.8	15.4	25.4	34.9	44.5*

Note: *Calculated using the production figure of 1989 and assuming the same growth in domestic demand as was experienced between 1985 and 1987.
Source: Based on Finnerty (1991a).

with an oversupply of labour. Its wage costs are now higher than those of China, Malaysia, India and the Philippines although still well below Singapore, Hong Kong and South Korea.

Thailand's investment policy is export oriented. Both domestic and foreign investors obtain extra incentives depending on their export shares. For example, when the company produces mainly for domestic consumption, at least 51 percent of the company must be Thai-owned. If at least 50 percent is exported, foreign ownership can be larger than 50 percent and companies can be wholly foreign-owned when all their output is exported. Exporting foreign and national firms alike can profit from export incentive schemes such as tax rebates on imported inputs.

Direct foreign investment has been rising rapidly throughout the 1980s. Its structure shows a highly diversified pattern with the highest share of textiles at 11 percent in 1987. In absolute terms, foreign investment in textiles experienced a peak in 1988.

Thailand's success in garments exports is reflected in the difficulties it has encountered in trade negotiations with the EC and especially with the USA. The bilateral agreement with the EC ran out at the end of 1991 and the one with the USA expired in 1988. Although some partial agreements have been reached, no full bilateral agreement has been concluded with the USA and negotiations appear to be conducted in an atmosphere of conflict.[4] An interesting development is that a Thai sewing thread firm has opened a plant inside the USA to circumvent USA quota restrictions.

The government takes active part in promoting exports by sponsoring firms to attend trade fairs and by co-organizing internal trade fairs. To facilitate export (and import) trade further a new electronic data interchange (EDI) system will be installed linking all major customs posts, thus speeding up trade transactions.

Research and development are stimulated by the Fabric and Garment Technology Group supported by the Textile Industry Division of the Ministry of Industry. This group undertakes research and offers technical training. Other such groups exist for fibre and yarn technology and for monitoring technical and quality standards for textile products. The Textile Industry Division itself was transformed into a National Textile Institute as a separate department under the Ministry of Industry responsible for implementing technological research, monitoring quality and offering consultancy on technical, management, pattern and style developments.

With regard to regulating investment, the government has been active in three problem areas. First, it is stimulating the location of new investment in areas outside greater Bangkok to reduce congestion and pollution.

Second, spinning and weaving factories are offered benefits such as exemption from import duties when establishing themselves outside Bangkok, thus simultaneously addressing the location issue and the lagging performance of the textile sector relative to garments. Third there is the problem of ageing machinery (due to very high tariffs on new equipment) coupled with old technology. With increasing wages, Thailand will have to maintain its competitiveness by upgrading its technology. In response to this, in 1990 the government reduced all tariffs on industrial equipment that was not produced in Thailand itself to a level of five percent. This has led to an upsurge of machinery imports (Finnerty 1991a).

In summary, Thailand's textile/clothing development has benefited from adequate government policies, a stable political environment and its geographical location *vis-à-vis* the NICs. Its problems, although requiring and receiving attention, are those of success.

4.3.2   Textile policies and performance in Bangladesh: privatization and foreign investment

Whereas Thailand has maintained a rather stable economic and political system, Bangladesh's industrial development has been influenced by drastic political changes. Policy with regard to the role of the state in industrial production has gone the full cycle from private ownership (before 1972) through nationalization (in 1972) to a period of privatization which started cautiously in 1975 and gained considerable momentum in 1982 and subsequent years (Chowdhury 1990). In 1972, 92 percent of total assets in the modern industrial sector were government-owned. Five major public industrial corporations, including the Bangladesh Jute Mills Corporation (BJMC) and the Bangladesh Textile Mills Corporation (BTMC) accounted for 75 percent of industrial production and employment. In 1982, amongst other privatization measures, formerly Bangladeshi-owned jute and textile mills were returned to their previous owners.

The structure of the Bangladesh textile and clothing sector is mixed in terms of firm size, ownership, market orientation and performance (Table 4.5). The textile sector is characterized by the nonintegrated coexistence of a large scale sector (78 firms)[5] with roughly equal participation by the private (37 firms) and public (41 firms) sectors and by a substantial small scale sector consisting of traditional handloom weavers (about one million), tie-dye, batik and screen workers. Only the small scale handloom sector is successfully exporting high quality fabrics. In addition, a large number of small firms engage in knitting. The clothing sector consists of some 760 apparel manufacturers. The main firms are mostly

Bangladeshi-owned; only three of the top ten firms have foreign participation and only one is more than 50 percent foreign-owned. Together textile and clothing industries provide 10 percent of total employment and 50 percent of industrial employment.

Table 4.4   Selected indicators, Bangladesh

	GDP constant 1985 prices	Number of garment establishments	Total exports (m. US$)	Apparel exports (m. US$)	Apparel as % of all exports
1982	372	43	768	11	1.4
1983	386	95	724	32	4.4
1984	391	180	932	116	12.64
1985	405	600	1000	126	12.6
1986	424	n.a	880	295	33.5
1987	441	658	1077	430	39.9
1988	453	713	1291	412	31.9
1989	–	–	1305	–	–
1990	–	–	–	–	–

Notes: GDP in billions of taka; (–) indicates end of series; n.a. indicates not available.
Source: World Bank (1990; 1991), Bhuiyan (1991).

Table 4.5   Selected statistics, Bangladesh textile and clothing sectors, 1988 and 1990

Sector	Employment (1990) (×1000)	Capacity (1990) (m mtrs/kg)	Production cloth (1988) (m mtrs)
spinning	57	88.6	–
weaving	1038	863.0	656.4
powerloom	38	174.9	106.4
handloom	1000	688.1	550.0
finishing	31	40.1	–
knitting	n.a.	481.5	187.5
dying & printing	n.a.	471.7	–
clothing	350	400.0	–
other	35	77.8	–
Total	1511	–	843.9

Note: Yarn produced in 1988 was 72.5 million kilos.
Source: Compiled from Bhuiyan (1991).

In the recent general policy thrust towards liberalization and export oriented growth the taka was devalued from 1985 onwards, but inflation
undermined these efforts (Table 4.4). Tariffs were simplified, import
restrictions were curtailed and foreign investments were encouraged by
adopting an investment code (1980) and creating export processing zones
in the port city of Chittagong and in Dhaka (1986). Specific export promoting measures (Khatun and Begum 1990; Bhuiyan 1991) included:

(a)   establishment of an Export Promotion Bureau (EPB) which, amongst
      other things, allocates export quotas and monitors the back-to-back
      letters of credit facility (export credits to exporters issued on the
      strength and security of the foreign importer), gives concessional
      interest rates for export credits and special rebates on duties and
      taxes to successful exporters and compensates garment manufactur-
      ers who use local fabrics;
(b)   bonded warehouse facilities (to facilitate imports for exports);
(c)   low rates of import duty on capital equipment: between 20 and
      75 percent depending on the location and only 2.5 percent if at least
      70 percent local raw materials are used;
(d)   simplification of import and export procedures.

Foreign investment was encouraged (Bhuiyan 1991) in the following ways:

(a)   a law was passed granting citizenship to foreign investors depending
      on the amount invested;
(b)   foreign industries can be set up without prior approval if project costs
      do not exceed US$ 3.3 million, foreign equity is below 49 percent
      and the industry is not on the 'discouraged' list;
(c)   100 percent foreign equity is allowed in the export processing zones
      and repatriation of capital investment including royalty and technical
      fees is permitted;
(d)   reinvestment of repatriable dividends is treated as new foreign
      investment;
(e)   tax holidays apply at various rates: from 12 years in the economic
      zones (after which firms enjoy 50 percent income tax exemption) to
      five years in developed industrial areas; tax exemption on interest
      payments for foreign loans and relief from double taxation; income
      tax exemption is granted to foreign technicians up to 50 percent of
      their salaries;
(f)   long term credit is available from industrial financing institutions;
(g)   tariff protection is possible for up to four years.

In response to these measures, the number of firms and value of exports of the clothing industry in Bangladesh has expanded rapidly (see Table 4.4) to make it the country's top foreign exchange earner. In 1986 it accounted for 33.5 percent of total exports, overtaking the share of jute (around 23 percent), its traditional export. This picture changes substantially if imports are taken into account, In 1989/90, for example, imports of inputs required for garment exports stood at 70 percent of the garments industry's export earnings (which at that time stood at 40 percent of Bangladesh's total export earnings) while jute presumably has a very low import content. This also implies that there should be considerable scope for the textile sector to supply the expanding garment sector.

However, the textile industry is lagging behind the apparel sector. While unable to meet domestic demand even at full capacity, capacity utilization stood at only 50 percent in 1989. In addition, the state of the machinery is generally poor, and most of its cotton requirements (more than 90 percent) are imported and of low quality (because of price and/or quality preferences). There is a mismatch (in terms of the count) between the yarn output of large scale spinners and the requirements of the handloom weavers. Consequently, imports of yarn and cloth (and second hand clothing) are high and competitive.[6] Indicative of these problems is that the government has reserved between 10 and 12 percent of the nation's export quotas for garments made from locally produced fabrics which garment manufacturers have been unable to utilize.

Government policy aims to increase self-sufficiency in cotton, to become an exporter of yarn and textiles (by increasing cotton production sixfold and almost doubling the textile output), and to raise the share of local fabrics inputs into export garments from 5 to 50 percent by 1995. Investments in the textile sector during the period 1985/86–1989/90 were very close to plan.

In summary, Bangladesh's garments export-led industrialization policy could (cautiously) be labelled successful. Much will depend on the outcome of the government's efforts to achieve better backward integration between the apparel and handloom weaving sectors and the textile sector and further upstream integration with the cotton sector.

4.3.3 Textile policies and performance in Sri Lanka: mixed results

Since 1977 Sri Lanka's industrial strategy has changed drastically from an import substitution approach to export led industrialization (ELI). Real GDP recorded substantial growth in the early 1980s of around 5 percent annually but levelled off later to 2.8 percent in 1988. The gap between merchandise imports and exports which stood at 77 percent of exports in

1982 closed gradually during the 1980s to 29 percent in 1988. Devaluation stayed generally ahead of domestic inflation, indicating changing relative prices between tradeables and nontradeables.

Key policy measures towards export orientation (Athukorala 1986; UNIDO 1988) included:

(a) Import trade and exchange payments were liberalized, accompanied by an exchange rate reform and tariff reform.
(b) Price controls were removed except for a few items.
(c) Measures to attract foreign investments were adopted: export processing zones were set up, an investment code protected foreign investments and free remittance of profits and dividends were permitted. However, it appears that foreign investment approval procedures are still rather selective (Athukorala 1986).
(d) Steps were taken to limit the expansion of public sector involvement in industry and to rationalize the operation of existing public sector ventures. This has been most effective in the textile sector. During the 1980s management of the five integrated textile mills owned by the state was entrusted to British and Indian managers while 60 of 70 existing powerloom workshops were privatized. These measures have been successful in turning these mills into profitable undertakings (although still substantially protected with an effective rate of protection larger than 100 percent in 1987).
(e) Emphasis was placed on export development with the enactment of the Export Development Act No. 40 in 1979. The export development policy package included direct cash subsidies, import duty rebates (including rebates on imported raw materials used in export production, concessionary rates on imports of equipment for companies registered by the Ministry of Textile Industries for local manufacture and subcontracting for exports and duty-free imports of machinery for companies which export 50 percent or more). Further, manufacture-in-bond (allowing exporters to import raw materials without having to provide bank guarantees), tax holidays on export profit (100 percent for a five year period and 50 percent for an additional ten years) were also included. Despite these measures, Abeyratne (1993) has shown that a consistent anti-export bias prevails in Sri Lanka's economy. Moreover simplification of shipping and customs procedures and various measures aimed at product and market development were introduced. This resulted in the creation of a Textile Training and Services Institute and a Clothing Industry Training Institute.

The increasing importance of textiles and garment production in Sri Lanka is shown in Table 4.6. Its share in total industrial production grew from 10.5 percent in 1980 to 35.7 percent in 1989, although in terms of value-added this was considerably less, from 15.7 in 1985 to 19.3 in 1989. Textile and garments exports gradually increased from 1985 to 1989 with a brief period of stagnation in 1988 which implies an average growth rate over the period 1985 to 1989 of 7.3 percent, which is rather modest in the Asian context. Cotton lint and cotton yarn are imported, as only 5 percent of the cotton requirements are locally grown. Exports consist mainly of garments (98 percent in 1989) with textile production servicing the domestic market.

Between the textile sector and the garment sector great differences exist in technology, ownership, production and export performance. The large scale textile sector is dominated by the state-owned National Textile Corporation which uses rather old equipment, while the small scale sector consists of privately owned handloom workshops. The handloom sector has suffered seriously from the foreign exchange shortages during the 1970s and also from liberalization, which started in 1977 and put 80 percent of them out of business.

The garment sector is privately owned, with around 350 export oriented establishments, most of which use modern equipment of a rather homogenous technology (Japanese) and are of medium size (100–200 sewing machines). Total employment was estimated at 175,000 in 1987. Most of the inputs for the garment industry are imported.

Total garment exports are quite small and although quota restrictions have been imposed by the USA and some European countries since 1980, these have not severely affected export growth (UNIDO 1988). Sri Lanka's low wage costs, which are amongst the lowest in the world (Table A.4), and its geographical position make it an ideal location for Asian investment for export production to the European market. Yet, despite its positive attitude towards foreign investment, Sri Lanka has not yet shown signs of becoming a major textile/clothing exporter. No doubt, the continuing civil war in the country has a major impact on its attractiveness to foreign investors. Moreover, an effective anti-export bias still prevails (Abeyratne 1993).

The garment sector in the free trade zones is a rather footloose industry. With most inputs into the garment sector imported, net export earnings are only a fraction of the gross export earnings reported in Table 4.6. For example, in 1980, 82.9 percent of total garment output was exported while the value of imported inputs amounted to 69.4 percent of output value (Athukorala 1986). Assuming that all imports are used for export

Table 4.6 Selected indicators, Sri Lanka

Year	Production			Exports		Textile & apparel sector as % of		
	GDP* constant 1985 prices	Yarn (1000 kg)	Fabric (m. mtrs)	Industrial (m. US$)	Textile & apparel (m. SDR)	All industrial exports	Gross industrial output***	Industrial value added***
1982	140.3	–	–	1014	–	–	–	–
1983	147.1	–	–	1061	288.1	–	–	–
1984	154.6	7780	41.3	1462	292.7	55.7	24.6	15.7
1985	162.3	7866	48.9	1316	338.5	60.7	29.2	16.0
1986	169.3	7573	42.5	1209	33.5	64.5	31.8	9.1
1987	171.9	8417	43.1	1394	381.8	62.9	33.6	19.3
1988	176.5	6592	43.1	1473	–	61.9	35.7	19.7
1989	–	–	–	1558	–	–	–	–

Notes: *   GDP in billions of rupees.
  **   This consists almost entirely of garment exports. In 1989 garments constituted 98 percent of exports.
  *** Includes leather.

Sources: World Bank (1991), Sri Lanka Central Bank (1989), Sri Lanka Ministry of Policy Planning and Implementation (1989).

production, this would imply that net garment exports consists of only 16.3 percent of gross garment exports. Yarn and fabric production stagnated in the 1980s, showing no signs of being stimulated by increasing garment production. The shallow nature of export composition is indicative of Sri Lanka's problem in industrializing.

4.4 POLICIES AFFECTING THE TEXTILE SECTOR IN SELECTED AFRICAN COUNTRIES

This survey of the policies and experiences of selected European and Asian countries has emphasized policies meant to influence the international competitive position with explicit and well-developed policies for the textile/clothing sector. Many African countries, however, have seen a decline in industrial performance in general and the textile/clothing sector in particular following the implementation of structural adjustment policy packages during the 1980s (Riddell 1990a). Before and during the continuing adjustment many countries experienced difficulties in supplying even the domestic market. For Africa as a whole, export earnings (excluding oil) declined in the first half of the 1980s (by a yearly average of 6.1 percent in the period 1980–4 and by 3.1 in 1985) while increases were recorded in 1986 and 1987 of respectively 9.5 percent and 3.6 percent (World Bank 1989a). With the exception of a few successful countries, shares of manufactured exports in total exports have increased little, and for some countries even declined between 1976 and 1986 (Table A.3).

At the same time, exports originating from African, Caribbean and Pacific countries (ACP) have been given special treatment in the GSP in general and by the EC, their major trading partner, under the umbrella of the Yaoundé and Lomé Conventions I-IV (1972–2000). For example, Article 130 of the Lomé convention provides ACP countries access to the EC market which is free of customs duties (and their equivalent) and Article 131 exempts ACP countries from any quantitative restrictions or measures having equivalent effects. But as McQueen and Stevens concluded 'despite being at the apex of the European Community's hierarchy of trade preferences, the ACP have seen their share of EC market fall since the first Lomé Convention was signed in 1975' (McQueen and Stevens 1989:239).

Therefore, in addition to trade policies, the following discussion will focus on factors to which this mixed performance should be attributed and, where data are available, discuss internal developments in more detail including sectoral and firm level experiences. The following countries will be discussed: Mauritius as a case of success (group IV of the UNIDO classification), Zimbabwe (group Ic) and Kenya (group Ib) as mixed performers and Ghana (group Ia) as a low performer despite its successful recovery. To a certain extent, the choice of countries and depth of discussion is dictated by available literature but, with reference to the classification developed in Chapter 3, a reasonable coverage of the spectrum is obtained.

4.4.1   Mauritius: export success through preferential access?

Mauritius, a small island located more than 1500 km to the east of Africa's mainland and with about two thirds of its population (roughly one million) of Indian descent, cannot be considered a typical African country in any sense. However, it is the most successful African country in terms of its recent industrial development away from an economy dominated by plantation based agriculture geared to the production of sugar for export.

Mauritius' industrial development policy began in 1964, four years before independence, with incentive schemes to encourage import substituting industries (Meier and Steel 1989:142). From 1970 until 1982 Mauritius opted for a dual strategy of export promotion (export processing zones) and continued import substitution, after which a period of economic liberalization started, indicating the exclusive pursuit of export promotion (Rogerson 1993). The period prior to 1982 had seen rather disappointing results despite the export processing zones (EPZ). First, the second oil shock and a sharp reduction in Mauritius' terms of trade ended the period of high growth in Mauritius (which stood at 8 percent per year since 1973). But more importantly, import substitution in such a small country cannot form the basis of industrial development: the final outcome of protection and export incentives produced an anti-export bias which exceeded the preferential trade margins granted to Mauritius under the Lomé Convention (McQueen 1990).

From 1979 onwards, under IMF/World Bank influence, liberalization measures were introduced with devaluation (leading to the adoption of a flexible system in 1981), elimination of quantity restrictions (in 1984 and 1985), tariff reform (1986), abolition of subsidies and price controls. This has increased export profitability. While wage controls were maintained, this has not been fully effective in keeping wage costs down as shown in Table 4.7. Wages are very low according to international standards. Labour costs were approximately US$ .48 per hour in 1987, placing Mauritius below countries like Thailand, Philippines and Malaysia but above Pakistan, Indonesia and Sri Lanka. Data available on the 1984 and

1987 period indicate that the ratio of exchange rate over labour costs actually declined (Table 4.7) suggesting an appreciation of the real exchange rate for the clothing sector.

Corporate taxes and income taxes were reduced drastically from 66 percent to 35 percent and from a maximum of 75 percent to 35 percent respectively. In 1985 the tax holiday scheme was adjusted to give companies established under the investment incentive scheme an option to pay corporation tax at a flat rate of 15 percent over the whole life of the company. This measure aimed at making it attractive to firms to stay beyond the years for which tax holidays applied. Dividends were made tax free for a period of ten years. The corporation tax on non-EPZ companies was reduced by 2 percent for each 10 percent of output exported, thus giving export incentives for all firms. In addition, the integration of EPZ firms into the rest of the economy was facilitated by the location of its firms near labour sources and not in separate enclaves.

Export performance has been unexpectedly good. The annual growth of total exports over the period 1982 to 1988 averaged 13.5 percent, with EPZ exports in clothing growing at an average annual rate of 29.7 percent. Clothing exports exceeded sugar exports from 1986 onwards.

However, the success of the economic reform package is not so straightforward and a number of qualifications have to be made with regard to factors contributing to the success, the nature of the success and problems arising from the success.

First, other factors have contributed to the apparent export success. Mauritius has enjoyed a politically stable democratic system within a multi-ethnic society and the general level of education is good (McQueen 1990). Further, the country's history and geographical location have created a substantial class of entrepreneurs and traders with links to Europe and Asia. Furthermore, a 43.5 percent improvement in the terms of trade over the period 1984–88 and sugar exports to the EC at prices around three times the international price have enabled local entrepreneurs to finance participation in the growing investments. As a consequence, 62 percent of production originates from enterprises with more than 20 percent local equity participation. Moreover, the World Bank estimates that the 'Hong Kong syndrome'[7] has contributed substantially to the upsurge in textiles and clothing investment (Meier and Steel 1989:244). Finally and most importantly the Lomé convention, ensuring quota and tariff free access to EC's markets, has stimulated direct foreign investment in Mauritius.

Second, the growth of the manufacturing sector is rather narrowly confined to clothing although recent new investments in the textile sector

Table 4.7 Selected Indicators, Mauritius

	1982	1983	1984	1985	1986	1987	1988	1989	1990
GDP (constant 1982 prices Rs × 1000m)	10.0	10.1	10.5	11.3	12.3	13.3	14.1	14.7	–
Exchange rate (Rupees/SDR)	12.0	13.3	15.3	15.7	16.1	17.3	18.6,	19.7	20.4
Consumer price index (1982 = 100)	100.0	105.7	113.4	121.1	123.0	123.7	135.0	155.7	172.7
Exchange rate/Consumer price index	12.0	12.6	13.5	13.0	13.1	14.0	13.8	12.6	11.8
Labour cost per worker, clothing (Rs th)	–	–	10.0	11.6	12.9	14.1	–	–	–
Exchange rate/Labour cost	–	–	1.53	1.35	1.25	1.23	–	–	–
Labour costs/Consumer price index	–	–	8.8	9.6	10.5	11.6	–	–	–
Exports (SDR m)	332	324	339	429	563	655	710	–	–
Sugar (SDR m)	211	206	169	188	226	255	244	–	–
Other (SDR m)	122	118	170	240	337	400	466	–	–
EPZ (SDR m)	103	98	141	209	308	380	440	–	–
Textiles (SDR m)	7	5	5	5	6	8	10	–	–
Clothing (SDR m)	73	69	104	162	249	313	347	–	–
Clothing as % of EPZ	71.0	70.5	73.7	77.3	81.0	82.3	78.8	–	–
Ratio of value added to gross output									
in clothing	–	–	31.9	33.9	33.8	33.2	–	–	–
in textiles	–	–	26.3	23.4	26.0	28.3	–	–	–
Employment EPZ	23870	25526	37573	53440	74015	87905	89080	–	–
Clothing	–	20446	–	–	–	–	77201	–	–
Clothing as % of EPZ	–	80.1	–	–	–	–	87.4	–	–

Source: IMF (1990, 1991), McQueen (1990), and author's calculations.

have increased vertical integration. Attempts to diversify exports have only met with modest success (in the production of watches and clocks).

Third, on one hand, the success so far obtained has reached its own limits in terms of labour shortages but on the other also requires sustained development for consolidation and integration. Labour shortages have already resulted in wage pressures, inflation and the need for further devaluation. Wage pressures arising out of labour shortages cannot be solved by measures manipulating the money-illusion effect of nominal wage increases; alternatives will have to be found to increase productivity and/or labour immigration. Increasing productivity by moving from low value standard commodities to high value, high quality production requires investments that are possible only for the larger firms possessing good linkages within the international trading system. For smaller firms to move in that direction, skill-intensive engineering and computer services need to be developed and intrasectoral linkages for subcontracting and the exchange of market information would have to be forged.

To consolidate and sustain manufacturing growth and to root the established enterprises more firmly in the national system, more growth is required in industrial services and horizontal and vertical linkages, thereby increasing the attractiveness for investors more interested in labour quality and industrial externalities of conglomeration than in cheap labour supply and EC market access.

4.4.2 Zimbabwe: uncertain future

Zimbabwe is a land-locked country bordering South Africa. Prior to independence (1980), the country was subjected to an economic boycott, which was only partly successful mainly because of its relations with South Africa. After independence, relations with the rest of the region were established under the umbrella of SADCC (Southern African Development Coordination Conference) and the larger PTA (Preferential Trade Area of Eastern and Southern Africa).

Both the industrial sector, one of the most advanced and diversified in sub-Saharan Africa, and the large scale commercial agricultural sector remain almost exclusively owned by the former white Rhodesian owners (now Zimbabweans) and by multinationals based in South Africa, although government equity participation in manufacturing (estimated at 16 percent in 1989) has reduced foreign ownership from 48 percent in 1985 to 25 percent in 1989 (Riddell 1990b:340). Higher-level skills are also still largely controlled by whites (Pakkiri, Robinson and Stoneman 1988). Zimbabwe's hourly wage rate for manufacturing was estimated at

US\$ 1.76 in 1983 which, given the fact that this has not changed drastically during the 1980s, puts Zimbabwe just below Turkey. Compared with other SSA countries Zimbabwe's wages are relatively high, but large inequalities exist between hourly wage rates and wages for skilled labour. Racial inequality being what it is, full-scale promotion of industrial development without structural change with regard to ownership would imply hard political choices for the black government.

Import substitution coupled with growth of domestic demand have formed the basis for manufacturing growth, with only a small role for exports. In the period just after independence, growth of domestic demand was the major source of growth, reducing import substitution and squeezing out exports (which became negative) as sources of growth (Riddell 1990b). Efficiency performance as measured by domestic resource cost ratios (DRC) and as reported by the World Bank (1987b) was mixed, with four sectors (accounting for 47 percent of total MVA), and an average DRC below unity in 1982. Within sectors widely diverging values of DRC were achieved but all sectors had efficient firms (with DRCs below unity). World Bank 1986 efficiency estimates for selected sectors, including the textile sector, are generally higher. Subsectoral import/export balance (or export surplus) was achieved in food, beverages, textiles, clothing and wood products with the overall export/import ratio for manufacturing at 33 percent. Overall integration of the manufacturing sector was high as early as 1976, when 34 percent of total inputs was produced by the sector itself.

Table 4.8 shows data for 1982 to 1989 on output and exports of the textile and clothing manufacturing sectors. The share of both textile (including ginning) and clothing exports in total manufactured exports and total exports has been quite small, respectively at 14.6 and 2.6 percent in 1986. The World Bank enthusiastically reported that while manufacturing exports declined in 1981 and 1982 by 16 and 22 percent respectively they picked up again in 1983 and 1984 by 11 and 26 percent respectively as a result of their policies (World Bank 1987b). However, this recovery was short-lived, and in 1986 manufactured exports declined once again. Clothing exports did increase in 1987 by almost 50 percent, but otherwise the overall performance suggests stagnation rather than dynamic growth. Real GDP barely outpaced population growth, manufacturing output followed the same pattern, and by 1987 total exports were back at the 1976 level. The value of the Zimbabwean dollar more than halved over the period 1982 to 1987 while annual inflation averaged 10 to 20 percent through the period. The general picture is that of a sleeping giant: compared to other African countries, Zimbabwe has a highly developed manufacturing sector but it seems unable to take off.

Table 4.8   Selected indicators, Zimbabwe

	1982	1983	1984	1985	1986	1987	1988	1989	1990
GDP (in 1985 prices; Z$ m.)	7297	7392	6619	7019	7220	7125	7378	–	–
Exchange rate (SDR/Z$)	0.99	0.86	0.68	0.55	0.49	0.42	0.38	0.34	0.27
Consumer price index (CPI)	62.3	76.7	92.2	100.0	114.3	128.6	138.1	155.9	–
Exchange rate times CPI	61.7	66.0	62.7	55.0	56.0	54.0	52.5	53.0	–
Manufacturing production (Z$ m)	1121	1360	1533	2118	2489	–	–	–	–
Volume index manufacturing output (1980 = 100)	108.7	105.8	100.7	112.2	115.4	118.1	123.9	130.9	–
Volume index textile output (1980 = 100)*	118.8	108.8	124.1	175.0	169.1	196.2	202.7	211.7	–
Volume index clothing & footwear output (1980 = 100)	118.6	109.2	99.9	111.5	73.0	119.5	120.2	144.5	–
Imports of textiles (SDR m)	44.4	36.9	32.2	–	–	–	–	–	–
Imports of clothing (SDR m)	1.2	0.4	0.7	–	–	–	–	–	–
Exports of yarn (SDR m)	1.1	2.8	9.7	8.6	10.3	11.3	–	–	–
Exports of fabrics (SDR m)	0.2	4.3	7.4	7.1	8.5	8.9	–	–	–
Exports of clothing (SDR m)	5.3	6.9	9.3	9.0	9.8	14.1	–	–	–
Value index of total exports (1976 = 100)	111	123	120	119	115	112	–	–	–

Notes: *   includes ginning.
        **   excluding cotton lint and ferro-chrome exports.
Source: IMF (1990, 1991), Reserve Bank of Zimbabwe (1990), Riddell (1990a), Wood (1988) and author's calculations.

Adjustment policies started in 1982 when 'Zimbabwe was hit by three simultaneous crises: the world slump, involving declining demand, at a falling price, for Zimbabwe's exports; the first year of a three-year drought estimated officially to have cost Z$680 million in that year alone; and (probably South African inspired) insurgency in Matabele land which

almost destroyed the nascent tourist industry and raised defence costs'
(Stoneman 1989:40).

Expenditure-switching and expenditure-reducing measures were
adopted. The Zimbabwean dollar was devalued (see Table 4.8) and the
resulting real depreciation of about 11 percent in 1983 made export production more profitable. Industrial export oriented policies were put in
place: export credit terms for industrial products were extended from three
to six months and an export revolving fund was established enabling firms
to import for the production of exports, thus removing the foreign
exchange constraint for export production. At the same time general
foreign exchange allocations to the industrial sector were reduced. As a
result, manufacturing output declined but total exports (as well as textile
and clothing exports) increased in 1983 and 1984 (World Bank 1987b),
although they have since declined again. Textile and clothing exports also
fell in 1985, but they increased substantially in 1986 and 1987.

These increased exports must be evaluated against the generally protected domestic market. The World Bank estimates Zimbabwe's (1986)
effective protection ratio for textiles (including ginning) as 1.74 and for
clothing as 1.43, compared to 1.33 for the manufacturing sector as a
whole. Despite the relatively high levels of protection, in both sectors very
efficient firms exist side by side with inefficient ones (World Bank 1987b).
Efficient firms can operate in a dual market, moving to exports when the
advantages for domestic oriented production are exhausted or when such
shifts are forced by, for example, foreign exchange allocation policies.

The Zimbabwean textile industry is relatively modern (see also section
4.2.2) and dominated by large scale producers with well-established
foreign linkages (both regional as well as overseas). The textile sector is
dominated by four large companies: David Whitehead (a Lonrho subsidiary with a weaving establishment in Botswana), Merlin (a local firm
with South African capital), Zimbabwe Spinners and Weavers (locally
owned) all three traded on the Zimbabwe Stock Exchange. Cone Textiles
(a privately owned Zimbabwean company with a subsidiary in Botswana)
is the fourth (Riddell 1990c).

South Africa had been a main export market, but a combination of protective measures in South Africa, including a total ban on textile imports
in the early 1980s, and poor prospects of local and regional demand have
provoked a shift in export sales to EC and US markets (Whitehead and
Cone). In addition, Whitehead and Cone have used their Botswana link to
penetrate the South African market. Spinweave's exports (75 percent of its
total production was exported to EC in 1988) began in 1983 when a UK
firm visited the country, and Merlin established a new spinning mill with

the explicit objective of exporting yarn to the EC and supplying quality yarn to its weaving section for fabric exports.

These companies moved with relative ease into the overseas export market. First, their level of technology and quality was such that they could supply the middle and lower segments of the EC market. Second, trade relations and the supply of market information were facilitated by good marketing contacts. Whitehead's contacts were organized by the Lonrho group, while Spinweave's contact with the UK and Cone's contact with German/Italian agents have been crucial for their market access. Third, domestic export oriented policies have contributed in terms of foreign exchange requirements and profitability. Fourth, a local supply of high quality cotton formed the basis of further upstream quality.

Zimbabwe's clothing sector is less dominated by foreign ownership (only 16 percent) and is more decentralized, with some 800 establishments. About 600 of these are informal sector operators employing fewer than 30 employees and producing about 20 percent of the sector's output. Of the remaining 200 firms only 30 are exporters, and 10 firms account for 80 percent of total sectoral exports. The largest exporter is Fashion Enterprise, which exports roughly 50 percent of its output. The EC is the main export destination (55 percent in 1988) followed by South Africa (20 percent), the USA (13 percent) and SADCC countries (11 percent). Details on the larger, non-exporting segment of the clothing sector are not available. Firms with a high DRC that coexist in this sector with firms with a low DRC are likely to be non-exporters. These firms would suffer considerably from liberalization of the domestic market.

Zimbabwe's exports enjoy tariff- and quota-free access to the EC market and a return to normal GATT rules could threaten Zimbabwe's position. However, some firms have joined hands in order to be able to respond in a flexible manner to small orders at short notice (most exports are air-freighted). Export quality and reliability have brought export orders larger than the industry can cope with. Because of the more favourable domestic prices, companies sell less than 20 percent of their output on the export market.

As reported by two leading firms, Fashion and Concorde (a foreign-owned firm, exporting up to 12 percent of its production), clothing manufacturers fear liberalization of the domestic market because this would eliminate a substantial part of the domestically-oriented industry and in the process ruin exports production which depends on a substantial domestic turnover.

Perhaps the cautious development of the textile and clothing sector is thus the result of relatively high wages, a protected domestic market, low (albeit mixed) efficiencies and reliance on tariff-free access to the EC especially for the clothing sector combined with export oriented policies, modern technology and well established trade contacts.

The future development of South Africa is also able to change the regional parameters drastically.

4.4.3 Kenya: inward-looking industrialization in an open economy

Kenya's colonial history, post-independence structure, and the nature of its industrialization invite comparison with Zimbabwe. Its economy is characterized by a predominant but dualistic agricultural sector, a high investment ratio, high levels of foreign participation and a very high degree of openness (van der Hoeven and Vandermoortele 1987). Industrialization in Kenya is based on import substitution.[8] Effective rates of protection for the whole manufacturing sector stood at 31 percent in 1968 and had increased to 51 percent in 1985, averaging 35 percent for local private firms, 57 percent for foreign firms, and 65 percent for parastatal enterprises (Sharpley and Lewis 1990).[9] This policy has produced mixed results since, while Kenya's manufacturing structure has moved beyond the 'early phase' of import substitution with many industrial linkages and substantial deepening towards production of intermediates and light capital goods, it shows many gaps and is dominated by private sector lobbies and is riddled with conflicts (not atypical for an import substitution regime) between producers and traders and between producers of inputs and users of inputs (for example between cotton producers and textile firms). These conflicts are articulated at the political level, while the implementation of government industrial policies may malfunction or be outright inappropriate (Coughlin and Ikiara 1988).

The ratio of manufacturing value-added to GDP stood at 12.6 percent in 1985 (Table A.3) which is in the upper range of SSA countries. Growth rates of manufacturing value-added were amongst the highest in SSA, especially in the period 1973–79 (10.8 percent) but fell substantially in the 1980s ((4.9 percent). Despite the import substitution policy, manufactured exports reached 20.5 percent of total exports (third highest in SSA excluding SACU) in 1976, but declined to 15.8 in 1986 (Table A.3). The share of textile and clothing in MVA stood at 12 percent in 1986 (Table A.3) with small textile exports and negligible clothing exports. Although no clothing imports were recorded (suggesting self-sufficiency in clothing), textile imports were substantially higher than textile exports leading to a negative trade balance in textiles and clothing combined.

The economy picked up again during the second half of the 1980s (Table 4.9) due to 'favourable weather conditions, a general improvement in Kenya's terms of trade (underlining Kenya's dependence on agricultural production and exports), and the effects of the restructuring programme in Kenya' (UNIDO 1990b). Export of textiles declined until 1986 (Table 4.9) and declined further in 1987 to US\$ 3.3 million (UNIDO 1990b). Garments exports, not reported in UN statistics, were restricted to one firm only (Stevens 1990).

The share of the textile/clothing industry in both total manufacturing MVA (1985) and in total manufacturing employment (1987) is 12 percent. Textile production has been growing steadily but clothing production more erratically (Table 4.9). Dyes and most chemicals are imported and a shift has occurred from cotton to synthetic fibres (UNIDO 1990b).[10]

Restructuring programmes started in 1980 (when import expenditures were almost double export receipts) with the first IBRD structural adjustment loan signed in 1980 (Hecox 1988). Table 4.9 shows that inflation was rather modest between 1982 and 1988 but that during 1982 to 1985 nominal wage increases undermined the effects of devaluation. Data on labour costs in textiles in Table A.3 confirm this.

In combination with the usual macroeconomic and international trade policies, industrial policy aimed to increase export orientation by reducing protection (lowering tariffs and particularly quantity restrictions on imports) and by strict controls on wages and prices. Specific export promoting measures (Hecox 1988; UNIDO 1990b) were the creation of an export credit and guarantee scheme, improvement of financial incentives for exports under the export compensation scheme (20 percent export subsidy on f.o.b. value), discontinuation of protective quantity restrictions, improved allocation of foreign exchange during the transition period to a market-based foreign exchange regime, and the recent creation of an Industrial Promotion Centre to encourage foreign investors.

During the 1980s further measures were taken, such as the reduction of corporation tax from 45 to 40 percent, replacement of sales tax by value-added tax, and reduction of the role of import licensing in favour of a simplified system of tariffs; discussions have also taken place on the controversial issue of divestment of parastatals (UNIDO 1990b).[11]

Apart from these general industrial policies, no particular textile and clothing sector oriented policies exist. Instead, policy towards the cotton sector, with world prices that are lower than domestic prices, and tight restrictions on cotton imports act as disincentives to exports.

Nominal tariffs for textiles and clothing combined averaged 58 percent in 1978 and increased to 65 percent in 1984 (Sharpley and Lewis 1990).

Table 4.9 Selected indicators, Kenya

	1982	1983	1984	1985	1986	1987	1988	1989	1990
GDP*	93.8	94.0	96.1	100.1	107.8	114.1	121.0	125.7	–
Exchange rate (Sh/SDR)	14.1	14.4	15.2	17.7	19.1	23.4	25.0	28.4	34.3
Consumer price index (CPI)	72.0	80.3	88.5	100.0	104.0	109.4	118.4	130.0	143.5
Real wage private sector**	100.0	95.1	90.7	89.4	–	–	–	–	–
Exchange rate over nominal wage	19.6	18.9	18.9	19.8	–	–	–	–	–
Quantity index manufacturing production***	–	163.6	170.3	178.2	188.7	199.4	211.4	–	–
% change	–	–	4.1	4.6	5.9	5.7	6.0	–	–
Quantity index textile production***	–	146.8	166.6	174.3	186.5	192.5	–	–	–
% change	–	–	13.5	4.6	7.0	3.2	–	–	–
Quantity index clothing production***	–	406.8	369.5	352.5	354.6	359.8	–	–	–
% change	–	–	–9.2	–4.6	0.6	1.5	–	–	–
Textile imports****	–	11.1	n.a.	12.7	18.3	–	–	–	–
Textile exports****	–	2.2	n.a.	6.5	4.5	–	–	–	–
Total exports****	936	937	1034	943	1170	909	1018	926	–
Total imports****	1468	1198	1348	1273	1457	1623	1802	1963	–

Notes: *   In 1985 prices in 1000 millions of TSh.
       **   1982 = 100
       ***   1976 = 100
       **** millions of US$.

Sources: IMF (1990, 1991), van der Hoeven and Vandemoortele (1987), Riddell (1990a), Grosh (1990), UNIDO 1990b, United Nations (1989), and author's calculations.

Effective rates of protection for polyester yarn and diverse fabrics ranged between 72 and 93 percent.[12] More variation is reported by Grosh (1990) (Table 4.10) who estimates nominal protection coefficients (NPC), effective rates of protection (ERP), domestic resource costs ratios (DRC) and the rate of return (ROR) for a number of firms (N) in the textile and clothing, footwear, and leather sectors by type of ownership. Effective protection and efficiency both have a positive influence on the rate of return. Thus, for example, the one private sector firm reported on enjoys a very high level of protection, but is so inefficient that its rate of return is almost zero. The possible behavioural relationship between high levels of protection and low efficiencies is not established by these data. Regrettably, no further information is available to analyse the causes of these diverging measures of protection and performance.

The textile industry operates at a high rate of capacity utilization (81 percent in 1986) displaying 'superior technological mastery in both spinning and weaving, with levels creditably near world best practice levels' (UNIDO 1990b:58, quoting the World Bank). Pack's detailed study on technological issues in the textile industry in Kenya gives a differentiated view, with productivity levels for spinning (of four sample firms) varying between 61 and 80 percent of world 'best practice' levels and for weaving between 41 and 84 percent (Pack 1987). This study attributes deviations from world best practice to, firstly, inadequate product specialization and secondly to lower levels of technological mastery. However, within sub-Saharan Africa as a whole, technological performance of Kenyan firms may well stand out positively.

Table 4.10   Average measures of performance for the textile and clothing/footwear/leather sectors by ownership (1984)

	NPC	ERP (%)	DRC	RoR (%)	No. firms
Textiles					
public	1.48	94.4	2.31	9.9	4
quasi-public	1.13	−17.9	1.16	2.1	2
private	1.73	616.8	16.56	0.6	1
Clothing/footwear/leather					
public	1.11	−38.2	2.68	−4.5	1
private	1.36	51.0	1.00	35.7	7

Source: Grosh (1990).

In response to strong government support for the new single-stop Industrial Promotion Centre aimed at encouraging foreign investors, only four foreign investors manufacturing garments under bond for exports have started production. Thirteen other projects for manufacturing under bond – mostly garment manufacturers – were fully approved by January 1990 (UNIDO 1990b). Thus, these new investments should enable local textile firms to sell to new export oriented garment manufacturers, significantly changing the focus and competitiveness of Kenya's textile industry (ibid.).

With increasing foreign investment in clothing, the share of government owned enterprises in textiles and clothing will decline even without privatization. At present, six textile firms out of a total of 53 are parastatals, and 14 are integrated mills. Five of the six have inexperienced, politically appointed management. Lower technical management positions are often filled by expatriates (Indian and/or European). Only one firm is mainly African-Kenyan owned. All other private firms are owned by Asian-Kenyans, often relying on expatriate (Indian) textile technicians and engineers.

The major constraints for the Kenyan textile industry (UNIDO 1990b:58) are:

(a) Lack of sufficient cotton at a good price and quality. Kenya produces medium staple cotton which increases weaving inefficiencies and results in low (non-export) quality fabrics. Supply of cotton is declining because of inadequate agricultural pricing and technological policies. Imports of quality cotton lint, for example from Tanzania, are hampered by cumbersome bureaucratic procedures in which the CLSMB has a major say. Export oriented firms prefer to import their requirements rather than use local inputs.

(b) Lack of specialization and economies of scale. Because of limited market development, firms often rely on one or a few wholesalers, trying to satisfy diverse demands. This leads to short runs and resetting the machinery with subsequent increases in down-times and inefficiency.

(c) Weak managerial skills. Only a few firms have multinational linkages with access to market information, skills and new product design. Management of costs of production and sales is generally weak.

Added to these are problems of equipment age, capacity imbalances within firms for different subprocesses, poor maintenance, medium quality of local mechanical and engineering firms, a general shortage of textile related skills, poor factory health conditions and increasing illegal imports of second hand clothing threatening to cause a collapse of domestic demand for new clothing.

To highlight the general discussion and to supply some comparative experience with respect to the Tanzanian textile sector to be discussed in the next chapters, details are provided below of two Kenyan firms, one private mill and one public sector mill. Choice of these firms was determined by data availability, but their highly divergent performances reveal something of the range of existing (in)efficiencies in Kenyan textile/clothing industry.

The private mill is an integrated mill, established in 1968, producing textiles and garments for the local market.[13] A subsidiary of an Indian-based firm and employing 2800 workers operating three shifts per day, it is the only firm in Kenya that exports garments. Exports of cloth are not possible because of technical problems in producing the long lengths of faultless cloth demanded by European clothing firms.[14] Export activities started in 1978 with a single product, synthetic trousers, but gained momentum only in 1986. The mill's main export outlet is the medium quality (and price) UK market but it is now diversifying its products (synthetic/woollen trousers and knitted garments) and markets (to include Germany). Transport is by sea or by air and poses no problems.

The public sector mill, Mount Kenya Textile Mills (Mountex) was originally established in 1974 as a private venture with foreign capital (about 75 percent Lonrho Group) in a minor industrial centre, Nanyuki (208 km north of Nairobi) with an initial capacity of 10 million square metres, employing second-hand, labour intensive machinery. It never took off properly. There were problems with the old machinery and low product quality affected sales, while a mismatch between the capacities of various production departments lowered its overall capacity. In 1978 it was taken over by the Government. Despite rehabilitation, the mill is still plagued by technological problems: old and technologically backward machinery with high energy consumption (some date back to 1954), a lack of spare parts and bottlenecks in production departments, especially in the weaving (warping section). Cotton supply is unreliable and is a major constraint in expanding output.

In addition, typical for public sector mills, the management structure is top-heavy and inexperienced, with a board of directors consisting mainly of high level representatives of public institutions with no textile experience. Even the general manager is a political appointee without experience in textile production. The middle management is a large and unbalanced team with great differences in competence. Employment has increased from 663 in 1986 to 1130 in 1990 without a corresponding increase in production. Workers receive only on-the-job training and possess little knowledge about the machinery they are using. Working conditions are very poor, with long uninterrupted shifts under poor conditions resulting in a high incidence of respiratory difficulties and high labour turnover. The production mix covers items of varying mark-up rates but the company has not considered specializing in the most profitable line of production.

Not surprisingly, financial performance has been poor, net losses being 28, 40 and 53 million KSh. in 1987 to 1989 which, expressed as percentages of total sales, are 28, 36 and 47 percent respectively. The financial situation is exacerbated first by the firm's inability to service its loans, thus accruing interest on unfulfilled interest payments, and second by the fact that its loans are fixed in foreign currencies and increase with every effective devaluation.

In summary, both private and public sector cotton-based textile and clothing industries have developed behind protective walls, but cotton supply bottlenecks have forced the industries to diversify into production using synthetic yarns and fabrics for the domestic market. Diverging indicators have been found for performance for both private and public firms. Exports have been very small for textiles and negligible for clothing but the new export promotion policy is changing this. As most of the export-oriented investments will not be able to use local fabrics because of quality limitations, integrating the domestic textile sector and these new ventures may prove to problematic. This emerging dualistic industrial structure reflects the outcome of dualistic policies, i.e. export promotion concurrent with an apparent reluctance to phase out import substitution promoting measures (in general or selectively) in the context of a generally dualistic economy in terms of ownership (private and public), income and forms of production.

4.4.4 Ghana: successful recovery, but what next?

Ghana's adjustment experience is often quoted as an example to other African countries. It was one of the early adjusters (starting in 1983) and has embraced the whole adjustment package quite seriously. While recognizing the positive effects of structural adjustment policies, this relative success was fundamentally conditioned by the increased supplies through increased imports (an outcome of IMF/WB approved economic reforms) and agricultural growth (caused by good rains). Rapid industrial recovery has been quoted as one of the outcomes (Meier and Steel 1989; Green

1987). Others are more cautious and, although recognizing the success of the economic recovery programme, they point out that real growth is still very low, that international debt is a tightening noose, and that the slow rise in urban living standards may lead to uncontainable political disruptions (Haynes 1989; Hutchful 1989). Indeed, figures presented in Table 4.11 show (from 1983 onwards) a continuous increase in real GDP and the foreign exchange value of exports (although declining in 1989), imports and gross manufacturing output (from 1984). Large devaluations stayed ahead of consumer prices and narrowed the gap between official and parallel market rates for foreign exchange.

The nature of industrial development during the period leading to the crisis has set the stage for the poor performance in the 1980s by creating an inefficient, capital and import intensive, predominantly large scale industry under a rather irrational system of protection without sufficient linkages within industry and between industry and agriculture; labour inefficiencies were high, especially in the public sector, government neglected the small scale sector, and little attention was paid to maintenance and replacement of capital assets (Killick 1989; Riddell and Taylor 1989). Reinforced by the general deterioration of the economy in the 1970s industrial production dropped by 1981 to 63 percent of its 1975 level with the manufacturing sector operating at around 20 percent of capacity. Particular problems in the industrial sector at that time were experienced in almost every aspect of production: obsolete plant and equipment, lack of raw materials, spares and ancillaries, inadequate financial resources, especially foreign exchange, poor industrial infrastructure, low productivity of capital and labour, low wages and salaries, depressed markets, a cumbersome import licensing system, overinvolvement of government in the productive sector and decision making and, finally, shortages of technical and management skills.

Manufacturing output reached its lowest level in 1984 before beginning to recover. Capacity utilization in textiles and garments showed fluctuations but in the last year for which data are given (1988) has 'improved' to 33 and 35 percent respectively, still substantially below the (still very low) average for the manufacturing sector (43 percent).

Ghana's textile industry comprises 138 medium or large scale enterprises and 223 small scale enterprises. Eight large scale vertically integrated enterprises account for almost 90 percent of spinning and weaving capacity. There are 4 large knitting mills. The remaining number of well over 100 firms, although classified as medium, is thus rather small in size. The 223 small scale enterprises are engaged in the production of hand screen printing, tie-dye and batik fabrics, and kente

Table 4.11   Selected indicators, Ghana

	1981	1982	1983	1984	1985	1986	1987	1988	1989
GDP (in 1985 prices, bn Cedis)	–	315.8	318.0	326.4	343.0	360.9	378.2	401.7	
Exchange rate (Cedis/SDR)	–	3.0	31.4	49.0	65.9	110.1	249.8	309.4	398.2
Parallel market to official rate	–	22.2	3.2	2.8	1.8				
Consumer price index (CPI)*	–	29.1	64.9	90.7	100.0	124.6	174.2	228.8	286.5
Exchange rate/CPI	–	10.3	48.4	54.0	65.9	87.4	143.4	135.2	140.0
Exports (fob, m US$)	–	607.0	439.1	565.9	632.4	773.4	826.8	881.0	807.2
Imports (cif, m US$)	–	588.7	499.7	533.0	668.7	712.5	951.5	993.4	999.0
Use of Fund reserves (m SDR)	–	68.4	316.6	525.1	638.0	642.3	610.9	566.4	572.9
Gross output manufacturing sector (constant 1975 prices, m C)	631.6	501.3	370.7	346.9	470.1	513.5	585.6		
Gross output textile and garments (constant 1975 prices, m C)	44.6	21.8	14.5	22.1	26.7	31.8	32.5		
Share of textiles & garments in gross manufacturing output (%)	7.1	4.4	4.0	6.4	7.7	6.2	5.5		
Capacity utilization total manufacturing (%)	–	–	27	18	25	28	38	43	
Capacity utilization textiles (%)	–	–	16	17	20	17	24	33	
Capacity utilization garments (%)	–	–	25	20	26	27	25	35	

Note: *1990 CPI was 392.4.
Sources: IMF (1990, 1991), Riddell and Taylor (1989), Meier and Steel (1989).

cloth weaving (Menako 1987). In contrast with other sectors where direct state participation can be high, state involvement in the textile sector has taken the form of joint ventures, with the Ghana Industrial Holding Corporation (GIHOC) holding 40 percent of the shares (Adomako 1990). Capacity utilization of the large firms has been estimated at 25 percent in 1986. The present installed capacity is capable of producing more than twice the domestic demand. Effective capacity was seriously reduced from the mid-1970s to the mid-1980s due to lack of spare parts and effective maintenance.

Ghana imports relatively large quantities of yarn, fabrics and clothing as well as cotton. The textile and clothing sector accounts for only 6 percent of MVA in 1985 (amongst the lowest in Africa). Thus although at present the sector cannot saturate domestic demand, solving the supply problems may lead to an effective overcapacity.

Machinery is outdated and in disrepair since spare parts are unavailable and firms have liquidity problems as a result of SAP related measures. Imports of raw materials are constrained while locally grown cotton does not cover the industry's requirements. On the demand side, second-hand clothing and synthetic fabrics provide significant domestic competition. The only feasible exports appear to be the high quality traditional fabrics produced by small scale industries.

Specific textile related policies include promoting local cotton supply on a commercial basis, encouraging and assisting small scale textile industries, rationalizing and rehabilitating the whole industry, stimulating linkages to for example ancillaries and maize starch (used for strengthening the warp during weaving), stimulating textile research by establishing a special textile research unit within the Industrial Research Institute and improving the training of textile technicians by upgrading the Tema Textiles Institute.

Behind the rather reluctant recovery of the manufacturing sector in general and the textile/clothing sector in particular are problems that either were not tackled by the ERP and SAP or arose from these policy packages. Technical constraints persist and although foreign exchange has now become available, problems have emerged not only in funding substantial rehabilitation and expansion but even in financing normal operations. One explanation for the lack of working capital is that repetitive devaluation and the resulting high rates of inflation have increased production costs enormously. Output prices are constrained by increasing liberalization (competitive imports) and illegal imports (especially second-hand clothing imports) and by domestic demand that has been suppressed as a result of the austerity measures. The further reduction of real wages lowers worker morale and productivity and also limits the industry's capacity to retain qualified and competent staff.

These problems have not affected all firms equally. Firms that use domestic inputs and/or export a portion of their output are less affected. Worst off are those firms that rely on imported inputs and produce exclusively for domestic markets. Small firms have an additional disadvantage in lacking sufficient leverage to obtain short and long term credit facilities.

It appears that lifting the most obvious constraints has uncovered more fundamental problems rooted in the industrial structure and originating from past economic policies; these will require more time to resolve.

4.5 CONCLUSIONS: COUNTRY EXPERIENCES AND THEIR POLICY IMPLICATIONS

After reviewing the policy experience of the above countries, this final section will first summarize, by regional groups, the salient points of the discussion on causes of success of the various countries and on the remaining constraints towards further development (section 4.5.1). Second, section 4.5.2 will identify the factors in economic policy with regard to textile and clothing sector development which are of general relevance. Finally, in section 4.5.3, the emerging policy issues will be compared to the general framework presented at the beginning of the chapter in Table 4.1.

4.5.1 Factors underlying successes and constraints

Belgium and Spain, have articulated their policies towards the sectors in the form of explicit and rather complete textile plans, recognizing the important role of the sector in employment and its balance of payments effects and aiming at (re)gaining competitiveness on EC and wider export markets. Factors that have been shown to be crucial were:

(a) Technological improvements including hard and soft automation: whereas Belgium has been able to reach the technological frontier, Spain has had only limited success in technological upgrading;
(b) Government assistance in the form of explicitly designed, all-embracing textile plans;
(c) Tripartite consultations, ensuring compatibility of objectives;
(c) Firm participation in sharing the costs of adjustment, ensuring commitment to the project;

(d) Selectivity and restraint: focusing on strengthening existing firms with potential, leaving aside strong subsectors and discouraging new capacity;

(e) Role of the EC in steering governments away from direct employment subsidies towards structural transformation;

(f) Sourcing towards nearby lower wage countries: Belgian firms have been able to divert part of their production to Mediterranean countries.

The Asian countries, Thailand, Bangladesh and Sri Lanka and one African country, Mauritius, have embarked on garment-led export oriented industrialization policies aimed at attracting foreign investment. The goal is to export standardized garments to the USA and EC quota markets while expanding the value-added content of exports by backwards integration between the clothing and textile sectors. Main factors that have contributed to the (varying degrees of) success are:

(a) Clear export orientated incentives in combination with measures encouraging foreign investment under acceptable investment codes: Thailand does not discriminate between domestic and foreign producers, Bangladesh and Mauritius favour foreign investment, while Sri Lanka is a bit ambivalent;

(b) Policies towards the domestic sector such as liberalization of imports of inputs and capital equipment;

(c) Measures aiming at backwards integration: most successful are Thailand and Mauritius. Bangladesh has developed an active policy on this issue (for both textiles and cotton) aiming to achieve results in the mid-1990s while Sri Lanka seems to be unable to tackle domestic inefficiencies;

(d) The MFA, in combination with the success of Japan and the four Asian NICs in industrialization, has created spill-over investments;

(e) Local entrepreneurial and skill endowments: Thailand and Bangladesh have a tradition in textile and garment production. Mauritius has a well established trading tradition while Sri Lanka's entrepreneurial class is not well developed;

(e) Political stability: Thailand and Mauritius have enjoyed stable political conditions, Bangladesh has been rather unstable while Sri Lanka is engaged in a continuing civil war;

(f) Wage costs: all countries have low wage costs although wages are rising in Thailand. However, the MFA quota system ensures that small wage differentials are not the most important determining factor in foreign investment;

(g) Small scale sector: the small scale (handloom) sectors in Thailand, Bangladesh and Sri Lanka offer considerable potential for export production and supply of general textile skills to the large scale sector.

The African countries, Zimbabwe, Kenya and Ghana, have little in common with regard to their textile policies. Only Kenya has started to develop garment-led export and foreign investment policies. Zimbabwe's unique political and geographical position gives it an advantage when narrowly focusing on entrepreneurial capacity and export potential, while Ghana is in the process of recovery from a rather deep crisis. Industrial policies in all three countries have been influenced by structural adjustment programmes. Key factors in recovery of the industrial sector have been:

(a) International import support to relieve acute foreign exchange shortages;

(b) Import liberalization: in Zimbabwe this took the form of an export oriented import liberalization policy whereas Ghana's and Kenya's liberalization replenished domestic supply by not only covering inputs for domestic production but eventually also consumer goods;

(c) Technological rehabilitation: technological degradation was most severe in Ghana, followed by Kenya. The issue is not so much to advance to a higher technological stage of textile production but rather to safeguard the sector's role in supplying domestic needs and selectively aim at raising quality to at least minimum export quality levels.

For the European countries, constraints that hamper further development in the desired direction are:

(a) Continuing wage cost competition from advanced exporting countries, some of which are also high quality market niche producers: for Belgium, expansion beyond the EC market will prove difficult even in market niches while Spain will face serious problems from both European countries and other textile and clothing producing countries;

(b) Limited adjustment: especially Spanish firms have not responded massively to the restructuring policies; protection is still considerable while domestic and foreign marketing capacities remain limited;

(c) Eastern Europe: the impact of political changes in Eastern Europe is difficult to forecast as there will be consequences for production, investment, demand and trade patterns. Figures on technology presented in Chapter 4 show that especially the USSR has acquired large quantities of modern technology;

(d) European integration: it is expected that individual European countries will be challenged by more imports from advanced textile and clothing producers when quota arrangements apply to Europe as a whole.

For the Asian countries and Mauritius some problems have arisen from success, while lingering constraints limit further development.

(a) MFA restrictions: especially Thailand but in descending order also Bangladesh and Sri Lanka have already experienced the enforcement of 'voluntary' export restrictions (VERs). Mauritius, as an ACP country, is not subject to such constraints;

(b) Rising wages: wage levels have been rising steadily in Thailand while it is moving into a more advanced stage of industrialization. Also Mauritius' wages seem to be on the rise, but here diversification will present more problems;

(c) Backwards integration: problems with backward integration from export garments into textiles are experienced least by Thailand, followed by Bangladesh and Mauritius and most by Sri Lanka. All Asian countries reviewed are trying to increase their capacity in growing quality cotton but so far with limited success. However, increased linkages of garments with the rest of the economy is essential to ensure that the country remains an attractive location even when wages increase and tax benefits have been reaped. In addition, linkages to the small scale sector remain underdeveloped;

(d) Protective policies for domestic producers: this is only a problem in Sri Lanka, where it will seriously constrain backwards integration not only because of resulting price differences but also because quality is lowered;

(e) Political instability: already discussed under factors of success.

African countries experience general problems in industrialization. Of the countries reviewed, Zimbabwe has the most solid industrial base, Kenya has progressed beyond the early phase of import substitution but has an unbalanced industrial structure, while Ghana's industries have suffered enormously in the recent past. Specific constraints are:

(a) Technological problems: aged machinery in poor condition. This is particularly a problem for Ghana and Kenya. Data on technology presented in Chapter 4 show that Zimbabwe has modernized most and Ghana least;

(b) Low management and skill levels: management was reported as poor in Ghana, mixed in Kenya and rather good for leading Zimbabwean firms, while specific technical textile skills are in short supply in Kenya and Ghana;

(c) Limited internal market: high quality markets in all three countries are rather small whereas the low quality markets are not conducive to improving firm efficiency. Furthermore, the availability of second-hand clothing has drastically reduced demand at the low quality end of the market in the case of Kenya and Ghana. Even before this is taken into account, Ghana's capacity in textile production exceeds total demand by a factor of two to one;

(d) Limited quality performance: as a consequence, quality performance is only achieved by firms planning or involved in export production. Zimbabwe is most advanced, while Kenya is in the process of stimulating export oriented industries in garments.

(e) Lack of integration: this becomes a problem when garment exports develop without accompanying textile and cotton developments, as is the case in Kenya.

(f) Lack of specialization: Kenya's lack of specialization results from underdeveloped marketing structures which lead to efficiency losses;

(f) Deteriorating performance: financial performance is poor and will deteriorate as liberalization measures proceed. DRCs were mixed in Zimbabwe and Kenya. No information is available for Ghana but the general picture that emerges is that Ghana's textile and clothing sectors are in the worst position.

(g) Small scale sector: Zimbabwe has a rather large small scale sector in garments and Ghana has a long standing tradition of handloom weaving and small scale processing. No clear policies seem to exist to preserve or to integrate this potential with the rest of the sector.

4.5.2   Major fields of economic policy

By and large, the EC countries have pursued sector- and firm-specific policies aiming at improving the competitiveness of their textile firms and moving away from the more defensive strategies of the past. Asian countries embedded their textile policies in a more general policy of export-led industrialization. The African countries were least specific in their industrial policies which are heavily influenced by macroeconomic stabilization and adjustment programmes. The findings of the previous section can be further analysed in relation to the role of the state, the role of the market, foreign linkages, technology and inter-sectoral linkages.

The role of the state

The role of the state can take many forms ranging from participation in production, design and implementation of policies to provision of supporting services (discussed in turn below) and may itself be shaped by both external and internal political factors. EC policy towards Belgium and IMF/WB policy for African countries have been important external political factors. Conditions internal to the country determine the balance of power and thus help to explain the nature of the state and of its actions as well as other limits to its range of action.

The emphasis of state intervention has shifted towards targeted policies and even firm-specific measures. For some countries this has implied a shift away from direct production for example in countries such as Ghana, Kenya, Bangladesh, and Sri Lanka. For most, the general focus of intervention (determining for instance, the level of effective protection) shifted from import substitution to export promotion. However, large differences exist between countries with respect to the relation between state and private sectors and this limits the scope for comparison.

As demonstrated explicitly by the case of Kenya, public corporations with local and politically appointed management are the worst economic performers. But state participation in production can take other forms. Especially where there is little local entrepreneurial capacity, few prospects for foreign investment and an inability to control and integrate foreign investment, state participation in the equity of private enterprises, foreign management of public enterprises and commercialization of public enterprises have potential gains that should not lightly be discarded in the fashionable wave of across-the-board privatization. For the textile/clothing sector, the apparent problems of backwards integration (discussed in more detail below) define a field in which government action may be desired. Assessment of the feasibility of these options, especially with respect to the degree of state control, is only possible after a more thorough analysis of the state in individual countries.

Ironically, in Ghana, while participating in production, the state has become incapable of providing supporting services to production, a role considered to be non-controversial and even essential regardless of one's ideological viewpoint. Infrastructural services, support for commerce and trade, education and health are all essential, not just for short term recovery but also for long term growth. With regard to the clothing-textile sector and in addition to general services, state involvement in technical training, technological research and commercial support has been part of the textile plans of nearly all the countries reviewed.

For economic policies towards industry the issue at stake is not the role of the state as such but the type, extent and scheduling of such policies. The export cum foreign investment oriented policies pursued in various degrees in all the countries reviewed involve direct and indirect transfers to firms, which may create dependencies similar to those developed under import substitution regimes when the state is not strong enough to gradually and selectively phase out such measures. Particular policies would include those that release the foreign exchange constraint for export production as in Zimbabwe. Full, indiscriminate liberalization of imports (especially second-hand imports) may do more harm than good once industries are accustomed to a protected environment, but gradual adjustment assumes a determined and capable state able to steer conflicting social forces in the desired direction.

It is thus not the size of the state that determines its effectiveness in economic planning and policy making but rather its strength as expressed by its relative autonomy with respect to major economic actors. Although it may be easy to reduce the size of the state and with that some major inefficiencies, strengthening the state is not a matter of better training or more policy advisors. Rather it is the result of socio-economic and political forces as they have been shaped by the past. A reorientation of such forces towards private enterprise does not affect the strength of the state but strengthens its servicing role to the private sector. Especially in that light, overemphasizing direct and indirect measures in favour of export development may prove countereffective in the longer run.

Role of the market

Structural adjustment policies have stressed the role of appropriate price signals given by free markets in resource allocation and production. Increased competition and better market information may also enhance efficiency and quality. Experiences with export oriented policies in the countries reviewed reveal that information on market requirements for quality and design have had an important role in the success of garment exports and has 'trickled' upstream into the textile sector.

There is no necessary conflict between free markets and a certain degree of state participation, as even under state ownership competition can be built into the system by individualizing public firms and making them function as private enterprises, thereby leaving aside other objectives (possibly incongruent with short term allocation efficiency) that government may want to pursue using public enterprises.

For textiles and clothing, a distinction will have to be made between domestic markets and export markets, and each of these should be further differentiated according to the quality requirements demanded by different income categories. The important role of the high quality export market in textiles and garments has been discussed in Chapter 3. As this is largely the high income market of Europe and the US, liberalizing access to these markets would be beneficial for the advanced textile producers amongst the developing countries such as the NICs, Thailand and to some extent Bangladesh. The developing countries of the ACP already enjoy free access and in fact benefit from investment relocation by more advanced countries in response to the MFA restrictions. The high quality end of the export market is out of reach for countries like Tanzania, leaving only the more standardized and lower quality segment, where cost compitition is most fierce.

The low quality end of the domestic market faces strong competition of second-hand clothing. But to what extent should these be liberalized or restricted? There is an apparent consumer interest in used garments but this threatens the local garment and textile industry and may generate losses in employment, income and productive skills. The obvious answer would be that local industries should specialize towards higher quality domestic and export markets. However the conditions in the textile/clothing system are such that quick transformation is impossible. An intermediate approach, allowing slower adjustment to regulated parameters is called for. But can the state administer such gradual change?

Technology

All of the countries reviewed have adopted policies for technological upgrading. Depending on the country, this has served different objectives, ranging from entering the race for the fashion market for Belgium, facing the challenge of low wage competition for many firms in Spain, venturing into the low to medium quality export market for firms in Thailand, Bangladesh and Zimbabwe, deepening the value-added component of the final product for firms in Thailand and Mauritius, and at the lowest end of the spectrum, revitalizing industries at the end of their lifecycle as in Ghana, Kenya and Sri Lanka. The scope for technological upgrading was widest and the need for it greatest in the textile sector. The garment sector is labour intensive, technologically simpler, and has a more limited scope for technological innovation. Thus, the type of technological upgrading depended on market orientation, factor endowments, sector and stage of industrialization.

Technological upgrading should not take place in isolation. Factors that have detracted from an industry's capacity and/or factors crucial to the new role a sector is envisaged to play should be addressed simultaneously. For instance, the physical rehabilitation of firms in Ghana, without restoring profitability, will slowly return the firms back to the starting point, leaving the country saddled with higher international debts.

Inter-sectoral linkages

Within the textile/clothing subsystem the main product linkages are cotton-yarn, polyester-yarn, yarn-fabric and fabric garments (see Figure 4.1). Another type of linkage is between firms within the same sub-sector and between firms belonging to different parts of the textile/clothing

Figure 4.1   The textile/clothing system excluding trade, transport and financial/ commercial services

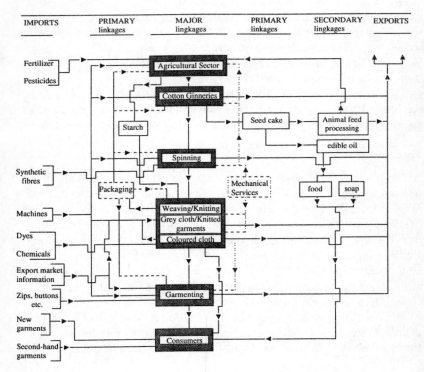

system. There can be a systematic lack of integration between firms such as between large and small scale firms, between firms supplying different type of markets (exports or domestic, high or low quality or different types of consumers in terms of culture), between firms with different ownership characteristics or there may simply be a general lack of integration. Between these different groupings a certain degree of clustering occurs, as shown in the case of garment exports below. The lack of integration reduces foreign exchange earnings because subsectoral linkages are replaced by imports; economies of specialization and flexibility also cannot develop without linkages between firms. Major instances of areas with linkage problems are discussed below.

Most developing countries experienced problems integrating the garments export sector and the domestic textile sector. The immediate reason given for this is that the domestic textile sector cannot supply fabrics of sufficiently high quality required for exports. But there are more fundamental causes. First of all there is a great difference in the complexity of technology and management required for garments and textiles, with more problems in the textile sector. Second, domestic markets are less sensitive to quality differences than export markets, possibly influenced by the low average income and lack of competition during past protective policy regimes. Third, for most developing countries the garment export sector *began* as an export sector, so that export market requirements were automatically incorporated. Fourthly, ownership is often different, with foreign investment flowing almost exclusively into garment exports. Finally, the MFA requirements on domestic input content apparently allow for non-domestic textiles, so that from the point of view of the foreign producer, it suffices to shift only the location of the garment manufacturing, leaving all other parts of the production and supply network intact.

A lack of integration between small scale and large scale producers is evident in Thailand, Bangladesh, Sri Lanka and Ghana, with their rather substantial handloom sectors.

The availability of local cotton has the immediate advantage of good supply even when foreign exchange shortages are severe. However, local cotton is not always of the right quality, and institutions and policies develop around the cotton sector that limit the flexibility of firms to choose their best options with regard to cotton inputs (for example in Kenya and Nigeria).[15] Such policies should be adjusted to reap the advantages of local cotton supplies wherever agricultural conditions make this possible.

Finally, firms often produce a wide range of products to satisfy the demands of their limited number of distributors (Kenya). This can be seen as a case of horizontal intersectoral linkages. Although this may be a rational response of firms to the prevailing marketing conditions in their countries (transaction costs), limited linkages between firms decrease efficiencies that could have been achieved by more specialization and reduce the overall flexibility of the system. Market development is therefore an important policy area.

Foreign linkages

Foreign linkages are broadly defined as including all linkages between the country and the outside world. Foreign linkages are often forged by foreign firms but not necessarily so. Most advantages arise from the substance of the linkage, such as marketing networks and possibilities, technology transfer, information on markets and technology, capital for inputs and investments through suppliers credit and other forms of finance and access to managerial and technical skills. Most disadvantages flow from the concrete form in which these linkages materialize in terms of foreign control and ownership, foreign dependency, high financial incentives and the outflow of surplus.

These disadvantages are not equal for all forms of foreign linkages. Inflow of foreign capital can take the form of joint ventures between the foreign investor and local private entrepreneurs or the state. Foreign managerial and technical skills can be acquired through management contracts. Marketing linkages can be organized to leave a substantial degree of autonomy with local firms. Countries using foreign investment to promote exports, such as Thailand, Bangladesh, Mauritius, Sri Lanka and recently also Kenya show a wide variety of such forms. Zimbabwe's particular ownership structure, although in other respects not desirable from the government's point of view, also allows some of the benefits of foreign linkages to be reaped.

Framework for textile policies

In general terms, three major types of policy experiences can be identified on the basis of the countries reviewed. The first type is followed by developed countries moving from defensive strategies through adjustment to new competitive strategies. The second is the competitive policy sequence followed by successful Asian countries (including Mauritius) as described in Table 3.4; the third is the policy sequence followed by African countries and some less successful Asian countries moving from protective policies to adjustment policies, aiming at increasing industrial exports rather than fullscale export-led development. Within these broad generalizations, individual countries will obviously differ and show elements of all three experiences. Spain, for example, shows some aspects of the structural adjustment policies of African countries, some successful Asian countries are strong competitors for developed countries even in their market niches while some African countries (Kenya and Zimbabwe) are beginning to orient themselves to export led development.

It is thus to be expected that the particulars of economic policy, classified in Table 4.12 for the group of developing countries reviewed, are quite different from those of developed countries (classified in Table 4.1). In addition, for countries under far-reaching SAPs such as the African countries, general adjustment and restructuring policies have a stronger impact than do export promotion policies as compared to countries with export-led development.

Comparing the classification for developing countries above with the classification for developed countries in Table 4.1, the main differences are that (a) no regional policies have been incorporated. Only Thailand had an explicit regional element in its policy package for investment and export promotion, (b) instead, an export orientation has been added to the classification, (c) employment preserving policies, which are a major objective for developing countries do not feature prominently in the policy packages of developed countries, (d) policies on mergers and cartels were not explicitly mentioned by developing countries, (e) privatization rather than state participation was the rule for most developing countries and (f) the impact of SAP policies has by no means been indiscriminately positive for industrial sector development in general or the textile/clothing sector in particular.

4.5.3 Firm strategies

Within the rather volatile economic environment of the 1970s and 1980s, the major actors in industry are governments, international institutions, and firms. Firms (depending on their initial conditions) will also adopt strategies in response to these changes. Their options consist of selective mixtures of five basic strategic possibilities: suffer (or enjoy) the impact without any adjustment, take defensive measures to soften the impact, move away from the area where the impact is felt, fight the change by creating a protected environment or adapt to take advantage of new possibilities.

De la Torre (1984) lists the major elements of strategic behaviour by firms from developed countries as (a) wage adjustment, (b) product and market shifts, (c) foreign assembly and subcontracting with no or very little importance of scale adjustments and direct foreign investment (with the exception of Japan). He identifies three different categories of firms. 'Growth' firms adopt a mixture of these strategies, attaching special

Table 4.12   Classification of public-policy measures to textile/clothing industry of developing countries

Policy objectives	Policy orientation		
	Affecting general industrial development	*General export development*	*Sector specific*
Improve the functioning of markets	Import liberalization Devaluation Price decontrol National investments in infrastructure Financial development	Real devaluation Improving input supply Simplify export procedures Open general licence system	Sponsor the collection and dissemination of information Promote joint industry research and productivity centres
Influence resource allocation	Incentives for industrial research and development Accelerated depreciation allowances Labour training schemes Internal terms of trade	Investment grants and concessions Fiscal advantages Foreign investment for exports Facilitating repatriation Export promotion schemes: export retention rotating foreign exchange fund trade centres	Subsidies and special grants for research and development Government procurement
Industrial restructuring and modernization	Privatization of parastatals Investment and dividend tax policy	Added incentives free trade zones	Rehabilitation plans Technological upgrading and related financing schemes Stimulation of linkages Improving local cotton supply

Table 4.12   continued

Policy objectives	Policy orientation		
	Affecting general industrial development	*General export development*	*Sector specific*
Influence competitive pressures	Import policy Simplification of tariff structure Wage policies	Trade arrangements	Multi Fibre Arrangement Lomé convention Policy on competitive imports such as second-hand clothing

importance to marketing policy. 'Comfortably surviving' firms also stressed the product and market side of strategic behaviour but were satisfied with their market share and did not 'go abroad' with their production. 'Struggling' firms took either very few strategic steps, leading them into serious problems, or took these steps rather late, enabling these firms just to survive. The 'growth' firms were least likely to be family-controlled and most likely to carry out multiplant operations.

A series of studies on industries under structural adjustment in African countries commissioned by UNIDO[16] concluded that those firms with the highest export/import ratios performed better under structural adjustment policies than others. This is hardly surprising, given the large devaluations that took place under these policies. The individual studies, however, showed that other, more fundamental explanatory factors, such as ownership structure and macroeconomic policies, need to be taken into consideration for a fuller understanding of industrial performance.

The case study on Tanzanian textile firms, presented in subsequent chapters, will show that these classifications cannot do justice to the variety of factors that explain firm performance. In other words, the important questions to be asked with regard to characteristics and developments of the textile sector have be answered by referring to factors outside the sector.

Notes

1. This section draws on de la Torre (1984), Finnerty (1991b) and UNIDO (1987), which in turn is based on Ramboer (1985).
2. This section is based on Fitzpatrick and Montague (1990) and UNIDO (1987), which itself is based on an unpublished report prepared for UNIDO by D. Montero, Madrid, 1985.
3. This section draws heavily on Finnerty (1991a) and UNIDO (1988).
4. For more details, see Finnerty (1991a:202–205).
5. The contribution of the top fifteen textile firms to output of the powerloom sector in 1988 was as follows: Of the total fabric production of 106.4 million metres, 56.3 million metres was produced by the top 15 firms which varied in size, with full capacity production ranging from 2 to 6 million metres. Of the total yarn production of 72.5 million kg, 24.0 m. kg originated from the top 15 firms, their contribution to output varying from .9 to 3.1 m. kg. They employed from 1500 to 3100 employees.
6. Large quantities of yarn, fabric and second-hand clothing imports enter the country illegally, leading to the closure of many smaller private textile mills. Yarn is smuggled from India to supply the needs of the handloom sector (which the local yarn producers are unable to meet because of different specifications). Fabrics are smuggled from the Far East.
7. Hong Kong based firms, faced by the uncertain future, are looking for other locations.
8. See for example van der Hoeven and Vandemoortele (1987), World Bank (1987a), Coughlin and Ikiara (1988), Sharpley and Lewis (1990) and UNIDO (1990b).
9. See Grosh (1990) for a more detailed analysis of protection and performance by ownership in Kenyan firms. For the textile and clothing sectors see Table 4.10.
10. Coughlin judges this to be the response of textile firms to inappropriate pricing policy with prices charged to domestic firms often 25 to 30 percent higher than the world price (Coughlin and Ikiara 1988:282), while UNIDO adds to the explanation shortages in supply of cotton coupled with the reluctance of government (through the Cotton Lint and Seed Marketing Board) to import cotton (UNIDO 1990b:57). Another reason may be that in fact strong consumer preferences exist in Africa for synthetic fabric.
11. An interesting study by Grosh in Coughlin and Ikiara (1988) and reprinted as Grosh (1990) shows that in 1984 private sector firms were concentrated in sectors with the highest effective protection (more than one third of private firms) and unprotected sectors (more than one third of private firms), public firms (politically appointed management) in moderately protected sectors and quasi-public firms (government owned with non-politically appointed management) in the least protected sectors. Firm efficiency as measured by DRCs was on average highest for quasi-public firms, mainly because of higher utilization of capacity. However without an analysis of factors responsible for these differences (for example the foreign exchange allocation system), it is difficult to draw hard conclusions for or against privatization. As Grosh cautiously puts it: 'the results suggest that the case for privatization is far from proven' (ibid:56).

12. As quoted in UNIDO (1990b) from Coughlin (1986), 'The gradual maturation of an import-substitution industry: The textile industry in Kenya', Report for the World Bank, Nairobi (mimeo).
13. This section is based on Stevens (1990).
14. In garments production, these faults are avoided by cutting around them.
15. Nigerian textile firms have started to grow their own cotton in response to uncertainties with regard to cotton supply caused on one hand by declining local cotton output due to a variety of problems and on the other by import restrictions resulting from foreign exchange shortages (Andrae and Beckman, 1987)
16. Countries included were Côte d'Ivoire, Ghana, Kenya, Morocco, Nigeria, Senegal and Zaire. Papers were presented at the Regional Workshop on Strategic Management of the Adjustment Process in the Industrial Sector in Africa held at UNIDO headquarters in Vienna.

5 The Tanzanian Economy and State

This chapter on the Tanzanian economy and state provides the historical and contemporary context for the case study on performance of textile firms in Tanzania in the 1980s. The current crisis in Tanzania is rooted in conditions and developments which had expressed themselves in several crises as early as the 1970s, albeit less severely, persistently and pervasively. At the same time, the nature of the present crisis is also the result of changes in internal and external conditions, some of which can be interpreted as responses to and outcomes of the experience of the 1970s, while others (such as the increase in international interest rates) are unrelated to Tanzania's developments. The chapter presents background information on the economy at large and the manufacturing sector in particular, to show that the experience of the textile sector is part of a general trend.

After presenting the overall developments of the economy and the industrial sector before the 1980s, the macroeconomic developments and policies during the 1980s are discussed, followed by a more detailed description of the manufacturing sector during the same period. The nature of the state and its role in industrial development are discussed separately at the end of this chapter.

5.1 TANZANIA BEFORE THE 1980s

In 1961 Tanzania (still called Tanganyika until 1964) gained independence from the British. It is basically an agricultural country with over 85 percent of the population living in rural areas. The population is growing at a rate of 2.8 percent per annum. The main industrial centres are in Dar es Salaam (the capital on the coast) and nearby Morogoro, Mwanza (Lake Victoria), Arusha and Moshi (Kilimanjaro), and Kanga (along the coast in the north). About 8 percent of the labour force are wage and salary earners. The 1989 per capita income was estimated at US$ 270. Basic social services were comparatively adequate, resulting in a literacy rate estimated at 90 percent, one of the highest among developing countries, and a life expectancy at birth of 53 which is in the higher middle range of African countries, but these deteriorated considerably in the 1980s.

From 1967 until recently, Tanzania was governed by a one-party political system,[1] officially aspiring to build a socialist state. A multi-party system was adopted in 1992 but elections were only to take place in 1994. The labour movement has been under the effective control of the Party since 1964 when the independent labour union TFL (Tanganyika Federation of Labour), was replaced by the NUTA (National Union of Tanganyika Workers), formally one of the mass organizations of the Party.

Real GNP growth per capita was modestly positive in the period following independence (2.0 percent over the period 1965–73), but became increasingly negative thereafter (from –0.9 percent over the period 1973–80 to –1.7 percent over the period 1980–7) (World Bank 1989a). Modest recovery seems to have taken place in the last years of the 1980s. While agricultural production has expanded since independence (although by only a meagre 0.2 percent annually over the period 1973–80), the average annual growth rates of industrial production and particularly manufacturing declined from 7.0 and 8.7 percent during 1965–73 to 1.8 and 2.6 percent during 1973–80 to become negative at –2.4 and –3.5 percent during 1980–7.

The economic structure (Appendix Table A.5) is dominated by a large agricultural sector involved in production for subsistence, exports (coffee, cotton, tea, sisal) and urban food supply. Agriculture's share in GDP stood at around 50 percent in 1964, declined to just above 40 percent in 1976 but actually increased during the 1980s to reach around 60 percent in the last half of the 1980s. The share of manufacturing showed the opposite trend, beginning at 6.9 percent of GDP in 1964, increasing to 13.0 percent in 1976 and declining to 6.1 percent in 1986.

The major political and economic event before the 1980s was the 'Arusha Declaration' in 1967, which defined Tanzania's path towards socialism and self reliance. Major means of production were nationalized, some overnight, including some textile firms, which, in 1973, were organized into the holding company TEXCO.

Other policy directives were issued on 'Education for Self-Reliance' and 'Socialism and Rural Development' (villagization in the form of 'ujamaa villages', i.e. cooperative production units). Wholesale trade was nationalized in 1970 and in 1971 the TANU guidelines (Mwongozo Declaration) were issued asserting the supremacy of the Party, and calling for new attitudes and practices in decisionmaking for both management and workers.[2]

During the 1970s a series of shocks led to three balance of payments crises which led to Tanania's first experience with import control systems (Green, *et al.* 1980). The first 'mini-crisis' in 1971–2 was caused by over-investment and capital flight. The Tanzanian government responded with a policy of import licensing and foreign exchange control and by the end of 1972 the crisis was under control. The second crisis came in 1974 with the fourfold increase in oil (adding US$ 54 million to the import bill) and grain prices, aggravated by a period of drought. For the first time in Tanzania's history the country imported substantial amounts of food. However, by the end of 1976 the situation was under control, partly because of the coffee price boom that started in 1976 when frost hit in Brazil, the world's major coffee exporter (prices per kilo increased from T.Sh 8.9 in 1975 to T.Sh. 22.2 in 1976 and T.Sh. 39.7 in 1977, leading to roughly US$ 100 million extra export revenue in 1976 and US$ 170 million in 1977 as compared to 1975).

The balance of payment problem re-emerged in 1978 when resuming medium and long term development efforts and with renewed increased investment to make up for the damage caused by the loss of strategic imports for spares and the maintenance of infrastructure and production. In addition, the East African Community also dissolved in 1977, which meant that Tanzania had to invest in new equipment and support structures for rail and air transport, and in communication systems. In the midst of this crisis the government began preparations for the Third Five Year Plan (TFYP, from 1974–9) and the Basic Industry Strategy. In line with these plans, import controls were relaxed in 1978. Imports rose rapidly (by 54 percent over 1977 imports) and the very same year saw the re-emergence of a serious balance-of-payments problem, revealing once more the basic structural problem of the economy: limited development capacity because of the sluggish performance of agricultural exports, and fluctuating primary commodity prices with an overall downward trend. This third crisis could have been a mini-crisis like the one in 1971–72. However, three factors combined to turn Tanzania's third crisis into a major one (World Bank 1984) leading into the the prolonged crisis period of the 1980s. First, the second oil crisis at the end of 1978 doubled the oil price, adding US$ 150 million to the import bill. Second, in 1978 the war with Uganda (Kagera war) erupted with an estimated total cost of US$ 500 million for which Tanzania received no external assistance. Third, the terms of trade over the period 1977–83 were declining continuously. The loss of income due to adverse movements in the terms of trade between 1978–82 was estimated to be 12 percent of GDP compared to the loss of each oil shock at 2 percent of GDP (IMF 1980). While this trend can be partly explained as a 'normal' correction on the peak price of coffee in 1977, terms of trade movements have been the most important external cause of the balance of payments crisis. The 'official' economic crisis had its impact on the expansion of the informal sector and parallel market activities (Maliyamkono and Bagachwa 1990). Already in the 1970s but especially during the extension of the third crisis into the 1980s (to be discussed later), the second economy grew. Increasing regulation, the government's limited implementation and monitoring capacity, the failure of both the modern sector and the traditional sector to supply satisfactory incomes, and the economic crises all contributed to the development of a thriving second economy (ibid.). While the state had penetrated the society and the market, the second economy penetrated the state sector, its administrative and productive apparatus, increasing inefficiency and corruption.

Thus at the end of the 1970s, Tanzania plunged into the deepest crisis of its history. As will be shown below, this crisis continued and expanded far into the 1980s and its repercussion are still felt.

Industrial sector policies and performance

Tanzania's attempts at accellerated state-led industrialization were at the basis of first and the third crisis. Donor support for this optimistic industrialization scenario was abundant. The desire for more rapid industrialization was quite understandable given the very insignificant pre-independence manufacturing sector (Rweyemamu 1973; Coulson 1982a).

The first major government initiative in industrialization took place with the 1964 Kampala Agreement which was formulated to achieve a better distribution of industries over the East African Custom Union. Although it was never ratified by Kenya, it induced some multinationals to locate in Tanzania (for example a tyre factory in Arusha) while aiming at the whole East African market. A second initiative was the creation of the National Development Corporation in 1964. In 1966 the NDC was to acquire control of key areas of the economy (Coulson 1982).

This formed part of the prelude of the major shift in government policy in 1967 set forth in the Arusha Declaration. Control over major industries was seen as an important instrument to further the goals of socialism and self-reliance. Important industrial sectors were identified as: iron and steel, machine tools, automobiles, cement, fertilizer, and textiles (Skarstein and Wangwe 1986). The Chinese-built parastal textile mill 'Urafiki' (Friendship), had already started operation. The creation of parastatal holding organizations for manufacturing activities opened avenues for vigorous pursuance of industrialization (not foreseen by policy). In fact the share of industrial investments increased rapidly during this period (Skarstein and Wangwe 1986).

Industrial expansion continued in the early 1970s under the Second Five Year Plan (SFYP, 1969–74) and the Third Five Year Plan (TFYP 1974–9), which included the policy of decentralization of industries (nine growth towns were designated excluding Dar es Salaam).

During the 1960s and until 1972, industrial growth surpassed the overall growth of the economy. Between 1964 and 1972 industrial value-added grew at an average annual rate of more than 10 percent. However, despite continued growth in industrial capacity in that period, shifts in income distribution caused consumer demand for basic commodities to grow more rapidly. Imports of such items therefore increased, and occasionally shortages arose, especially in 1972–3 (Green, *et al.* 1980). The constraint to increased production therefore shifted from the demand side to the supply side in the form of limited productive capacity.

The first explicit industrial strategic planning effort began towards the end of the second five year planning period and resulted in the Basic Industry Strategy (BIS).[3] BIS was a twenty year plan, starting in 1975, although implementation was delayed to 1976 after the first oil crisis ended. The term 'basic' was to indicate those industries with the most linkages with the rest of the economy, including both interindustry linkages and linkages with final demand for mass consumer goods.

Table 5.1 shows the massive increase in industrial investment during the last half of the 1970s. It also shows the declining share of manufacturing in GDP during the period 1974–5 and 1979–80 (and beyond), indicating the problems of an import dependent manufacturing sector during balance of payment crises. Industrial employment shows none of these trends and continued to grow steadily throughout the crisis periods. The public sector share in manufacturing value-added grew to almost 60 percent in 1982.

In hindsight, these goals seemed to be rather ambitious, with too much emphasis laid on the technical sophistication of the planning exercise and too little on the creation of a robust and efficient manufacturing sector, assisted by pragmatic policies with serious attention to implementation problems. At the time, however, the general mood prevailing among national policy makers and external economic advisors was more optimistic with regard to the role industrialization could play.

5.2 THE ECONOMY IN THE 1980s

The economic crisis continued unabated during the 1980s and in fact intensified with the long period of drought that lasted from 1980 until

Table 5.1 Investment, value added and employment in industry, 1963–80

Year	Industrial investment T.Shs. m (1966 prices)	Industrial investment as % of total investment	Employment in industry (more than 10 workers)	Employment in industry as % of total wage employment	Value added in manufacturing as % of GDP value-added	Share of public sector in total manufacturing
1963			22212	6.5	3.4	
1964			23583	6.7	7.1	
1965			25729	7.7	7.7	
1966	153	15.6	29390	8.7	8.1	5
1967	174	14.8	34157	9.9	8.4	14
1968	206	16.2	42387	11.7	8.6	18
1969	151	13.2	43396	11.8	9.3	22
1970	281	17.0	48314	12.9	9.3	26
1971	268	13.5	53516	13.6	9.8	29
1972	185	11.0	62118	15.3	10.0	33
1973	204	11.8	63355	13.4	10.1	32
1974	277	15.6	69974	14.5	10.0	35
1975	294	17.9	73218	15.6	9.5	39
1976	520	26.6	75003	15.7	10.5	37
1977	719	37.2	78090	15.7	10.4	39
1978	779	36.7	81216	15.9	12.2	34
1979	962	36.9	86500	14.5	10.8	31
1980	781	33.8	91133	15.1	8.8	37
1981			102842	16.1	7.4	48
1982			106956	15.8	5.4	57

Source: Compiled from Skarstein & Wangwe (1986).

1985. From 1986 onwards, economic recovery plans were implemented with the assistance of IMF and the World Bank, which makes the period thereafter distinct. High levels of food imports were again required from 1980 to 1985, peaking in 1980 (increasing tenfold from the previous year). Imports remained necessary in 1986/7 (94 thousand tons) and 1987/8 (85 thousand tons) although substantially less (TET 1988). Export prices for coffee fell by a further 30 percent from 1980 to 1981, picked up slowly and a bit erratically until 1985, peaked again in 1986 and fell to their lowest level for the decade in 1987. Export volumes of the major crops fluctuated during this period; levels of production were low.

Explanations for this poor agricultural performance have pointed to: the low real prices for commercial crops, the lack of inputs, the lack of incentive goods, the poor functioning of the marketing and distribution system, and a withdrawal by peasants into subsistence, and the second economy (World Bank 1987c, 1991; TET 1988; Maliyamkono and Bagachwa 1990).

Overall developments in the economy at large reflected these downward trends in agricultural performance. Table A.6 (Appendix) shows that as GDP declined, exports declined from US\$ 571 million in 1980 to US\$ 395 million in 1989. Inflation fluctuated around 30 percent throughout the period but came down slightly in 1989. This rather stable, albeit high inflation rate, was achieved despite the very large devaluations that began modestly in 1983 and intensified from 1986 onwards. This may be due to the government's ability to contain its deficit by controlling expenditure (World Bank 1991), later combined with import liberalisation and an own-import scheme which wiped out windfall profits for traders (World Bank 1987c).[4] Export earnings covered only one third of imports from 1985 onwards and exhibited no recovery even in 1989. Imports, already at the level of absolute necessities, reached their lowest value in 1985. The manufacturing sector, underlining its import dependent character, recorded large negative growth rates in terms of manufacturing gross output to recover only somewhat in the last three years of the 1980s but stagnating after that.

The import starvation of the economy, itself the result of (among other things) the poor performance of the productive sectors, expressed itself in declining productivity, reinforced by a process of de-capitalization (World Bank 1984). Roads, communication infrastructure, water systems, the railroad, the air transport fleet, and the capital assets of industries all showed considerable depreciation with few or no resources available for maintenance, repair, or replacement, let alone rehabilitation. Even Tanzania's achievements in basic social services such as education and health started to be affected.

Under these regressive conditions, with industry declining and agriculture stagnating, the structure of the economy changed to increase the share of agriculture from about 50 percent to 60 percent and to reduce that of manufacturing from its highest value of 13.5 percent in 1978 to 6.1 percent in 1986 (recovering to 8.6 percent in 1989).

The gap between savings and investments increased significantly during the decade. The share of national savings in GDP, which stood at around 16 percent before 1980, declined to 11.4 in the period 1981–3, to 8.6 in 1984–5, and even became slightly negative in 1986–90. Investments followed a quite different trend. Before 1980, levels of gross domestic investment as high as 24.7 percent (1976–80) were achieved. This also declined in the 1980s (18.4 in 1981–3; 15.5 in 1984–5) and began to increase toward the end of the decade (21.1 in 1986–90).

The resource gap shows that in the late 1970s Tanzania became increasingly dependent on foreign inflows for its development efforts. During the crisis in the first half of the 1980s the resource gap became smaller as investment declined faster than national savings. The drastic increase in the resource gap during the last half of the 1980s shows that the recovery is fully foreign financed and was even accompanied by the complete disappearance of national savings. Moreover, as noted above, exports did not increase significantly. Thus, although it is difficult to estimate the longer term outcomes of this approach to recovery, it is definitely too early to be even cautiously optimistic with regard to sustainable development in the 1990s.

Total formal sector employment increased throughout the whole period. The growth pattern by sector showed more diverse trends. Employment in manufacturing actually expanded, although output declined. Employment in other services expanded rapidly, accounting for the larger part of total formal employment increases. Between 1978 and 1984, formal private sector employment declined slightly, parastatal employment declined a bit more (but nowhere near its decline in output) and government employment expanded tremendously. This seems to contradict the earlier quoted fact of restrained government expenditure. However, as will be shown below, real wages decreased even faster than employment expansion.

Urban informal employment declined during the same period from 570 thousand to 460 thousand. But thereafter, relaxed government regulations, increased demand, and improved input supply all contributed to a very rapid expansion of informal employment to reach an estimated one million in 1988 (World Bank 1991). This implies an annual growth rate of approximately 20 percent over the four years 1984–8.[5]

Wages and salaries in the formal sector did not follow the trends in inflation. On the contrary, the average real wages of government employees in 1986 were estimated to be less than 18 percent of their real value in 1975. For example, by 1987 a university professor received the equivalent of US$ 70 per month. At the same time, wage differentials between different categories of workers decreased. Private sector and parastatal wages for both skilled and unskilled labour were generally higher than for government employees. In 1990, simple, unskilled informal sector activities generated incomes about four times those paid by the government salaries for unskilled labour (World Bank 1991). Under these circumstances, additional sources of income became essential for those dependent on formal wages. Families started to cultivate plots of land in and around the town, and/or offered cars, rooms, or houses for rent. Others began small scale trade and transport services. Rent seeking and corrupt activities increased. Absenteeism not only increased but was officially tolerated. This situation, which is still acute, has considerably lowered productivity and morale. It is surprising to find that certain services still function at all and that, within these constraints, civil servants continue to work.

Peasant incomes do not appear to have increased significantly, although overall welfare has improved mainly through the increased availability of consumer goods from 1984 onwards (Collier and Gunning 1989). Persistent inefficiencies in marketing institutions have been quoted as one hindrance to increased farmer incomes (World Bank 1991).

Macroeconomic policy responses

The crisis of the late 1970s led to several structural adjustment programmes of the 1980s culminating in the Economic Recovery Programme (1986) and its successor, and resulting in general liberalization and deregulation. These programmes were: the National Economic Survival Programme (NESP) from 1981–2, the Structural Adjustment Programme (SAP) from 1982–5, and the two Economic Recovery Programmes, ERP I from 1986–9 and ERP II (or the Economic and Social Actions Programme, ESAP) from 1989–92. The first two of these had little impact, although a gradual policy of devaluation was implemented over the period 1981 to 1985 with average values as follows: 8.3 (1981), 9.4 (1982), 11.7 (1983), 16.3 (1984), and 17.2 (1985). A mild attempt was made to liberalize the economy.

The *Economic Recovery Programme* (ERP, 1986–89) continued previous structural adjustment efforts (URT 1986:13). However, it was much more ambitious in terms of the size and extent of the changes proposed.

While SAP attempted gradual adjustment, the ERP was a shock treatment aiming at a complete restructuring of the economic system. It is second only to the 1967 Arusha Declaration in its effects on the economic environment, moving the economy from a regime of administrative controls towards market orientation. The major economic objectives of the programme were:

(i)   to increase the output of food and export crops through appropriate incentives for production, improving marketing structures, and increasing the resources made available to agriculture;

(ii)   to rehabilitate the physical infrastructure of the country in support of directly productive activities;

(iii) to increase capacity utilization in industry through the allocation of scarce foreign exchange to priority sectors and firms;

(iv)   to restore internal and external balances by pursuing prudent fiscal, monetary and trade policies (URT 1986:13).

For the manufacturing sector more detailed policies were spelt out. To be considered a priority, an enterprise's activity would have to contribute towards at least one of the four objectives:

(i)   increase the availability of consumer goods whose scarcity acts as a disincentive for productive activities, and has demoralizing effects on the population as a whole. Soap, textiles, shoes, food and beverages are prime examples of such consumer goods;

(ii)   increase the supply of intermediate inputs and raw materials, in support of agricultural production, transportation or the manufacturing of key consumer goods, as described in (i) above;

(iii) generate net export earnings;

(iv)   generate additional public sector revenue. Beer, soft drinks and cigarettes are prime examples of activities contributing to this objective.

The industrial rehabilitation programme was aimed at carrying out comprehensive repairs and replacements of equipment to restore the production capacity of priority enterprises. This implied providing recurrent input requirements, necessary spare parts and components to the key enterprises, and supplying raw materials. Specific targets were set for some incentive goods industries, industries producing intermediate inputs and raw materials and those generating revenue for government.

For the textile sector the target was formulated to increase the manufacture of textiles to meet domestic requirements and leave a surplus for export. Under the present system of taxation with 100 percent sales tax on textiles, the textile sector in fact qualified as a priority industry on three of the four criteria.

The key policies of the ERP I included:

(i)   raising producer prices by 5 percent per year in real terms or to 60 to 70 percent of the world market price, whichever is higher;
(ii)   improving the system of foreign exchange allocation;
(iii)   pursuing an active exchange rate policy in order to remove the overvaluation of the shilling within three years;
(iv)   further de-confinement of imports and internal trade.

The Economic and Social Action Programme (ESAP or ERP II, 1989–92) was adopted in July 1989 to strengthen the achievements of ERP I, while addressing the problems experienced during its implementation. The social sector has been given special attention with a sub-programme, the Priority Social Actions Programme (PSAP). The aim is to rehabilitate social services through peoples' participation in operation and management of these services (URT 1990b).

In general, the objectives of ESAP are the same as those of ERP I. Rehabilitation of the physical infrastructure, in particular transport and communication, has been emphasized. The transport and communication sectors have been constraining recovery in other sectors (e.g. agriculture). ESAP also incorporates a specific target rate of inflation of below 10 percent. The industrial sector is now recognized as in need of being 'revamped' rather than in need of more foreign exchange for increased capacity utilization.

In addition to the emphasis to particular industries spelled out in ERP I, small scale enterprises are also mentioned. In contrast with ERP I, public revenue generating industries no longer appear in the list of specially emphasized industries.

An investment code was adopted in 1990, to create an enabling environment for potential domestic and foreign investors. It offers guarantees against nationalization, five year tax holidays on both corporate taxes and personal income tax for the owner, and provisions for remittances. It designates controlled areas normally reserved for public investment or joint ventures, and reserved areas in which only public investment is permitted. It further reserves some small scale retail and service activities for local investors only, and designates areas where foreign investment is only welcomed above a certain specified amount (URT 1990c). These policies have had mixed results. Success in improving the balance of payments is far from being achieved. The exchange rate has moved drastically in the 1980s from T.Sh/US$ 8.2 in 1980 to T.Sh./US$ 196 in June 1990 and further to T.Sh./US$ 230 in June 1991. Yet, exports are stagnating or only growing slowly, while imports are expanding. Even in 1989, exports covered only 32 percent of imports. Tanzania's external debt, including arrears, is estimated to be US$ 5.09 billion (as of December 1989), of which 17 percent (or US$ 881 million) is arrears. The ratio of debt service to merchandise exports is 94 percent, with interest payments accounting for 49 percent of exports.

In addition, as will be shown in the next section, the manufacturing sector has not really recovered. Many inefficient firms still exist and capacity utilization, although increasing, is still very low.

Moreover, social services such as health and education have further declined. To a large extent they have effectively been privatized. Private tutoring has become an essential complement to free education for those aiming to move to higher levels of education, while medicine is often priced beyond the reach of the general public.

On the other hand there have been a number of positive developments. First, after years of stagnation and decline, economic growth has picked up since 1984 and especially since 1986. The 1989 real growth rate of GDP of 4.4 percent (1976 prices) is the highest for the decade (Table 6.5). Real per capita incomes have also increased during this period.

Second, the combination of fiscal and monetary policies adopted since 1986 and the liberalization of imports have succeeded in checking the rate of inflation. Although the 23.8 percent rate of inflation in 1989 was above the 10 percent target set in ERP, it was the lowest for the decade and surprisingly low when considering the substantial devaluation during the period.

Third, the liberalization of both the internal and external markets has contributed considerably to the increased supply of wage goods in the economy. The dominant role of the National Price Commission has receded as the number of controlled items was reduced from over 400 items in the early 1980s to the fewer than 10 items at present (constituting less than 15 percent of the CPI basket).[6] From mid-1991, price controls and confinement will apply only to petroleum products and fertilizer.

Fourth, foreign exchange has become much more available since 1986 with the introduction of more import funding schemes and facilities such as the Open General Licence (OGL) scheme introduced in February 1988. This, however, came about through massive inflows of foreign exchange as balance of payments support (from US$ 490 million in 1985 to US$

850 million in 1989 with US$ 400 million specially earmarked for balance of payments support).

5.3   THE MANUFACTURING SECTOR IN THE 1980s

In 1980 the manufacturing sector began to contract. With the exception of 1984, negative growth rates were recorded until 1987, when a modest recovery took place (Table 5.2). Consequently, the utilization of capacity which had started to fall in the late 1970s (Skarstein and Wangwe 1986) sank to an average level of 37 percent in 1986 (with levels as low as 21 percent for paper products and 25 percent for textiles (Mbelle 1989). World Bank estimates of capacity utilization in 1985 are even lower. Based on a sample of 48 firms, total capacity utilization was estimated at 30 percent with some sub-sectors as low as 10 and 20 percent, while attainable capacity was estimated at 53 percent (Table 5.3). During this period of foreign exchange scarcity, the sector's share in exports declined from 28.1 percent (in 1980) to 8.0 percent (in 1986) (Table 5.2), thus aggravating the foreign exchange shortage.

Despite contracting production, with the exception of 1981, employment actually increased until 1986 (when employment dropped 8.3 percent). The average annual growth in employment between 1979 and 1985 was 5.6 percent. The years 1987 to 1989 again saw modest increases in employment. As a rough measure for productivity, the manufacturing GDP (in 1976 prices) per worker declined from T.Sh. 28,990 per worker in 1979 to T.Sh. 15,420 per worker in 1985 (53 percent of its 1979 value). In 1989 it still stood at only T.Sh. 17,853 per worker.

Investment in the manufacturing sector declined faster than in the economy at large. The share of total (economy wide) investment declined from 24.7 percent of GDP in the period 1976-80 to 15.5 percent in 1984–5, the share of manufacturing investment in total investment declined from 36.9 percent in 1979 to only 12.2 percent in 1985. This appears to be a logical response to over-capacities and foreign exchange scarcity. However as most investment funding in the past was specially earmarked for that purpose by donors, it also reflects a change in donor attitudes towards import support for recurrent imported inputs.

Within these general trends of decline and partial recovery, some sub-sectors performed relatively better than others, leading to changes in the manufacturing 'structure'.[7] The Basic Industry Strategy had as one of its goals, to shift the almost exclusively final-goods-oriented structure of manufacturing towards basic industries such as chemical, iron and steel,

Table 5.2 Performance of the manufacturing sector in Tanzania, 1979–89

		1979	1980	1981	1982	1983	1984	1985	1986	1987	1988	1989
1.	Manufacturing GDP (1976 prices m.T.Shs)	2 821	2 683	2 382	2 304	2 103	2 159	2 075	1 991	2 075	2 187	2 299
2.	Manufacturing GDP(%, 1976 prices)	12.4	11.5	10.2	9.8	9.2	9.1	8.6	7.9	8.0	8.1	8.1
3.	Manufacturing growth rate (%, 1976 prices)	3.3	–4.9	–11.2	–3.3	–8.7	2.7	–3.9	–4.1	4.2	5.4	5.1
4.	Manufacturing employment (number)	97 309	100 993	104 226	100 671	115 394	121 671	134 557	123 334	124 210	125 001	128 769
5.	Manufacturing employment (as a % of Total)	15.6	16.0	16.8	16.8	16.8	16.6	18.0	17.8	17.7	17.8	18.1
6.	Manufacturing value added (m.T.Shs)	2 927	2 909	3 308	3 204	3 620	4 417	4 968	6 413	11 062	18 308	–
7.	Manufacturing value added (as a % of total)	8.5	7.1	5.8	–	–	–	–	–	–	–	–
8.	Manufacturing investment (as a % of total)	36.9	33.8	21.7	21.3	15.1	13.2	12.2	–	–	–	–)

Table 5.2 continued

	1979	1980	1981	1982	1983	1984	1985	1986	1987	1988	1989
9. Manufacturing Gross Fixed Capital formation (m.T.Shs)	1 865	1 955	2 561	3 022	2 509	2 614	4 289	5 095	14 115	–	–
10. Manufacturing Gross Fixed Capital formation (expressed in US$ equivalent)	227.4	238.4	308.6	324.9	226.0	170.8	245.1	155.8	219.5	–	–
11. Manufacturing exports (as a % of total)	22.3	28.1	13.7	19.1	19.8	17.3	10.2	8.0	11.6	22.0	–

Note: Manufacturing exports include petroleum products for 1988 and 1989.
Source: Economic Surveys (various issues), United Republic of Tanzania.

Table 5.3 *Structure of Tanzania's manufacturing sector* (%)

	Number of Establishments				Persons engaged				Gross output				Net Value Added				Capital Formation	
	1965	1978	1985	1988	1965	1978	1985	1988	1965	1978	1985	1988	1965	1978	1985	1988	1985	1988
31	24.4	14.4	23.5	22.8	27.8	24.5	27.8	34.2	38.2	25.9	31.8	22.7	44.7	22.4	33.3	24.9	17.8	24.5
32	30.9	22.2	24.5	23.3	43.3	38.0	40.2	37.3	43.9	29.2	19.8	24.4	26.6	31.5	19.9	17.7	23.8	29.3
33	15.8	39.7	17.3	17.0	9.1	11.1	5.3	4.4	3.2	2.6	2.4	2.4	6.0	3.3	3.0	3.1	2.0	3.0
34	3.9	3.0	7.8	8.7	1.3	3.8	4.6	4.6	1.2	4.6	5.8	4.6	1.7	6.6	7.0	4.9	3.6	6.6
35	4.1	3.8	8.9	9.4	2.9	6.8	6.7	6.1	2.7	13.4	14.6	17.7	4.4	11.1	15.2	25.5	7.6	12.9
36	1.6	5.2	2.1	2.6	1.2	3.4	3.6	3.9	0.7	2.8	5.2	6.6	0.9	3.1	1.5	6.2	8.6	10.7
37	3.3	0.3	7.7	7.9	1.1	1.2	4.8	4.5	1.6	4.2	9.8	12.2	1.5	7.7	9.1	9.2	3.3	5.6
38	14.9	9.0	6.5	6.6	12.6	9.8	6.2	4.2	8.2	16.2	9.9	9.0	13.8	12.4	10.1	8.3	33.1	7.3
39	1.1	2.4	2.1	1.9	0.7	1.5	0.9	0.9	0.3	1.2	0.7	0.4	0.4	1.9	0.6	0.3	0.2	0.3
	100	100	100	100	100	100	100	100	100	100	100	100	100	100	100	100	100	100

Sources: Computed from Economic Survey (various issues), United Republic of Tanzania.

31 Food, beverages & tobacco
32 Textiles, clothing & leather
33 Wood & wood products, incl. furniture
34 Paper & paper products, printing & publishing
35 Chemicals & chemical products, petroleum, coal, rubber & plastic products
36 Non-metallic mineral products except petroleum products & coal
37 Basic metal industries
38 Fabricated metal products, machinery & equipment
39 Other manufacturing industries

and iron based industries. This is not easy to gauge from Table 5.3, as the developments in the 1980s reflect a mixture of capacity expansion and capacity utilization.

Taking the sectors of food, beverages and tobacco, textiles, clothing and leather goods, and wood and wood products as final consumer goods; paper and printing, chemicals, plastics and fossil fuels, and non-metallic minerals as intermediate goods; and basic metals and fabricated metals and equipment as capital goods, the following picture is obtained for the years 1978, 1985, and 1988. The respective shares of consumer goods industries were 57.2, 56.2, and 45.7. This development was however composed of a fast decline of the textile sector from 31.5 percent in 1978 to 19.9 percent in 1985, and an initial increase of the food sector from 22.4 percent in 1978 to 33.3 percent in 1985, followed by a decline in its share to 24.9 in 1988. The intermediate goods sector shares were respectively 20.8, 23.7, and 36.6 with the expansion mainly due to chemicals. The shares of the capital good sector in value-added declined from 22.0 percent to 19.2 percent in 1985 and 17.5 percent in 1988.

These developments in terms of value added were not reciprocated in terms of employment. The consumer goods sector shares in employment in 1978 were 73.6 percent, in 1985 73.3 percent, and in 1988 75.9 percent. The share of this sector's employment increased while its share in value-added declined. Moreover, while its shares in value added fluctuated around 50 percent, the employment shares were up in the 70 percent, reflecting the relative labour intensity of this sector. The share in employment of the intermediate goods sector were respectively 14.0 percent in 1978, 14.9 percent in 1985, and 14.5 percent in 1988. The shares of employment of the capital goods sector were 11.0 percent in 1978, 11.0 percent in 1985, and 8.7 percent in 1988. Thus rather limited variation has occurred in these figures on employment shares. The final consumer goods sector remains the dominant employer.

On average, firm-level efficiency has been very low, although with substantial individual differences (World Bank 1987c). Partly this can be explained by the low rates of capacity utilization. Table A.6 gives the aggregated results at sub-sectoral level. Actual long-run DRCs are only within a reasonably efficient range for the food sector (1.48) and the beverage and tobacco sector (0.93).[8]

Some subsectors such as leather, plastics and pharmaceuticals, and chemicals and fertilizers, produce at negative value-added when measured at world prices.[9] When allowance is made for low capacity utilization by recalculating the DRCs for the case of attainable levels of capacity, non-metallic mineral products, and to a lesser extent textiles, approach more efficient (but still uncompetitive) levels of production with long-run DRCs respectively of 1.45 and 1.74.

There is little difference between the private and the public sector, with actual long-run DRCs respectively 3.12 and 2.35. However, while the public sector on aggregate is less inefficient than the private sector, when beverages and tobacco are left out of the sample, the public sector is more inefficient, with a long-run DRC of 3.93 as compared to the unchanged value of 3.12 of the private sector.

The effective rates of protection in 1984 include the effects of non-tariff barriers (first column, Table A.7). The data for 1987 (second column) give the rates effective protection based on tariffs only. From the differences, it may be concluded that before liberalization, non-tariff protection was much more important than tariff protection but that with the progressive elimination of non-tariff barriers the tariff structure will influence relative prices and effective protection.

The industries reported in Table A.6 were surveyed again at the end of 1989 in order to assess how they have fared during the Economic Recovery Programmes in the latter half of the 1980s (World Bank 1991). The more efficient firms in 1984 (with DRC) responded better to liberalization increasing the value of their production over the period 1985–90 (by 28 percent). Moreover they were also less foreign exchange intensive and relied less on credit as compared to the inefficient firms. Further evidence presented by the World Bank (1991), points at the fact that firms which were also medium-scale, privately-owned, and export-oriented have tended to expand output significantly.[10] An easy interpretation of these findings is that during foreign exchange shortages, those firms using less foreign exchange would perform better than those using more. Because they are more profitable, they would also require less credit. Further, the large devaluations raised the input costs of foreign exchange intensive firms faster than those of other firms, while exporting firms obtain higher prices for their output. Private sector firms that have weathered the hardship years are bound to be more resourceful in adjusting to liberalization. While these observations are interesting, they appear to be used in justifying past economic policies. The real problem however, is in understanding the dynamics of inefficient firms and locate ways to improve their performance, so as to avoid a serious loss in industrial capacity and know-how.

Factors explaining trends in manufacturing performance

The dismal performance of the manufacturing sector from 1980 until 1986, and its stagnation (or reluctant recovery) at very low rates of capacity utilization from 1987 onwards can be explained as an interplay of factors arising from the environment, the nature of industrialization, and firm specific conditions, much in line with the general approach to industrial performance developed in Chapter 2. Explanations have tended to emphasize the first two factors more than the last, but all three are important.

The *environment* of the manufacturing sector can be further differentiated into physical, economic, and social environments, all of which are influenced by the policy environment. Deterioration of physical infrastructure (roads, transport, communication, electricity and water supply) and the social environment (as affected by the development of a second economy that interferes in various ways with the formal economy) have been mentioned above and will be discussed again for the textile sector later in this chapter. The economic environment before 1986 was particularly affected by the type of protection offered to industries and by the foreign exchange constraint and its management by government. Policies with regard to these two issues will be discussed below. After 1986, structural adjustment polices further influenced industrial performance by introducing different systems of foreign exchange management (as discussed later in this chapter) and policies with regard to exchange rates, credit, and import liberalization including tariff reforms.

However the combined effects on the industrial sector are ambiguous. On the supply side, import liberalization and increased availability of foreign exchange has had positive effects, but exchange rate policy (devaluation) and a restrictive credit policy, have caused further problems. It can be argued that for some firms the combined policy package has transformed the foreign exchange constraint into a credit constraint. On the demand side, the effects of ERP are equally ambiguous. Demand in general has increased as GDP has grown, but import liberalization has resulted in large quantities of competitive imports, thus restraining effective demand for locally produced goods. This will be demonstrated more convincingly for the case of the textile sector in the next chapters.

The nature of industrialization has resulted in a fragile manufacturing sector. The present industrial structure is basically the result of industrialization efforts in the late 1960s and the 1970s. During the 1980s this structure did not change much. The investment drive was halted by crisis conditions, while public sector firms that were unable to cope with the changing conditions were saved from bankruptcy by government support. The nature of industrialization has been described by various authors (Coulson 1982b; Green 1982; Bienefeld 1982; Perkins 1983; Skarstein and Wangwe 1986; World Bank 1987c). All agree that Tanzania followed an import substitution strategy. In the particular context of Tanzania's policy of 'self reliance' the concept of import substitution obtained an ideological dimension. Within this broad strategy and at various points in time, different substrategies have been emphasized such as small-scale industrialization, balanced spatial distribution of industrialization, appropriate technological choice, and industrial integration.

However, in the light of the management and planning skills, and foreign exchange availability, a contradiction developed between ideology and practice. The concept of self reliance in industrialization acquired a paradoxical connotation; in the first place, since industrial planning was carried out with the help of foreign advisors, most of the new investments were foreign financed and the management and technical skills were foreign as well. In the second place, the industrial structure that evolved was very dependent on imported inputs, only partially integrated (through 'vertical slices' such as the cotton-clothing chain), regionally dispersed, predominantly medium to large scale, capital intensive, and with the private/public dichotomy primarily expressed in ethnic terms, i.e. Asian/African. In the third place, tariff walls and other protective devices sheltered the sector from world competition so that the self-reliance of the industrial sector was never tested. Of these, the issues of technology choice (Perkins 1983; James 1989; Skarstein and Wangwe 1986) and foreign exchange dependency (Wangwe 1984; Mbelle 1988; Mbelle and Sterner 1991) have obtained a great deal of attention. Green (1982) provides a wider evaluation of Tanzanian industrial development including, for example, factors underlying the lack of technical inefficiency, such as the quality of management and related X-inefficiency.

These contradictions have been the explicit focus of policy debate, particularly in the formulation of the BIS, but have never been resolved, partly due to the emerging crisis of the 1980s and partly to implementation problems originating in the public sector decision-making process and the objective constraints identified above. In this sense, Tanzania's industrialization process can be labelled 'aborted' when one takes the viewpoint of the theoretical intentions of the BIS at the time of their development including the uncertainties with regard to future developments of the national economy and international events, or as 'overextended' when a simplistic *ex post* view is adopted.

Whatever value judgement one prefers with regard to past industrial policy, little disagreement exist about the resulting structure of industry in Tanzania and the way in which this structure interacted with the crisis conditions of the 1980s. Moreover, no one doubts that the leading role that industrialization played in the 1970s should be removed from the policy agenda to allow for a period of re-adjustment. However when looking for actual solutions, 'structural adjustment' acquires a different meaning depending on whether the 'overextended' or 'aborted' view is adopted. The former would take a short term perspective, adjusting the structure to prevailing realities in the 1980s, and taking the historical opportunity to: bring the industrial sector back into an 'appropriate' size (closure of unprofitable firms), change the ownership structure (privatization) and adjust the economic environment (liberalization). The latter view would maintain a more long term perspective and try to: salvage what remains of the industrial structure (rehabilitation) and promote more marginal changes such as commercialization rather than privatization, allow gradual exposure to world market conditions, and gradually reorient towards export production. Paradoxically, in theory and in official publications such as World Bank (1991), the World Bank has espoused the former view while in practice they are implementing elements of the latter (see Chapter 3) much in line with what the Tanzanian government itself views as most desirable (URT 1990d).

Firm-specific factors that have influenced industrial performance are located along dimensions of ownership, management characteristics, scale, age, market orientation, and skill requirements. These factors will be discussed in more detail with reference to the textile sector in the next chapter. With regard to ownership, there is not only the distinction between public and private but also, with reference to the private sector, foreign versus local and whether a firm is part of an economic group or operating on its own. Management, especially in the public sector, can be contracted to foreign managers. Alternatively, foreign managers can be employed for specific functions within a locally owned and managed firm. Scale, in combination with lack of management skills, can affect efficiency negatively. Age of machinery, together with lack of maintenance and repair (due for example to foreign exchange shortages) affect quality and performance in general. Market orientation in combination with an economic environment that is shifting towards an open economy influences adjustment costs as well as adjustment potential. When available skills are boasted by training facilities and incentive schemes, quality, machine maintenance, and productivity can be improved.

The three sets of factors discussed above are, of course, interrelated, with the main lines of causality running from the more general to firm-specific factors. Macro-policies that have most seriously affected the pattern of allocation of resources to the industrial sector over time are those dealing with foreign exchange allocation and protection through tariffs and otherwise. These policies will be detailed below.

Foreign exchange management and allocation

Industrial development through the strategy of import substitution depends on foreign exchange for the purchase of capital goods and imported inputs. Such industrial development becomes dependent on the amount of foreign exchange generated by the exporting sectors of the economy which, in the case of Tanzania, is predominantly the agricultural sector. Foreign exchange saved by the process of import substitution itself is limited to the net foreign exchange impact of such import substituting industries which is often only a small fraction of output.

Foreign exchange for the purpose of investment often comes in the form of long term loans specifically for that purpose and thus without direct consequences for the allocation of foreign exchange earned from exports. Apart from the consequences of debt servicing, this can potentially lead to (and indeed, this has been a common experience) industries established with the help of foreign loans requiring more foreign exchange for their recurrent inputs at economic levels of capacity utilization than is available from exports. Such can be the misallocation of foreign exchange under a managed system where planning capacity or planning control is insufficient.

Since investment projects by their nature require time to become productive, the foreign exchange constraint can become more severe over time. This can lead to the paradoxical situation in which existing industries have overcapacities, while new industries are being established.

Which firms face foreign exchange shortages depends on the particulars of the foreign exchange allocation system. Under an equitable distribution system, a foreign exchange shortage should develop simultaneously for all foreign exchange users. When foreign exchange is allocated according to most efficient use of foreign exchange measured in world prices and taking into account both inputs and outputs of the firm, shortages should develop first for inefficient users. Such a system of demand (of foreign exchange) regulation also maximizes the supply of foreign exchange.

In practice no clear system of priorities exists and arbitrary decisions can at times mean that efficient firms may face more serious shortages than inefficient firms. Thus, it results in a misallocation of scarce resources.

Foreign exchange shortages are experienced both by governments and by individual economic actors such as firms. Therefore management of the constraint is practised not only at national but also at firm-levels.

Firm-level responses to foreign exchange shortages can be directed at increasing the supply of foreign exchange and at better utilization of the available foreign exchange. Without such responses at firm-level, downward spirals develop moving from lower production to lower profits (or even losses), to reduced working capital, less spending for maintenance, lower depreciation allowances, lower input purchases and neglect of capital stock, and finally to reduced output and lower attainable capacity. Costs (especially wage and salary costs) cannot easily be adjusted to levels of output. Short term loans cannot be repaid (and are changed into long term loans in the case of parastatals), sales tax payment delays occur, and illegal transactions become attractive.

Some firms manage to readjust their production to less foreign exchange intensive products such as, in the case of textiles, grey fabrics instead of finished cloth. Others make use of special contacts with high level civil servants to lobby for foreign exchange allocation to their firms (this was confirmed in various interviews). Some firms enter into barter arrangements and are able to exploit the new export incentive schemes not only to export but also to obtain foreign exchange for domestic production, which is still more profitable.

For many firms, the liquidity situation becomes problematic and positive changes in the foreign exchange situation cannot be exploited because of lack of working capital to purchase foreign exchange and even lack of productive capacity. Rehabilitation expenditure is necessary first, but this means investment finance and new loans in a situation where the liquidity of the firm is already a problem. The irony now becomes that more state support is necessary at the beginning of the period of liberalization and privatization. The unattractive alternative is to close down potentially viable enterprises.

At national level, the foreign exchange allocation system, established in 1971 to deal with the impact of the first oil crisis, functioned more or less satisfactory until 1982, when it collapsed into crisis decision-making. Shortages had become so acute that foreign exchange had to be distributed on an emergency basis without even short term planning.

The allocation of the increased supply of foreign exchange resulting from the adoption of the Economic Recovery Programme (URT 1986) according to the agreed criteria discussed above has been complicated by the existence of various schemes to allocate foreign exchange. From the mid 1980s, the sources of foreign exchange in Tanzania have increased considerably:[11] in 1990 there were six main sources. Apart from the traditional sources of Bank of Tanzania ('free resources') and loans and grants, own source foreign exchange was allowed in 1984, export retention schemes were expanded during the 1980s, Preferential Trade Area (PTA) arrangements began in 1987 and the 'new' Open General Licence (OGL) was introduced in 1988.

Accountability for the funds disbursed under the CIS and OGL was very poor. This has implied an effective subsidy when enterprises participating in the schemes did not fully pay their domestic cash-cover of the foreign exchange. Moreover, before unification, application of the official exchange rate under these schemes also implied an extra subsidy when compared to the auction rate or the parallel market rate. These (inappropriate) mechanisms have allowed many enterprises to survive the adverse consequences of liberalization and the unfair competition of illegal imports.

Foreign exchange auctioning was introduced in 1993, followed later in that year by the unification of the offical exchange rate with the auction rate. The OGL system was thereby abandoned and most commodity import support schemes are to be phased out. In terms of facilities and conditions of usage, the economy has moved from the restrictive foreign exchange regimes of the 1970s and early 1980s, towards a market orientation supported by large inflows of balance of payments support from bilateral and multilateral donors (almost one third of the total import bill). The new system has taken away the advantages that enterprises were enjoying. Because of the illegal imports and poor infrastructure they now face effective negative protection on the domestic market and many enterprises are in serious problems. The consequences under the new system of the large inflows of foreign aid on the exchange rate and the resulting possibility of an anti-export bias have not yet sufficiently been analysed. The export duty drawback scheme (established in 1988), which allows exporters to reclaim their import taxes on imported inputs used in their export production, does not function properly because of bureacratic constraints and, even if efficiently implemented, would not cancel potential Dutch disease effects of large inflows of foreign aid.

5.4 THE TANZANIAN STATE, INDUSTRIAL DEVELOPMENT AND THE PARASTATAL SECTOR

The previous sections have shown the increasing role of the Tanzanian state in running the economy. The new neoliberal critique on the overextended role of the state in the economy in Tanzania (and other developing countries) has close parallels (and obviously also stark contrasts, particularly in terms of reforms) with the neomarxist critique that developed in the 1970s.[12] Both base their critique on an analysis of conflicting interests of various groups in the society. The economic system as it evolved in the late 1960s and the 1970s, is largely the outcome of a political process in which both the progressive developmentalists and the opportunists could see their interests provided for, at least as far as the formal system was concerned. The actual working of the economic system became more and more influenced by the political economy of opportunistic elements with the role of the progressive leaders increasingly limited to furnishing the ideological fabric.

The development of the state after independence has been characterized by a continuous penetration of the state into different spheres of society and spatially into the regions, districts and villages (deemed necessary for legitimation and control), and by attempts at economic development (partly out of genuine concern for economic welfare and legitimation). The year of the new constitution and CCM (1977) perhaps signifies the culmination of the degree of autonomy the state elite achieved with respect to the rest of the society. But although the autonomy of the state became stronger when viewed from the outside, internally it was transformed into dependency on individuals and groups (including the parastatal lobby). This internal dependency developed into the basis for softness of the state. On the other hand, the stakes many of these individuals and groups have in the state system became its main source of hardness leading to its characterization of an authoritarian state (Shivji 1982). Civil servants at various levels and sectors in the state apparatus had different private interests in the system, different opportunities, and indeed different motivations ranging from opportunism to job commitment, or some curious mixture of both.[13] Instruments and institutions were expanded in attempts to increase control. But with the incorporation of larger sections of society, the state became overextended beyond its control capacity and was more and more penetrated by society. Because of the limited control capacity of its ideology and institutions,[14] and in the absence of delivery of economic progress, the state itself became target for exploitation. Hyden (1982) explains this as an 'economy of affection' with strong family and ethnic ties in a pre-capitalist society. In contrast, van Donge (1994) shows that in the private sector, these family and ethnic ties can in fact lead to an economy of distrust when entrepreneurs wish to stay clear of their obligations arising from the 'economy of affection'. Civil servants also sometimes feel 'strangled' by their affective obligations.[15]

Within the optimistic atmosphere of the early 1970s, the internal contradictions were less visible. The dual process of increasing control and development carried on. Villagization started in the first half of the 1970s and with regard to the industrial sector this process culminated in the adoption of the BIS around the same time as the culmination of political control in 1977. Subsequent developments, such as declining terms of trade and the Uganda war, triggered what was at first interpreted only as a full scale economic crisis. A last attempt was made to tighten the political grip on the situation in 1982. However, the economic problems were too severe and the crisis manifested itself also in the political realm.

From the second half of the 1970s onwards, the autonomy of the state has been increasingly challenged by the development of the second economy with its uncaptured activities, groups, individuals and psychologies, both outside and within the state apparatus. During the 1980s, the autonomy of the state was further reduced by increasing external pressure from the IMF, World Bank and donor countries.

Thus, the internal contradictions of this political and economic outcome, coupled with the objective socio-economic conditions in the agricultural and the manufacturing sector, and with international economic developments, finally led to the loss of the (temporary) relative autonomy of the state elite with regard to international powers, i.e. the IMF, World Bank and donor countries, who then started to redefine the basic economic and political structure of the country (Doornbos 1991; Shaw 1991).[16]

In Chapter 2 it was argued that the state plays an important role in socializing individuals to conform subjecting to the particular relations of production in the society. Industrial development was characterized by extensive state participation in production. The increasing gap between ideology and practice, with individual and family based opportunism prevailing over the presumed nationwide ujamaa ideology, and the conflicting requirements of controlling and coopting the workers, made this process of socialization ineffective. Exit options from the ujamaa ideal showed up as low productivity and absenteeism, reinforced by very low wages (necessitating other sources of income), and facilitated by political protection against dismissal, the Mwongozo Declaration, limited possibilities for effort-related incentives (by law), and often inadequate management.

The state and public enterprises

This view of the Tanzanian state also explains the development as well as the persistent support for public sector enterprises: the parastatals. Parastatals were supported not only for developmental and ideological reasons but also for opportunistic and nationalistic reasons. The industrial sector began with a very small base. The underdeveloped African managerial and entrepreneurial class could be expanded through state capitalism as alternative to the Indian entrepreneurial and commercial class. Support from workers could be obtained by offering formal wage employment. Managerial positions were created for a growing state elite. Control was obtained over many sectors of the economy. It is therefore understandable that a strong lobby existed within the state for continued support of this sector, even at the costs of subsidizing many of its ventures, and in the face of obvious inefficiencies. Despite continuous pressure for privatization and outright closure of public sector firms by the donor community led by the World Bank, and despite the adoption of rather rigorous donor 'advice' in most other areas of the economy, very little has happened in this respect. Apparently, the parastatals are at the core of the state elite's position.

The parastatal sector

In 1966, there were 43 parastatals in existence, with two thirds of their assets in electricity and mining and only ten percent in manufacturing. The Arusha Declaration signalled a period of rapid increases in both the number and assets of parastatals. Their number increased to 73 in 1967, 380 in 1979, and even expanded during the crisis period (over 425 in 1988).

Assets expanded correspondingly, doubling at first (in 1967 and 1968) mainly through nationalization. Asset expansion continued between 1969 and 1971 to reach about 5.5 times the 1966 value, through the establishment of new firms and capacity increases of existing ones. After 1971, this expansion slowed and began to concentrate on holding companies, regulatory bodies, non-commercial organizations, regional transport and trading companies, and district development corporations. However, major investment in the textile sector took place under the public sector holding company for textile firms, TEXCO, during the 1970s and 1980s.

Parastatal value-added as percentage of GDP rose from about 2 percent in 1964 to 7 percent in 1967, 9 percent in 1972 and to about 13 percent in 1988. This last figure is not atypical for developing countries. However, the number of parastatals in Tanzania is uniquely high and in terms of fixed capital formation Tanzania also scores very highly. In the early 1970s, this stood at 50 percent of total investment and declined to a still substantial 35 percent in the beginning of the 1980s as compared to an average of 27 percent for developing countries.

The total contribution of the parastatal sector to value-added is 12.8 percent. The sector is very diverse in scale (ranging from one company employing more than 6,000 workers, to large to medium scale firms such as TEXCO's subsidiaries and smaller companies with fewer than 30 workers), and in functions, such as manufacturing firms, marketing boards, hotels, consultancy firms, trade associations, and non-commercial parastatals such as the University of Dar es Salaam.[17] Parastatal employment dominates formal employment in transport (87 percent), mining (55 percent), commerce (53 percent), manufacturing (47 percent), and construction (36 percent). In terms of value-added, parastatals are most dominant in the manufacturing sector (47 percent).

Almost all ministries have parastatals under their control, including the Offices of the President and the Prime Minister. About one third of all parastatals are under the Ministry of Industry and Trade, which employs 10 holding corporations (including the National Development Corporation, NDC, with 22 firms and TEXCO with 12 firms) to supervise 89 firms. The remaining 54 firms fall directly under the control of the Ministry.

The supervision and control of parastatals is very complex. There are about 20 different supervisory and control agencies that at various levels and in different ways formally interfere with the functioning of parastatal enterprises. Six were created to deal exclusively with the parastatal sector as a whole. Four of these six deal only with the operations of existing parastatals. The most important of the four is the Standing Committee on Parastatal Organizations (SCOPO), which has a staff of about 45 persons. It reports to the Office of the President and presents detailed advice on organizational, personnel and training issues, including the definition of salary scales and incentive schemes. It is often criticized for its tendency to over-regulate and to demand too much uniformity between parastatals. Any deviation from its guidelines has to be approved by SCOPO.

The second of the four committees is the Tanzanian Auditing Corporation (TAC) with as parent ministry the Ministry of Finance and Planning, and staffed by 230 professional auditors. By law parastatals have to submit their accounts to TAC for auditing within three months of the end of their financial year. TAC also produces an annual report evaluating the quality of accounts, often with recommendations on management practices.

Parastatals must submit their audited accounts to the Parastatal Organization Committee (POC) of Parliament (the third committee dealing with operations) within eight months of closing their books. POC reviews TAC findings and can call managers for questioning.

The fourth institution dealing with the operations of the parastatals is the set of Parastatal Monitoring and Supervision Units located in the parent ministry of each parastatal. However, apart from the unit in the Ministry of Agriculture, these have been largely ineffective because of the low priority given to them.

Two other bodies were designed to deal with public sector investment and financing, and sectoral planning. The first one, under the Treasury wing of the Ministry of Finance and Planning is the Office of the

Commissioner for Public Investments, which has wide ranging powers to advise government on new investment, financing, and the operation of parastatals. It is staffed by 26 professionals. However, its performance has been below standard; many investments have been passed without proper appraisal since it has not come forward with recommendations on how to improve poor performance of parastatals. The second body is the Office of the Commissioner of Sectoral Planning under the planning wing of the Ministry of Finance and Planning which is to advise on sectoral development planning.

Besides these specific committees there are bodies within individual parastatals, and (national) bodies which deal with certain aspects of the parastatals. The former comprise the Workers' Council, Management Committees or Board of Directors, and the General Manager. Holding companies, where they exist, form a layer between groups of individual enterprises and the national institutions. The Workers' Council is composed of representatives of workers and management, and approves corporate plans and budgets. The Boards of Directors of holding companies and independent parastatals are responsible for corporate policy and plans, budgets, annual accounts, financial statements, capital investments and financing – all appointments except the General Manager, who is appointed by the President. Board members are mostly civil servants, sometimes supplemented by outsiders. The Management Committee of enterprises under holding companies has the same responsibilities as the Board of Directors but its composition also includes workers and representatives from management. The Chairman of the Management Committee is appointed by the Board of the holding corporation. General managers are the principal executives of the parastatal, responsible for the day to day running of the operation.

Bodies with more general functions are, first of all, the various banks: the National Bank of Commerce (NBC) allocates foreign exchange and short term credit; the Bank of Tanzania (BoT) provides foreign exchange licences and approves requests for expatriate staff; the Tanzanian Investment Bank (TIB) provides medium and long term credit and is responsible for monitoring of industrial projects; and the Cooperative Rural Development Bank (CRDB) provides credit to the agricultural sector and is responsible for monitoring projects.

Second, the Ministry of Labour and Manpower has various labour monitoring functions, including the settlement of labour conflicts through its Permanent Labour Tribunal. Third, the Parliament is responsible for the legislation that creates and dissolves parastatals. Fourth, the President appoints chairpersons of Boards of Directors and the general managers of holdings and independent parastatals. Fifth, the CCM has its own Standing Committee on Parastatals for policy formulation and advice to the parent ministry. Sixth, there is the Registrar of Companies, which reviews and approves the accounts and financial statements of parastatals established under the Companies Ordinance (which includes most subsidiaries of holding companies).

There are also three advisory bodies: the National Productivity Council, the Tanzania Bureau of Standards and the Tanzania Legal Corporation. And finally, there is the Price Commission, which in the recent past controlled the prices of many items but presently covers only a few strategic prices.

Table 5.4 summarizes important control functions and the related control institutions. A very large number of institutions are involved in reviewing and approving budgets and corporate plans and in performance monitoring. Other important decision-making areas such as investments, and especially appointments are controlled by a more limited number of agencies.

On paper this appears to be excessive. However, as the World Bank (1988) notes, most of these institutions (with the exception of TAC) did not perform their functions well, either by not doing what they are supposed to do or by doing it in an excessive bureaucratic and interfering manner (*in casu* SCOPO). This was the case in particular with relation to performance monitoring, investment analysis, and accountability processes. Second, control over day to day functioning acquired an extra dimension by extra-statutory controls and the individual interference of highly placed government officials in matters of appointments, procurement of local and imported goods and inputs, and allocation of commodities and services (Mihyo 1987).

This excessive control over the parastatal sector by government has been explained by Mihyo (1994) as a natural outcome of the Morrisonian model of public enterprises.[18] He argues that this has been further aggravated by the lack of market control over the parastatal sector, and that its lack of performance has created further dependencies on and provided additional leverage to government institutions and individuals. Effectively, accountability to Parliament has been reduced because parastatals resort to the supremacy of the Party and presidential decrees, and can play upon insecurities faced by members of Parliament who disagree with government. This general picture is consistent with the above analysis of the nature of the state.

Thus the emphasis of the application of control has shifted from control for efficiency to control for resources. In this context, it is only to be

Table 5.4   Parastatal oversight functions and structures

Key overview functions	Institutional location in Tanzania
Set policy for parastatal sector	National Assembly; CCM; Office of the President
Set policy for subsectors	Parent ministries; Holding companies
Review and approve budgets and corporate plans	Workers' Councils; Boards or Management Committees; Holding Companies (where applicable); Parent ministries; Registrar of Companies (where applicable); Ministry of Finance and Planning
Review and approve: subventions	Holding company, Parent ministries, Ministry of Finance and Planning, Board of Directors
investments	Holding Company, Parent ministry, Board of Directors, Ministry of Finance and Planning, Investment banks
dividends	Holding Company, Parent ministry, Board of Directors, Ministry of Finance and Planning
Appoint General Manager of major company	Parent ministry provides short list, President makes choice
Appoint General Manager of subsidiary	Appointed by Board of Directors of holding company
Appoint Board of Director	Directors appointed by parent ministries, some few parastatals by laws stipulate appointment of users or creditors; Chairman appointed by President
Appoint Management Committee	Board of Directors of holding company appoints directors and chairman; parent ministry approves
Performance monitoring	Board of Directors or Management Committees, holding companies, parent ministries, Ministry of Finance and Planning, TAC, POC, CCM, credit-supplying and investment-analyzing banks, other central ministries, Presidents' Office, Presidential commissions
Analyse sectoral trends and macroeconomic impact	Ministry of Finance and Planning

Source: World Bank (1988).

expected that accountability faded into the background. As early as 1982, in the Structural Adjustment Programme, the Tanzanian government explained the lack of performance of the parastatal sector along these lines:

In general, there is inadequate accountability at all levels of decisiontaking. The elaborate internal and external control system over parastatal activities, which exist on paper, are in reality very weak. Motivation of both managers and workers has been found to be inadequate as evidenced by problems of discipline in a number of firms and this is compounded by the absence of effective incentives either moral or material (URT 1982b:42).

The debate on the parastatal sector in the 1980s

The debate on the future of the parastatal sector in Tanzania has been conducted, in the first place, between the World Bank and the Tanzanian government. However, not only have views and positions shifted over time; it is also possible to identify within the World Bank and especially the Tanzanian government different views, which in the latter case can be attributed to different interest groups such as the parastatal managers themselves, holding companies, the parent ministries, Party, etc. The debate has concentrated on the size and form of, and the centre of control over the parastatal sector, with the World Bank arguing (against the Tanzanian government) for smaller size and more market control.

The first economic policy document by the Tanzanian government dealing with the crisis, URT (1982a), makes only cursory mention of the crisis in the parastatal sector, putting the largest part of the blame on external developments (even ignoring the disruptive effects of the Uganda war). The decline in output and productivity in various productive sectors and services is mentioned, as is the need to control recurrent expenditure for ministries, regions and parastatals.

The document outlining the SAP (URT 1982b), drafted as an economic policy document intended to attract IMF support and written partly in collaboration with IMF sponsored foreign advisors, is much more open and critical (see section 6.5.3). It proposed restoring the profitability of the parastatals through a new material incentive system and second, asked for a general rationalization of decisiontaking and more effective control and accountability systems. However, in practice this meant introducing more control by involving more institutions in the process. For example, the Commissioner for Public Investment and the Commissioner for Economic Planning (at that time still under the planning ministry) were given a role in investment decisions and yearly budgeting cycles so that 'parastatals would for the first time be brought into the annual budget procedure and special skeleton accounts will be published for scrutiny by the Government, Parliament and the Party' (URT 1982b:44). No mention is made of possible closures and divestures.

The 'Country Economic Memorandum on Tanzania' (World Bank 1984), cautiously, and for the first time, introduces the idea of rationalizing the parastatal sector with more than institutional reforms. Donor funded projects at various stages of implementation are to be critically assessed, involving 'the cancellation or redesigning of some projects still at an early stage of implementation; postponing the completion or start-up of new plant and closing down some existing operations' (World Bank 1984:85-86).[19] Also new is the application of the 'net foreign exchange situation' as a criterion for closure. The importance of the private sector is mentioned as is the fact that they should benefit from the general measures proposed under recovery programmes.

In 1986, this view was phrased more strongly in the 'Report to the Consultative Group for Tanzania on the Government's Economic Recovery Programme' (World Bank 1986).[20] According to the World Bank, 'work carried out by the Bank and the Government on the domestic costs of different parts of the industrial sector suggests that the sector must be extensively restructured as recovery proceeds' (World Bank 1986:20). Reference here is made to the industrial sector survey presented in World Bank (1987c). The report continues to say that 'it also means accepting the scaling down and closure of wasteful plants (including those that are state owned) and of borderline ones that are unable to improve their productivity' (ibid:20).

These two documents represent only the World Bank view. The official document titled 'Economic Recovery Programme' (URT 1986) outlines the negotiated outcome between the Tanzanian government and the World Bank. In the introduction to the ERP, mention is made of the fact that upon the recommendation of a commission appointed in 1982 'several parastatals have been disbanded' (URT 1986:11).[21] None of the six mentioned is in manufacturing and, in the actual description of the ERP, the section on parastatal reform refers only to the agricultural marketing system. But, while the World Bank's strong views on privatization and disinvestment were successfully held at bay by the Tanzanian government, the economic policies of devaluation, liberalization, and restrained credit expansion adopted since 1986 have generally added more pressure on parastatal performance, shifting governmental parastatal support from indirect subsidies (through protection and price control) to direct subsidies to keep the public enterprises from bankruptcy. Thus, structural adjustment policies in the latter half of the 1980s have made the drain on resources by the parastatal sector more visible even in cases where actual performance remained the same, adding fuel to World Bank's arguments.

The strongest attack on the parastatal manufacturing sector came from the World Bank in 1987 with its report 'Tanzania: An Agenda for Industrial Recovery' (World Bank 1987c).[22] This report was based on research that had started in 1985 and its results were already referred to in the report to the Consultative Group (World Bank 1986). It painfully exposed the disastrous situation in a many of Tanzania's manufacturing industries, using DRC ratios as the main analytical tool. It introduced a very explicit comparison of the public with the private sector, showing the superiority of the latter. Four broad areas identified as major reasons for the disappointing public enterprise performance were: (i) the political nature of decision-making structures; (ii) political patronage and nepotism; (iii) shortage of skilled labour; and (iv) lack of control. The statement that all these problems 'are closely linked to society and the political structure of Tanzania' (World Bank 1987c (II):58), may be interpreted as a forerunner to the 'democracy shock' that followed at the end of the 1980s.

The World Bank recommended that restructuring should take place in: (1) expanding firms (currently economically efficient enterprises), (2) currently economically inefficient enterprises, and (3) emerging firms (under new policies of general liberalization). Category 2 consists of: (a) firms that require streamlining (displaying a mixture of efficient and inefficient activities; these firms should abandon their inefficient activities unless they can be made efficient), (b) firms that require restructuring (with some activities that are potentially viable being revamped while all others are closed), and (c) contracting firms (in which all activities are unviable and which should be closed down). Further decentralization is recommended to individual enterprises but with the role of holding companies reduced to facilitating operations, and the role of parent ministries reduced to formulating sectoral policies and participating in the boards of directors of holding companies. The role of the Treasury should be in monitoring the financial performance of industries and their impact on the national budget.

Outright privatization of public enterprises was not (yet) recommended although 'any practical reform process should be guided by the ultimate objective to increase the role of the private sector in the future' (World Bank 1987c (II):56) and 'the extent to which Tanzania's manufacturing sector can be revitalized on a sustained basis will largely depend on the Government's intention to draw on the resourcefulness and ingenuity of private sector entrepreneurs' (ibid.:59). At the same time, the World Bank argues that the parastatal sector is expected to continue playing an important role in Tanzania's industry. Thus, the World Bank favoured restructuring and revitalizing the parastatal sector in order to achieve financial, economic and management efficiency.

By 1988, the World Bank had taken a first step towards recommending privatization (World Bank 1988). The idea that the parastatal sector would continue to play an important role was replaced by the recommendation that parastatal firms be limited to public utilities, natural monopolies, and financial institutions, and that commercial parastatals either be divested or 'be allowed to fend for themselves without preferential treatment but with greater freedom to respond to competition and form joint ventures or enter into management contracts' (World Bank 1988:44). The World Bank reported that increased institutional control had had relatively little impact 'in part, because they have not gone far enough and in part because they have failed to attack more fundamental problems such as lack of competition and inadequate managerial accountability and autonomy' (ibid.:iii). It specified four causes for the lack of performance as:

–   The institutional environment of parastatals has not been altered sufficiently to enhance managerial accountability and autonomy.
–   Both managerial and financial resources are too thinly spread over too many parastatals. The size of the parastatal sector should be reduced.
–   Measures are required that: impose greater financial discipline, make it clear that commercial parastatals are not required to perform social services, and eliminate all artificial barriers to entry into commercial activities.
–   The present regulatory system does not reward managers for maximum commercial performance but rather for compliance with regulations and procedures. To force a change in this system, authority must be shifted upwards and downwards: downwards to give the manager greater authority and simultaneously greater responsibility to perform, and upwards to be able to keep managers effectively accountable.

These attacks on the parastatal sector followed the implementation of the ERP measures, which visibly put most parastatals into problems. However, it cannot be demonstrated conclusively that the timing constituted a deliberate strategy, an instance of sequential decisionmaking or occurred by sheer coincidence.

In response to the 1988 World Bank report on parastatals, the Tanzania Association of Parastatal Organizations (TAPO) which can be interpreted as the lobby group of the parastatal elite, submitted a report to the President (TAPO 1989).[23] Without explicitly mentioning the World Bank, TAPO comments that 'in our view, we should rather take the initiative to bring about such a parastatal reform on our own instead of giving too much initiative to external agencies' (ibid.:48). The report calls for a redefinition of the 'commanding heights' of the economy as employed in the implementation of the 'Arusha Declaration' to include only those parastatals that are 'strategic', or 'nationally significant', or 'natural state monopolies'. These parastatals should continue to receive government support, which amounts to significantly more government support than recommended by the 1988 World Bank report. TAPO argues that while commercially viable parastatals outside this definition should face private sector conditions, those that are non-viable should be allowed to 'go into partnership with other viable parastatals, cooperative organizations, domestic private investors or foreign investors' (ibid.:48). This implies a considerably more conservative approach to parastatal reforms than the 1988 World Bank position. Using the tide of times, TAPO further argues for increased autonomy from the government and the Party through the formation of a Public Enterprise Board (PEB) to absorb the activities of SCOPO, the Commissioner for Public Investment and POC. The increased autonomy should be based on an explicit code of conduct 'governing the relationship between PEB, the Party, the State House, PMO [Prime Minister's Office] and the parent ministries' (ibid.:49).

In the spirit of taking the initiative as suggested by TAPO, the government installed a task force to formulate proposals on the parastatal leather sector (under the holding corporation Tanzania Leather Associated Industries, TLAI) prior to the outcome of a World Bank study on the same sector. This task force was mainly composed of the 'owners' within government along with a representative from the parent ministry, Ministry of Industries and Trade (MIT), the Ministry of Finance, National Bank of Commerce (NBC), Tanzania Investment Bank (TIB), and Tanzania Industrial Studies and Consulting Organization (TISCO) – the parastatal leather sector includes the earlier cited Morogoro Shoe Factory which has been 'operating' at below one percent of its capacity. The report (URT 1989) recommended continuing and strengthening the holding corporation, and continuing all its subsidiaries through financing its short term and long term capital requirements, strengthening management, and other supportive measures. While restructuring is suggested for a few very marginal activities, privatization or private sector participation is out of the picture altogether. The external control structure is not commented upon at all.

On the other hand, the World Bank study on the textile sector (URT 1990d), which was officially under the auspices of MIT, was carried out by a British group of sectoral experts. It offered recommendations ranging from the micro-level (individual and machine level) to the general environment, including changes in the control structure of the parastatal sector and economic policies and suggestions for communicating the rehabilitation programme to the general public. The report takes a much harder position than any of the earlier World Bank documents. In particular, of the thirteen establishments discussed, it recommends closure of three, divestment of seven, and retaining only four in the public sector – three because of their monopoly position and one because it has traditionally been the flagship of the public sector and has been the most efficient textile mill. Correspondingly, the role and size of TEXCO will have to be reduced compatible with the diminishing number of its subsidiaries. For implementation of these and other recommendations the report calls for the creation of an Action Committee (AC) directly under the President with a very strong and independent chairperson who would also be appointed as chairperson of TEXCO.

The World Bank and Tanzanian government negotiated document on the country's second economic adjustment programme (URT 1990c), points out that 'the role of parastatals in the Tanzanian economy is still crucial, particularly at this stage of development' (ibid.:15). Acknowledging the problems with performance, the report notes that 'some steps have been taken to restructure and abolish some of them' (ibid.:15) (This is basically the same position taken in ERP I, discussed above). It continues that 'the restructuring of the [industrial] sector will include consolidation and streamlining of activities, rehabilitation of plant and machinery and, when appropriate, the phasing out of inefficient activities (ibid.:24). Significant is the use of the term 'activities' rather than 'firms' when talking about streamlining, restructuring and phasing out. Privatization is only tentatively hinted at by the statement that 'joint ventures and the role of the private sector will also be encouraged' (ibid.). However, mention is made of sectoral studies being undertaken in for example the leather, textile (see above) and agro-processing sector, as well as of crucial decisions to be taken on the basis of concrete proposals for individual enterprises. Thus, 'it is expected that the studies and actual restructuring will be finalized during ESAP' (ibid.:15). Given the apparent disagreement between the World Bank and the Tanzanian Government, it is unlikely that restructuring will proceed as smoothly as this suggests.

In the following year the World Bank notes that 'inefficient enterprises have managed to survive in the much more competitive environment created by ERP; no inefficient enterprise surveyed in the original survey [i.e. World Bank 1987] has closed down' (World Bank 1991:93). In explanation, it points to the increasingly important role that financial institutions, including the Treasury, have played in supporting ailing industries. Thus, it concludes that 'industrial parastatals, on the whole, have therefore not been forced to undertake a major restructuring, in spite of the pervasive inefficient nature of a large segment of the sector' (ibid.:96). It recommends that 'to reduce budgetary costs and improve efficiency in the industrial sector and throughout the economy the government needs to adopt a comprehensive programme of parastatal reform and actively pursue private participation and outright sale of government-owned enterprises' (ibid.:ii). This is the strongest version of the official World Bank view on parastatal restructuring: it acknowledges that very little has been achieved towards the World Bank's desired outcome and that much stronger action is required, including 'outright sale', i.e. privatization.

In that same year (1991) official Tanzanian policy took the first steps towards privatization. Financial sector reform started with the passage of the Financial Institutions Act which allows for domestic and foreign private participation in banking activities; the enactment of the Loans and Advances Realization Trust (LART) Act to deal with the transfer (from the national banks) and recovery of non-performing debts; and with the issuance of the Parastatal Reform Policy Statement which establishes the Parastatal Reform Commission, outlines priority objectives and a programme of privatization. In 1992, the legal framework was amended (Public Corporations Act) to facilitate sales of state-owned enterprises. Thus, in 1992 the foundations for a privatization programme had been laid.

From 1991 onwards several cases of privatization were started and some finalized. However, the ambivalence and reluctance of parts of the Tanzanian government and the Party towards privatization has found its expression in the cumbersome decision-making process which involves many stages and institutions and the unrealistic conditions imposed during the bargaining process. On the other side, private investors, dreaming of a buyers' market, attempt to obtain unrealistic consessions. Moreover, many practical problems are still unresolved such as valuation of assets, transfer of debts, the institutional framework, and the selection of attractive rather than poorly-performing assets for sale. As in the early years of independence, preference seems to be given to foreign private investors rather than to the local Asian community. Although privatization has seriously started, the process will be lengthy and the final outcome is as yet unclear. Above all, the impact of privatization on long-term development cannot be assessed at this point in time.

5.5   CONCLUSIONS

This chapter has described the historical and contemporary context of the textile sector in terms of general economic developments and more specifically, the development and performance of the manufacturing sector. It has provided details on two important sets of policies that steer resource allocation and partly determine performance of the manufacturing sector, i.e. foreign exchange allocation and protection. The nature of industrialization as it developed in the 1970s must be seen as one of the major contributing factors to the fragility of the industrial sector.

The nature of the state in Tanzania has developed in mutual interaction with economic developments, in particular towards more control over its resources and an increasing internal softness, eventually leading to the generally low level of productivity, which in turn has led to further economic problems and changes in the nature of the state. In addition, it has been shown that despite increasing pressures by the World Bank, the government has undertaken no fundamental changes in the size or the control of the parastatal system. In the new, more competitive environment it has continued to provide direct financial support to ailing public enterprises. Although the government has succumbed to World Bank pressure in virtually every respect, it continues its support for the parastatal sector, which thus appears as a core interest to the ruling elite. How long it will be able to do so, however, remains to be seen.

With regard to the concepts of 'embeddedness' and 'hardness/softness' of the state developed in Chapter 3, it can be concluded that if the Tanzanian government has no alternative other than maintaining its large manufacturing parastatal sector, it will have to become harder towards itself in order to perform its tasks within the limits of its own resources in terms of finance and human capacities. This could go hand in hand with a changing conception of the 'commanding heights' of the economy into the direction of disciplined implementation of consistent economic policies and away from direct control of productive assets. The extent to which this can be achieved by the contending internal forces within the state elite, by the imposed conditionality of the IMF, World Bank, and donor countries, or by some mixture of both, will determine the success of the eventual outcome in the medium and long term. Industrial development and accumulation in general will have to be carried by the state at large and cannot be imposed exclusively from outside.

While it appears that the above analysis of the Tanzanian state in some respects implies a 'predator state', the present analysis characterizes the Tanzanian state as a form of monopolistic state capitalism. The 'predator' analysis of the neoclassical political economy (assuming an ideal market as reference point) aims to show the impossibilities of the ideal of socialism. However, both show the prevailing forces of opportunism. The neoclassical political economy takes opportunism as a building block of free market ideology, ignoring thereby the monopolistic outcomes of state power and capitalist power in fully developed capitalist states such as the US, which they take as their concrete reference point. The present analysis does not accept this as a final outcome.

Notes

1. In 1977, the CCM (which stands for 'Chama cha Mapinduzi' and translates into English as 'People's Party of Revolution') became constitutionally the single party of Tanzania.
2. The Mwongozo guidelines have been interpreted to have produced an anti-management attitude of workers. Managers trying to achieve greater productivity were accused of anti-socialist attitudes. In this view, the guidelines have thus contributed to the general inefficiencies in public enterprises and administration (van Cranenburgh 1990). However, it seems unlikely that one document can exert such influence. Rather, it should be seen as an expression of underlying realities and an opportunity for instrumental use of the guidelines within these realities.
3. See Skarstein and Wangwe (1986) and Roemer *et al.* (1975).
4. Own funded imports, which allow unrestricted imports from own foreign exchange however acquired, in 1984 initially accounted for 40 percent of all imports and after the introduction of the Open General Licence Scheme in 1988, for 30 percent (World Bank 1991).
5. Van Donge (1992) provides a detailed account of processes of accumulation in the informal agricultural trade sector, showing both the dynamics as well as the limitations to further expansion of such developments.
6. As from 1990/1, ten items remained under price control and confined: farm implements, electric cables, cement, sugar, galvanized corrugated iron sheets, tyres and tubes, petroleum products, fertilizers, reinforced steel and beer. A further six items remained confined but not price-controlled. These were: gunny bags, bicycles and spares, khanga, kitenge, uniform materials, pipes and pipe fittings.
7. Quotation marks are used here to signify that most of these effects were in terms of capacity utilization, rather than capacity *per se*. The resulting structural breakdown in Table 5.3 therefore partly reflects short term developments.
8. This positive result for beverages and tobacco could be influenced by the effect of high international prices because of taxes in exporting countries.
9. Erroneously expressed by the source as 'infinite' for both ERPs and DRCs in Table A.6.
10. This combination of factors applies to only a few private sector firms. There were only 12 private sector (as compared to 36 public) firms in the whole sample to begin with. Moreover, the differences between private and public

firms and between larger and smaller firms in terms of expanding or contracting are not so large. The conclusions are therefore presented as more robust than justified.

11. See de Valk (1992) for more details on the procedures and operation of these schemes.

12. See Alavi (1972), Freyhold (1980), Othman (1980), Saul (1980), Shivji (1982), and de Valk (1992).

13. When dealing with Tanzanian officials one is often impressed with the work being done despite the difficult working conditions and involvement in other income generating activities.

14. Although Tanzania's ideology claims to be grounded on African traditions at village level, the selected set of values and traditions were not necessarily the only values at village level; neither were they necessarily applicable to the nation-state as a whole (Kunz 1991). After all, processes of identification that take place at village level are based on socio-psychological acculturation in small, recognizable communities.

15. Casual personal observations and interviews have confirmed this. In fact, not only entrepreneurs but many of those who have achieved some degree of success feel their obligations too weighty and at the same time difficult to ignore without appearing insensitive to the family. Furthermore, members of the (wider) family claim the right to be assisted even beyond the established rules of the formal system.

16. Shaw, for example, speaks of a 'democracy shock' following the oil shocks of the 1970s and the liberalization shock of the 1980s; and Doornbos speaks of state formation under supervision.

17. For a complete list, see World Bank (1988).

18. A Morrisonian type of public corporation is an enterprise with an independent corporate personality which operates at a distance from government with a semblance of autonomy and is accountable only to parliament through government on matters of policy. Such accountability is limited to matters on which the government has influence (Mihyo 1994).

19. Two projects mentioned in particular are the National Bicycles Company and the Morogorro Shoe Factory. The former factory has been completed but is closed down at present, while the latter has been completed but has never functioned properly.

20. The consultative group consists of donor countries and institutions involved with Tanzania.

21. This was part of a general drive towards more efficiency in the whole public sector, which resulted in the retrenchment of over 20 thousand government employees.

22. Surprisingly, personal interviews revealed that this report has been largely ignored by Tanzanian policy makers and academics, who tried to disqualify it in terms of the methodology used. However, irrespective of short-comings of DRC-based efficiency measures, the report contains much justified criticism. Perhaps it was too much to bear at one time.

23. This report was based on the 1988 TAPO conference on parastatal performance. Its 1986 and 1987 conferences were also devoted to parastatal performance.

6 Performance of the Textile Sector in Tanzania

6.1 INTRODUCTION

The textile sector in Tanzania is the second largest manufacturing sub-sector in terms of value added (in 1978 it ranked first) while in terms of employment and gross capital formation it is the largest (see Table 5.3). Generally speaking, about two thirds is public and another third is in private hands. It consists mostly of medium scale enterprises using rather outdated and run-down technology. Its capacity was built up in the 1970s but also in the 1980s capacity was added. Employment levels are inflexible downwards and with declining capacity utilization have become excessive from the firm point of view.

As will be shown in this and the next chapter, during the 1980s the textile sector suffered from a supply constraint showing up as under-utilization of capacity due to lack of foreign exchange. This led to short-ages of spare parts and recurrent imported inputs. Combined in many cases with poor management, these shortages led to a neglect of mainten-ance, declining attainable capacity, low or negative profitability, and poor quality. Under economic liberalization, liquidity problems also intensified. When faced with import liberalization, the gap between the constrained supply and potential local demand narrowed, with the local market increasingly served by second-hand clothing imports. Given the low quality of the output of most firms, the average ability to export is very low. For enhanced export performance, improved technical management must precede the rehabilitation or investment in new technology required.

However, as this will show, firms differ greatly in performance. This is the result of elements of the sectoral structure and of diverging individual characteristics discussed in Chapter 7 and analysed in Chapter 8.

6.2 GENERAL OVERVIEW OF THE TEXTILE SECTOR

The structure of the textile sector for the years 1978 and 1983 is given in Table 6.1. The focus in this study is on spinning and weaving. The declining shares of spinning and weaving in gross output and value-added

213

Table 6.1   Structure of the textile industry by ISIC subsector in Tanzania 1978,
1983 (%)

	No. of establishments		Persons engaged		Gross output		Value added	
	1978	1983	1978	1983	1978	1983	1978	1983
Spinning, weaving, etc.	41.5	58.5	73.8	72.5	72.5	56.6	83.6	59.8
Made-up textiles except apparel	29.3	11.1	8.6	8.1	6.0	5.6	4.5	7.6
Knitting mills, carpets & rugs	18.9	18.3	4.5	8.9	11.5	26.1	7.6	28.5
Cordage not elsewhere classified	10.4	12.1	13.1	10.5	10.0	11.7	4.3	4.1
Textiles	100.0	100.0	100.0	100.0	100.0	100.0	100.0	100.0

Source: Computed from 1978 and 1983 Census of Industrial Production.

but not in persons engaged show declining capacity utilization without a corresponding employment reduction.

Woven and knitted fabrics constitute the main end products of the sector. Yarn is an end product only when exported, and given the fact that exports of yarn are small, almost all yarn is converted into woven or knitted fabric. Net average imports of woven fabrics over the period 1985 to 1988 stood at 20 percent of production, which is quite significant considering the vast underutilization of capacity in weaving. All knitted fabrics are produced in the private sector.

Textile bags constituted a monopoly in Tanzania until bags were allowed to be imported in 1985 because their shortage had become a constraint to the marketing of agricultural production. Average imports over the period 1985 to 1988 were more than double local production.

Average imports between 1985 and 1988 were generally much higher than imports in previous years, reflecting the impact of the import liberalization policy. Synthetic woven fabrics constitute the main component of imported fabrics, since local production of synthetic fabrics is low and demand is high, especially for women's clothing.

At the onset of the crisis in 1980, exports of yarn increased suddenly but this was not sustained in the years that followed (Table 6.2).[1] The quantity and value of yarn exports increased substantially in 1983 and 1984,

Table 6.2 Exports and imports of selected textile products in value ('000 ECUs) and quantity (tons) between the EC and Tanzania, 1980–90

	1980	1981	1982	1983	1984	1985	1986	1987	1988	1989	1990
Exports to EC											
Yarn											
value	721	106	214	1 091	3 584	2 265	1 919	3 353	2 692	2 318	4 382
quantity	332	25	98	412	1 036	686	800	1 337	1 120	1 059	2 020
Woven cotton fabrics											
value	0	0	241	770	401	1 299	1 916	3 066	2 434	2 834	2 953
quantity	0	0	63	201	115	372	625	1 028	783	952	1 022
Quantity of yarn and woven cotton fabrics	332	25	162	613	1 151	1 058	1 425	2 357	1 903	2 011	3 042
Knitted fabrics											
value	20	297	0	819	980	620	901	813	627	297	62
quantity	10	82	0	226	246	155	352	317	223	95	25
Clothing											
value	5	52	36	194	605	990	307	792	2 021	1 775	2 695
quantity	1	6	1	22	68	120	78	157	418	359	445
Imports from EC											
Second-hand clothing											
value	158	251	364	285	376	2 027	3 532	4 567	3 658	5 199	4 024
quantity	318	470	568	459	593	2 363	4 283	5 189	5 846	7 457	4 919

Source: Eurostat (EC), unpublished.

declined in 1985 and 1986, but picked up again from 1987 onwards (almost doubling in 1990) although at lower prices.[2] Woven cotton fabrics were first exported in 1982 and increased from 1985 onwards but also at declining prices.[3] The quantity of yarn and woven cotton fabrics exported taken together show a more smooth pattern of increases (the dip in yarn exports in 1985 and 1986 might be explained by the increase in exports of woven fabrics which require export quality yarn). The quantity and value of exports of knitted fabrics was relatively stable between 1983 and 1988 but declined suddenly in 1989 and 1990. Clothing exports increased from ECU 5000 in 1980 to ECU 2.7 million in 1990. On the whole, export performance is very erratic and represents only a small proportion of output. Textile imports are substantially higher than exports, with the improving exports of grey cloth still far below imports of synthetic fabrics.

Second-hand clothing imports from the EC started at 318 tons in 1980, increased dramatically in 1985 and 1986, and peaked at 7457 tons in 1989. This last figure amounts to approximately two and a half metres per person, which amounts to about half of the average demand for fabric in Tanzania. This is one of the main factors that need to be considered when comparing textile producing capacity with demand.[4]

Figures 6.1 to 6.4 show the trends in total production and capacity in weaving (1980–89) and those of the public sector only (1974–89), as well as the increasing underutilization of total capacity in the 1980s. Capacity utilization decreased gradually from more than 80 percent for the public sector in 1978 and above 50 percent of the combined sectors in 1980 to less than 20 percent for the public sector and slightly above 20 percent for the combined sectors. Weaving capacity in the public sector kept increasing into the late 1980s, while total production in weaving declined (Table 6.3).

6.3   FIRM-SPECIFIC PERFORMANCE INDICATORS

This section presents available information on the performance of individual textile firms with regard to output, capacity utilization, profits, labour and machine efficiency, product quality and exports.

6.3.1   Output

Table 6.4 shows the quantity of production in weaving by firm from 1980 to 1988. The public sector textile mill, Friendship, accounted for around 50 percent of all weaving throughout the period 1980 to 1988. The slight upturn of production in the public sector in 1988 seems to have been caused solely

Figure 6.1   Total production and capacity cloth in the textile sector, 1980–89
(m.m²)

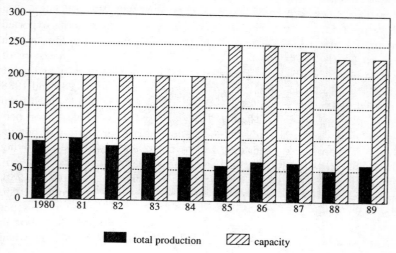

total production   capacity

Figure 6.2   Capacity utilization in the textile sector, 1980–89

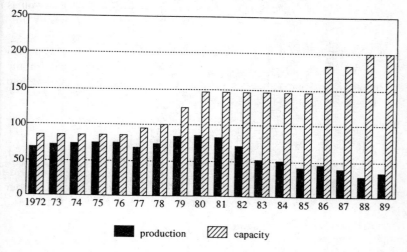

production   capacity

by the higher output of this mill (percentage changes of weaving production
are calculated in Appendix, Table A.13). The monotonous decline in production is in many instances a reflection of the negative rates of change for
most firms, although there are large fluctuations.

Figure 6.3   Production and capacity in the textile sector, 1972–89 (m.m²)

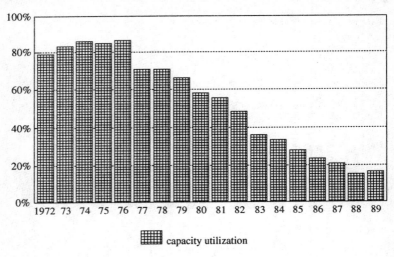

capacity utilization

Figure 6.4   Capacity utilization in the textile sector, 1972–89

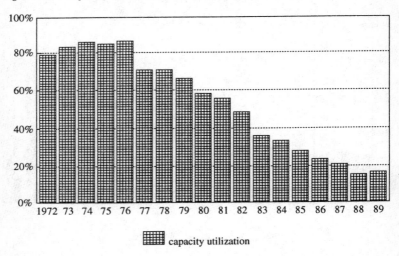

capacity utilization

The private sector produced the greatest share of cotton yarn in 1985 (66 percent), but thereafter public sector output expanded faster than that of the private sector, so that in 1988 the private and public shares were respectively 26 percent and 74 percent. Total production increased almost

Table 6.3   *Textile production 1974–89, private and public (million metres)*

	1974	1975	1976	1977	1978	1979	1980	1981	1982	1983	1984	1985	1986	1987	1988	1989
Public	72.0	72.5	73.1	66.1	71.7	82.4	83.8	80.9	69.0	50.1	48.0	39.4	42.6	29.1	27.3	32.3
Private(a)	14.0	14.6	9.9	12.9	1.3	2.6	9.2	15.1	17.0	9.9	9.0	26.6	19.4	32.0	36.7	38.7
Private(b)				8.5	11.2	14.4	9.3	19.1	17.3	25.3	21.2	16.8	19.3	22.8	25.0	
Total(a)	86.0	87.0	83.0	79.0	73.0	85.0	93.0	96.0	86.0	60.0	57.0	66.0	62.0	61.0	64.0	71.0
Total(b)	86.0	87.0	83.0	74.6	82.9	96.8	93.1	100.0	86.3	75.4	69.2	56.2	61.9	61.0	50.1	57.3
Total capacity			90.0				200.0	200.0	200.0	200.0	200.0	252.0	252.0	241.0	230.0	230.0

Notes: Private (b) is based on the Ministry of Industries and Trade's budget speeches, and Economic Surveys for 1988–89; Total (b) adds public and private (b) with missing values from private (a). Preference is given to series (b) because it uses independent estimates for a number of years for private sector ouptut as supplied by the Ministry of Industries and Trade, whereas series (a) is calculated as the residual of the total output after deducting the public sector output. Using residuals especially when relatively small introduces large errors.

Source: Bureau of Statistics (Selected Statistical Series 1951–85); Economic Surveys (various issues), URT; Ministry of Industries and Trade (Budget Speeches and Reports); TEXCO (Annual Reports).

Table 6.4   Production of woven fabrics by firm 1979–88 (1000 m²)

	1979	1980	1981	1982	1983
PUBLIC:					
Friendship	29 748	27 014	24 179	19 634	19 527
Mbeyatex					
Mutex		1 667	4 227	7 535	3 541
Mwatex	20 490				3 770
Polytex					
Sunguratex		13 460	11 911	10 593	7 441
Kiltex (Arusha)	5 698	5 250	5 014	5 209	4 614
Kiltex (DSM)					
Morogoro Canvas					
Subtotal	26 188	50 125	48 166	47 516	39 000
PRIVATE:					
Tanganyika Textiles		1 863	2 286	2 455	2 283
Calico					
JV Industries					
CIC					
Sunflag					
Ellen					
Polyknit					132
Tangamano					65
Subtotal		1 863	2 286	2 455	2 480
TOTAL	26 188	51 988	50 452	49 971	41 479

sixfold in 1987 as compared to 1985. In the public sector this increase was in the first place attributable to Morogoro Canvas and secondly to Polytex; in the private sector to Sunflag and A to Z, in that order.

Knitted fabrics are produced only by the private sector. Total output has remained rather constant but there have been quite some changes at the level of the individual firms. Cotex and Sunflag show declining trends, while A to Z is producing more. Polyknit shows no clear trend (much depends on the availability of polyester inputs).

6.3.2   Capacity utilization

Friendship has been the most successful public sector firm, although rates of capacity utilization declined during the 1980s (from 85 percent in 1980 to 42 percent in 1988; Table 6.5). Of the old textile firms in the public sector, Mutex never really took off, while Mwatex, Kiltex and Sunguratex

Table 6.4 continued

	1984	1985	1986	1987	1988
PUBLIC:					
Friendship	17 088	14 553	17 293	14 552	
Mbeyatex					138
Mutex	5 292	1 140	2 307	1 435	1 364
Mwatex		10 305	6 430	4 278	1 945
Polytex			1 063	2 569	6 586
Sunguratex	9 046	7 535	4 524	2 512	3 305
Kiltex (Arusha)	184	3 218	1 512	1 934	2 354
Kiltex (DSM)		2 517	2 517	496	756
Morogoro Canvas	2 004	2 887	3 903	4 226	4 137
Subtotal	36 053	44 682	36 809	34 743	35 137
PRIVATE:					
Tanganyika Textiles	1 634	2 068	1 922	1 553	765
Calico		1 564	1 606	1 178	638
JV Industries		2 129	2 279	2 220	2 592
CIC		2 793	3 459		6 335
Sunflag				4 099	5 288
Ellen	203	219	76	72	116
Polyknit	169	31	384	117	30
Tangamano	85	98	35	72	
Subtotal	2 092	8 903	9 726	27 356	17 012
TOTAL	36 141	51 927	44 241	59 094	49 432

Source: Central Bureau of Statistics (internal data files), TEXCO Reports (1979 to 1988), URT (1990d), own data.

saw their capacity utilization rates decline to around 10 to 15 percent in the years of the ERP (1986–88).

Of the new firms, only Morogoro Canvas reached satisfactory levels of capacity utilization (between 33 percent in the starting year 1984 and 70 percent in 1987); Polytex is still having problems in approaching normal levels of capacity utilization.

The first five firms of the private sector listed in Table 6.5 are medium scale firms, the last three are small scale. The medium scale private sector does not show the low utilization rates recorded in the public sector, although here too, experience is mixed. A clear declining trend is visible for Tanganyika Textiles, Calico is rather stable, while JV Industries, CIC and Sunflag seem to be recovering in the last two years from lower utiliza-

Table 6.5   Capacity utilization in woven fabrics by firm 1979–88 (%)

	1979	1980	1981	1982	1983	1984	1985	1986	1987	1988
PUBLIC:										
Friendship		85	77	69	56	56	49	42	49	42
Mbeyatex									1	1
Mutex		8	19	34	16	24	5	10	7	6
Mwatex	45						22	14	9	4
Polytex								7	16	41
Sunguratex		62	55	49	34	42	35	21	12	15
Kiltex (Arusha)	34	31	29	31	27	1	19	9	11	14
Kiltex (DSM)							63	63	12	19
Morogoro Canvas						33	48	65	70	69
PRIVATE:										
Tanganyika Textiles	41	51	55	51	36	46	43	35	17	10
Calico							46	47	35	48
JV Industries							21	22	22	25
CIC							33	41		75
Sunflag									27	34
Ellen						34	37	13	12	19
Polyknit					4	6	1	13	4	1
Tangamano					32	43	49	17	36	36

Note: Using more recent estimates of maximum capacity made by URT (1990d).
Source: Calculated from Table 8.6 and Table A.12.

tion rates. Of these, only CIC is at the normal level of capacity utilization of around 70 percent.

Of the small scale firms, Polyknit seems least successful (much depends on whether they can import polyester yarn or not), Ellen and Tangamano experienced a difficult time respectively in 1986 and 1987 but both recovered to some extent in 1988.

6.3.3   Profits

Data on profits are notoriously hard to come by. Moreover, the definition of profits used by firms often differs, while the Bureau of Statistics does not receive direct information on profits but calculates profits as a residual. Within these limitations the following can be said on the sector as a whole and on individual firms.

First, the findings show that, for the whole sample 1986, 1987 and 1988 have been years of decrease in overall profitability with 1986 having the most pronounced decrease. Before 1986 only 1983 showed a slight deterioration. At least 45 percent of the firms made losses in 1986, 50 percent in 1987 and 42 percent in 1988. This is considerably higher than the 38 percent average over the whole period 1980-88 and definitely higher than the average before 1986 (33 percent). It seems that in the last three years the overall picture has became worse. To what extent this is the result of the ERP cannot be assessed at this point in a straightforward manner as the performance of firms is to a large extent also the result of past policies and firm level decisions.

Second, the private textile sector was already experiencing a downward trend from 1985 onwards and in fact no significant improvement took place during the years of ERP. The year 1988 saw a further worsening of their situation. The small scale private sector (consisting of Ellen and Polyknit) has doen worse than the larger private firms which did not perform badly in the years 1985 to 1988.

Third, profitability in the public sector decreased in 1986 and increased in 1988. This result is not contradicted by the data from the Central Bureau of Statistics presented below.

Fourth, the findings definitely do not corroborate any view that profitability has been restored during the years of ERP, the period 1986 to 1988.

Table 6.6 shows data from Central Bureau of Statistics for a sample of firms on sales, gross profit and pretax net profit as percentage of sales. The only public sector firm that has positive profits, i.e. Friendship, shows a declining trend of pretax net profit over sales (which became negative in 1988). All other public sector firms have negative values for this indicator. For the public sector as a whole, pretax net profit over sales becomes more negative with time, reaching values as low as –390 and –309 percent in 1987 and 1988.

For the private sector the picture is quite different. With the exception of Coast Textiles and Cotex (Zanzibar), all private firms shown in the table have recorded positive rates of profits in at least one year. Of 25 entries, 13 show negative pretax net profits over sales, 10 were positive and 2 were zero. For the private sector as a whole, the figures indicate a declining trend from a positive value of profit rates in 1985 to negative levels in 1987 and an improvement to low but positive levels of profit again in 1988. When the figures for Cotex (Zanzibar) are excluded, it appears that 1987 was a difficult year but that during 1985, 1986 and 1988 positive levels of profit were realized.

Table 6.6   Gross profit, pre-tax net profit as percentage of sales, public and private firms (1985–88)

Firms	Gross profit as % of sales				Net profit as % of sales			
	1985	1986	1987	1988	1985	1986	1987	1988
PUBLIC								
Kiltex	−7	−7	−21	−63	−44	−53	−84	−125
Mbeyatex		19	46	24		−1266	−1688	−327
Mutex	−74	9	−16	−40	−460	−565	−945	−1791
Mwatex	7	−35	−167	−263	23	−137	−704	−1696
Polytex		−600	−98	−93		−1255	−1580	−384
Sunguratex	0	2	−3	−78	−5	−20	−55	−189
Friendship	22	26	19	8	11	7	4	−3
PRIVATE								
A to Z	−3	5	23	24	−13	−14	−22	2
Coast Textiles	19	−50	−700		0	−100	−1600	
Cotex (Zanzibar)	45	44	38		−20	−340	−545	
JV Textiles	27	25	20	18	11	0	−3	−4
CIC	37	31	32	22	6	1	8	−2
Sunflag		42	21	23		21	4	14
Tanganyika Textiles	0	2	−7	25	2	−1	−11	19
Total Private	24	28	20	21	4	−13	−24	2
Total Private(*)	19	27	20	21	5	6	−3	2
Total Public	7	−25	−23	−46	−16	−164	−390	−309
Total	12	−4	−6	−19	−10	−105	−248	−185

Note: *excluding Cotex (Zanzibar).
Source: Calculated from Table A.18.

6.3.4   Best practice, firm-level efficiency estimates for spinning and weaving

Following the approach developed in Chapter 2, the input coefficients for labour and capital (empirically measured) for bboth spinning and weaving can now be used to calculate the relative total factor productivity (RTFP) for spinning in Tanzanian textile firms relative to British 'best practice' firms using similar technology. The CES production function estimate with =0.5 and =0.6 is taken as the most appropriate function (Pack 1987). But for the sake of testing the sensitivity of the estimates to variations in the elasticity of substitution, CES production functions with =0.2 and with =1 (which is the same as a Cobb-Douglas function) have been used.

The results for spinning (Table 6.7) show that, while all RTFPs are far below 'best practice' standards, some Tanzanian firms such as Friendship, Ubungo Spinning, CIC, Mbeyatex, and Kiltex (Arusha) are in line with those of the four Kenyan firms, all of which have RTFPs above 60 percent. Friendship stands out above the others (including the Kenyan firms) with an RTFP of 87 percent relative to technology from the 1950s. However, a large fraction of firms falls below the RTFPs of the Kenyan firms. The lowest value is recorded by Sunflag, followed by A to Z and Mwatex. The low values scored by Tanzanian firms do not necessarily imply that Kenyan firms on average perform better, since the above four Kenyan firms are not a representative sample of the Kenyan textile industry. It is interesting to note that both public and private firms show a large diversity in their performance with very inefficient and reasonably efficient firms in both sectors.

A similar analysis can be made for technical efficiency in weaving. Weaving technologies can be distinguished by the way the weft is inserted and the degree of automation (see Chapter 3).[5]

Kenyan firms are included in Table 6.7 as an additional check on the results based on the hypothetical firm. Data on these firms have been disaggregated into different technologies by firm. For Tanzanian firms this was not possible, since the labour productivity measures were on a firm-wide basis. This necessitated calculation of a weighted average of machine efficiency over different technologies by firm. The results are shown in Table 6.7.

First of all, it can be concluded that the difference between the calculations of RTFPs using different values of labour input for the hypothetical firm is not so large, while the ranking of firms remains intact and their relative differences change very little. The result is thus not very sensitive to the precise value of the labour-input coefficient. The results based on the lowest value of the labour-input coefficient will be taken as the better ones.

Second, even more than in the case of spinning, RTFPs vary greatly between firms, with the lowest values for Sunguratex and Mwatex (at 15 and 14 percent respectively) and the highest for JV Textiles (68 percent), Kiltex (Arusha) (66 percent), CIC (62 percent) and Sunflag (58 percent). Friendship, which is amongst the best Tanzanian firms in spinning, scores rather low in weaving (38 percent). Mutex (54 percent) and Polytex (37 percent) confirm their rather poor performance recorded in spinning. Cotex (DSM) is amongst the poorest performers.

Third, unlike in the case of spinning, the private sector seems to perform better in weaving.

Fourth, as in the case of spinning, all firms are considerably below 'best practice' standards (represented by the hypothetical firm).

Table 6.7 Relative Total Factor Productivity (RTFL) of spinning and weaving in Tanzanian firms (1988)

	Spinning			Weaving			
	CES (= 0.5) RTFP	CES (= 0.2) RTFP	Cobb-Douglas RTFP	CES(= 0.5) RTFP (L/Q = 0.00002)	CES(= 0.2) RTFP (L/Q = 0.00002)	C-D	CES(= 0.5) (L/Q = 0.000015)
Kenya A	0.71	0.92	0.56				
automatic				0.84	1.05	0.69	
Kenya B	0.61	0.77	0.51				
automatic				0.71	0.88	0.59	
non-automatic				0.56	0.75	0.39	
Kenya C	0.80	0.89	0.76				
automatic				0.55	0.69	0.44	
non-automatic				0.41	0.48	0.38	
Kenya D	0.64	0.75	0.57				
automatic				0.61	0.81	0.46	
Sunguratex	0.48	0.53	0.45	0.28	0.39	0.18	0.15
Friendship	0.87	0.87	0.89	0.47	0.47	0.45	0.38
Ubungo Spinning	0.65	0.82	0.53				
A to Z	0.39	0.45	0.33				
CIC	0.62	0.80	0.43	0.75	0.82	0.80	0.62
Sunflag	0.29	0.36	0.27	0.71	0.71	0.64	0.58
Mbeyatex	0.79	1.04	0.58				
Kiltex (Arusha)	0.72	1.04	0.25	0.79	1.00	0.67	0.66
Mutex	0.51	0.67	0.43	0.65	0.80	0.49	0.54
Polytex	0.62	0.84	0.42	0.45	0.47	0.44	0.37
Mwatex	0.41	0.59	0.21	0.29	0.32	0.26	0.14
Cotex (DSM)				0.34	0.34	0.36	0.27
Cotex (Iringa)	0.58	0.70	0.49				
Calico				0.65	0.77	0.66	0.54
JV Industries				0.52	0.54	0.51	0.42
JV Textiles				0.81	0.99	0.70	0.68

Note: The RTFP has been calculated relative to a hypothetical firm with labour input coefficients equal to 0.00002 and 0.000015 respectively (which is equivalent to 50 and 67 thousand metres of weft inserted per labour-hour) and machine efficiency of 68 percent.
Source: Kenyan firms from Pack (1987) and Tanzanian firms from own calculations based on data in Table 8.13.

Fifth, there is little correlation between the performance in spinning and weaving for the eight firms appearing in both samples, with a simple correlation coefficient between $RTFP_{sp}$ and $RTFP_{we}$ equal to 0.22.

Finally, there is considerable room for improvement in all cases in both spinning and weaving. In weaving, no firm has an RTFP above 81 percent while in spinning eleven of the thirteen firms are below 70 percent. However, before passing definite judgements, better insight is required into the reasons why the performance is as low as it is. This will be attempted in the next chapter.

Other estimates of firm level efficiency

A number of estimates of efficiency in Tanzanian industry have been made. At the level of the manufacturing sector Skarstein and Wangwe (1986) concluded that efficiency in the manufacturing sector has been declining, especially in the late 1970s. Measures of both capacity utilization and partial factor productivities confirm this.

Three studies that have analysed efficiency in the textile sector will be discussed here. These are Mbelle (1988) covering the period 1976 to 1984, de Valk and Mbelle (1990) covering the period 1980 to 1988, both using a production function approach, and World Bank (1987c) estimating DRCs. Mbelle's conclusions in the first two studies will be presented first, followed by those of the World Bank.

a)   Mbelle found that value-added per worker in the textile industry has been declining drastically, especially in the 1980s. Capital productivity has declined as well. Low levels of capacity utilization brought about by the shortage of imported inputs etc. have contributed significantly to declining efficiency.

Mbelle also used production function estimates of the entire textile sector (1980-88) to identify the types of input with the highest marginal output elasticity (marginal product defined in terms of percentages). The inputs used in the analysis were: capital (proxied by energy consumption), labour (actual labour hours worked), domestic inputs (cotton yarn) and imported inputs (US dollar equivalent of imported inputs). The marginal elasticities in order of importance were domestic inputs, labour, capital and imported inputs. This contrasts with the 1974 to 1984 estimates, in which imported inputs ranked first, followed by capital and then labour.

In addition, Mbelle found that while the observed textile output could be produced using between 46 percent and 69 percent of the observed amounts of inputs used in the 1970s, during the period 1980 to 1988 observed textile output could be produced using between 22 and 93 percent of the observed input amounts. This is not a very significant result as the former interval is fully included in the latter.

Between 1980 and 1988, labour inputs (actual labour hours worked) increased (as measured by the trend in labour elasticity), as well as imported inputs usage. Since average output declined significantly during this period, the continued application of labour (either through increased employment or by maintaining existing levels) meant declining labour efficiency. This is opposite to the situation in the 1970s in which the trend of labour elasticity (and foreign exchange) showed a decrease – and capital (the trend of its elasticity) an increase. There was a general decline in efficiency (though 1988 presented a slight improvement over preceding years such as 1985). The magnitudes of the 1980s are lower than those of the 1970s. In 1980 the firms could have, on average, produced the same observed output using only about 85 percent of the observed input amounts. In 1988, on the other hand, only about 58 percent of the observed input amounts used could have produced the observed output (in 1985 this was 50 percent). The efficiency performance of the individual firms does not show any particular pattern, although some public firms have higher efficiency performances than private firms.

Mbelle's finding that no clear difference exists between the public and private sector is confirmed by the calculations presented here. However, since the particulars of these firms necessary for identification are missing, a firm by firm comparison with the efficiency estimates calculated in the present study is not possible. Furthermore, the small sample size makes generalization less meaningful. Above all, the differences in production technology between firms and between processes (which, as detailed in the two preceding sections, affect the comparison) have not been taken into account.

Changes in technical coefficients over the period 1980 to 1988 were calculated. There have been no significant changes in input coefficients for labour, domestic and imported inputs. There have been some efforts to reduce import content. Mbelle argues that this can be partly attributed to firms substituting domestic yarn for imported rayon). However, there has also been a shift towards the production of grey cloth and towards reducing the use of dyes and chemicals, as evidenced by the lower quality of coloured fabrics. The capital input coefficient has increased. However, as Mbelle notes, this result should be interpreted with caution, because the proxy for capital (electricity consumption) is less than optimal and the increase in the capital coefficient could also mean decreased capital utilization (with relatively higher energy overheads), or simply higher electricity consumption due to an aging plant and machinery.

(b) As part of its study of the industrial sector (World Bank 1987c), the World Bank estimated firm level efficiency using the method of domestic resource cost ratios. As was explained in Chapter 2, the DRC as a measure of inefficiency captures (but does not distinguish between) all sources of inefficiency, including underutilization of capacity. This last source of inefficiency has been eliminated in the estimation of attainable DRCs, which calculates the DRC at attainable capacity. The sample included eight textile firms, two of which were private sector firms. Although firms were not identified by name, three of the public sector firms are easily recognized by their product: Morogoro Canvas, Tanzania Bag Corporation, and Blankets Manufacturers. On the basis of the efficiencies achieved, public firm four can probably be identified as Friendship Textile Mill.

Only one of the firms surveyed (Friendship) has a long run DRC near unity. The other firms are all economically inefficient and use more value than they produce (according to the definition of DRC). Morogoro Canvas and 'Private 2', with their rather new capital equipment, show large differences between long run and short run DRC. The public sector firms have a much lower actual long-run DRC (1.80) than the private sector (3.81). However, since the private sector sample consists of only two firms, generalizations are impossible.

6.3.5 Product quality

On-site assessments of product quality were made by textile experts. Quality is reported as 'very poor', 'poor', 'fair', 'good', and 'very good'. In the classes qualified as 'good' and 'very good', at least part of the output would be acceptable in the low to medium quality export market. 'Fair' and 'poor' signify locally acceptable quality. The qualification 'very poor' signifies that a large fraction of output can be classified as rejects or scrap. With respect to the final output (woven cloth or yarn), of the 25 firms evaluated, one firm had very poor quality output, five recorded poor, nine fair, eight good, and two very good quality.

Any quality reducing factors in the early links of the long value chain from cotton growing through ginning, spinning, weaving, processing and garmenting have their effects on the latter links. Thus, maintenance of quality under generally deteriorating circumstances becomes increasingly difficult. In addition, as it happens, the processing stage is also the most foreign exchange intensive production process, adding further difficulties to maintaining quality in that particular stage of production. For the public sector, this leads to a tendency of shifting exports to earlier links in the chain, i.e. from garments towards grey cloth, yarn and cotton and to lower average prices for the processed cotton products. For the private sector, in order to control input quality, there is a tendency towards backward integration. One firm is even contemplating engaging in cotton growing.[6]

6.3.6   Exports

Eight public sector companies (of which two very small) and six private sector companies reported exports in 1988. Data on exports by firm are rudimentary in the sense that different units of measurement are used between years and firms, and time series and even incidental data on quantity and value of exports by firm have not been made available.

Yarn exports appear to be the most feasible, followed by grey cloth. Most firms have exported to benefit from the foreign exchange retention schemes which allow them to buy dyes and chemicals to produce for the more profitable local market. With the large devaluations and import liberalization the export market has become more attractive in recent years.

Of the public sector firms, serious exporters are Morogoro Canvas, Friendship, Ubungo Spinning, and Ubungo Garments. However, exports have not been achieved without costs to the firm in all cases. For example, for Friendship to be able to export woven fabric, a special export line has been set up utilizing the best machinery with special efforts to control quality which, as estimated by the production department, leads to cost increases of about 60 percent over normal production. Ubungo Garments has entered into a special arrangement with a US firm to produce on contract (for five years). They have been unable to provide the quantity agreed, and due to the small margins negotiated and the initial costs of this project, have incurred losses. At present they have managed to negotiate some contracts in Europe as well. The substantial exports of Morogoro were initially the result of lack of demand in the local market for its heavy fabrics. Export prices were so low at the ruling exchange rate that they produced at a loss. Meanwhile, export prices have gone up. However, there are accusations of incorrect practices with foreign transactions.

The private sector firms CIC, Sunflag, A to Z, Calico, and JV Textiles have been successful exporters. Cotex (DSM) is less successful. In addition to yarn and grey cloth mentioned above, the knitted garments exported by Sunflag, A to Z and JV Textiles such as T-shirts have a good market in the

EC. JV Textiles also exports towels, linen and T-shirts to Scandinavia, and some of its products are also exported to Tanzania's neighbours. A to Z, in addition to T-shirts, also exports yarn cotton fabric and lace to the EC. Part of their new equipment has been purchased by means of a barter deal with a British firm which also takes care of their foreign exchange requirements for production. Calico exports grey cloth and kitchen towels to the EC. CIC exports mainly yarn (to the EC and Australia) but also various fabrics such as bedsheets and pillow covers. Chapter 8 will provide further analysis with regard to the question of why firms export.

6.3.7 New investments

Apart from extensive rehabilitation of all plants under its authority, new projects that TEXCO has considered are: (a) the Central Base Workshop, which should produce at least 70 percent of all the spare parts required, establish a technical service unit for all public sector mills, and control and regulate imports of spare parts, (b) the Textile Training and Research Institute to be located in Morogoro, which would offer courses lasting from 18 months to three years, and (c) the Denim Project, to be located in Moshi, which would be a fully integrated textile mill with an annual production of about three million linear metres exclusively producing denim for exports (TEXCO 1986). On the advice of several World Bank missions, all these projects have been shelved.

Private sector investment is primarily oriented towards supplying the export market. Below the investment plans of private firms, as reported in URT (1990d), are summarized:

– *A to Z*: Plans to invest in a polyester chips plant with a capacity of 30 tons per day in order to supply the local market, as well as the regional export market. In addition, modernization of weaving looms and finishing equipment at the Moshi plant is foreseen. The foreign exchange for these transactions would come from suppliers credit and barter arrangements.
– *Calico*: Installation of modern shuttle-less looms of widths suitable for the EC export market.
– *JV Industries*: Replacement of 94 shuttle looms by 40 air-jet looms complete with ancillary equipment to produce standard grey sheeting for the export market. A World Bank loan is requested.
– *JV Textiles*: Plans to install a spinning plant to control the supply and quality of yarn.
– *Cotex (Ir.)*: First priority is to rehabilitate existing equipment. After that has been accomplished, new investments will be considered.

- *CIC*: Intends to expand weaving department to produce high quality cloth which can be used for garments for exports. Financing of the foreign exchange component by use of barter arrangements and the seed capital retention scheme.
- *Sunflag*: Intends to invest in machinery to produce khanga and kitenge for the local market. These ideas are still in an early phase.

Thus, private firms which are already successful in exporting are also dynamic in the sense of expanding their export activities. The public sector on the other hand, although forever wishing to undertake new projects, is restrained by the World Bank's and other donors' conditions. Instead, efforts are concentrated on rehabilitation and rationalization.

6.4 CONCLUSIONS

The present chapter's detailed, firm specific information on various indicators of performance has emphasized measures of efficiency, with firm level data on output, profits, capacity utilization, product quality, exports and investment provided as well. The efficiency measures calculated here are mostly direct measurements of technical inefficiency based on comparison with 'best practice' firms. As shown in Chapter 2, these measures of technical inefficiency relate closely to the concept of X-inefficiency by focusing on the subprocesses spinning and weaving separately and by eliminating the effects of different technologies in use and of the degree of capacity utilization. It allows estimation of how much improvement in firm performance would be possible by better management.

The other measures of efficiency for Tanzanian textile firms employed in two other studies – the generalized Farrell measures employed by Mbelle and DRC ratios employed by the World Bank – could not be compared directly with the data employed in this study. Moreover, these measures, in the way they were calculated, require the valuation of capital, which is at best very unreliable and at worst impossible. The DRC ratio can be estimated either with assumed sunk capital costs, thus eliminating the measurement problem of capital (short-run DRC), or with some rough estimate of capital cost (long-run DRC). Neither of the two methods has shown the refinements of the 'best practice' approach which measures capital in terms of quantity, differentiates between different subprocesses, and evaluates performance relative to comparable technologies.

On the other hand, the DRC ratio, when based on all costs, measures the total viability of the firm while the 'best practice' approach only deals with technical inefficiency. In this sense, both methods are complementary (see also the discussion in Chapter 2 on the relation between DRCs and X-inefficiency). Moreover, Farrell measures inefficiency with the help of multi-input production functions, allowing for the identification of marginal elasticities of all inputs. This would give some clues as to which constraints are binding to further growth (although also assuming substitutability between inputs). The 'best practice' approach as employed here only deals with labour and capital inputs and thus only measures the inefficiencies (Farrell measure E_1 or E_2, identical for homogeneous production functions such as CES) based on these two inputs.

The three empirical approaches to efficiency measurement all show that no simple classification of private and public sector firms is possible along the dimension of efficiency. This impossibility was amplified in the light of the very small samples employed by the two other studies. Large individual differences between firms have been measured. However, the present study, employing a much larger sample of firms, shows that in weaving the efficiency difference between private and public firms is more pronounced than in spinning.

One firm that stands out in all three studies is Friendship Textile Mill. It has the highest efficiency in Mbelle's studies, and the various DRCs calculated by the World Bank are lowest. However, in the calculations carried out here Friendship does not perform very well in weaving, although in spinning it is one of the best firms in Tanzania.

A final empirical observation on firm performance is that for private sector firms there seems to be a strong relationship between product quality, exports, and new investment.

The next chapter will present the available information on factors that may explain the firm level differences in performance.

Notes

1. This excludes exports to non-European countries. Although exports were reported to Eastern European countries, to Mozambique, and to the USA (garments from 1988 onwards), the bulk of trade is with the EC.
2. This could reflect lower quality, since the decline in average price from 3459 ECU per ton in 1984 to 2169 ECU per ton in 1990 seems to be too large to be explained only by price movements. Another possibility is that it represents a lowering of the price by Tanzanian exporters made possible by the depreciating Tanzanian shilling.
3. The average price decreased from 3487 ECU per ton to 2889 ECU per ton in 1990. The price of woven cotton fabrics per ton in 1984 is only very little

above the price of yarn per ton in 1984 (3459 ECU). The price for woven fabric per ton in 1990 is even substantially below the price of yarn per ton obtained in 1984. If this can be explained as quality effects, it would make sense to improve yarn quality first before increasing exports further.

4. This will be done in the next chapters.

5. Technologies are respectively non-automatic, automatic, air-jet, and rapier weaving. The data for weaving are in a different form and it is impossible to directly compare firms with the 'best practice' firms used in spinning. Instead, a hypothetical firm has been used, with a labour input coefficient (at 0.00002 with its reciprocal of 50000 metres of weft inserted per labour-hour for rapier technology) below the lowest value recorded in the Tanzanian sample (0.000031) and machine efficiency of 68 percent. The value of 68 percent has been chosen so as to ensure that, in the sample of Tanzanian firms, no firm would have an RTFP lower than its capacity utilization since this would be contradictory.

6. Based on interviews in Arusha. This has already happened in the case of Nigerian firms although not for identical reasons (Andrae and Beckman 1987).

7 Macro-, Meso-, and Micro-Factors Affecting Performance

7.1 INTRODUCTION

This chapter presents the factors that will be used to explain the performance of the firms in the textile sector. Following the theoretical framework developed at the end of Chapter 2, explanatory factors can be distinguished by the level at which they are formed: (a) mega-factors: technological developments, international trade flows, and the performance of other countries; (b) macro-factors: the impact of structural adjustment policies such as devaluation, credit policy, liberalization, allocation of foreign exchange and credit, price developments in relation to cost structures, and the role and nature of the state; (c) meso-factors: sectoral characteristics such as concentration, spatial distribution of production, demand, and institutions of market control; and (d) micro-factors: firm characteristics such as ownership, location, management, size, export share, age in relation to depreciation, financial structure (foreign loans), technology.

The mega- and some of the macro-factors have already been addressed earlier when discussing technology, international developments, the role of international institutions, and the state. Macro-factors will be discussed in section 7.3, meso-factors in section 7.4 and micro-factors in section 7.5. This is preceded by an overview of constraints as they have been perceived by the managers of public and private firms, the public sector textile holding corporation TEXCO, and the National Bank of Commerce (NBC). Chapter 8 analyses performance in relation to macro- and micro-variables in more detail with the help of regression analysis.

7.2 CONSTRAINTS TO PERFORMANCE

Tanzania's industrial development has been affected by various constraints. Firm-level constraints may differ from what appears to be the overriding constraint at the macro-level. Chapter 5 on the economic and industrial development of Tanzania has noted that as early as 1973 a

235

foreign exchange crisis had manifested itself. Reluctant private sector investment was replaced by public investment, shifting the constraint of investment finance to factors related to shortcomings in industrial management. Wangwe (1979) and Mbelle (1982) reported that at the end of the 1970s and the early 1980s the industry was basically supply constrained: the shortage of foreign exchange was mentioned by firms as their first constraint, while the second problem experienced was with the supply of water and electricity. In 1986, TEXCO's Corporate Strategic Plan (TEXCO 1986) identified 26 problem areas in relation to the weak performance of its group companies. Of these, 19 are external and 7 internal problems. The following list presents their account in summary form as an indication of the type of things that may negatively affect industrial production. The list is (understandably) silent on problems of technical, financial and commercial management and related inefficiencies.

(a) Price control and confinement policy: Prices of textiles and related products may be reviewed annually if producers request it. The procedures are cumbersome and sometimes confusing. Up to nine months may elapse between the initial request and the review. In the meantime, producers must continue producing and selling at old prices. However, the price of cotton fibre, the basic raw material, is not controlled. This allows the TCMB to fix its price and determine the effective dates of this price almost at will. The gaps between the effective dates of the reviewed prices of cotton and sisal and the corresponding prices of bags, textiles and allied products have been widening year after year.

(b) Rate of inflation: Inflation has been varying around 30 percent per annum, pushing up production costs. The protected market has enabled producers to pass on inflationary effects to consumers because of chronic shortages. Since late 1985 this is no longer possible because the liberalization policy has effectively undermined the market for locally produced products with cheaper imports.

(c) Scarcity of foreign exchange: Between 1980 and 1985, the foreign exchange required to import spares, dyes and chemicals was never met, and the gap continues to exceed 90 percent. Machine efficiency and productivity and, very importantly, the quality of products have gone down.

(d) Cotton and sisal fibre supply: In 1985 'the Government decided to pay cotton growers higher prices than those prevailing in the world market, forcing the TCMB to recover the losses arising thereof from the domestic textile industry in terms of price increases ranging from

60 percent to over 250 percent above the world market prices' (TEXCO 1986:70). Even as world prices declined, domestic prices for cotton have shot up from TSh. 17.0 per kg in 1983 to TSh. 81.0 in 1986 and for sisal from TSh. 2200 per ton in 1985 to TSh. 6500 in 1986. 'This kind of price increases coupled with the recently introduced liberalization policy and presence of "mitumba" (second-hand imported clothing) will eventually force the entire textile industry to a total collapse' (ibid.:36).

(e) Bureaucratic export-import procedures: With regard to export procedures TEXCO complains of lost and misplaced documents and undue delay in notifying the parties concerned which result in late execution of orders. With regard to import procedures, there is the additional problem that 'the existing procedures are so lengthy and cumbersome that it sometimes takes more than a year to get a Letter of Credit opened after the Bank of Tanzania has granted its approval and confirmation facilities have been secured' (ibid.:37). Missing and/or misplaced documents also delay customs clearance, which leads to heavy demurrage charges.

(f) Location, transport and logistic problems: 'Most of the mills within the TEXCO Group of Companies have had their locations determined by the government on the basis of socio-political and macro-economic considerations. Those locations, therefore, necessarily impose locational advantages and disadvantages to the companies' operational costs' (ibid.:64). Dar es Salaam, Arusha, and Moshi-based mills are at an advantage in terms of both domestic and imported input supply and the marketing of final goods. Dar es Salaam has a water supply problem, but this may emerge in Arusha and Moshi as well if no adequate measures are taken. The second-best location, in the major cotton growing zone and near the second largest domestic market, includes the mills in Mwanza, Musoma and Tabora. However, 'those mills are faced with serious lack of trucks which are about the only means by which their cotton requirement could be transported. This mode of transport happens to be very costly and unreliable because of the poor mechanical condition of most of the trucks in the country and the seasonality of the roads in those regions' (ibid.:42). Additional disadvantages are posed by problems in power supply and the difficult connections to the major ports. The location of the mill in Mbeya is considered to have major disadvantages being far from markets, major ports and supply of good quality cotton. Railway transport is cheapest and could minimize the costs of long distances, but it is not sufficiently available.

TEXCO estimates that the TEXCO group could keep the whole National Railway System occupied.

(g) Confinement policy: Passed in 1981, this policy confines all textile products and blankets produced by TEXCO Group to the Regional Trading Companies (RTCs) to enhance an equitable distribution of commodities in short supply. This has resulted in the following problems for the mills:

 – Transport problems: the costs of transport to the RTCs have to be born by the mills.

 – Liquidity problems: because of the poor financial position of most RTCs they have ordered commodities they could not purchase or for which they paid late. For the mills this had the 'obvious effect of choking the liquidity position of the mills' (ibid.:43). This in its turn has negatively affected the profitability position of the mills.

 – Political problems: 'It has been common for regional authorities to force their respective RTCs to buy certain products without any consideration to their saleability' (ibid.:44). RTCs 'cover up their mistakes by accusing TEXCO ... of producing poor quality products thereby tarnishing the political image of the group' (ibid.:44).

 – Marketing problem: 'The textile mills, therefore, are under the mercy of the RTCs in so far as marketing of their produce is concerned' (ibid.:77). No active domestic marketing policy can be pursued by the individual mills or the TEXCO group as a whole.

(h) Power supply: The supply of power represents a devastating problem for most of the mills. From 1980 to 1985, TEXCO companies 'lost over 260 million metres of linear cloth worth over T.Shs. 13.0 billion on account of power failures alone' (ibid.:45).

(i) Water supply: Most affected by inadequate water supply are the Dar es Salaam based mills, especially Kiltex and Sunguratex. The existing pumping station cannot supply enough water because of the increased demand for water from other industries and the increased population.

(j) Fuel supply: Due to foreign exchange shortages fuel has been in short supply. This has been aggravated by the difficult transport situation and inadequate storage facilities. Especially affected were Mwanza, Musoma and Tabora, even at times when industrial diesel oil is plentiful in Dar es Salaam.

(k) Demand structure: Rough estimates indicate that total domestic demand for textiles is around 400 million metres, while total rated capacity is 258 million metres: 188 million meters for the public sector and 70 million meters for the private sector. An estimated 5 percent of the population has a high propensity to buy fashionable wear with little consideration for costs, while the rest are more cost-conscious, with fashion considerations taking second priority. With liberalization this means that the high income segment prefers high quality, imported garments and the middle and low income segment has turned to 'mitumba' (imported second-hand clothing). Competition from 'mitumba' is most threatening for the TEXCO Group as it affects 95 percent of the population. For effective competition with 'mitumba', local producers will have to find ways to lower their production costs. Competition with the private sector in the domestic market is seen as especially unfair 'because of the *competition's ability to cheat the government*' (ibid.:95). These problems are most serious for garment factories, e.g. Ubungo Garments Ltd (UGL). The market for kitenge and khanga, school uniforms and institutional buyers has been less affected. TEXCO states that its production costs, especially labour, electricity and cotton lint, are too high and its quality too low to allow it to penetrate the markets of Europe and the USA. The export of yarn, grey and bleached cloth is feasible, however.

(l) Financing: 'the only source of future equity financing is dividends from profitable mills and funds from willing private partners' (ibid.:68). For working capital, the National Bank of Commerce is the only source. The NBC has introduced credit ceilings, and interest rates have gone up significantly, thus limiting the availability of short term credit and increasing its cost. Working capital requirements are large because the mills are forced to buy all of their inputs on a COD (cash on delivery) basis, while at the same time they are compelled to extend 45 days' credit to customers. In addition, price increases in inputs can be passed on to output prices only once a year through the Price Commission.

(m) Labour turnover: 'Because of the infancy of the textile industry and the backward nature of the industrial base in general, the textile labour market is significantly small' (ibid.:69). Textile mills must train their own operatives to cater for labour turnover. The TEXCO Group's greatest needs are in engineering, textile technology, accountancy and management. There is a rapid turnover of higher technical personnel as TEXCO Group of Companies loses professionals to the better paying private sector. Local training facilities for engineering, accountancy and management produce too few graduates to meet total local requirements. Textile technologists need to be trained abroad.

Incentive schemes do exist, most of which were established independently by individual mills. Some are effective, some ineffective and some seem to have negative effects. In 1981 the government introduced a general policy on incentives with the paper: 'National Policy on Productivity, Incomes and Prices'. This policy is administered by the National Productivity Council. However, these incentives do not stop the labour drain to the private sector. 'Given the rigidity of the SCOPO (Standing Committee on Parastatal Organizations) directives, the parastatal sector always suffers and will continue to do so as the private sector continues to grow' (ibid.:77).

(n) Purchasing and material management: Lack of coordination between stores, users and purchasing staff has led to procurement of less important and/or unwanted items and in other cases to over-procurement, leading to liquidity problems and waste. Lack of storage skills have led to depletion of safety stocks resulting in stoppages and wastage attributable to poor storage and theft. Lack of material handling equipment has led to spoilage and waste.

(o) Factory floor transportation: Poor factory design in the old mills and damaged factory floors have resulted in inefficient factory floor transportation.

(p) Dependency on imported inputs: About US$ 10 million annually is required to import critical inputs such as precision and specialized spare parts and accessories, dyestuff and chemicals and, for the polyester plant, synthetic fibre.

(q) Monitoring agencies: The excessive number of monitoring and control institutions includes Boards of Directors/Management Committees, SCOPO, and 'literally every officer in the Parent Ministries' (ibid.:71), factory branch chairpersons and secretaries of the CCM, area and regional chairperson and secretaries of the CCM and regional authorities in general.

(r) Management information system: The current management information system supplies more or less the same information to the mills' CEO's and TEXCO head office. This leads to duplication of efforts and to the handling of issues by TEXCO that could be handled by mill executives themselves.

TEXCO's strategy for 1986 to 1990 as formulated in their corporate strategic plan 1986–90 in response to this overwhelming list of problems, is to centralize further, to increase management, control functions and training, to issue more manuals, and to obtain more privileges from government.

In 1988, the ninth General Managers Conference was held by TEXCO. The TEXCO contribution to the conference report summarized the situation as follows:

The major causes of this poor performance and decline in productivity to almost all of the group companies include the following:

1. There has been a persistent power shortage for Mwatex, Mutex and Tabora Spinning Mill;
2. Lack of adequate water supply which affected most of our Dar es Salaam mills including Kiltex, Sunguratex and Friendship;
3. Lack of foreign currency to purchase the vital inputs and spare parts for almost all the mills;
4. Liquidity problems which at present affect virtually all group companies;
5. Increase in the cost of loan financing, especially foreign loans, mainly due to the everdepreciating Tanzanian shilling against other stronger currencies, coupled with increased bank interest rates;
6. Glut of market by imported cheaper goods especially garments and agricultural bags;
7. Management failure, in some cases, in taking timely decisions to solve production problems which are within their capability and in taking cost control measures (TEXCO 1988:1).

This is no longer the list of problems noted in 1986. TEXCO notes demand as well as supply problems and acknowledges management failures. The demand problem is seen to originate in cheap imports made possible by liberalization. Another new item on the list is the increased local currency costs of foreign loan financing. Foreign exchange shortages are no longer at the top of the list. Apparently, the liquidity problem has recently become stronger. NBC's response during the conference elaborated upon the problems in financing working capital. They are much more critical of TEXCO. Nine factors are discussed as having contributed to the financing problem, ranging from the influence of policy measures on liquidity to bad planning, ineffective management and embezzlement. These nine factors show in detail how the soft budget constraint operates (see section 7.3 on credit for the complete list). However, it can also be read as an attempt to put the blame elsewhere and not on the tight credit controls exercised by the NBC. Together, the lists of TEXCO and NBC show how disastrous the performance of the industries has been during the last years.

Primary data, collected in 1988, on perceived constraints to performance for a sample of firms in the textile sector are summarized in

Table A.7 (Appendix). The most important problem perceived by public and private managers has been the lack of domestic credit. Shortages of foreign exchange for spares and inputs is ranked second, closely followed by interruptions in the supply of electricity.

Interviews held in 1993 revealed that the excessive competition from illegal imports constituted a major demand-side problem. Firms lost their domestic market shares unless they themselves would also evade sales and profit taxes by using parallel market outlets. Implicit subsidies under the system of import support prevailing during the 1980s had allowed them to survive. But the elimination of these subsidies from 1992 onwards resulted in serious liquidity problems for most of the firms interviewed. The export market is an option for only a few efficient firms. This brings out the underlying importance of firm level factors: the managerial and technological capability to produce quality at competitive prices.

Concluding, over time the most important constraint has been the supply of foreign exchange. It has negatively affected the supply of utilities, the road and transport system, capacity utilization, levels of attainable capacity, profits and the liquidity of firms. This in turn has created an environment in which low productivity, inefficiencies and corruption prosper. Thus, other constraints have developed which will persist for some time even if the foreign exchange constraint has been eased.

With the macroeconomic adjustments in the late 1980s, a constraint in the supply of credit has developed because of the poor performance of industries, cost increases, devaluation and tight credit policy. This was reinforced by the pressure on prices by illegal competitive imports. However it seems that the credit constraint is of a less structural nature than the foreign exchange constraint. Macroeconomically speaking (and all other things being equal, which of course they are not since especially the price of foreign exchange has increased drastically), it is difficult to imagine how a credit constraint could develop if all foreign exchange would be earned from exports of goods and services and the money supply would be adjusted to the changes in the level of imports made possible by these exports. But when foreign exchange is made available in excess over exports, it is possible that credit starts to play a restrictive role. Expansion of domestic credit seems a necessary companion for increased availability of foreign exchange from abroad which, after all, is also an expansion of credit. When foreign credit is expanded without an equivalent expansion in domestic credit, anything between the following extreme situations may happen: the first possibility is that inflation may drop if excess demand in domestic currency is shifted towards purchasing foreign exchange. However, the second possibility is that if this excess demand does not shift to foreign exchange (for example because of the restricted list of allowed imports from the point of view of those with excess domestic currency), inflation continues and foreign credit remains unutilized. In reality, when domestic credit is restricted while foreign credit expands, something between these extremes may occur. Some redistribution of purchasing power towards foreign exchange will take place, thereby reducing inflation, and some amount of foreign exchange will prove difficult to spend because those interested in specific commodities allowed to be imported do not have the cash. In practice this implies that consumer demand may shift to imported goods while producer demand remains unsatisfied.

It has been shown how the liquidity constraint has reinforced low performance and how in the case of the public sector the credit constraint has been operating as a soft budget constraint thereby increasing the debt burden of firms. This, in turn, puts further pressure on firm performance.

Other interrelationships also exist between the constraints. Constraints in one area lead to constraints in other areas, which then become independent of their initial cause. For example, foreign exchange shortages cause low capacity utilization, leading to financial losses which increase the demand for credit and lead to the neglect of capital stock and decreasing attainable capacity.

While the overriding importance of the foreign exchange constraint draws attention to macroeconomic balances between, on the one hand, imports for investment, recurrent imports, and consumer goods and exports on the other, it does not follow that this macro-constraint is unaffected by micro-performance. Macroeconomic balances are aggregates of microeconomic outcomes with microeconomic performance in its turn affected by macroeconomic constraints.

7.3 MACRO-FACTORS AFFECTING PERFORMANCE

Policy packages aiming at economic adjustment during the 1980s have been discussed in Chapter 6. In this section, impacts of these policies on the allocation of foreign exchange to firms, allocation of credit, and the impact of changes in prices on cost structures of firms will be discussed. In addition, available information on problems with the supply of infrastructural inputs will be presented.

Foreign exchange allocation

From the Tanzanian perspective, management of the constraint is necessary both at national and firm levels. Chapter 5 has listed the various foreign exchange schemes in operation. The number of ways to obtain foreign exchange are quite diverse and controlled partly by firms, donors, overseas suppliers, the parallel market and the Tanzanian government.

The firms experiencing the most severe shortages are not necessarily the most inefficient ones. As was mentioned in Chapter 6, some firms have been quite successful in exporting, thus augmenting their foreign exchange supply by utilizing retention schemes. However, official allocation takes into account the amounts received from such sources (see Appendix, Table A.8) which in fact introduces a negative incentive to firms diversifying their foreign exchange supply. Most firms spread their risks over all facilities. The most commonly used facilities are export retention, OGL, revolving seed capital and free resources.

Firms were asked to report on their sources of foreign exchange. Within the limits posed by the reliability of the responses[1] the following comments can be made:

1. Before 1984 requests exceeded foreign exchange allocated (by a factor of more than four in 1983). Thereafter allocations collapsed and foreign exchange requests disappeared. They began again in 1986, when the official allocation system was reintroduced but the system collapsed after one attempt at planned allocation in the first half of 1987, and there was a further decline in 1987 and 1988.

2. In absolute terms, total reported allocations decreased between 1979 and 1984, when they were at their lowest. In the period 1986 to 1988 they increased substantially, especially in the last two years.

3. The sources of foreign exchange have become increasingly diversified over the years, so that the allocation system became similarly complex and difficult to administer. In the early years of the 1980s (1979–82), the BoT allocations were the only (reported) source of foreign exchange.

4. Import support declined in 1984 but became increasingly important from 1985 into the period of the ERP when it amounted to about 50 percent of total reported allocations. This decline in import support in 1984 is corroborated by an evaluation of Dutch commodity import support (NEI 1987).

5. Supplier credit became an important source of foreign exchange and in 1984, the year when all other sources seemed to have dried up, it accounted for 96 percent of total reported allocations. In 1985 it fell considerably and in 1986 and 1987 no suppliers' credit was reported. In 1988 suppliers' credit was back in the picture again.

6. Barter trade appeared in the figures for the first time in 1985, the crisis year of the negotiations with IMF. Together with the drop and subsequent disappearance of suppliers' credit, it signals the lack of perceived creditworthiness of Tanzania in the eyes of its foreign private suppliers.

7. Export retention played a role in 1986 and 1987, after which it seemed to decline again. The introduction of the OGL system and the World Bank's lack of support for the programme despite its earlier positive recommendations may have caused its decline.

8. Too few private firms are represented in these data to allow sources of foreign exchange in the private and the public sector to be compared. It appears that the public sector has been able to tap more sources of foreign exchange than has the private sector. It is particularly surprising that the import support programme has reached the public firms better than the private firms.

Table A.8 gives complete official information on foreign exchange allocation in the first half of 1987, the only time that the official system was in fact applied. Because this table can be assumed to present complete coverage, a comparison can be made between the private and the public sector and between firms within this sector. First, the private sector requested more foreign exchange than the public sector, was recommended a higher proportion by the Ministry of Industries, had roughly the same proportion of import licences pending, had received more import support (though very small amounts), had higher export retention, was allocated and, finally, had more foreign exchange resources at its disposal. Per 100 metres installed capacity, the private sector was allocated US$ 3.9 as against US$ 2.3 for the public sector. Second within the public sector, Friendship received the highest allocation in absolute terms. In terms of US$ allocated per 100 metres installed capacity, the highest allocation was to Morogoro Canvas (8.7) followed by Polytex (3.1), Friendship (2.9) and Kiltex (2.4). Third, within the private sector the highest absolute allocation was to JV, but in relative terms (per installed capacity) the highest allocation was to MB Textiles (11.4) followed by A to Z (7.9), JV (5.2) and Calico (4.4). Finally, it is not clear on which criteria the above allocations were based. For example, firms that use synthetic inputs have different import requirements, but this does not seem to have been the overriding criterion.

Credit policy

So far, in discussing the negative effects of an undifferentiated credit policy on production, no distinction has been made between private and public sectors. The discussion of a supply constrained economy was conducted at a high level of abstraction without reference to the realities of Tanzania. One of these realities is the emergence of parallel markets and the differentiated response of private and public firms to that.

Parallel market operations and corrupt practices in public sector firms tend to benefit individuals working for the parastatal at the expense of consumers, government and the firm. Private sector firms are able to profit from parallel markets at the expense of consumers and government but not of the firm, so capital is accumulated and liquidity of the firm maintained. In addition, private firms generally tend to rely much more on own sources of capital.

Therefore, tight credit policy affects public sector firms much more than private sector firms, but expansion of credit to the public sector by itself could easily lead to a continuation of transfers from the public to individuals in the parastatals. This implies that credit expansion for production to public firms should be accompanied by measures to ensure that firms' interests are served rather than individual interests.

Credit rationing takes place in two forms: firstly by raising the price of credit, i.e. the rate of interest, and secondly by limiting access to credit facilities through more stringent requirements of creditworthiness or absolute credit ceilings, possibly differentiated by sector. Until 1989, the highest lending rate has been below the inflation rate.

The National Bank of Commerce (NBC) is the most important source of credit in Tanzania and therefore also the main financial watchdog in charge of implementing the credit constraint measures in the economy.

A high proportion of credit has gone to the marketing boards. This has been a hot issue in negotiations with the IMF. Credit had to be extended to pay primary producers for food and export crops. Credit to marketing boards represents more than half of the total credit allocated and definitely competes with other sectors. Credit allocation nearly doubled from 1987 to 1988 for all sectors except financial institutions. Given a rate of inflation of around 30 percent, it seems a misnomer to talk of a credit squeeze. Credit to the industrial sector as a whole has increased more slowly than total credit allocated in the years 1984 to 1986 but was still above the rate of inflation. After 1986 industrial credit increased even more rapidly. It is difficult to observe a credit squeeze.

Perhaps the lending to the TEXCO group of companies has been more restrictive than to the rest of the industrial sector. Table 7.1 gives the data.

Credit to TEXCO group companies has been fluctuating strangely when compared to the allocations to the whole industrial sector. Certainly the year 1986 demonstrates something of a credit squeeze. However this was followed in the next year by a vast expansion of credit resulting in a

Table 7.1 *Lending to TEXCO Group of Companies, 1985–88 (m. TShs)*

	June 1985	% incr.	June 1986	% incr.	June 1987	% incr.	June 1988	% incr.
Industrial Sector	1 946	n.a.	2 622	35	4 730	80	9 911	110
TEXCO	274	n.a.	207	–24	964	366	1 465	52
TEXCO (% of Total)	14		8		20		15	

Source: National Bank of Commerce (1988).

20 percent share in total credit allocated to the industrial sector. In 1988 TEXCO's share was in line again with the percentage for 1985.

In the General Managers Conference Report (TEXCO 1988), TEXCO's contribution starts the section on liquidity as follows:

The problem of liquidity is at present affecting practically every company in the group ... The problem has become extremely serious to the extent of making many companies within the group unable to maintain a continuous flow of raw materials ... Already some companies are working with negative working capital (TEXCO 1988:5).

Most companies in the group are heavily indebted to the Tanzania Cotton Marketing Board (TCMB). TEXCO mentions the low utilization of capacity and its causes as a group of factors, the effects of which have been compounded by the increase in prices of finance, essential inputs and utilities combined with the credit squeeze.

Surprisingly, low output prices are not mentioned in the section on liquidity and TEXCO states in the section on trade liberalization that 'the problems being faced are not a result of trade liberalization ... competition is healthy and where it thrives consumers' sovereignty is strengthened' (ibid.:6). The increase in input prices is cited as part and parcel of the same trade liberalization policy that 'has enabled ...[TEXCO]... to get the necessary dyes, chemicals, sewing thread, buttons, electrical equipments, suiting materials etc.' (ibid.:7).

Yet, in the same section, it is argued that 'our mills are exposed to unfair competition' (ibid.:7) because, while imported final goods are not price controlled, the prices of locally manufactured textiles are still controlled by the Price Commissioner.

But price controls in Tanzania have protected the producer more than the consumer, being based on the principle of 'cost plus' pricing separately for each mill. Thus, only the positive elements of trade liberalization are accepted.

The problems of financing working capital have been elaborated upon in the contribution to the General Managers' Conference report (TEXCO 1988) by the National Bank of Commerce, which, as an outsider, is much more critical. The NBC discusses nine factors as having contributed to that problem. Together they show how the soft budget constraint operates in detail:

1. Some industries have been established with inadequate equity capital. This forces such companies to divert working capital provided by the NBC to uses contrary to the NBC's lending conditions. Companies remain borrowers for long periods and increasing interest further aggravates the problem.
2. Some companies have been established without proper feasibility studies and planning. Cost overruns during project implementation due to delays have made the projects nonviable right from the start.
3. Foreign exchange constraints have reduced capacity utilization, causing losses that are then financed by increased borrowing, increasing the costs of production even further. The continuing devaluation has increased the cost of foreign inputs. Where inputs have been obtained through suppliers' credit this was even more true. Higher working capital financing was sought from the NBC.
4. Companies with foreign loans have been forced to seek additional working capital to meet maturing foreign loan repayments, contrary to the NBC's policy for working capital financing.
5. Trade liberalization has depressed sales and forced companies to extend longer credit periods. This had led to higher working capital requirements and costs thereof.
6. Working capital has been diverted to capital expenditure such as the purchase of automobiles.
7. Weak management and a lack of experience in the line of activity in some companies has led to misuse of working capital funds provided by the NBC. Mismanagement can cause great losses and erode valuable investments in the company.
8. Accounting personnel are weak in some companies.
9. Some companies have experienced embezzlements/thefts of working capital funds provided by the NBC, perpetuated by some dishonest staff in the accounting and supplies departments.

Together, the lists of TEXCO and the NBC show how disastrous the prospects for the industries are if no additional measures are taken to lead the firms gradually to adjust to a more open economy.

In fact, some companies have been unable to pay sales tax, and wages have been delayed. One firm was allowed to sell without sales tax so that it could pay its workers. Short term loans have been given to some firms to be able to survive in the last years under ERP.

One further aspect of the credit squeeze and the general situation of illiquidity in the whole economy is that everyone wants to borrow from everyone else but no one is willing to lend. This has caused a general slowdown in transactions and further threatened the viability of production. Producers face the dilemma of either increasing finance costs through offering suppliers' credit to customers while having to pay cash for delivery to input suppliers, or not being able to produce at all.

Companies have become inefficient and nearly bankrupt because of the macroeconomic environment. Now they are exposed to very stringent conditions in a policy environment which very rapidly has made life even more difficult. Without remedies, they will not survive.

In conclusion, it is hard to defend the point of view that credit *per se* has been the key factor in causing the collapse of textile industries. Only the year 1985 would lend support to such a statement. The alternative that suggests itself, supported by the observations of the NBC on causes of illiquidity, is rather that the general decline in profitability and the increasing debt burdens have brought the firms so many problems that the only way out would be to resort to financing the losses. The apparent credit squeeze comes about by an increase in demand for credit rather than a decrease in the supply.

The best answer to the question of the extent to which credit has been an effective constraint can only be given on the basis of firm by firm analysis. The data for such an analysis could not be obtained, not from the firms themselves and not from official sources.

Pricing policies

Various pricing policies designed to stimulate aggregate production were adopted, especially during the ERP. In agriculture, the incentives included raising producer prices. In industry, input prices have generally increased, but output prices have not followed the rise in costs.

An analysis of changes in cost structures over time can trace the effects of policy changes and macroeconomic variables on relative costs. When important macroeconomic variables such as the price of foreign exchange are adjusted and accompanying policy measures are implemented to ensure a more liberal trade regime, domestic prices will change. In fact, 'getting the prices right' is often seen as the immediate objective of policy changes, since from there everything will fall into place. But while most economists would agree that prices indeed do matter, the degree to which they matter is an issue of debate. Thus, whatever one's position, detailed analysis of price developments under structural adjustment is necessary to establish at least some of the consequences of economic policy.

A complicating and important issue in practice is *which* prices matter. In an economy of shortages and government controls, a parallel economy will develop with parallel price mechanisms. The parallel market and the official market should however not be seen as separate entities but more as a symbiotic (or parasitic, if one likes) system where prices in one are partially determined by what happens in the other.

For example, the minimum wage has been declining steadily in Tanzania, and is now less than US$ 15 per month. At the same time, labour regulations make it very difficult for employers to fire people, resulting in overemployment and therefore higher wage costs than necessary from the point of view of maximizing the firms' profit. In addition, payments in kind add substantially to the actual wage rate. However since labourers cannot survive on such low wages, additional market activities must be undertaken during or outside working hours, often in collaboration with other family members. This in turn is facilitated by over-employment. The price of labour to the firm is thus determined by income-earning options outside the firm for the labourer and the family group. What could thus be viewed as inefficiencies of labour, can in fact be considered as compensation for low wages in the form of allowing labour inputs to be used in parallel market activities outside the firm's interests.

Another example would be where firms, even public enterprises, can only survive when part of their output is sold illegally, i.e. without paying sales tax. Given the high rates of sales tax (100 percent in some cases) this makes an enormous difference, the benefit of which is reaped by both seller and buyer. In such cases, what is then the average output price?

With the above qualifications in mind, a detailed analysis of the cost structure of the output of different firms over time will shed some light on issues such as:

- Have wage costs declined relative to other input costs? This is not just a question of wage levels but of the total wage bill. Especially in public enterprises, the level of employment is not adjusted to output, so the share of wages in the cost of one metre of cloth reflects a variety of wage and surplus labour combinations depending on the level of output.

– Have prices of directly imported inputs risen faster than other inputs? This could be expected given the steady devaluation of the shilling. The assumption here is that other prices do not adjust directly and/or completely to price changes of imported items. Such an assumption is a necessary (but not sufficient) condition for depreciation to be an effective policy for structural adjustment. Particularly interesting is the relationship between prices for domestically produced exportable commodities, such as cotton and cotton yarn, and prices of imported inputs such as dyes and chemicals.

– What has been the trend for finance costs? Firms with high foreign debt servicing will face enormous increases in such costs expressed in Tanzanian shillings.

– What is the trend in depreciation? If firms would like to replace their physical assets after these have been depreciated, the foreign exchange equivalent in Tanzanian shillings should be available. This implies that the existing capital stock should be revalued in line with devaluations. But the final amount reserved for depreciation should not just cover the present depreciation charges but also the now-deflated accumulated depreciation of the years before the particular devaluation. Whether this is possible depends on the way firms have kept their saving on the depreciation account: some may have been able to export their capital one way or another but it is unlikely that public enterprises have been able to do so. If these firms are serious about replacing physical capital, enormous increases in the current amounts for depreciation would arise. Failure to replace leads to consumption of physical capital and a postponement of the problem. New loans or rehabilitation programmes would be required when the capital stock is worn down.

– The cost of local credit will depend on the rise in interest rates and the amount that firms have borrowed domestically. Interest rates have been rising to the level of inflation so real interest rates are close to zero. However the increases in input prices necessitate larger amounts of working capital. This is reinforced by the general stickiness in transactions because of the constraint in domestic credit facilities: everyone wants to buy on credit but no one is willing to grant credit. Delivery time increases, and underutilization of capacity results.

Some relative and absolute changes in prices result automatically from changes in macroeconomic policies, others depend in addition on partially controlled responses by institutions and still others depend on actual practices of individual firms. In other words there are automatic and behavioural determinants of price responses to policy changes.

For example, while exchange rate adjustment (other things being equal) will directly change prices of imported goods, the local price for cotton is only partly related to the export price since the price of cotton lint also depends on decisions by the TCMB. Prices for output of firms, say kitenge, are partly influenced by cost increases due to inflation and partly by fragmented market conditions, prospects for continued government support (or discontinuation thereof) for parastatals, government control of illegal import practices and consumer demand, and practices with regard to depreciation of capital assets, which vary from firm to firm.

Below, the impact of tariff and sales tax, liberalization and deconfinement of trade, and large scale devaluation on prices will be discussed. The impacts of all these changes together will then be demonstrated by showing the cost developments over time for three firms.

(a) Tariff and sales tax

Import duties vary from 25 to 60 percent. Using the current exchange rate, import prices (the basis for computation) are converted in local currency prices. Import duties therefore increase with the exchange rate and this necessitates the prefinancing of larger amounts of local currency, increasing working capital requirements. The duty paid is then normally passed to the consumer by raising prices. Thus higher duty means higher prices and further erosion of the domestic market for local manufactures.

Sales tax, like import duty, is imposed before the manufactured product leaves the premises of the manufacturing firm. In other words sales tax is paid irrespective of actual sales (once output figures have been obtained). In 1990, the sales tax for textile products ranged from 30 to 100 percent. The sales tax increases the price of the commodity to the final consumer by a corresponding amount.

As the government has been restricted on budgetary aspects, e.g. bank borrowing (as part of the ERP policies), it has resorted to increasing duties and sales tax for a group of imports and local manufactures. For example, sales tax jumped by about 100 percent for some textile products. While these increases have meant more revenue to the government, they have considerably eroded domestic demand (and hence the market).

The combined effects of duty and sales tax on prices can be demonstrated by comparing a local manufacturer and an importer of khanga. To arrive at the domestic price of imported khanga, first 60 percent duties have to be added; then, over the total another 100 percent sales tax, after which a 20 TSh CCM levy is added. The final price for a pair of Khanga amount to 725 TSh. At the current wholesale price of between 700 and 800 shillings, a rational trader ceases to operate. Hence some mechanism must make the trade profitable. The most common way is through under-declaration of quantity and hence evasion of import duty and sales tax.[2]

For locally manufactured khanga the sales tax is currently TSh 79,000 per bale i.e. about TSh 526 per pair. This implies that in effect a locally manufactured khanga is charged approximately 50 percent more sales tax than an imported one. Hence a local manufacturer is at a disadvantage due to unfair competition. This is reinforced by irregular imports and second-hand clothing imports discussed below.

(b)   Liberalization and deconfinement of trade

The import of various textile products has been allowed (especially second-hand clothes) since the partial trade liberalization in 1984 and further relaxation in 1986. These imported textile products are offered at prices far below the price of locally manufactured textile products (especially second-hand clothes) for the following reasons:

(i)   Under-declaration of value reduces import duties paid.

(ii)   Products channelled through charity organizations are exempted from duties. Given that the corresponding charity organization in the country of origin obtains most of these materials free, these goods enter the country at zero cost (except for shipping costs which are cheap and may even be subsidized).

(iii)   Complete evasion of import duties: In the few cases in which information on attempted evasions was made public, these involved imported textile products worth hundreds of millions of shillings. With the volume of imports increasing, the cases of interceptions made public are only a fraction of actual cases.

(iv)   The cost of producing second-hand clothes is almost nil, as most of these have been worn and discarded. The price charged domestically corresponds only to freight cost and the trader's margin. The inability of domestic textile manufacturers to compete with imported second-hand textile products has meant the erosion of the domestic market base for domestic producers. Given the small market size (effective demand), increases in prices (e.g. to accommodate rising costs of production) are certainly going to shrink the market further. Given the availability of cheap alternatives, domestic manufacturing is likely to collapse. (An estimate of total demand for textiles is made later in this chapter).

Internally the liberalization of trade has been effected through reducing the number of items with controlled prices from 2000 (in the early 1980s) to fewer than 10 (June 1990).[3] The immediate effect of this type of liberalization is to increase the price of commodities as domestic traders (especially middlemen) are allowed to set their price at will. Even if these prices would reflect scarcities (rather than monopolies), firms would need time to adjust.

(c)　Effects of exchange rate adjustments on prices

The most dramatic price change has been in that of foreign exchange, which has increased by a factor of ten in only a few years. The Tanzanian shilling maintained a rather stable exchange rate with the US$ until 1981, after which year the shilling was devalued, modestly at first but rather drastically from 1986 onwards (Table A.6). Since the adoption of the ERP the Tanzanian shilling has been devalued three times: in 1986, in November 1988, and most recently in December 1989. In addition to the devaluations the shilling was allowed to depreciate to the level of 230 TSh/US$ in 1991.

Direct effects of exchange rate adjustments on the textile industry consisted first of sharp increases in the price of imported inputs such as dyes, chemicals, and spare parts. Second, the price of cotton (a tradeable item) rose proportionally with the devaluation. Third, lowering the value of the shilling increases the burden of loan repayment for those loans with foreign components. Every textile firm in the country has imported machinery. This has meant substantial foreign borrowing, once encouraged by low interest rates and a favourable exchange rate. Loan servicing was manageable (with difficulty) until 1985. But after the substantial devaluation of June 1986 and further exchange rate adjustments, the debt burden increased very substantially, making loan servicing impossible. Given the current cash flow problems facing the manufacturing sector in general and the textile industry in particular, default on servicing loans is inevitable. Left on their own, the textile firms cannot possibly honour such commitments. There is thus a need to secure government help in dealing with this 'micro-debt crisis'.

(d)　Examples of firm level impact of price development on cost structure[4]

The impact of devaluation on firms depends on a number of firm specific parameters. First the difference between the shares of exports and imported inputs in total output determines whether the firm will gain or lose from devaluation in a static sense. Of course a firm can alter its input and output mix to some extent so as to direct the changes to its advantage.

Second, unlike new firms, old firms have less foreign debt and are therefore less affected by this aspect of devaluation. However, their need to replace capital stock may be more urgent, and depreciation allowances may have been set aside in local currency (if at all). Older firms will also require more maintenance and (foreign produced) spare parts.

Third, the type of ownership (local or foreign) and the type of foreign financing also determine access to foreign finance and the possibility to save in foreign currency. Some firms are allowed to repay their foreign debts in kind to the same institution that supplied its machinery and is still supplying its imported inputs.

The combined effects of all these price movements are highlighted below with the help of three examples, one private and two public firms. These are Friendship Textile Mill, an older, relatively efficient public firm with a rather low level of exports and with Tanzanian management; Morogoro Canvas, an efficient, new public mill with a high level of exports and foreign management; and Tanganyika Textiles, a medium scale, rather inefficient private sector firm producing only for the domestic market. This selection reflects a reasonable spectrum of the differences that exist within the textile sector, which is fortunate, since data availability has inhibited the presentation of other private firms.

Cost structures have been analysed by grouping costs into broad categories and expressing these as percentages of total costs, total value of production and as costs per metre of output. The broad cost categories depend on data availability and include the following: cotton lint, cotton yarn, polyester yarn, dyes and chemicals, energy, maintenance, wages, salaries, depreciation and finance costs. There are important differences in the nature of these inputs:

- Cotton lint and cotton yarn are domestically produced and exportable and their price is therefore likely to follow the trend in the exchange rate.
- Dyes, chemicals and most polyester yarn are imported and their prices are directly linked to the exchange rate. However substitution may occur when shortages in these inputs (coupled with high prices) would affect production.
- Energy, especially oil, is imported but its price is regulated. Its price therefore reflects institutional discretion rather than automatic market behaviour.
- Maintenance is a mixed item of local and foreign costs. Substitution is possible to some extent, but lack of working capital and foreign

exchange may lead to neglect of maintenance activities, thus eating away at the capital stock.

-   Wages and salaries are a domestic input, although wage and salary goods can be exportables or imports. Wage rates and salary scales are determined by a complex set of relationships in which the price of foreign exchange does not figure prominently.
-   Depreciation differs from firm to firm. Sometimes it is based on historical value of capital which does not reflect the true replacement costs, sometimes on adjusted values. There is therefore a difference between how depreciation appears in the actual figures and how it should appear in order to save enough for replacements.
-   Finance costs are a mixture of domestic and foreign loans costs. Most firms have both, as even old firms have received some loans for rehabilitation and new machinery.

In the following pages, cost items have been represented in three ways: (a) as a percentage of total costs so that only relative changes are monitored and overall inflation is eliminated, (b) as a percentage of total value of production, to eliminate to some extent the effect a large change in one cost item would have on the others, (c) in Tanzanian shillings per metre of fabric to obtain a measure that also shows inflation.

All these measures are sensitive to capacity utilization, as some costs are more or less proportional to capacity utilization and others are more constant *vis-à-vis* the level of production. Therefore capacity utilization is also shown for each firm to allow for a better interpretation of the results.

Friendship Textile Mill

Friendship Textile Mill is an old, publicly owned mill with few foreign loans. It is located in Dar es Salaam and has had few infrastructural problems compared to the other parastatals. Also it is treated favourably in terms of foreign exchange allocation. Its capacity utilization has therefore been much higher than the others (see Table 6.5 and Table 7.2). Nevertheless, its attainable capacity has declined to about two thirds of installed capacity. Its capacity utilization declined steadily, from 85 percent of installed capacity in 1980 to 42 percent in 1988.

Tables 7.2 and 7.3 summarize the cost structure of the Friendship Textile Mill. Figures 7.1 and 7.2 display the most important cost items over time. It is obvious when inspecting Figure 7.1 and Table 7.3 that depreciation follows a rather strange pattern, distorting the shares of the other cost items.

Figure 7.1   Friendship cost structure (as % of total costs per metre)

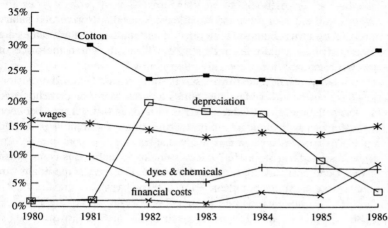

Source: de Valk (1992).

*Table 7.2   Friendship Mill capacity utilization and cost structure
(% of value of production)*

	1980	1981	1982	1983	1984	1985	1986	1987	1988
Capacity Utilization*									
Attainable capacity (m. mtr.)	32.2	31.2	27.3	27.7	21.3	21.2	21.2	22.0	22.0
Capacity utilization (%)	92	87	88	71	92	80	69	79	66
Utilization of installed capacity (%)	85	77	69	56	56	49	42	49	42
Cost Structure (% of value of production)									
cotton	34	29	25	38	30	23	33	22	29
dyes & chemicals	12	10	5	8	10	8	8	4	17
energy	13	13	11	19	17	16	16	16	15
maintenance	6	4	3	5	4	7	5	4	3
wages	17	16	15	20	18	14	17	9	11
salaries	10	13	12	19	10	13	12	6	8
depreciation	1	1	20	28	22	9	4		
overheads	9	12	12	18	12	10	11		
finance costs	1	1	1	2	4	3	9		

Dyes and chemicals have gradually declined as percentage of total costs. Since this is a directly imported item, this is most probably due to a reduction in the use of dyes and chemicals. Second, despite the persistent complaints by firms about the high price of cotton, the share of cotton costs in total costs has actually declined slightly. Third, the percentage share of wages has remained rather stable over the years. One would expect a reduction because of relative cost increases in other items. Given the fact that wages have not risen very fast, this points towards increasing inefficiencies in the use of labour. Fourth, finance costs have risen faster than other costs, especially recently. Data availability does not allow for conclusions on the years 1987 to 1989. But it seems likely that this trend is continuing. Fifth, overheads started to rise in 1987 but it is unclear whether this is the beginning of a trend or a sudden, incidental increase. Finally, the reasons for the depreciation pattern are not clear. Even if there has been a revaluation of capital in 1982, depreciation figures should not decline so rapidly again.

Table 7.3 and Figure 7.2 reveal further that after 1986 the costs of cotton and dyes and chemicals have risen faster than other items (which is to be expected in times of fast depreciation).

Table 7.3 shows the trends of average prices and total costs (excluding depreciation, finance costs and overheads since these were not available for the last two years). In 1987 the average price of output, which almost doubled, compared to rather modest cost increases, must have increased

Figure 7.2   Friendship cost structure (in TShs per metre)

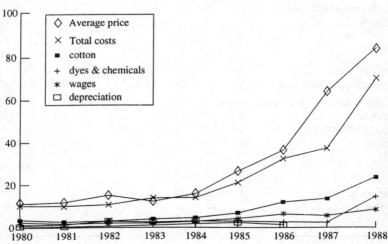

Source: de Valk (1992).

Table 7.3   Friendship Mill cost structure (TShs/mtr)

	1980	1981	1982	1983	1984	1985
cotton	2.9	3.0	3.5	4.8	5.0	6.5
dyes & chemicals	1.0	1.0	0.7	1.0	1.6	2.1
energy	1.1	1.3	1.6	2.4	2.8	4.3
maintenance	0.5	0.4	0.4	0.6	0.7	1.8
wages	1.4	1.6	2.1	2.6	3.0	3.8
salaries	0.9	1.3	1.6	2.4	1.7	3.7
depreciation	0.1	0.1	2.8	3.5	3.8	2.5
overheads	0.8	1.2	1.6	2.2	2.1	2.7
finance costs	0.1	0.1	0.1	0.2	0.7	0.7
Total	8.8	10.2	14.5	19.6	21.4	28.3
Total excl. last 3 items	7.8	8.7	10.0	13.7	14.9	22.3
Average price	8.5	10.3	14.1	12.5	17.0	27.9

Table 7.4   Selected indicators for Friendship Mill

Year	1983	1984	1985	1986	1987	1988
Exports (M. TSh)	2	3	24	1	98	25
Export as % value prod.	1	1	5	0	10	2
Dyes and chem. (M. TSh)	18	3	4	4	4	210
Cotton lint (M. TSh)	93	98	112	176	246	351

profitability. In 1988 the picture was reversed with costs increasing sharply compared with modest output price increases.

Figure 7.2 shows how total costs per metre and average price per metre have changed over time. Output prices were higher than costs throughout the 1980s, except for 1983. In addition the positive margins have increased over time (especially in 1987 and 1988) both in absolute and relative terms. It should be stressed that this excludes depreciation, overheads and finance costs. When these are added for 1980 to 1986 there has been a positive margin only in 1981 and rather large negative margins in 1983, 1984 and 1986.

This implies that the local output price has risen faster than average input price. But some inputs are imports or exportables. This could indicate that earnings from exports are larger than expenditure on imported and/or exportable inputs (direct effect) or exports have risen as a percentage of total output (indirect effect). The data on the value of exports, dyes and chemicals (imported input) and cotton lint (exportable input) for the years 1983 to 1988 by Friendship are shown in Table 7.4 (million TSh's).[5] However, the value and quantity of exports have fluctuated. The encouraging increase in 1987 was not sustained in 1988. On the whole, the increase in operational margin noted above does not seem to be attributable to higher exports.

Therefore, if the policy of devaluation is to provide price signals encouraging exports, then these results suggest that the policy has failed at least for this firm. Nevertheless, exports have definitely increased in 1987. If the explanation for this could not be found in an 'automatic' price reaction and in purely coincidental factors, than it would have to be explained as an institutional attempt to make a policy work, against the odds. The next chapter will return to this issue.

Morogoro Canvas

Morogoro Canvas Mill, a relatively new mill, started production in 1984. Designed to supply Morogoro-based factories with canvas, its customers failed to purchase their planned requirements from the mill, and Morogoro Canvas had to search for other markets.

Exports (see Table 7.5) at first were promoted to earn foreign exchange for the purchase of foreign inputs through retention schemes to produce for the domestic market. But by the end of 1988, more than half of the mill's production went to exports, which by then were also promoted for their higher returns after the large devaluations had taken place.

Because of the high share of exports in total sales, Morogoro Canvas is exceptional in the sense that one would expect this firm to suffer less or even gain from devaluation, especially after adjusting its export share to

Table 7.5   Morogoro Canvas Mill capacity utilization and exports (% of total sales)

	1984	1985	1986	1987
capacity utilization spinning	46	67	77	72
capacity utilization weaving	47	65	70	70
capacity utilization processing	26	35	26	31
exports (% of production)*		0	7	39

Note: *54 % of production was exported in 1988.

the new situation. Table 7.5 shows that the export share did increase rapidly from 1986 onwards.

Capacity utilization (see Table 7.5) has been high in spinning and weaving and low in processing. This has been both due to marketing problems and a strategy to save foreign exchange (processing is heavily dependent on imported inputs).

No quantitative information was obtained on finance costs, but during an interview it was confirmed that the high shilling values of the current foreign loans will pose enormous problems for this firm if no solutions are found.

The cost structure is shown as a percentage of total costs in Table 7.6, and as a percentage of value of production in Table 7.7. No information on quantity of production was obtained. The following observations can be made about Tables 7.6 and Table 7.7 and the accompanying Figures (7.3 and 7.4).

First, from the figures on depreciation it appears that capital was revalued in 1986. Second, cotton costs increased as a percentage of the value of output until 1987 and declined slightly in 1988. Since cotton prices in fact rose in 1988, this implies that the average output price for Morogoro Canvas increased faster. With the high export share, this is not implausible. Third, wages have declined in importance as input cost both compared to total costs and to value of production (respectively 2 percent and 3 percent in 1987 and 1988). These low shares reflect a rather modern technology in combination with high labour efficiency. Fourth, the cost of chemicals decreased before 1986 and increased afterwards (see Table 7.6 and Table 7.7). The relative

Figure 7.3   Morogoro Canvas cost structure (as % of total costs per metre)

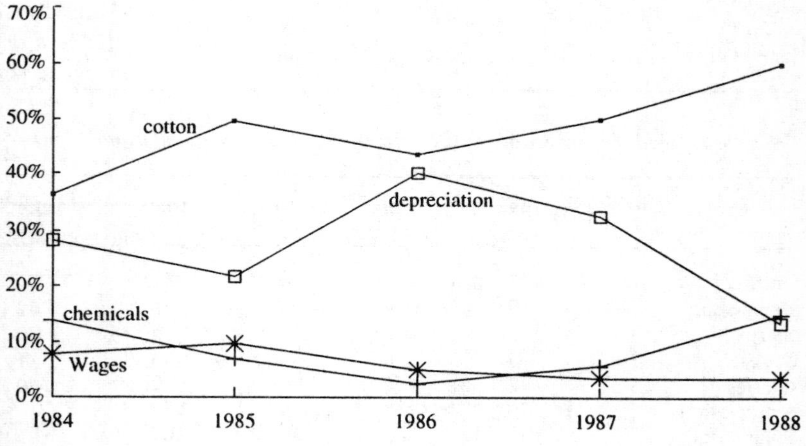

Source: Based on data in Table 7.6.

Figure 7.4   Morogoro Canvas cost structure (as % of total value)

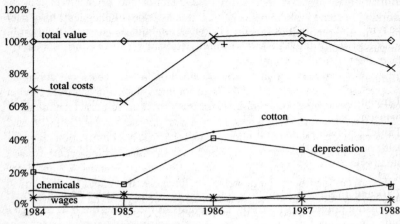

Source: Based on data in Table 7.7.

Table 7.6   Morogoro Canvas Mill cost structure (% of total costs)

	1984	**1985**	**1986**	**1987**	**1988**
cotton	36	49	43	49	59
chemicals	14	7	2	5	15
energy	12	10	9	9	8
wages	7	10	5	3	3
salaries	3	3	2	2	2
depreciation	28	21	40	32	13

Table 7.7   Morogoro Canvas Mill cost structure (% of value of production)

	1984	**1985**	**1986**	**1987**	**1988**
cotton	25	31	43	51	48
chemicals	10	4	2	6	12
energy	8	6	9	9	6
wages	5	6	5	3	3
salaries	2	2	2	2	2
depreciation	20	13	40	33	10
Total costs	70	63	101	103	81

costs of chemicals is lowest in 1986, whereas 1987 saw the lowest capacity utilization in processing. A combined quantity and price effect may be working in some years in opposite direction as prices of chemicals have risen fast. Finally, reported total costs (i.e. excluding finance costs and overheads) surpassed value of production in 1986 and 1987.

Tanganyika Textiles Manufacturers

Tanganyika Textiles Manufacturers is a small to medium size private firm engaged in weaving and processing. Its capacity utilization (see Table 7.8) was at its highest point in 1982 but declined thereafter; in 1988 it dropped drastically to 17 percent. The years of the ERP show a steady decline.

The following observations can be made on the basis of Table 7.8 to 7.10 and Figures 7.5 and 7.6. First, Tanganyika Textiles Manufacturers was using polyester yarn in the early years of the 1980s but later phased it out, switching fully to domestic cotton yarn when foreign exchange became increasingly scarce. Second, dyes and chemicals (another imported input) declined in relative terms and increased very little in absolute terms, which means that quantities must have been reduced as prices were rising. Tanganyika Textiles Manufacturers has therefore shifted its production away from the foreign exchange intensive inputs. Despite this, capacity utilization has been falling. Third, depreciation has been a very small fraction of total costs. Apparently, no revaluation of

Table 7.8   Tanganyika Textiles Manufacturers, cost structure (% of total costs)*

	1980	1981	1982	1983	1984	1985	1986	1987	1988
Capacity utilization (%)	41	51	55	51	36	46	43	35	17
cotton yarn	22	41	48	44	47	56	59	59	69
polyester yarn	28	14	1	5	3	0	0	0	0
dyes & chemicals	5	3	6	3	3	2	3	3	2
energy	5	5	5	7	5	7	8	5	6
maintenance	4	4	6	6	6	4	3	4	3
wages	31	25	29	30	30	25	24	25	15
salaries	3	3	3	3	4	3	2	2	2
depreciation	0.5	0.4	0.4	0.4	0.3	0.2	0.2	0.2	0.2
pol. + dy. & ch.	32	17	7	8	6	2	3	3	2
cot. + pol. yarn	49	55	48	48	50	56	59	59	69

Note: *Minor cost items not included in the table.

*Table 7.9   Tanganyika Textiles Manufacturers, cost structure
(% of value of production)**

	1980	1981	1982	1983	1984	1985	1986	1987	1988
cotton yarn	19	32	34	30	38	49	51	50	65
pol. yarn	24	11	0	3	3	0	0	0	0
dyes & chem.	4	3	4	2	2	2	2	2	2
energy	4	4	4	4	4	6	7	4	5
maintenance	4	3	4	4	5	3	2	3	3
wages	26	19	21	20	24	22	21	21	14
salaries	3	3	2	2	3	3	2	2	2
depreciation	0.4	0.3	0.3	0.2	0.3	0.2	0.2	0.1	0.2

Note: * Minor cost items not included in the table.

capital was carried out to reflect higher replacement costs resulting from currency devaluations. Fourthly, as in other firms, wages increased much more slowly than either output price or total input costs. Fifth, the costs of cotton yarn per metre of fabric increased rapidly, from TSh. 1.8 in 1980 to TSh. 44.4 in 1988; yarn costs doubled between 1987 and 1988.

Figure 7.5   Tanganyika Textiles cost structure (as % of total costs)

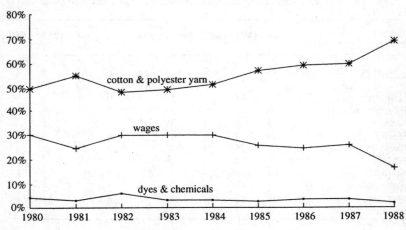

Source: Based on data in Table 7.8.

Figure 7.6 Tanganyika Textiles cost structure (in TShs per metre)

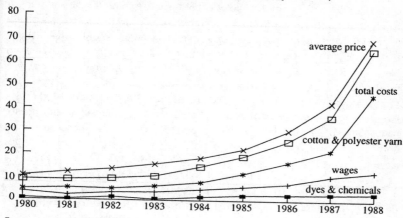

Source: de Valk (1992).

Total reported costs have increased faster than the average price, so that margins, certainly in real terms, have declined (see Figure 7.6). Since some costs have not been reported (for example overhead costs and finance costs) actual profits based on these figures would become negative.

From the firm-level data in the previous pages, the following conclusions can be drawn. First, the general trend is one of decreasing profit margins. Secondly, the only exception, the Friendship Mill, is also an exception in

Table 7.10 Tanganyika Textiles, cost structure (TSh/mtr)

	1980	1981	1982	1983	1984	1985	1986	1987	1988
cotton yarn	1.8	3.4	4.2	4.3	6.4	10.2	14.5	20.2	44.4
pol. yarn	2.3	1.1	0.0	0.5	0.4	0.0	0.0	0.0	0.0
dyes & chem.	0.4	0.3	0.5	0.3	0.4	0.4	0.7	0.9	1.2
energy	0.4	0.4	0.5	0.6	0.7	1.3	1.9	1.6	3.7
maintenance	0.3	0.3	0.5	0.6	0.8	0.7	0.7	1.3	2.1
wages	2.5	2.0	2.6	2.9	4.0	4.5	5.8	8.4	9.9
salaries	0.3	0.3	0.3	0.3	0.6	0.6	0.6	0.8	1.5
depreciation	0.0	0.0	0.0	0.0	0.0	0.0	0.1	0.1	0.1
average price	9.6	10.7	12.3	14.5	16.8	20.8	28.3	40.3	68.4
co. + pol. yarn	4.0	4.5	4.2	4.8	6.8	10.2	14.5	20.2	44.4
Total costs	8.2	8.3	8.8	9.8	13.6	18.0	24.7	34.0	64.2

capacity utilization and allocation of foreign exchange. Thirdly, finance costs are generally increasing, this includes, but is not limited to, the servicing of foreign commitments. Fourth, depreciation costs increased erratically depending on firm practices. When viewed as savings in domestic currency for replacing old equipment, past savings may be wiped out by devaluation. New depreciation charges must cover both exchange rate induced losses and the higher prices for imported capital equipment. Fifth, there have been drastic increases in the relative price of cotton. Sixth, there have been drastic increases in relative prices of imported inputs, but to some extent substitution has taken place by using less imported inputs and/or selling more unprocessed cloth (processing is the more import-intensive production stage). Seventh, wage and salary costs have gone down relative to other costs, despite declining capacity utilization coupled with employment levels which are rather inflexible downwards. Therefore wage and salary *rates* have declined even faster. Finally, most industries will face serious problems in continuing production if remedial measures are not taken.

Most of these changes can be understood as the normal effects of liberalization and devaluation. However the firm level effects can be quite devastating. For example, Morogoro Canvas is facing serious problems in servicing its foreign loans.

7.4   MESO-FACTORS AFFECTING PERFORMANCE

Under-utilization of capacity (or rather strategic over-capacity) is a typical feature of oligopolistic sectors (see Chapter 2) and indeed played a strategic role in the early phase of industrialization in Tanzania in the 1960s (Rweyemamu 1973). However, demand expansion during the early 1970s overtook supply. Expansion of the number of firms and the resulting installed capacity followed demand with a lag and reached its peak in the latter half of the 1980s. Despite the expansion of the number of firms, the degree of concentration of the sector is still high. The consequences of concentration for competitiveness are more serious when taking account of the high transportation costs between regions (horizontal differentiation). The peak in installed capacity occurred at a time when local demand was no longer growing and was increasingly being satisfied by imports. Individual firms controlled the market by their relation with marketing networks, which had developed over time. Firms attempt to control their economic environment on the demand side by product specialization and on the supply side by a tendency towards increasing vertical integration and horizontal networks (or integration).

The present section described the textile sector in terms of some general characteristics. The next section will focus on sectoral factors relevant to firm conduct and performance. These are (a) the degree of concentration of capacity and production, (b) demand, (c) spatial structure of capacity in relation to population, (d) vertical and horizontal integration, (e) marketing structure, and (f) the supply of infrastructural inputs. Apart from the last, these factors tend to enhance the degree of control that firms exert over their environment including their output market.

Sectoral concentration indices for capacity and production

In Chapter 2 (section 2.2.3) formulas were presented for calculating indices of concentration, the Gini-coefficient (GC) and the Herfindahl index (HI). Below these indices are calculated for the distribution of installed capacity and production in weaving. The data for installed capacity are drawn from Table A.5 and data for production (1987) from Table 6.4.

$$HI_{cap} = 0.099, \qquad HI_{prod} = 0.143$$
$$HI_{cap}^{r},19 = 0.52931, \qquad HI_{prod}^{r},17 = 0.412213$$
$$GC_{cap} = 0.502, \qquad GC_{prod} = 0.580$$

GC and HI can be compared as follows. GC approaches unity for the case of full concentration and zero when all firms are the same (even for the case of two firms). HI declines very quickly from one for full concentration to values close to zero. For example: with one firm per sector HI=1, with two equal-size firms per sector HI=.5, for three equal firms per sector HI=.333. Thus, with equal firms, HI measures the share of each firm. Inequality between firms will be superimposed on the effect of the number of firms. HI thus includes both the effects of the number of firms as well as the inequality between the firms, and it moves in the same direction as the Gini-coefficient as inequality increases. In order to compare HI better to GC, the effect of the number of firms can be removed by comparing the actual HI to the HI obtained for the same number of firms but with equal firm size ($HI_{19}=0.0526$ and $HI_{17}=0.0588$ where 19 and 17 stand for the number of firms used in the calculation for capacity and production respectively). $HI_{cap}^{r},19$ is now defined as HI_{19} divided by HI_{cap} (with a similar definition for $HI_{prod}^{r},17$). With this definition HI^{r} not only excludes effects of the number of firms but also moves in an opposite direction (between 0 and 1) when compared to GC.[6]

Both measures show that production is more concentrated than capacity, indicating that larger firms tend to use more of their installed capacity. The

Gini-coefficient indicates a rather unequal distribution but this offers no clues with regard to economic implications. The Herfindahl index is used in the calculation of the average mark-up under oligopoly, as shown in equation 2.12 in Chapter 2. Making some simplifying assumptions on the elasticity of demand and the degree of collusion (e=1 and a_i=0, so that their combined effect becomes unity) HI measures the mark-up over unit costs expressed as percentage of the price. With $HI_{prod} = 0.143$, a mark-up of roughly 14 percent does not appear as excessively high. However if a_i=1 (which means that total output would increase respectively decrease by the amount by which firm (i) increases or decreases its output), the mark-up rate would become 29 percent, which is quite high. This indicates a moderate level of concentration and does not rule out collusive behaviour.

Spatial distribution of capacity and its relation to population

The nationwide indices for concentration give only limited insight in the nature of market dominance of particular firms. High transport costs due to long distances, poor transport infrastructure and poor communication networks have created a degree of regional protection. Table 7.11 identifies four regions and their hinterland: Lake Victoria, Kilimanjaro, Tanga, and Dar es Salaam. These regions are assumed to be serviced in the first place by their own textile firms.

Capacity per head in the three main regions, Lake Victoria, Kilimanjaro, and Dar es Salaam, at 12.1, 13.6 and 15.1 metres per head respectively, is roughly comparable to the nationwide capacity per head of 12.8 metres. Tanga has a lower capacity per head (6.7 metres) first of all because it is smaller than the other regions and secondly because its market may be partly serviced by firms of other regions. The Lake Victoria region is serviced by two large public sector firms. In the Arusha region there are two private sector firms and one public sector firm. One would expect that these private sector firms would benefit from some degree of collusion. The Dar es Salaam region has the largest number of both public (5) and private (4) textile producers. But even these numbers are quite small and collusion would be feasible. Thus hotelling effects (horizontal product differentiation) would tend to strengthen the possibilities for collusion.[7]

Demand and effective capacity

To assess the implications of the overall concentration of production and the regional capacity per head of the population (hotelling effects) it is necessary to know the absolute size of domestic demand for locally produced textiles and its relation to total effective capacity. Therefore this section estimates demand for textiles, compares this estimate with others, and provides initial estimates of effective productive capacity in textiles.

Demand per capita (Table A.9), can be taken as approximately 0.9 kg corresponding with about 4.5 square metres. This estimate is consistent with Figure A.2, with estimates made by the FAO as quoted in URT (1990d), and with World Bank estimates (World Bank 1987c). It sharply contradicts the estimates of up to 25 metres per head (Table A.9) made by the Ministry of Industries and Trade (URT 1990d) based on figures about second-hand imports that are not confirmed by EC data. In Table A.9 other imports based on the same unreliable data are included and lead to a jump in per capita consumption of 100 percent to 8 metres per person in 1988. TEXCO also postulates a very high per capita textile consumption of 16 meters per head but this is not supported by the evidence (TEXCO 1986). Thus, per caput consumption is taken as about 0.9 kilo. This is equivalent to 20700 tons or 100.5 million metres for the whole population.

Table 7.11   Regional capacity and population

Regions	Population	Capacity (million mtr)	Capacity (metres/head)
Lake Victoria[a]			
Centre	3 204 454	82.2	25.7
Hinterland	3 597 508		
Total	6 801 962	82.2	12.1
Kilimanjaro[b]			
Centre	2 460 374	33.5	13.6
Tanga[c]	1 283 636	8.6	6.7
Dar es Salaam[d]			
Centre	3 221 637	120.6	35.3
Hinterland	4 766 104		
Total	7 987 741		15.1
Tanzania	22 533 758	288.2	12.8

Notes: (a) Centre regions are Kagera and Mwanza; Hinterland regions are Mara, Shinyanga, and Kigoma.
(b) Centre regions are Arusha and Kilimanjaro.
(c) Tanga is the only region.
(d) Centre regions are Dar es Salaam, Coast region, and Morogoro; Hinterland regions are Lindi, Mtwara, Ruvuma, Dodoma, and Iringa.

Source: Table A.5 for data on capacity and Bureau of Statistics (1988) for 1988 population data.

The sector should be able to produce about 288.2 million linear metres for the domestic market, which corresponds to 345.8 million square meters. A number of factors are at work that effectively reduce this capacity. First, engineering capacity is never reached so that a normal attainable capacity utilization of about 80 percent can be assumed. Second, inefficiency (relative total factor productivity as calculated in Chapter 8) reduces capacity by a factor of 46.4.[8] Third, power and water problems lower capacity another 34.7 percent.[9] Fourth, at any given time 10 percent of all machines will normally be off-line. Together these factors reduce the effective installed capacity to $345.8 \cdot (1-0.2) \cdot (1-0.347) \cdot 0.464 \cdot 0.9 =$ 75.4 million metres or about 3.28 metres per caput.

This figure is very close to what was actually produced: 61.9 in 1986, 61.0 in 1987, 50.1 in 1988, and 57.3 in 1989. Other constraints to production, such as foreign exchange and credit, could account for the difference of roughly 15 million metres (which is less than one third of the installed capacity of Mwatex). If these constraint could be released and production increased above this level, competition would start between firms and with imports; price, taste, and quality would then become important parameters.[10]

Vertical and horizontal integration

Vertical integration has been described in Chapter 2 as arising from minimization of transaction costs. In an economy with poorly developed infrastructure, and a small, protected industrial sector, transaction costs are usually high. Quality and timely delivery of inputs cannot easily be ensured. When, in addition, upstream sections of the value chain are characterized by oligopolistic conditions, the resulting economic rents can be captured be vertical integration.

As will be shown later when discussing individual firm characteristics, both private and public sectors incorporate integrated textile firms. The public sector however is more integrated than the private sector, since all the public sector integrated mills were actually built as such. The private sector mills have grown more organically into integrated mills in response to their needs and opportunities. Integration in the public sector however derives from the logic of comprehensive planning, including transaction costs minimization at the theoretical level rather than as a pragmatic, economic response to increase profits and control of the economic environment.

Horizontal integration taken the form of economic groups in the private sector. Four economic groups are involved in the eight private firms while one of the eight is part of a multinational group and another two enjoy good foreign linkages through their owners.

The public sector can also be viewed as an economic group, in the first place through its holding company TEXCO and more generally through the facilities (and constraints) that public sector firms enjoy from government in terms of finance and marketing. In both cases, being part of an economic group increases control over the environment. However, horizontal integration in the public sector does not necessarily enhance efficiency and profitability, since the internal logic of the state (as discussed in Chapter 5) in combination with the functioning of public enterprises (as discussed in Chapter 2) does not produce such outcomes.

Even in the private sector, increased control has not produced high levels of efficiency. More research specifically on these issues and including the detailed operation of economic groups would be required, however, to derive the connection between vertical and horizontal integration and economic efficiency. Here, only their existence is noted and their effects on control of the economic environment in general. Chapter 8 compares their performance to their ownership structure.

Market structure

Control of the market is further strengthened by vertical product differentiation through quality and design characteristics and by product specialization. Public sector integrated mills specialize more and more in khanga, kitenge, and fabrics used in army and school uniforms. The public sector had its own marketing structure in the form of regional trading companies, but most public sector firms consider this a hinderance rather than an asset. Many private firms, some of which have emerged from trading activities themselves, have established longstanding relations with wholesale and retail networks, apparently to mutual benefit, with the traders supplying market information to the producers, i.e. prices, quantities and design characteristics.

Problems with the supply of infrastructural inputs

The erratic supply of infrastructural inputs has greatly affected production (see also Wangwe, 1979; Mbelle, 1988). Some firms have been affected more than others. Electricity supply has been a major problem for Taboratex, Mutex and Mwatex, and water has been a major problem for the Dar es Salaam based mills Sunguratex and Kiltex (DSM), for Mwatex (on the border of Lake Victoria!), and to a lesser extent for the mills in Morogoro, Polytex and Morogoro Canvas. No private sector firm has been seriously affected by these inputs; any private firm affected to the same extent as the above mentioned public sector firms would have gone bankrupt long ago.

Table 7.12 summarizes information on the use of water and electricity, and problems experienced with the supply of these inputs. The actual values of energy and water use per ton of output are respectively called the specific energy requirement (SER) and the specific water usage (SWU). These depend on the type of processes carried out in the firm and are therefore firm specific. Whether or not requirements are high, normal or low can only be judged by experienced engineers.

The Dar es Salaam mills Sunguratex and Kiltex, located almost next to each other, have experienced increasingly severe water problems as the city expanded. Friendship, in a different area of Dar es Salaam, has been supplied reasonably well through some adjustment in the water supply routes. All three mills have been affected by frequent power cuts. The Morogoro based mills Polytex and Morogoro Canvas also reported water problems and power interruptions. Mills located in Arusha and Tanga experienced no problems in the supply of utilities. Mwatex and Mutex, both on Lake Victoria, have had a combined water and power problem, which for Mwatex was less severe in the beginning of the 1980s. Despite the water supply problems of many mills, water use remains very inefficient; only Sunflag is an efficient user.

Water usage was inefficient for both public and private sector firms. Although the price of water is low and therefore the direct costs of inefficient use are not very significant, inefficient water use under conditions of shortage leads directly to production losses. In the case of energy, public sector firms were much more inefficient users, with higher than necessary energy bills. The problem of inefficient energy usage was aggravated by the low level of capacity utilization causing standing losses.

A rough estimate of production losses resulting from inadequate supply of utilities would be about 100 million metres per year, calculated on the basis of full capacity. When attainable capacity is taken to be 70 percent of full capacity the estimated losses would be 72.7 million metres per year.[11] About 82 percent of these losses are accounted for by four public sector firms: Mutex (15.4 percent), Mwatex (36.9 percent), Sunguratex (12.1 percent) and Kiltex (17.2 percent).

7.5   MICRO-FACTORS AFFECTING PERFORMANCE

Micro-factors affecting firm performance (see Chapter 2) mainly concern the behaviour of managers and labour (principals and agents). The behavioural theory of the firm in particular is concerned with the motivation of labour through identification with the firm's goals and personal pride in

Table 7.12 Water and energy use and supply problems

Firm	Water use m³/ton	Electricity use GJ/ton	Efficiency of usage	Problems
Public				
Friendship (Dar es Salaam)	479	105.8	Energy use about normal, water use excessive	Frequent power cuts
Sunguratex (Dar es Salaam)	387	240	Both water and energy use should be 50% less	Processing limited to 30% due to water shortage
Kiltex (DSM) (Dar es Salaam)	107	n.a.	Water use is excessive	Processing limited to 15% due to water shortage
Kiltex (Arusha)	171	105.1	Energy use too high, water use excessive	No supply problems
Taboratex (Tabora)	n.a.	n.a.		No electricity supplied yet since 1984
Mutex (Musoma)	908	328.9	Both water and energy use are excessive	Low production: gets only half of power requirements
Mwatex (Mwanza)	645	244.4	Both water and energy use are excessive	Only one quarter of required electricity supplied
Tanzania Sewing Thread (Morogoro)	780	98	Both are excessive; should be at 150 m³/t resp. 40 GJ/t	No supply problems
Polytex (Morogoro)	340	124.7	Energy use about right, water use excessive	Problems with water supply: loss of 1.5 days/month

Table 7.12 continued

Firm	Water use m³/ton	Electricity use GJ/ton	Efficiency of usage	Problems
Private				
CIC (Tanga)	n.a.	66.6		No problems reported
Tanganyika Textiles (Dar es Salaam)	108	23.9	Water use twice the needed amount	Frequent power cuts major cause of low productivity
JV Textiles (Dar es Salaam)	157	67.8	Water usage too high; energy usage efficient	No major supply problems
A to Z (Arusha)	162	52.9	Water use about 300% too high; energy use is efficient	No major supply problems
Sunflag (Arusha)	122	84.7	Efficient use of water and energy	
Kilimanjaro Blankets (Tanga)	n.a.	n.a.		No supply problems

Note: n.a. = not available.
Source: Compiled from Ministry of Industries and Trade (URT 1990d).

the job and the role of society therein, whereas the evolutionary theory of the firm, in a Schumpeterian vein, stresses the importance of the entrepreneur in both normal and search routines. Some firms are better at this than others. De la Torre (1984) identifies 'growth firms', 'surviving firms', and 'struggling firms' in the private textile sector in the UK (see Chapter 4).

While concepts developed in behavioural theories in principle apply to any kind of organization (including those in the public sector), theories of public enterprises have shown that both workers and managers tend to dissociate themselves from the goals of the firms. Subsequent analysis of the state and its relation to public enterprise has given more evidence of this dissociation. Within the literature the main divide with regard to ownership and performance is along the public-private line. However, various forms of ownership and management exist within both the private and public sector which bear on the nature of behaviour and the range of possible actions. The extent of international connections at this level also has important consequences for firm conduct and performance in terms of foreign exchange availability, export market information, and finance capital.[12] Thus, factors of ownership, management, and international relations influence both the nature and scope of firm conduct. Firm level details on ownership and management are given in Table 8.3; details on international relations arising partly as a consequence of ownership and management relations and partly as a consequence of trade relations.

The conduct of labour can be influenced by wages and incentives relative to other firms (see Table 8.3) in addition to the more general influences identified by behavioural theories. Labour conduct can be measured, to some extent, by information on labour turnover (see Table 8.3) and the incidence of absenteeism, about which no systematic information is available.

However, as discussed at the end of Chapter 2, in addition to conduct related factors, structural factors can be identified at the firm level which translate the impact of changes in the economic environment differently depending on their firm by firm incidence. For example, UNIDO took the firm level export/import ratio as the core of its analysis of firms' success during structural adjustment. But there are other micro-factors that need to be considered when analysing the firm level impact of changes in macrovariables under a policy of liberalization. These are first factors related to improvements in production performance required to face domestic and international competition, such as age, type, technological diversity, and technical condition of the firm's machinery (Table 8.3).

Second, financial factors play a role in adjustment problems, especially with regard to the large devaluations of the Tanzanian shilling. Foreign loans need to be repaid in hard currency using revenue raised in domestic currency. To compensate for devaluation, profits would have to rise at the same rate as the devaluation. However the opposite, i.e. a profit squeeze, has been the result of liberalization. (Data on foreign loans by firm are given in Table 8.5 insofar as these are available.) The situation is worse when it comes to savings put aside for physical capital replacement, i.e. depreciation charges. Past savings are eroded to virtually nil, while new depreciation charges must cover both lost past savings as well as higher foreign prices for capital goods because of devaluation. The older the machinery is, and thus the more in need of replacement, the more acute this problem is. In reality, replacement becomes new investment, financed through new foreign commitments.[13]

Finally, there may be some firm level factors that have a negative influence on performance *per se*. One example is that of wrong location with regard to cotton supply and markets such as is the case for Mbeyatex and Mutex. However, it may also be argued that this is an outcome of the ownership dimension, i.e. by the fact that these firms are owned by the state which has multiple objectives, not all of which are economic. Another example would be firm size, but here as well the large firms are public ones and the small firms are private. Once again, the explanation can be sought in the internal logic of the state, which in this instance seems to prefer large scale enterprises.

7.6 CONCLUSIONS

This chapter has reviewed macro-, meso-, and micro-level factors affecting the performance of textile firms. The foreign exchange constraint, which affected capacity utilization and maintenance activities, was replaced in later years by a credit constraint, showing the poor liquidity position of many firms. This was shown to be the combined result of actual foreign exchange allocation, pricing policies (including the price of foreign exchange and money, and prices of competitive goods), and problems with the supply of infrastructural inputs. It was argued that meso-factors (in addition to commodity import support) have contributed to firms' survival. Especially TEXCO's account of constraints and the differences of opinion on on credit between TEXCO and the NBC shed light on the processes involved in lobbying between different coalitions within government. Micro-level factors were reviewed mainly as preparation for a detailed analysis of performance in the next chapter. The next chapter will present a cross-section analysis of micro-factors affecting performance, supplemented by a time series analysis of macro-factors affecting performance.

Notes

1. Seven firms did not indicate how much foreign exchange was received. In addition, some of those who responded did not provide the information for all years requested. The results are also distorted by the fact that reporting is more complete for the more recent years. And, of course, no firm admitted the possibility of obtaining foreign exchange outside legitimate channels.

2. In February 1988 the Tanzanian Daily News reported that between June and December 1987 collected customs import duty and sales tax averaged about 400 million shillings per month, but when collection procedures were strengthened in January 1988 an average of 1.5 billion shillings per month were collected. Strengthening procedures included suspending and/or transferring some customs officials. Goods covered included new and second-hand clothes as well as khanga.

3. See Chapter 5, note 6 for a list of these items.

4. The source of data for this section is the author's own survey unless otherwise stated.

5. The figure for dyes and chemicals in 1987 as it has been reported is probably wrong as it was a repetition of the figure for 1986.

6. Both GC and HI move in the same direction if HI is redefined by subtracting HI^{rel} from unity.

7. The above analysis is only a first approximation. It does not take into account differences that exist between regions in terms of income per caput, income distribution, demand composition between rural and urban dwellers, and the role that regions play in trade with their hinterland. Neither are transport costs calculations available to show the extent of regional protection. Furthermore some regions have not been allocated to a particular textile producing region since it was unclear how these regions are in fact serviced.

8. This is calculated as the weighted average of the RTFP in Table 6.7 using installed capacity (Table A.5) as weights. The RTFP of Mwatex and Sunguratex has been taken as .3 because the low value calculated in Table 6.7 was based on overall machine productivity (including stoppages for interruptions in supply of utilities).

9. This corresponds to the ratio of the estimated loss of about 100 million metres over total installed capacity of 288.2 million metres.

10. One omission in the calculation of demand and supply has been imports other than second-hand clothes. Since these would enter both in the estimation of demand and supply the above analysis is not affected by this omission.

11. Based on the observations in Table 7.24, the following percentages for production losses relative to full capacity output have been used: Friendship 10 percent, Sunguratex 70 percent, Kiltex (DSM) 85 percent, Mutex 50 percent, Mwatex 75 percent, Polytex 5 percent, Morogoro Canvas 5 percent, Tanganyika Textiles 10 percent. When these percentages are applied to full capacity figures for weaving (electricity) or processing (water) in Table A.5, a loss of 103.8 million metres per year is obtained. However, when there have been other capacity reducing factors at work, such as faulty machinery or foreign exchange shortages, this figure should be adjusted downwards to reflect losses with respect to attainable capacity. If attainable capacity is a bit arbitrarily put at 70 percent, the estimated losses would decrease to 72.7 million metres per year.

12. These international relations include those between private firms and donors who, during the 1980s, developed a taste for private sector assistance, for example through the Commodity Import Support (CIS) Programme.

13. See de Valk (1992) for information on rehabilitation requirements. As some firms are in fact proposed for closure, the data on rehabilitation give only restricted information on capital replacement requirements. De Valk (1992) also gives information on which (parts of) firms are proposed for closure.

8 Performance Analysis of Textile Firms in Tanzania

8.1 INTRODUCTION

The aim of this chapter is: first, to obtain a better understanding of the different aspects of textile firms' performance and the relation between them; second, to identify more systematically the factors that have affected performance; and third, to analyse the interrelationships that may exist because different levels of explanation were employed in the analysis and some explanatory factors may cluster.

The theoretical framework developed in Chapter 2 has identified structural and behavioural micro-factors, sectoral meso-factors, national macro-factors and international mega-factors. The preview of explanatory factors in Chapter 7 has proceeded from the macro- to the micro-factors. Below the opposite direction will be taken, i.e. from micro-factors upwards. First, in section 8.2, the various performance indicators developed in Chapter 6 will be further refined in order to make a cross-sectional comparison and aggregation (for 1988) possible. Second, in section 8.3, these performance indicators will be discussed in relation to firm-specific explanatory factors with the help of regression analysis. The first performance indicator to be analysed is the relative labour coefficient, followed by the RTFP (relative total factor productivity which measures technical management), residual capacity underutilization (after allowance for RTFP, measuring all other factors which have been labelled organizational management), gross and net profitability (measuring financial management), export performance and finally investment performance. All these indices are combined in a total performance index. Third, in section 8.4, a time series analysis will be undertaken for exports of the whole sector and for net profits and capacity utilization of public sector firms (no time series data for the private sector were available) relating performance in terms of exports, net profits, and capacity utilization to sectoral and macro-factors such as the exchange rate, the overall balance of payments, interest rate, inflation and price. Finally, the chapter shows that the public/private dichotomy is in some respects false, since the question is more complex, as is the relationship between capacity utilization and domestic and export demand.

Table 8.1 Performance indicators, 1988

| | Technical | | | | | Organizational | | |
| | Spinning | | Weaving | | RTFP average | Capacity util. | Org.[1] perf. index | Org.[2] index excl. ut. |
	RLC	RTFP	RLC	RTFP				
Public								
Sunguratex	3.4	47.7	26.0	28.0	38.4	15	53.5	100.0
Friendship	1.1	87.2	2.0	46.6	66.9	42	90.2	100.0
Ubungo Spinning	4.6	64.7			64.7	19	29.4	29.4
Mbeyatex	5.2	78.6			78.6	1	1.3	1.3
Kiltex (Arusha)[4]	37.2	72.0	3.6	79.0	75.5	14	17.7	17.7
Mutex	7.0	51.2	4.0	64.8	58.0	6	9.3	18.6
Polytex	9.0	61.9	2.8	45.1	53.6	41	90.6	95.7
Mwatex	35.9	41.1	4.8	29.4	35.3	4	13.6	54.3
Morogoro Canvas[5]					72.8	69	94.8	94.8
Private								
A to Z	4.7	39.1			39.1	28	71.6	71.6
CIC	5.7	61.9	2.0	75.3	68.6	75	99.6	99.6
Sunflag	9.1	29.0	1.6	70.7	49.9	34	48.1	48.1
Cotex (L)	4.0	57.5			57.5	32	55.6	55.6
Cotex (DSM)			3.5	33.5	33.5	29	86.4	86.4
Calico			3.0	65.5	65.5	48	73.3	73.3
JV Industries			2.4	51.7	51.7	25	48.4	48.4
JV Textiles			2.8	81.5	81.5	55	67.5	67.5

Table 8.1 continued

	Financial			Export	Investment	Total	
	Gross prof. as % of sales[3]	Net prof. as % of sales	Fin. index	Exp. index	Inv. index	Total perf. index A	Total perf. index B
Public							
Sunguratex	−28	−91	6.0	0	0	30.5	45.0
Friendship	15	1	67.4	80	0	72.7	75.7
Ubungo Spinning	−60	−162	0.9	100	0	47.7	47.7
Mbeyatex	26	−645	0.0	20	0	25.6	25.6
Kiltex (Arusha)[4]	−32	−89	6.3	0	0	31.1	31.1
Mutex	−18	−1135	0.0	0	0	21.0	23.9
Polytex	−126	−750	0.0	40	0	46.4	47.9
Mwatex	−149	−793	0.0	0	0	15.3	28.0
Morogoro Canvas[5]	21	−3	60.2	100	0	74.3	74.3
Private							
A to Z	22	−5	56.9	60	75	57.6	57.6
CIC	26	2	67.6	80	50	77.7	77.7
Sunflag	27	13	90.5	100	25	62.8	62.8
Cotex (I.)				0	0	51.4	51.4
Cotex (DSM)	−5	−49	18.1	20	0	43.8	43.8
Calico				20	50	66.3	66.3
JV Industries				0	75	48.9	48.9
JV Textiles	20	3	70.5	40	25	70.6	70.6

Notes: (1) Organizational performance is total capacity utilization divided by RTFP weaving or by RTFP spinning when weaving is not appropriate; (2) Organizational index excluding the effect of problems in the supply of utilities; (3) Gross and net profit rates are based on three year averages; (4) Gross and net profit rates are for Kiltex (Arusha) and Kiltex (DSM) combined. They are only used to calculate the overall performance index for Kiltex (Arusha) but excluded in other analyses; (5) The RTFP for Morogoro Canvas has been estimated on the basis of Table 10.7. The corresponding organizational and total indices are based on this estimate. *Source:* Based on tables presented in Chapter 8.

8.2   FIRM PERFORMANCE (1988): CONSOLIDATION

Chapter 6 discussed various performance measures. This section summarizes these measures in order to clarify the linkages and complementarities between some of them. To this end some further refinement of these indicators is required.

The simplest performance indicator is the relative labour coefficient (RLC). When combined with the relative capital coefficient by means of the methodology employed in Chapter 6, the first measure of performance, the relative total factor productivity (RTFP) or 'technical performance' is obtained.

Technical performance is one of the factors limiting full utilization of capacity (as discussed section 7.4.3 for the case of the whole sector).

After accounting for technical performance, one can identify the residual underutilization of capacity, referred to here as 'organizational performance' and encompassing all non-technical factors that limit capacity utilization. Thus, the first index of organizational performance (OPI-A) is defined as overall capacity utilization divided by the RTFP for weaving (or divided by the RTFP for spinning when there is no weaving). It includes performance with regard to internal organization[1] arranging for supply of inputs, utilities, credit and foreign exchange and other matters of organization that allow effective use of capacity. To exclude the effects of problems in the supply of utilities, a second organizational index (OPIB) is defined by dividing OPI-A by a factor that takes into account the estimated percentage loss in production (Table 7.12).[2]

Combined with technical and organizational performance, financial performance determines final profitability. Financial performance relates to cost control, price setting and marketing, optimal stock management, etc. The initial measure of financial performance employed here is gross profits over sales (GP/S), and the second is net profits over sales (NP/S). This last measure is converted into an index by employing an exponential transformation that ensures that highly negative values do not dominate the more 'normal' values.[3]

Export performance can be measured by the proportion of sales exported. Export performance is to some extent an outcome of financial performance (highest revenue), organizational performance (supply of foreign exchange), and technical performance (quality achieved). However, it requires special market linkages and networks, and a special effort in quality control. Moreover, the highest attainable level of exports is not necessarily optimal from the firms' point of view. In this respect, public sector firms are different from private sector firms as, on the one hand, national objectives to increase exports may determine a public firm's export efforts while, on the other, even without exports such firms may obtain foreign exchange from government. For private firms, exports are more essential for survival. Given the rough information supplied by firms, export performance has been rated on a scale of 0 to 100 in steps of 20, using personal judgement where necessary.[4] An index of 100 implies that 50 percent of sales or more is exported.

Investment performance, measuring firm level innovation and dynamism, is based on the information supplied in section 6.3.7 and has been somewhat subjectively rated on a scale of 0 to 100, in steps of 25, to reflect the general nature of the information.

The total performance index (TPI) is composed of technical, organizational, financial performance (all weighted by a factor 100) and export and investment performance (both weighted by a factor 10). Two versions (TPI-A and TPI-B) are shown using OPI-A and OPIB, respectively, in its definition. Ignoring the differences between indices A and B, the total performance index (TPI) can be written as:

$$TPI = 100 \cdot RTFP + 100 \cdot OPI + 100 \cdot FI + 10 \cdot EI + 10 \cdot II \text{ over } 320 \qquad (8.1)$$

Technical and organizational performance are independent. Financial performance is at least partially determined by the former two, although it is not possible to say precisely to what extent. Moreover, many other factors related to financial management enter into this indicator and, as will be shown, it is dominated by servicing (foreign) loan commitments, a variable independent of technical and organizational performance. Therefore, financial performance has also been assigned a weight of 100. The low weights for export and investment performance are justified first, because export performance contributes to capacity utilization, second, because investment results from successful performance in the other categories and third, these data are more subjective than the other data. While it may be argued that the actual choice of weights is rather arbitrary, to exclude export and investment performance altogether would sacrifice information relevant to overall performance. Besides, the overall performance index is the least important the indices used here, as the analysis will mainly concentrate on the composing indices. Finally, although this study has shown that it is necessary to disaggregate the concept of performance to understand firm performance, an overall performance index constitutes an initial summary of the differentiated indices. The results are shown in Table 8.1.

Efficient firms exist in both private and public sectors whatever criterion is used. Moreover, little difference seems to exists between the aggregate

public and private sector in terms of technical performance. The private
sector ranks first in overall organizational performance, where the divergence between the public and private sectors is highest, with a ratio of
1.80. When problems with water and electricity supply are eliminated this
index drops to 1.32, but the fact remains that on the whole, the private
sector performs better on the organizational index. The private sector
scores very much better on its financial performance, with a ratio of 3.88.
The export performance of the public sector is higher (a 1.28 ratio in
favour of the public sector), while investments in the private sector are
only in a planning stage, thus making quantified comparison impossible.
Overall performance of private sector firms is higher than public sector
firms by about 48 percent but when the adjusted organizational index (B)
is used in the calculation of the overall index (B) this percentage is 35.
Although these results are not without interest in their own right, the available disaggregated data on both firm performance and explanatory factors
allow us to go beyond comparisons between the public and private sectors.
This will be undertaken in the next section.

8.3 MICRO-FACTORS AND CROSS-SECTION ANALYSIS OF PERFORMANCE (1988)

Chapter 2's discussion of theories of the firm focused first, on the consequences of the possibility of market control by oligopolistic firms (the structure-conduct-performance model), and second, on the consequences of
ownership on performance (managerial model, principal-agent theories, and
public enterprise theories). The former issue has been addressed qualitatively
in section 7.4, while the latter can be addressed here, at micro level, in a
more quantitative manner. The underlying concern with regard to ownership
is the assessment of the degree to which the owners' rationality permeates all
levels of the firm under different ownership and management arrangements.
The more differentiated concept of performance employed in this study
(as developed above) permits a more detailed analysis of the diversified
forms of ownership and management in the Tanzanian textile sector.
Macroeconomic factors that bear on performance will also be incorporated.

8.3.1 Relative labour productivity

The generally high relative labour coefficients reported in Table 8.1 may
indicate low inherent labour productivity (low skills, low motivation, high
degree of shirking), and poor technical, organizational and financial

management. For example, poor quality control in the early phases of production (such as opening, mixing, and cleaning cotton lint) leads to yarn, weft, and warp breakages and other interruptions in later phases for which labour is required.

Poor machine maintenance causes labour to be idle. Organizational failures may lead to irregular production flows. Financially, the low cost of labour may reduce the cost awareness with regard to labour use.

The nature of socialization in the family and wider society are important determinants for the process of identification with firm's objectives (see Chapter 2). A possible explanation of the lack of identification with the firm objectives could be the prevalence of a traditional 'economy of affection' in modern society. In the absence of satisfactory remuneration and decent working conditions, modern society's values lose much of their attraction. This will be reinforced by the demoralizing influence of 'rent seeking and outright corruption which have increased significantly since the early 1980s hand in hand with the decline in real salaries of civil servants' (World Bank 1991:24). Thus the nature of the state, coupled with low wages and poor working conditions will partly explain the low productivity of labour, although the strength of the influence would be difficult if not impossible to estimate.

Textile sector wage costs in Tanzania were at the very bottom of the international scale (see Table A.4). In comparison to Kenya where wage costs have increased, Tanzania's wage costs may have come down. The World Bank (1991:20) reports that in 1984 the real wage in Tanzania was only one third of its 1978 value, with formal wages for unskilled labour about equal in the private and parastatal sectors (World Bank 1991:23). However, from interviews with private firm managers it appears that workers receive benefits in kind as well, such as meals and medical treatment.

Most private sector firms reported that they prefer to attract experienced workers to minimize on job training (see Table 8.2). Most public sector firms have good training schools and facilities. One would therefore expect unskilled workers to go initially to public sector firms to receive training, and then to look for a better paid, private sector job (labour-switch effect). The higher labour productivity in the private sector would then be explained by its higher incentives, which attract more capable workers and induce them to work better. Moreover, labour turnover would then be lower for firms with higher incentives and lower relative labour coefficients.

To test the relations between relative labour coefficients and incentives, labour turnover, training facilities and overall management performance, regression analysis has been used. One would expect a positive sign for training and a negative sign for incentives and management. The

Table 8.2   *Relative total factor productivity, ownership, management and technology*

	RLC	RTFP	Labour Turnover	Incentive Schemes	Training Facilities
Public					
Sunguratex	14.7	38.4	17	2	4
Friendship	2.0	66.9	–	–	–
Ubungo Spinning	4.6	64.7	15	1	1
Mbeyatex	5.2	78.6	–	–	–
Kiltex (Arusha)	20.4	75.5	45	0	3
Mutex	5.5	58.0	23	1	
Polytex	5.9	53.6	55	2	
Mwatex	20.4	35.3	5	0	
Morogoro Canvas	–	–	–		
Private					
A to Z	4.7	39.1	21	–	
CIC	3.9	68.6	5	4	
Sunflag	5.4	59.9	100	1	
Cotex (I.)	4.0	57.5	2	–	
Cotex (DSM)	3.5	33.5	2	3	
Calico	3.0	65.5	68	–	
JV I	2.4	51.7	20	1	
JV Textiles	2.8	81.5	20	1	

coefficient of labour turnover will be positive if it is a proxy for the general degree of inexperience of workers. If, additionally, a positive correlation would exist between turnover and training this would further confirm the existence of the labour switch effect. But the coefficient of labour turnover will be negative if efficient firms are better able to shed inefficient workers. The data allow a full equation (including all variables) to be estimated for a sample of only 11 observations. The results are shown in Table 8.3.

The coefficients of incentives, turnover and training are all significant, while that of management is not significant. As expected, the sign of the coefficient of the incentive variable is negative. The sign of the turnover variable is negative, contrary to the expectation that higher labour turnover would lead to higher labour inefficiency. One explanation could be that unproductive workers are dismissed, leaving behind the more productive ones, but the evidence needed to confirm this is not available. The sign of

Technology			Residuals of regression	Residuals as % of prediction	Ownership[a]	Management[b]
Diversity	Age	Condition				
3	18	med.	−13.1	−25.6	Tx/P31%[d]	Tanz.
1	33	good	5.6	9.1	Tx	Tanz.
1	7	good	1.8	2.8	Tx	Tanz.
3	7	v. good	14.2	21.9	Tx	Tanz.
3	25	v. good	7.7	11.4	Tx, LG	Tanz.
4	11	good	2.5	4.5	Tx	Tanz.
2	5	v. good	−17.5	−24.5	Tx	Tanz., Belgian
6	17	poor	5.7	19.4	Tx	Tanz.
1	8	v. good	—	—	TL	Dutch
4	27	med.	−6.9	−15.0	I[c]	I, N–O
1	7	v. good	−4.3	−5.4	I, LG, V	I, O-M
4	9	good	−8.0	−13.8	I, Mn, L	I, N–O
3	22	med.	11.8	25.5	I	I, O-M
3	22	med.	−12.2	−26.4	I, LG, S	I, O-M
3	15	good	0.3	0.5	I, LG, S	I, O-M
1	35	med.	3.2	6.5	I, LG, V	I, N–O
2	5	v. good	9.5	13.3	I, LG, V	I, N–O

Notes: (a) The following abbreviations have been used: TEXCO (Tx), local group (LG), multinational group (Mn), Tanzania Leather Associated Industries (TL), Indian (I), very large group (V), large group (L), small group (S).

(b) The following abbreviations have been used: O-M means that the firm is managed by the owner, and N-O means that management does not directly involve the owner. Friendship is seen as the flagship of TEXCO and is treated with priority in many aspects including management.

(c) Kenyan-based.

(d) Sunguratex is 31% privately-owned.

Sources: Based on Table 8.1 and own data.

the coefficient of training is positive. Since training only occurs in the public sector, this indicates higher labour coefficients in the public sector. The coefficient of management is the least significant of all and has unexpectedly a positive sign. This indicates that as far as this sample is concerned, firms with better overall performance tend to have higher labour coefficients.

Table 8.3   *Regression results of RLC on labour turnover, incentive schemes, training facilities, and overall management performance*

Regressant	Incentives	Labour Turnover	Training	Managment (TPI–B)	Adjusted R^2	D–W
RLC	–3.11 (93.6)[os]	–0.14 (89.6)	3.01 (95.0)[os]	0.16 (66.8)	0.52	2.23

Notes: The abbreviation 'os' indicates that a one-sided test of significance has been used.
The figure between brackets indicates the highest level (in percentage) at which the coefficient is significant.
Source: Based on data in Table 10.4.

There are thus three effects: the 'pull' effect of incentives (higher labour efficiency with higher incentives), the 'labour push' effect of dismissal (higher labour turnover leading to higher efficiency), and the 'labour switch' effect (labour trained at public mills switches to private mills). Further, there is an enormous difference between public and private sector labour coefficients, as shown in Table 8.2. This difference is mainly caused by three public firms with greatly underutilized capacities, Sunguratex, Kiltex, and Mwatex. Finally, the average labour use is about 6.8 times higher than in British 'best practice' firms. This is feasible because of the very low wages in Tanzania.

8.3.2   Relative total factor productivity

To explain differences in technical performance two sets of factors have been used: technical factors relating to machines and to technical management, and factors related to firm ownership and management. Technical performance has been measured by relative total factor productivity. The average RTFP for spinning is higher for the public sector, and for weaving it is higher for the private sector. The differences are not very significant given the few observations. RTFP for spinning and weaving taken together showed no difference between public and private sectors. This combined RTFP will be used in the subsequent analysis because it covers more firms.

Table 8.3 gives available evidence on technical factors, i.e. average age, condition, and diversity of origin of the machines, and on types of ownership and management. It might seem that the condition of the machines in the textile sector is on average quite good. However, most firms with very poor machine condition do not feature in the sample.

Whereas the information on technical factors is easily quantified, types of ownership and management are not. The only simple dichotomy is in terms of public or private ownership. However, as discussed in section 7.5 and detailed in Table 8.3, within the private sector the nature of ownership and thus management is quite diversified and although within the public sector forms of ownership are more homogenous, there are differences in management arrangements especially with regard to the use of foreign management. To quantify these differences would involve too many arbitrary choices. Instead, after establishing the relation of technical performance with technical factors in a quantitative manner, a more qualitative discussion will trace the influence of ownership and management factors on technical performance in the next section.

Relative total factor productivity and technical factors

To obtain an indicator for technical management independent from the RTFP, an index has been derived based on the age and the condition of the machines. With neutral technical management, machines up to 8 years old are expected to be in very good condition, from 9 to 15 in good condition, from 16 to 25 in medium condition, and in poor condition if 26 or more years old. Deviations of the condition of machines from this scale are assigned with a technical management index different from zero, its value depending on the number of classes below or above the normal machine condition. For example, a 33 year old machine is expected to be in poor condition with neutral technical management (index=0). When it is in good condition, the technical management index is put at two because the condition of the machine is two classes higher than expected.[5]

To assess the explanatory value of technical factors with regard to technical performance, RTFP has been regressed against diversity, age, and technical management. Diversity and age are expected to have negative coefficients and technical management a positive one. The results of the regression are shown in Table 8.4. The explanatory power is not very high with an adjusted R^2 of 0.53. However, all the sign are as expected and the coefficients become significant at levels of respectively 96.5, 99.4, and 96.3 percent for a one-sided test and 93.0, 98.7, and 92.5 percent for a two-sided test.

Inspection of the residuals (see Table 8.3) allows for a discussion of firm-specific factors that could be used to explain large deviations from predictions based on the estimated regression equation. First, differences exist between the public and private sector, with the standard deviation of residuals of 5.4 for the public sector and 3.9 for the private sector. Apparently, the technical factors used as explanatory variables in the regression have more explanatory power for the private sector than for the public sector.[6] The average residual of the public sector is marginally positive, that of the private sector negative. Inclusion of a dummy variable for public or private ownership produced very low significance for its coefficient.[7]

Second, three public and two private firms, Sunguratex, Mbeyatex, Polytex, Cotex (I), and Cotex (DSM), all show 20 percent or greater deviations from the predicted values. It must be remembered that these are deviations from a trend, set by the explanatory factors based on the particulars of the sample analysed. Firms may do better or worse than expected due to particular firm-specific circumstances.

The RTFP of Sunguratex is about 25 percent less than its predicted value. If this is caused by the persistent water problems, then this implies that these problems have crept into the estimation of the RTFP. Interruptions in the supply of utilities lead to higher labour coefficients as workers have to be available anyway, and to higher capital coefficients due to start-up times and to the fact that small interruptions may be counted as part of the effective machine time.

Mbeyatex scored about 22 percent above its predicted value. Mbeyatex has not really started to be operational, using only one percent of its capacity. Its machines were still brand new and management attention could be focused fully on the low level of output. One would therefore expect higher than predicted values.

With 25 percent, Polytex and Sunguratex deviate farthest from their predicted value in the public sector. Technically, Polytex has been running their machines at too high speeds, which leads to excessive breakages and reduced

Table 8.4   *Regression results of RTFP on technology factors*

Regressant	Diversity	Age	Technical management	Adjusted R²	D–W
RTFP	−4.2 (96.5)[os]	−1.2 (99.4)[os]	10.2 (96.3)[os]	0.53	2.15

Notes: The abbreviation 'os' indicates that a one-sided test of significance has been used. The figure between brackets indicates the highest level (in percentage) at which the coefficient is significant.
Source: Own calculations.

efficiency. On the management side, there are many internal problems in Polytex. Conflicts have developed between the expatriate (Belgian) technical management and the Tanzanian management. The Tanzanian management complained that the technical management was incapable of working with the Japanese machines at Polytex. However, the financial management indicator was the lowest in the whole sample supporting the view that the rest of the management was not very effective either. Thus, this rather new mill is under-performing badly because of a management problem.

Cotex (Iringa) has done 25 percent better than predicted. Previously, this firm belonged to a group of textile firms including Cotex (DSM) and DSM (Zanzibar) but split from the group in 1988 to be under sole ownership of one of the former directors of the larger Cotex group. It is active only in spinning. Most workers have been with the firm from the start in 1979 and the mill manager is a very experienced expatriate supervised by the owner's son.

Table 8.5   Financial performance indices, foreign loans, management dummies, foreign exchange allocation per unit of capacity and output

	Gross profit rate	Net profit rate	Foreign loans	Management dummy	For. ex. per capacity (US$/100m.)	For. ex. per output (US$/100m.)
Public						
Sunguratex	−28	−91	2 926	0	1.4	9.3
Friendship	15	1	18	0	2.9	6.9
Ubungo Spinning	−60	−162	87	0		−
Mbeyatex	26	−645	3 334	0		−
Mutex	−18	−1135	5 974	0	1.5	25.0
Polytex	−126	−750	8 552	0	3.1	7.6
Mwatex	−149	−793	5 366	0	0.7	17.5
Morogoro Canvas	21	−3	2 926	1	8.7	12.6
Private						
A to Z	22	−5	172	1	7.9	28.2
CIC	26	2	250	1	3.3	4.4
Sunflag	27	13	30	1	13.2	9.4
Cotex (DSM)	−5	−49	0	1	4.0	13.8
Calico					4.4	9.2
JV Industries					5.2	20.8
JV Textiles	20	−3	133	1	5.2	9.5

Table 8.6   Regression results for gross profit rates

Regressant	RLC	Export index	Capacity utilization	Management dummy	Adjusted R^2	D-W
GPR	−10.3 (97.7)^{os}	0.11 (<25.0)	0.17 (<25.0)		0.38	2.29
GPR	−5.7 (97.3)^{os}			41.4 (91.9)^{os}	0.47	1.71

Notes: The abbreviation 'os' indicates that a one-sided test of significance has been used. The figure between brackets indicates the highest level (in percentage) at which the coefficient is significant.

Source: Calculations based on data in Table 8.5.

Cotex (DSM) has done 26 percent worse than predicted. Its technical management is very poor, a fact born out by the high weft and warp break-age rates and poor quality of the end product, with 40 to 50 percent disposed of as seconds or scrap. While technically Cotex (Iringa) has out-classed Cotex (DSM), in terms of overall performance the picture is reversed. Cotex (Iringa) performs poorly in organizational matters and exports (in the absence of financial information from Cotex (Iringa)). The location (Iringa), rather out of the way for most purposes, may have something to do with the difference.

Relative total factor productivity and factors of ownership and management

There are two ways to explain technical performance based on types of ownership and management. Types of ownership and management can be taken in addition to the technical factors. Since types of ownership and management cannot be quantified, straightforward regression analysis including these factors is impossible. However these factors can be used to explain the residuals of the regression using technical factors similar to the analysis of the large residuals (outliers) above. Alternatively, technical factors could be seen as an outcome of types of ownership and management. In that case, the full values of RTFP should be analysed in relation to types of ownership and management. For the private sector each approach will be followed. The public sector shows too little variation in types of ownership and management to go beyond some general observations.

Regrettably, Morogoro Canvas, one of the two public sector firms that employ foreign management, provided none of the data needed to calculate the relative factor productivity.[8] Morogoro Canvas is under full foreign management. The author's own judgement, upon visiting this firm, is that it is very well managed, including its technical management. But well informed sources have alleged that illegal transfers from the firm's export revenue to foreign management have taken place. Polytex, the other firm employing foreign technicians, has performed very badly. The two forms of foreign management are very different, and as isolated cases, their experiences cannot be generalized.

But clearly, monitoring and controlling the owner-management relationship in the public sector can be problematic. Taking a purely opportunistic view of managers' behaviour, the foreign manager will probably benefit from optimal performance of the firm and from maximizing foreign linkages. This combination would enable foreign management to divert maximum flows to its own pockets. One solution would appear to be to limit foreign employment to technical management, as in the case of Polytex. However, the owner-management problem remains, since an opportunistic local manager's interests and actions can be just as antagonistic to the optimal performance of the firm.[9] Local interest networks both within and outside the firm are stronger while linkages with the foreign sector take a different form. Shortages boost the market power of the supplier,[10] and linkages to the parallel market are more feasible.[11] These conditions may foster conflicts between top management and technical management which will be intensified when technical management is foreign, perhaps under contractual obligations to reach certain standards, and not part of the opportunist interest network of local top management. To what extent this applies to Polytex cannot be ascertained given the limited information available.

The private sector shows more variation with regard to types of ownership. Only one firm is part of a local group owned by an African Tanzanian (IPS). All others are owned by either Indian nationals or non-nationals. Within the sample for which performance indices have been calculated (see Table 8.3), there is one multinational firm (Sunflag), one foreign private firm that is not managed by its owners (A to Z), three firms that are part of a rather large and diversified local group (CIC, JV Industries and JV Textiles), two firms that are part of a small local group (Calico and Cotex-DSM), and finally one firm which is owner-managed (Cotex-Iringa).

Technical performance and factors of management and ownership can be compared by inspecting the residuals of the regression. The residuals show which firms have higher (positive) or lower (negative) than expected technical performance. Taking the residuals as percentage of RTFP, the ranking of the firms is: Cotex-Iringa, JV Textiles, JV Industries, Calico, CIC, Sunflag, A to Z, Cotex-DSM. The only fact related to ownership-management characteristics (see Table 8.3) standing out in terms of performance is that the two foreign firms are poor technical performers relative to the rest (after allowing for technical factors such as age, etc.).

When ranking the private firms according to the average technical performance index, a different picture is obtained. The ranking becomes JV Textiles, CIC, Calico, Sunflag, Cotex-Iringa, JV Industries, A to Z, and Cotex-DSM. The firms which are part of a group now have moved up. A glance at the 'age' column in Table 8.3 shows that the first four firms in this ranking are also the four firms with the newest machines. There appears to be a correlation between the age of the machines and the fact that a firm belongs to a larger group. Simple explanations would be better access to finance, foreign exchange, and other business expertise such as the acquisition of market knowledge for inputs, machines and outputs, and successfully lobbying the government and foreign donors. The owner-manager variable, an important factor in the management and organizational theory of the firm, appears evenly throughout the ranking, with no clear relation to technical performance.

8.3.3 Organizational performance

Under-utilization of capacity can be partly explained by the relative total factor productivity. The unexplained residual of actual capacity utilization captures all other causes of under-utilization of capacity. This is labelled the organizational performance index (OPI-A). Thus actual capacity utilization is realized as a combination of two factors, i.e. capacity utilization = (RTFP)·(OPI-A).[12] A high value for OPI-A indicates few, relatively minor capacity reducing factors other than RTFP. A low value for OPI-A implies important problems, for example demand problems or supply constraints such as foreign exchange shortages, lack of working capital, or an inadequate supply of utilities. Using data on capacity utilization and RTFP, the organizational performance can be calculated (Table 8.1). The effect of water and electricity problems on capacity utilization is accounted for in an adjusted measure of organizational performance (OPI-B). Large problems with utilities or RTFP will suppress all other constraints, making the adjusted organizational index high. Other problems are not acute because their constraints have not yet been reached.

Whereas no significant differences between public and private RTFP values existed, the organizational index (as a result of large differences in capacity utilization) shows large differences in average values (average OPI-A public 38.2 and private 68.8) and standard deviations (the standard deviation in OPI-A is 33.6 for the public sector and 17.0 for the private sector). When problems with utilities are accounted for, the average values of the public and private sector come closer (average OPI-B public 52.1 and private 68.8) but the standard deviation of the public sector actually increases (standard deviation of OPI-B is 38.6 for the public sector and 17.0 for the private sector). Thus, the public-private ownership dichotomy appears as a significant dividing line.

The main explanation for both the low average value and high standard deviation lies in the problems experienced by Mbeyatex, Mutex, Kiltex (Arusha), and Ubungo Spinning. Mbeyatex, as noted above, still has not started full operation. Water and electricity problems at Mutex show up again as organizational problems because, to a great extent due to earlier water and electricity problems, Mutex has been unable to raise enough finance to expand production to reach the utility constraint. Kiltex (Arusha) has three different vintages of machinery. The RTFP has been measured with the greatest weight attached to the new machinery. Much of the old machinery is inoperable partly because of a lack of spare parts but mainly because of a lack of finance to purchase enough cotton to keep both the new and the old machines occupied (URT 1990d). Ubungo Spinning's management claims that right from the start the mill has been ill-funded. However, later inefficiencies in management have added to the weak financial position.

Thus the working capital constraint appears to be the main factor explaining the low organizational performance of three of the four low performers. However, since this financial constraint accumulated through a combination of inefficiencies, problems with utilities, and lack of foreign exchange, simply refinancing and rehabilitating these mills would not present a long term solution. In the private sector, such mills would have gone bankrupt. The existence of such acute working capital constraints is therefore a public sector phenomenon, explaining both the low average value and the high standard deviation in comparison with the private sector.

The private sector experienced few or no problems with the supply of utilities, with both organizational indices equal. However, variation in this sector, although less than in the public sector, is substantial. Lowest values were recorded by Sunflag, JV Industries, and Cotex (Iringa). Foreign exchange or working capital cannot be the problem for either Sunflag or

JV Industries, given the amount of exports achieved by Sunflag and JV Industries' affiliated company JV Textiles and given the type of owner-ship. Sunflag reported that demand problems led it to switch from 3 to 2 shifts, cutting its employment by 20 percent. (The possibility of a demand side problem was already noted in section 7.4.3). Sunflag's experience may reflect a general problem, since although JV Industries mentions no demand side problem, the JV Company has shifted its attention away from the domestic market. Whether this is a push (lack of domestic demand) or a pull (higher export prices) effect, or a combination, cannot be assessed on the basis of the available evidence. Cotex (Iringa) is a case apart. It split from the Cotex Group of Companies in 1988 and is now under improved management. Just before the break, 40 percent of its ringframes were stripped of some vital parts to be used in Cotex (Zanzibar) where machines were damaged by fire. Since then, capacity utilization has increased to 58 percent, and technical efficiency has been improving. Thus, its low organizational performance is attributable to past problems of management inefficiencies and ownership conflicts and has been improving since 1988.

Foreign exchange shortages were found to be of little importance in explaining the exceptionally low organizational performance of the four public and three private firms discussed above. The question now becomes whether this is particular to these firms or whether it applies more gener-ally. Foreign exchange allocation data are given in Table 8.5. On average, the private sector has been performing better, has received more foreign exchange per unit of installed capacity, and, curiously, less per unit of output produced.

The lower public sector performance and higher allocation per unit of output is confirmed by the negative value of the simple correlation coefficient between OPI-B and the foreign exchange allocated per unit of output (−77 percent). This implies that those firms that perform poorest have obtained the highest allocation of foreign exchange per unit of output. Regressing OPI-B against foreign exchange allocated per unit of output gives a coefficient of −1.5, with a t-value of 4.24, and an adjusted R^2 of 0.57. The conclusion must be that foreign exchange, as a recurrent input, cannot explain low organizational performance. However, this may not always have been the case. Even in the period when the research took place, some individual discrepancies may have existed. In any event, both firm-level and economy-wide foreign exchange shortages of the past have contributed strongly to low organizational and technical performance. Shortages have affected the supply of utilities, maintenance and replace-ment expenditures, leading to lower machine efficiencies and reduced capacity as machines go off-line. Section 8.4 presents a time-series analysis of performance to reach firmer conclusions although not using precisely the same performance measures employed here.

8.3.4 Financial performance

Financial performance is measured by two different indicators (Table 8.5). First, the gross profit rate (GPR) expresses the difference between revenue and operating cost as a percentage of revenue. Second, the net profit rate (NPR) takes into account all costs and is defined as net profit before tax as a percentage of revenue. To smoothen out yearly fluctuations three year averages have been used. Table 8.5 shows how large the differences are between these two indicators. The main reason for these differences is the financial costs involved in servicing loans and especially foreign loans.

Differences in gross profit rates between firms can be explained firstly by differences in labour efficiency as measured by the relative labour coefficients. A negative sign is expected for the relation between RLC and GPR. Second, it could be argued that capacity utilization would influence gross profit rates, because lower rates of capacity utilization lead to higher RLCs (given the prevailing labour practices). Third, export performance may influence gross profits if higher or lower export prices are realized. However the price ratio between production for the export and domestic markets changed in favour of exports (to be in balance roughly around 1988). The effect of exports therefore may be small and unclear. The last explanatory factor is management, for which a dummy variable has been introduced. All private sector firms and Morogoro Canvas (foreign management) have been given a value equal to one, the remaining public sector firms a value equal to zero. The influence of this dummy variable is assumed to be positive. The regression results are shown in Table 8.6.

The relative labour coefficient is negative, as expected, and highly significant. Both export index and capacity utilization have insignificant coefficients. These results are not surprising since the influence of capacity utilization on gross profits should be small (especially when labour effects have been accounted for by including RLC),[13] and the price effect of exports relative to production for the domestic market is not strong. Therefore, they have been omitted from a second equation which includes the management dummy. The sign of the coefficient of the management factor is positive, as assumed, but its significance is on the low side, at 91.9 percent for a one-sided test.

Net profits as a percentage of sales reflects the actual financial performance of the firm more closely. The first factor able to explain net profits is

Table 8.7   *Regression results for net profit rates*

Regressant	Capacity Utilization	Foreign Loans	RTPF	OPI A	OPI B	Water & Elec.	Adjusted R²	D–W
NPR	6.17 (97.60)[os]	−0.10 (>99.00)	–	–	–	–	0.80	
NPR	–	−0.10 (>99.00)	−0.67 (<25.00)	4.89 (>99.00)	–	–	0.85	2.34
NPR	–	−0.10 (>99.00)	0.56 (<25.00)	5.36 (>99.00)	–	–	0.92	2.11
NPR	–	−0.10 (>99.00)	0.65 (<25.00)	–	5.23 (>99.00)	271.0 (86.70)[os]	0.93	2.05

Source: Calculations based on data in Table 8.5.

the level of foreign loans that firms have acquired.[14] The second factor is capacity utilization. With low capacity utilization and high levels of foreign loans, the effect of different labour coefficients becomes negligible, so RLC is not assumed to be an explanatory factor. The management variable is closely correlated to the level of foreign loans and has therefore also been omitted. The first equation in Table 8.7 thus includes only capacity utilization (assumed to have a positive effect) and foreign loans (assumed to have a negative effect). Both coefficients are significant and of the proper sign. The coefficient of foreign loans in particular is highly significant.

The second and third equation differentiate capacity utilization into two factors, technical performance and organizational performance, each of which is assumed to influence net profits positively. Because of the relatively high value of the Durbin-Watson coefficient, a Cochrane-Orcutt first order correction method has been used. The results (third equation) show that technical performance has very little influence on net profits. Organizational performance however is highly significant, higher than the coefficient of capacity utilization in equation one. Overall explanatory power of the third equation is as high as 92 percent.

The fourth equation has further differentiated organizational performance into the adequacy of water and electricity supply and the residual organizational performance (OPI-B). The explanatory power of the equation increases slightly, the significance of the coefficient of OPI-A is higher than that of OPI-B in the third equation (not visible in this presentation), and the coefficient of water and electricity supply is positive and significant at a level of about 87 percent for a one-sided test. Although this level of significance is not very high, it shows the tendency of the supply of utilities to influence net profit rates.

8.3.5 Export performance

Both public and private sectors are exporting, with the average export performance of the private sector 28 percent higher than the public sector. Available data on exports by firm show a strongly increasing trend during the 1980s for all firms for which more than one year of information was available. A large number of factors could possibly contribute toward high export performance such as quality, technical management, overseas contacts, commercial management, government pressure, and relative prices in the export and domestic market. Exporting also requires good management. It is hard to define firm level indices on the basis of the available data that capture all these characteristics. The one that comes closest is the total performance index, which itself is a weighted average of the other performance indices summarized in Table 8.1. Assuming that this index is meaningful in the way it was defined, it should be able to explain at least part of the variation in export performance.

Table 8.8 shows the results of a regression of the export index on the total performance index (TPI-A). This index explains 45 percent of the total variation and its coefficient is highly significant.[15]

Table 8.8   Regression results of export performance on total management performance

Regressant	Total performance index A	Adjusted R^2	D–W
Export index	1.39 (99.00)	0.45	1.99

Notes: The figure between brackets indicates the highest level (in percentage) at which the coefficient is significant.
Source: Own calculations based on data in Table 8.1.

8.3.6   Investment performance

Only the private sector firms have investment plans. Of the private firms included in the performance analysis, only Cotex (Iringa) and Cotex (DSM) have no investment plans. These firms are in a process of internal reorganization after the change in ownership. Both are still in financial difficulties, which could be the reason why they do not invest (as confirmed by Cotex (Iringa)). The most ambitious investment plans are for A to Z and JV Industries, both of which intend to replace old equipment with new, enabling the firm to produce for exports. An explanatory factor for these investments could be found in the low technical performance of the machines caused by age. In addition, A to Z wants to move upstream into the production of polyester chips from which polyester fibres can be made. The envisaged plant would be able to serve the whole East African market. CIC and Calico, both of which have quite modern and well maintained equipment, plan to invest in very modern equipment for the purpose of penetrating the export market in the high quality segment. Sunflag and JV Textiles, both with new equipment in good condition, have different reasons for their investments. Sunflag aims at producing 'khanga' and 'kitenge' for the local market, whereas JV Textiles wants to move upstream into spinning to control the quality and supply of yarn to its weaving departments in order to be able to achieve higher quality for exports (vertical integration). Thus, little generalization appears to be possible.

Commercial feasibility and access to finance are major determinants of investment. One source of finance is the firm's own funds, which depend on the profitability of the existing venture. The five private sector firms for which data are available display no relationship between net profit rates and investment. Only A to Z plans to finance its new investment from internally generated funds (that is coupled with supplier credit).[16]

Firms that are part of a network, be it a group of firms or a more informal business network may have access to finance through their network. JV Textiles and JV Industries, CIC, and Calico are all part of a local group and have owners belonging to the Indian business community (Table 8.3) while Sunflag is part of a multinational textile firm. However, only the JV Group mentions this source of finance (for the local currency component). Regrettably, the available information on its investment plans and its financing is rather vague. Given its international character, an appropriate mixture between own finance, foreign and local finance is likely to be sought.

The third source of finance is international development finance. The foreign component of the investment proposals of the JV Group is to be financed in the form of a foreign loan (World Bank). CIC's investment is financed by the Dutch Development Bank and the East African Development Bank. Calico is looking for soft (foreign) loans to finance its expansion. Thus, it appears that investment finance for the three private sector firms which are also part of a local group, is mainly supplied by development banks related to the development aid circuit.

8.3.7 Total performance

Table 8.1 shows total performance by firm measured by TPI-A (using an organizational index that includes problems with the utility supply) and by TPI-B (excluding the effects of utilities). Figure 8.1 shows by firm how total performance is built up from its main composing parts. Total performance will be analysed qualitatively in relation to factors of ownership and management.

The average TPI-A for the public sector firms excluding Friendship and Morogoro Canvas was 31.1 percent. This becomes 40.5 percent when Friendship and Morogoro Canvas are included. On the other hand, all private firms except Cotex (DSM) and JV Industries scored above 50 percent on the TPI-A, and the private sector average was 59.9 percent, which even rises to 62.6 percent when Friendship and Morogoro Canvas

Figure 8.1   Performance indicators by firm

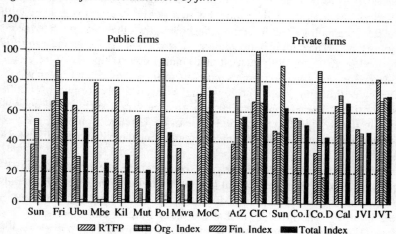

Source: Based on data in Table 8.1.

are included (as firms with good management). The average TPI-A of the private sector was 48 percent higher than that of the public sector, and even when the effect of the supply of utilities is excluded (TPI-B), this still amounts to 35 percent.

In the private sector CIC is the top performer (according to the TPI-A), followed, at some distance, by JV Textiles. Both firms belong to large, local, Indian-owned groups and employ rather modern technology. The main difference between them is that CIC is owner-managed where JV Textiles is not. Third comes Calico, another firm that belongs to a local group of Indian ownership, although smaller than the others. Calico has modern equipment and is owner-managed. Next are Sunflag and A to Z, the firms with international, Indian ownership and delegated management. This contradicts Perkins' earlier conclusions that private firms use more appropriate technology and that those firms doing so (public or private) are more efficient (Perkins 1983).

At the bottom are Cotex (Iringa), JV Industries, and Cotex (DSM). The two Cotex firms have recently experienced some ownership and management problems and are now in the process of catching up. Cotex (Iringa) is a single private firm, managed by its owner, although slightly at a distance. Cotex (DSM) is part of a small local, Indian-owned group but has very old equipment. Finally, JV Industries belongs to the same group as JV Textiles but has old machines, and low RTFP and capacity utilization.

Summing up, the group of high performers is formed first by those private firms that belong to local, Indian-owned groups, and employ modern technology and second by two public sector firms, one with modern technology and foreign management, the other with outdated technology and Tanzanian management. The second performance group is formed by the firms with international, Indian ownership. The third group, comprising the poor performers, consists of three private and seven public firms. Within this group the lower tail is exclusively formed by public sector firms. The reasons for poor performance vary. Especially discouraging is the low performance of Polytex and Ubungo Spinning, each of which have considerable technical potential at their disposal but cannot take off.

With regard to the public-private sector debate, the problem with the public sector is not so much that it is unable to perform. After all, the performances of Friendship and Morogoro Canvas are amongst the best in the industry. The problem is that too many failures are tolerated for too long. For a deeper understanding of this, the analysis has to draw on the discussion of the Tanzanian state offered in Chapter 5.

8.4 MACRO-FACTORS AND TIME SERIES ANALYSIS OF PERFORMANCE

Figure 8.2 shows the links between explanatory micro-factors and macro-factors. All components of the total performance index are influenced by macro-conditions. First, RTFP is affected by the age and poor maintenance of the capital stock, each of which is influenced by general foreign exchange shortages. RLCs are high, reflecting low labour incomes but also high labour turnover.

Second, organizational performance measures all other constraints to higher capacity utilization apart from RTFP. Amongst these are problems with the supply of utilities, themselves indicating the lack of resources to improve such facilities. When these factors are isolated, other constraints remain (organizational index B) such as credit and/or foreign exchange, and possibly for some firms a demand constraint.

Third, the level of foreign loan commitments is one of the three factors influencing the net profit rate. The rapid devaluation of the Tanzanian Shilling multiplied the domestic value of foreign loans. Liberalization kept the domestic price level in check and finance costs as a percentage of sales increased substantially. For firms producing for the domestic market, all imported inputs increased in price in proportion to the devaluation, thus undermining profitability.

Fourth, export performance has been affected differently for public and private firms. Private firms initially exported to obtain foreign exchange under retention schemes. Later on, with the ongoing devaluation, export prices became attractive. Public sector firms, although not insensitive to the incentives that apply to the private sector, face in addition a public sector drive towards exports by government decree. Such an export effort may conflict with firm-level objectives. For example, technical conditions of the older firms make the cost price of exports (of minimum quality) 50 percent higher than the cost price of domestically acceptable production. Moreover, domestic prices were more attractive than export prices in the first half of the 1980s.

Fifth, investment performance is directly related to the profitability of investment which in turn is determined by commercial and trade policies and the development of local demand.

Therefore, of the three main factors contributing to the total performance index, financial performance and organizational performance are most directly related to macroeconomic policy variables (see section 8.4). RTFP's link to macro-variables is more indirect and long term.

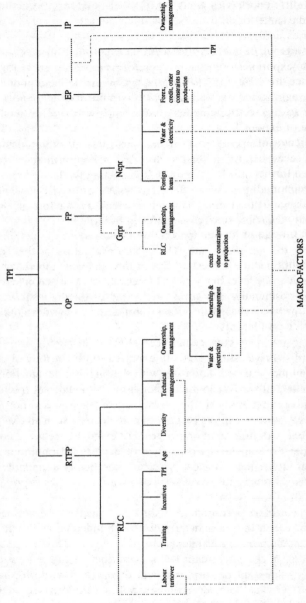

Figure 8.2 Total performance index and explanatory variables

Note: TPI = Total Performance Index; RTFP = Relative Total Factor Productivity; OP = Organizational Performance; FP = Financial Performance; EP = Export Performance; IP = Investment Performance; RLC = Relative Labour Coefficient; Grpr = Gross profit; Nepr = Net profit; Forex = Foreign exchange.

Whereas cross-section analysis was able to deal with explanations of firm level differences with regard to micro-factors, macroeconomic variables are the same for all firms, so that their impacts can only be traced in a time-series analysis. In Table A.6 time series data (1974–88) are presented for a group of public sector firms on net profits and capacity utilization.[17] Also export performance (section 8.4) and private sector investment performance are clearly related to macroeconomic policy variables. Data (1980–90, aggregated over all textile firms) exist for the various subsectors of the textile sector on exports to the EC (Table 6.2). From these the total value of exports of woven and knitted fabrics and yarn will be taken as the indicator of export performance. Investment data are available for the public sector but not for the private sector so that this indicator will not be analysed further.

Macroeconomic variables included in the analysis are the exchange rate, overall balance of payments, national consumer price index, and interest rate. Additionally, the average price of textiles is also available. For all these data, time series exist from 1974 to 1988.

8.4.1 Profits

The cross-section analysis has shown that profits were related to capacity utilization, which was later differentiated into reduced capacity utilization due to RTFP, supply of utilities, and organizational performance. Since no time series data on these last three variables are available, capacity utilization will be used as the first explanatory factor for which a negative sign is assumed. Moreover, the high significance of foreign loans is an effect of the rapidly devaluating Tanzanian shilling. Devaluation also

Table 8.9   Regression results of profits on price, capacity utilization and exchange rate

Regressant	Exchange rate	Price (deflated)	Capacity utilization	Interest	Adjusted R²	D–W
Profits (deflated)	−48.1 (99.0)	1773 (<25.0)	8.3 (88.0)ᵒˢ	−13.9 (40.1)	0.97	2.15

Notes: The figure between brackets indicates the highest level (in percentage) at which the coefficient is significant. The abbreviation 'os' stands for a one-sided test.

Source: Calculations based on data in Table A.19.

increases the cost of imported inputs such as dyes and chemicals and domestically produced tradeables such as cotton lint (see section 7.3 on cost structures). The exchange rate is therefore taken as the second explanatory variable with, by assumption, a negative sign.

The average price of textiles is the third explanatory variable. Curious as this may sound, the relation between price and profits is not straightforward. Under the system of administered prices that prevailed in Tanzania during the period of observation, a positive mark-up over costs for each firm was ensured. With declining capacity utilization and as a consequence declining profits, the price was adjusted upwards (the simple correlation coefficient between capacity utilization and price is –75 percent). Thus, to that extent the coefficient of capacity utilization captures the effect of the price variable. The remaining effect of price on profits may thus be weak, although positive. To eliminate the effect of inflation on profits and price of textiles the national consumer price index has been used as deflator to obtain profits and price at constant prices.

The results of the regression (Table 8.9) show that first of all the signs of the coefficients are as expected. Second, the highly significant and negative influence of the exchange rate on profits stands out loud and clear. Capacity utilization is not highly significant even for a one-sided test, but cannot be ignored as an explanatory variable. The coefficient of the price variable is insignificant, in line with the explanation given above. Interest rates have little explanatory power for profits given their low level of significance.

8.4.2 Capacity utilization

Capacity utilization (CAPU) was found to be a variable that, although not highly significant, could not be excluded from the explanation of trends in

Table 8.10   Regression results of capacity utilization on balance of payments and lagged profits

Regressant	BOPOV	PROFC(–1)	Adjusted R^2	D–W
CAPU	0.08 (>99.0)	0.012 (>99.0)	0.73	1.49
CAPU	0.12 (>99.0)		0.49	1.21

Source: Calculations based on data in Table A.19.

profits. Capacity utilization itself is composed of RTFP, effects of utility supply, and a remainder of factors captured by the second organizational index. Time series data on these component parts of capacity utilization are not available. Instead, as in the case of profits, data on capacity utilization for the public sector (1974–88) are used. The foreign exchange constraint influences capacity utilization by reducing the effective capital stock as well as its utilization because of recurrent imported inputs. To capture these macroeconomic effects the overall balance of payments is used as an explanatory variable (BOPOV). A second explanatory variable is the availability of working capital to finance production. Working capital is assumed to depend on the level of profits in the previous year. Thus, in the section on profits, the financial performance of the firms is partially explained by capacity utilization, while in this section the financial performance of the previous year (PROFC(–1)) is used to explain capacity utilization. The spiral effects of such a model could be broken by credit from suppliers, customers, banks, or from government. However, time series on credit are not available so that capacity utilization will be regressed against BOPOV and PROFC(–1). The results are shown in Table 8.10.

Referring to the first equation in Table 8.10, both coefficients are highly significant, and the adjusted R^2 is 0.73. The Durbin-Watson coefficient is rather low, indicating positive autocorrelation of the residuals. However, the pattern of autocorrelation is such that its effect on the estimated coefficients is small.[18] When the regression is calculated using the 'unlagged' profit variable, the significance of the coefficients and the overall explanatory power declines, giving some support to the specification employed. When in the second equation the lagged profits variable is dropped, the adjusted R^2 is almost halved while the coefficient of balance of payments variable remains highly significant and of the same order of magnitude.

8.4.3 Export performance

Two different hypotheses on the relation between exports and the exchange rate can be formulated. First, shifts from production for the domestic market to production for the export market (or vice versa) depend in part on the relative prices prevailing on the respective markets. Accordingly, the exchange rate has a positive effect on exports and domestic inflation a negative effect. In combination, they define the effective exchange rate (see Chapter 2). The effective exchange rate has a more significant positive effect on exports than the nominal exchange rate.

Table 8.11   Regression results of exports on exchange rate, national consumer price index, and effective exchange rate

Regressant	Exchange rate	Consumer price index	Effective exchange rate	Adjusted R²	D–W
Exports	−112.2 (>99.0)	17.4 (>99.0)		0.78	2.31
Exports			8648 (<25.0)	−0.12	1.73

Notes: The first equation is estimated with the maximum likelihood method; the second equation has corrected for autocorrelation by transforming the regressant using an estimate of the first order autocorrelation based on the residuals of the ols-estimate.
Source: Calculations based on data in Table A.19.

Alternatively, under an economic regime with foreign exchange shortages (overvalued domestic currency implying higher domestic prices) and foreign exchange management through (amongst others) exports retention schemes, firms would export to earn foreign exchange in order to produce for the domestic market. Higher domestic prices would then lead to higher production for the domestic market requiring more imported inputs and thus inducing firms to export more in order to obtain foreign exchange. The effect of higher exchange rates would be higher prices for imports and thus, if anything, negative. For the same reasons, the effective exchange rate would have a negative influence on exports induced by import requirements.

The highly significant coefficients, negative for the exchange rate and positive for the national consumer price index, and the insignificance of the effective exchange rate (Table 8.11) confirm the view that firms exported to purchase imports in order to produce for the domestic market during the survey period. This is further confirmed by a cross-section regression analysis of capacity utilization on exports, with a highly significant coefficient of exports (97.8 percent for a one-sided test).

8.5   CONCLUSIONS

This chapter started with the construction of technical, organizational, financial, export, and investment performance indices, and combined these into a total performance index. No clear difference between public and private sectors exist for the technical performance index (RTFP) and the export index (EI). The largest difference between the public and private sectors was found to exist in investment and financial performance. Organizational performance also showed great differences along this line. The gap between public and private performance on this index became considerably less when problems with the supply of water and electricity were eliminated from the organizational index. The resulting total performance index (TPI) was 48 percent higher for the private sector. The same index, but without the effects of water and electricity supply, was 35 percent higher. Finally, despite the large differences in performance between the averages of the public and private sector, for each index public firms existed that were amongst the highest performers of the private sector.

A cross-section analysis was then used to investigate the relation between the various performance indices and micro-factors appropriate to each. Analysis of the relative labour coefficient of each firm revealed support for the hypothesis that private firms benefited from public sector training facilities through a 'labour switch effect' influenced by a 'labour pull effect' – the attractiveness of higher incentives in the private sector. Evidence suggests that the high rates of turnover in the private sector could be explained by the 'labour push effect' of higher labour efforts demanded by the private sector.

Firm by firm differences in technical performance could be explained by the diversity and age of technology and technical management, i.e. the ability to keep machinery in a condition higher than expected on the basis of age. Particular deviations from the trend set by these explanatory factors could be explained by supplementary firm-specific information. Within the private sector, the analysis shows that firms belonging to an international or local economic group rank higher on the technical performance index than do others. This was explained by better access to various inputs, including finance to purchase modern equipment.

Analysis of organizational performance including all capacity reducing factors other than technical performance proceeded in a more qualitative fashion, using firm-specific information to explain particularly low values. Some evidence was reported on an emerging local demand constraint (in line with the analysis of section 7.4.3). The analysis also revealed that foreign exchange as a recurrent input was not a significant factor in explaining the 1988 organizational performance. This, however, does not preclude its importance as a major explanatory factor for the more structural changes that have occurred in the industry as subsequent time-series analysis aims to demonstrate.

Financial performance was analysed on the basis of gross profits (financial operational performance) and net profits (total financial performance including financing). Gross profits were found to be negatively influenced by the relative labour coefficient and positively by a private management dummy variable, but not by capacity utilization (as expected) or export performance. The latter finding can be explained by the fact that export prices were not significantly higher than domestic prices in 1988. The time series analysis on export performance summarized below supports this conclusion. Net profits were explained by the amount of foreign loans to which firms were committed and by the degree of capacity utilization. The factor capacity utilization was then further differentiated into technical performance, effects of water and electricity supply, and the residual organizational performance. Of these, only water and electricity supply and residual organizational performance were found significant, underlining the relatively small effect of technical performance in determining net financial performance.

Export performance was shown to be related to total performance. Although its coefficient is highly significant, residual variation is 55 percent, showing that it does not fully account for export performance. However, on the basis of the available micro-data, no clear pattern of additional factors could be established.

Investment performance, relevant only for the private sector, has been analysed qualitatively in relation to investment objectives and sources of investment finance. Investment objectives varied so greatly that no generalization was feasible. It was found that only one firm relied mainly on own generated funds for investment finance. Another possible source of finance for those firms that belong to a local group would be the group itself. Regrettably, no information was available for further analysis on this point. Three of the five private firms investing (all part of a local group) have sought investment finance from sources related to the development aid circuit, including banks that operate on commercial conditions. The extent to which a firm's financial trustworthiness as member of a larger economic group is related to its access to such finance cannot be assessed.

Analysing total performance with regard to ownership and management variables, three groups were identified. The group of highest performers consisted of three private firms, all belonging to local, Indian-owned, groups using modern technology, and of two public firms, one with modern technology and foreign management, the other with outdated technology and Tanzanian management. The outstanding performance of the latter public firm has been attributed to its choice of appropriate technology (Coulson 1982b, Perkins 1983). However, in addition, this firm received priority treatment in the allocation of foreign exchange, as well as priority for the appointment of (Tanzanian) quality management. The group of medium performers consisted of two private firms with international, Indian ownership. The group of lowest performers was composed of three private and seven public firms, with the lower end of the spectrum exclusively occupied by public sector firms. In view of the presence of public firms in the highest as well as the lowest group, the conclusion was drawn that the low performance in the public sector was due to its incapacity to deal with cases of poor performance rather than that the public sector was unable to perform *per se*.

The micro-factors used in the cross-section analysis were viewed in relation to macro-economic variables such as the exchange rate, the national consumer price index, the overall balance of payments, the rate of interest, and to a sectoral variable, namely the average domestic price of textile products (see Figure 8.2). Based on this, a time series analysis was applied to profits and capacity utilization for the public sector (no time series data were available for the private sector), and to exports of the whole textile sector.

Profits (in constant prices) were found to be negatively (and highly significantly) related to the exchange rate and positively to capacity utilization, although of lower significance. The relationships between profits and textile prices (in constant terms) and the interest rate were found to be insignificant but with the expected sign.

Capacity utilization, itself an explanatory factor of profits, was explained by the overall balance of payments and previous year's profits. Both coefficients were highly significant and of the expected (positive) sign.

The analysis of export performance showed that during the period of observation firms exported primarily to obtain foreign exchange that would enable them to produce for the more profitable or otherwise more feasible domestic market. The coefficient of the effective exchange rate was found to be insignificant. This explanation contrasted with the alternative explanation of exports as a response to higher export prices relative to domestic prices.

Thus, macroeconomic linkages with microeconomic institutions were articulated on the supply side in terms of the quantity and price of available foreign exchange, available credit, and physical infrastructure. This has both a short term effect, i.e. limitations to expansion of utilization of effective capacity, and a long term effect, i.e. with regard to restructuring and revitalizing the textile sector. Additionally, the public-private ownership dimension in the textile sector obtains a macro-character when viewed in light of current pressures for privatization. The findings of this chapter, coupled with the analysis of the Tanzanian state, demonstrate that this issue of ownership cannot be isolated from its ethnic dimension. On the demand side two issues were raised: firstly, the relation between export demand and domestic demand, and the underlying production decisions of firms; secondly, the level of demand in relation to effective productive capacity. Evidence suggests that local demand was emerging as a constraint to further capacity utilization. In Chapter 7, it was shown that the gap between the level of overall effective demand and capacity was quite small (section 7.4.3). This issue is complicated by the possibility of regional concentration (section 7.4.2), and other forms of market control such as forward vertical integration through formal (economic groups) and informal linkages (sections 7.4.4 and 7.4.5). The concluding chapter of this study will place the issues raised in this summary in perspective within the overall theoretical framework developed in Chapter 2.

Notes

1. See section 7.2.2 for examples of internal problems that can occur. The borderline between technical and organizational problems is not always clear.
2. The organizational index, excluding the effects of problems in the supply of utilities, has been calculated using data from Table 7.12.
3. The exponential transformation is required to differentiate better between those firms that have higher profit rates. This occurs at the expense of differentiation between those firms with very low profit rates. The definition of the financial performance index is:

$$FP = 50 \cdot 1.3^{(NP/S+10)/10}$$

Net profits over sales is shown as NP/S in the equation. This transformation ensures that, on a scale of 0 to 100, a profit rate of −10 percent becomes 50 percent, that the firm with the highest profit rate scores 90 percent, that those firms with profit rates between −10 and 12.6 percent are spread over the 50 to 90 percent range, and that the firms with highly negative profit rates score 0 or very close to zero.

4. On this scale, the numbers roughly correspond to the share of exports in total sales divided by ten.
5. Technical management, thus defined, combines a number of factors. Some of these are: the type of technology in relation to technological capability (i.e. choice of technology), the availability of spare parts for the particular vintage, the amount of foreign exchange available for maintenance and repair and the degree of capacity utilization (can lead to low morale and idle machines can

easily be neglected or cannibalized). To assess the relative importance of these factors, a more detailed firm-level study would be required.

6. Larger dispersion in performance of the public sector firms is possible since, in contrast to the private sector, even very poor performers are kept alive.

7. This was done in three ways. First, the dummy (0 for the public sector firms and 1 for the private sector firms) was added to the other explanatory variables. Second, the technical management variable was dropped and replaced by the dummy. Third, the residuals were regressed against the residuals. In no case did the dummy produce t-values higher than .3, while in the first two cases the overall explanatory power of the equation decreased. The coefficient was negative in all cases in agreement with the average values of the residuals for the public and private sector obtained in the original equation (see Table 8.2).

8. On the basis of the estimated equation in Table 8.4, the predicted value of RTFP for Morogoro Canvas would be 72.8. This leads to an overall performance index of 78.7 which would be the highest public sector performance and the second of the whole sample after CIC.

9. Even the showcase firm Friendship has suffered from financial mismanagement (URT 1990d).

10. For example, interviews with management of Mwatex and Mutex confirmed that production levels near attainable capacity would quickly saturate the regional market.

11. See the Appendix for some examples of corrupt practices.

12. Since in most cases capacity and capacity utilization are measured in terms of metres of fabric, the RTFP for weaving has been used. In the remaining cases, the RTFP for spinning has been used.

13. Differentiating capacity utilization into RTFP and organizational performance is not possible since RLC is part of the definition of RTFP.

14. It would have been more accurate to use the amount of foreign exchange required to service these foreign loans. The assumption here is that this is roughly proportional to the level of foreign loans. Variations due to different years and conditions under which these loans were acquired are thus not taken into account.

15. The weight of the export index itself in the total performance index is 10, which compared to a total weight of 320 is only 3 percent. The regression is therefore not tautological.

16. This is precisely how they have successfully financed previous investment. The suppliers credit has been repaid with the help of barter arrangements.

17. These firms are Friendship, Sunguratex, Mwatex, Mutex and Kiltex (DSM and Arusha combined).

18. The pattern of autocorrelation was found to be cyclical with a few cycles. The cause of the autocorrelation is the nature of the data of capacity utilization: sudden increases of capacity with a lagged output response.

9 Conclusions

The debate between advocates of liberalization and export orientation and those of an industrial development which is more guided by the use of protection and state investment has largely been conducted at an ideological and macroeconomic level paying little attention to the concrete problems and constraints that firms face in day-to-day business. Meso-policy approaches for developing countries, in particular the recommendations arising from the academic 'discovery' of flexible specialization in developed countries, appear to assume away the differences that exist between them with regard to the conditions of production and markets. This book has analysed firms' performance in great detail with due attention to explanatory factors arising at all levels of analysis and against the background of the international and African comparative perspective. On this basis, this last chapter discusses the broad implications for industrial development of African countries and the textile sector that can be drawn from specific conclusions on Tanzanian textile firms. The major question for industry in almost all adjusting countries is to what extent liberalization is a positive policy for both short-term and long-term industrial development. Related questions concern the pace and extent of liberalization measures and the need, nature and feasibility of complementary measures to help firms adjust. Concretely, should all inefficient firms be eliminated by quickly-introduced liberalization or should liberalization policy be based on careful assessment of the long-term potential of firms and the industrial sector at large, with due consideration of the complexities that arise in the adjustment process? In other words, how can liberalization be beneficial rather than destructive for industrial development?

A major question is to what extent alternative policy approaches are based on the experience of developed countries or of newly industrializing countries and to what extent the factors underlying their success can be found or reproduced in less developed countries. This concerns in particular the role of exports as an engine of growth and the role of the state, based on the NICs' successes, and the view that flexible specialization can form the basis of a new paradigm for industrial development in developing countries. Innovative policy interventions designed typically for developing countries' conditions carry with them the risk of failure, which calls for a cautious approach with intensive monitoring and research. This risk can be reduced only by a thorough understanding of the problems of industrial production and of the few successes that have been achieved. This is one of the major contributions of this book.

The first part below summarizes the approach taken in this book, presenting and integrating the main empirical and theoretical conclusions reached in the individual chapters. The second part draws lessons from this study for the development of the textile sector of African countries, and that of Tanzania in particular, and of African industrial development in general.

9.1 SUMMARY

The central purpose of this book has been to understand the problems of industrial development by a detailed analysis of performance of firms. The theoretical approach of this study has been that performance of manufacturing firms has to be understood as the outcome of an interplay of factors at four distinct levels. These were defined as the international, macro-, meso-, and micro-levels. The international level comprises factors such as developments in technology and trade, international institutions and the policies of other countries. At macro-level the main factors are macroeconomic policies and constraints and the role of the state. Sector-level factors that influence performance are the structure of ownership, marketing arrangements and the regional structure of production and demand. At micro-level, performance is affected by structural and behavioural characteristics of individual firms such as technological capability in relation to the particular vintages installed, management capability, ownership structure and location with regard to supply of inputs (utilities, cotton), and to demand.

To apply and empirically verify the ideas developed in this study, a particular sector, the textile sector, and a particular country, Tanzania, were chosen. To explain performance, the concept of performance had to be defined in a manner that allowed for both comparison and differentiation.

Comparison, inherent in the concept of performance, has been addressed at the international and at the firm level. At the international level, countries were compared with regard to technological performance, policies and achievements, particularly in exports. This comparison included industrialized countries, NICs, industrializing countries and the differentiated impact of the international institutional framework for textile trade. Indices were constructed characterizing the technological development of countries and sectoral development with regard to foreign trade related performance (UNIDO's classification developed for successful countries). Different policy sequences shaped the development of the textile sector of European, Asian and African countries. Thus, African countries, and Tanzania in particular, could be placed in the context of the world system.

At the firm level, comparison has been addressed first, in a general overview of selected case studies of African countries, depending on available secondary evidence, and second, in the elaborate case study of textile firms in Tanzania. Technological performance has been defined in relation to 'best practice' firms employing similar technologies.

The concept of performance has been differentiated theoretically and empirically. Theoretically, performance was differentiated by a closer investigation of the concept of rationality and its relation to performance in an overview of theories of the firm. Rather than rejecting one theory wholesale in favour of the other, an eclectic approach has been taken selecting elements of each theory when considered appropriate. Thus, neoclassical concepts were used for the specification of measurement of technical performance in a 'best practice' approach. The structure-conduct-performance model, with its emphasis on sector-wide outcomes of individual decisions, showed the relevance of the meso-level. The rigidity of the logical sequence of determination of structure-conduct-performance has been challenged by the recently emerging new industrial economics which shows how causality can be reversed and identifies elements that fall outside the whole structure-conduct-performance framework.

The early managerial theories stressed the importance of separation of ownership and management, which could be usefully extended to its extreme expression in the public sector. The more comprehensive organizational theory of the firm in combination with the new institutional economics supplied more general principal-agent concepts applicable to all levels of a firm's hierarchy and incorporated elements of the transaction costs concepts applicable to issues of vertical and horizontal integration. Partly in agreement, behavioural theories of the firm placed more emphasis on the role of human behaviour and its determinants, including on one hand the role of the entrepreneur in coordination and innovation, and on the other the role of the state in terms of socialization. Structure-conduct-performance models, new industrial economics, organizational and behavioural theory in combination led to the recognition of both intra- and inter-firm interactions as well as the influence of the wider economic environment. This found its expression in theories of the public firm and recent empirical studies explaining differences in industrial performance of the Asian and Latin American NICs.

With the exception of the public enterprise model mentioned, all theories discussed above took the micro and/or sectoral level as their point of reference. Because macro-micro linkages and *vice versa* remain underdeveloped, the theoretical discussion presented in this study has devoted attention to various aspects of these linkages. Elements of macroeconomic policy and their impact on the microeconomic environment were discussed in terms of both their short term and long term consequences. In addition, the role of the state in economic development was reviewed in light of the recent debate on the successes of the NICs. It was argued that macro-analysis should be backed up by micro-analysis to obtain adequate understanding of impacts of macro-level changes. Moreover, the possibility for aggregated micro-outcomes to have short and long term impact on macroeconomic variables was indicated.

The theoretical framework adopted at the end of this theoretical tour reflects these dimensions. It is comparative and considers the role of international institutions, in particular the Multi-Fibre Arrangement, IMF, and the World Bank. It incorporates the role of the state, effects of macroeconomic policies and variables, micro-factors such as structural and incidental characteristics of firms, their interaction, and finally the ability of firms to affect macroeconomic variables, firstly through their performance and secondly through their lobbying to influence macroeconomic policy decisions.

Empirically, different aspects of performance were specified as technical, organizational, financial, export, and investment performance. Differentiating and comparing firms has been achieved by constructing indices for each of these aspects of performance. An appropriate linear combination of these indices was defined as total performance. Cross-section data covering the largest part of the textile sector in Tanzania were available, enabling the measurement of both these indices and a range of microeconomic explanatory variables. In addition, time-series data were available for a group of public sector firms on profits (financial performance) and capacity utilization (combination of technical and organizational performance), for aggregate textile exports of the whole sector, and for a number of macroeconomic variables such as the exchange rate, overall balance of payments, national consumer price index, rate of interest and the average price of textiles, a sectoral variable.

Analysis of performance began with a historical account of Tanzania's economic and political development, emphasizing industrial development. The nature of the Tanzanian state was reviewed to elucidate its role in processes of socialization, in the particular form of industrial development which has evolved (public sector industrial development), and in the shaping of macroeconomic policies, in particular the structural adjustment policies of the 1980s, culminating in the public sector debate between the

World Bank, the Tanzanian government, and some of its constituting parts.

Focusing on the textile sector in more detail, a combination of quantitative and qualitative evidence on both micro- and macro-factors affecting firms' performance led to a preliminary analysis focusing on the primacy of the constraints that have affected the development of the sector, on the impact of structural adjustment policies on cost structures of firms, and on the impact of the system of foreign exchange allocation and of credit policy.

The performance indices were taken as starting point for a quantitative analysis aimed at first explaining the cross-section variation of firms over these indices with the help of micro-factors. Secondly, these micro-factors were understood to be related to macro-factors leading to a time series analysis tracing the effects of macro-variables on three performance indicators: profits, capacity utilization (both defined for a group of public sector firms) and the exports of the whole sector.

It was shown that the main factors affecting firm performance (in the absolute sense) are found at micro- and macro-level. At micro-level, the main issues are technology, management, ownership, supply of utilities, access to foreign exchange and credit. At macro-level, the protected economy allowed for the development of inefficiency, and foreign exchange scarcity was progressively felt in input procurement and maintenance, limiting capacity utilization and effective capacity, and reducing financial viability. Trade and monetary policies of the latter half of the 1980s added to the problems of firms.

How firms fared under these circumstances depended on their micro-characteristics. Successful private firms were those that could resort to wider economic networks, domestically and/or internationally. For most public firms, this interaction between micro- and macro-factors resulted in a downwards spiral, which found its bureaucratic expression in more governance structures controlling and interfering with these firms, thus fuelling the downwards spiral. Morale sank at all levels with the general decline in wages and salaries and the bankruptcy of Tanzania's ideology. Corruption and other manifestations of the second economy further undermined the formal productive sector. While the Tanzanian nation state has proved very stable, and legitimization of the ruling elite as such is not strongly challenged, the value system of the Tanzanian state was seriously undermined. This, together with the failure of the state functions of accumulation and distribution (whatever its causes), has caused general lack of motivation. Cases have been cited where the productive apparatus itself suffered from actions by individuals with decision-making powers. Thus, rather than the state as a contest place for competing interests (the liberal view), or state power as the target of dominant interests for appropriation of surplus (the Marxist view), the almost perverse perspective of the state appears where the state apparatus becomes the target for opportunist individuals in the state elite to appropriate benefits at the expense of the productive (surplus generating) state system itself. Ironically, this has been the outcome of what was intended by some respected leaders as Tanzanian ujamaa (self reliance) and socialism.

The role of international institutions in Tanzania's development has been highlighted at various points, in particular the debate between the World Bank and the Tanzanian government. Detailed recommendations to privatize the public sector textile mills eventually emerged but have not yet been accepted. The coordinated actions of the donor community earlier to push the Tanzanian government to accept IMF conditionality, resulting in a further worsening of the crisis in the years just before the Economic Recovery Programme, were accepted in 1986.

Import support was one of the instruments with which to make the Tanzanian government accept the conditionality. The period of over investment in the late 1970s had been supported by development aid. When overcapacities developed, aid programmes had shifted to import support to supply the required recurrent imported inputs. This was withdrawn 1984/5 to be resumed in late 1985 when the IMF conditions were accepted. The evidence does not support the view that donors used import support to favour private sector firms when the international climate had shifted towards private firms. However, data on investment finance reveal that private firm investments are largely financed from aid-related sources.

Tanzania's textile sector has been compared to that of other countries in terms of technological advancement, trade performance and policies affecting performance of the textile sector. While technological development has been relatively advanced in some African countries, especially those in northern and southern Africa, most African countries are technologically stagnant compared to the highly dynamic international environment, with rather small installed capacities per capita in both spinning and weaving. Three waves of technological innovations have left most firms largely untouched. The first wave consisted of better spinning (open end) and weaving (shuttleless) technologies. The second wave consisted of automation based on electronics, and the third and most recent wave consists of microelectronic, computer-aided applications in production (for example robotics), monitoring and design. Corresponding changes in comparative advantages and trade patterns have gone unnoticed in Tanzania with its inward looking production focus. However, export markets still exist for standardized products for firms capable of reaching the required quality standards. Some firms (predominantly private ones) have jumped at these opportunities. For spinning and weaving separately, a technological ladder has been constructed classifying African countries in four technology groups. The highest group is at a technological level comparable to the sub-top of the world. The bottom group is unsuccessful in textile production, with old technology, no technological change and small textile sectors in relation to the population. For both spinning and weaving, Tanzania belongs to the second to last group (of four) on the technology ladder for African countries. About 70 percent of all African countries are at or below this level.

Again with the exception of northern and southern African countries, little success has been achieved in textile exports in Africa. A textile development ladder was constructed for Asian countries by UNIDO on the basis of export performance. Most African countries are in UNIDO group 1, the 'infant' stage. Subsequent differentiation of this group in three classes (1a, 1b, and 1c), also based on trade performance, revealed that most are in the lowest group (1a), showing no or very little exported textiles or clothing. Tanzania was classified in group 1c, the top of UNIDO's group one and, according to the UNIDO development model ready to move along to group 2. Most African countries (22 of the 28 surveyed) are below Tanzania's position on the trade ladder. However, its import-export ratios increased, indicating stagnation and decline, and a reversal of UNIDO's development sequence. More recent figures show that Tanzanian textile exports are again picking up. Thus, the development path suggested by the UNIDO classification does not appear to be the route that African countries follow. Instead, the available evidence suggests other routes: (a) backward linking from clothing exports into textile exports, (b) self sufficiency in both clothing and textiles with some exports, followed by decline, (c) initially only cotton exports while progressively forward linking into textiles and apparel, and (d) success in clothing leading to increasing textile imports. From this it appears that *a priori* no particular development path can be identified.

The model of development implied in UNIDO's classification was based on the analysis of the experience of successful Asian countries. It therefore does not necessarily (and perhaps was not intended to) apply to countries facing other historical conditions, particularly those of structural adjustment and decline of the manufacturing sector and the textile/clothing sector with it, and those arising from very low income per capita and rather fragile manufacturing sectors.

Most African countries have no special subsectoral textile policies and its industrial policies are dominated by structural adjustment policies.

This contrasts both with the European countries implementing specific textile plans, and with the countries adopting an industrial export orientation, i.e. the Asian countries and African countries such as Mauritius and, to a lesser extent, Zimbabwe and Kenya. In general terms, three major types of policy experiences can be identified on the basis of the countries reviewed. Firstly, policies followed by developed countries moving from defensive strategies through adjustment to new competitive strategies. Secondly, successful Asian countries (including Mauritius) follow a competitive policy sequence. Thirdly, the policy sequence followed by African countries and some less successful Asian countries moves from protective policies to adjustment policies, aiming at increasing industrial exports rather than full scale export-led development. Within these broad generalizations, individual countries obviously differ and show elements of all three experiences. Spain, for example, shows some aspects of the structural adjustment policies as implemented in African countries, some successful Asian countries are strong competitors for developed countries even in their market niches while some African countries (Kenya and Zimbabwe) are beginning to orient themselves to export-led development.

Concrete conclusions for specific theories of the firm can be drawn as well. While sectoral structure, such as the spatial structure of demand and supply and the resulting oligopolistic structure, has contributed to the survival of private sector firms, little evidence has been found for oligopolistic price or quantity competition. Indeed, this would be unlikely in an economy facing supply constraints. Other forms of strategic interaction between firms have been limited to attempts towards market control through varying degrees of vertical integration with marketing activities. This took place in a wider industrial structure characterized by economic groups, surpassing the borders of the textiles and garments sector. But it could equally be argued along the lines of reasoning of transaction cost economics that formation of economic groups and ensuing market control have been responses to various types of market failures. In that case, structural characteristics would find their explanation in factors related to firm behaviour and performance. For the private sector these developments have contributed to their survival, but public sector firms have felt their integration into a state controlled economic group, including the public sector marketing agency (Regional Trading Companies), more as a restriction to their production and marketing efforts. Considered in a longer time perspective, structure, behaviour, and performance must be seen as mutually interactive, each pervasively influenced by macro- and micro-factors. The direction of causality, subsectoral scope, and exclusive focus on meso-structural factors of the structure-conduct-performance model are contradicted by these considerations.

Instead, the results tend to support behavioural explanations (in particular the evolutionary model of the firm), coupled with elements of principal-agent theories and transaction cost economics, stressing the role of technological and management capability, in interaction with structural characteristics of the firm (such as technology and location) and the economic environment, government policies, and the nature of the state. Sectoral factors (but not of the type stressed by the structure-conduct-performance model) have played only a minor role in the period under study.

9.2   GENERAL LESSONS: TECHNOLOGY, TRADE AND TEXTILE POLICIES

Present-day 'conventional wisdom' is embodied in the model of an open economy following a policy of export-led industrialization. While export-led industrialization was successful under quite different circumstances than those prevailing in poor African countries, it is still justifiable to ask to what extent aspects of these experiences can be transferred. Indeed, the present analysis has also shown that some African firms are able to penetrate world markets. However, the most general lesson of this study has been that a differentiated approach to performance is required both in terms of aspects of performance (technological, organizational and financial performance, exports, and investment) as well as with regard to individual characteristics of firms. This implies that exclusive reliance on macroeconomic policies is too rough and imprecise as an instrument for industrial development.

Also for industrialized countries, sectoral and micro policies have played an important role. The emergence of a new trade pattern in a major segment of the textile/clothing sector, in which industrialized countries have resumed leadership and developing countries closer to the main industrial markets have started to play an increasingly important role, has been the result of a combination of government support, technological change, a new product mix and a niche marketing strategy.

Consequently, a large part of the market has been effectively closed to less advanced producers, not only because comparative cost advantages between low and high labour cost countries have declined but also because of requirements of quality management, production speed and market responsiveness based on detailed market information. Increasingly, the remaining export option for less advanced textile producers has become the market for more conventional, slower moving products as well as less processed intermediate textile products.

A rather wide range of technological choice exists both in terms of scale of production as well as capital labour ratios. Because of the dynamic innovation in the rest of the world, a large supply of second-hand machinery should be available for profitable use in countries that have large wage cost advantages.

Although international trade institutions in the textile/clothing sector are designed to protect and promote developed countries' producers (a tendency reinforced by pervasive non-tariff barriers to trade), for small exporters a market remains reserved as the quantity restrictions imposed under the Multi-Fibre Agreement do not (yet) apply. The position of ACP countries under the Lomé convention offers good possibilities for export expansion, although other non-tariff barriers may be more difficult for them to overcome. The opportunities on the EC market are confirmed by the export experience of Tanzanian private firms.

Therefore additional questions arise as to what extent individual African countries can and/or should climb the technological ladder in textile/clothing and other manufacturing sectors, and to what extent they will be able to increase their exports in the conventional and advanced product markets. Which development path should they choose and which macro and sectoral policies and firm level measures would be required to stimulate such developments? These questions are first are answered for the Tanzanian textile sector before the more general case of African industrial development is addressed.

Implications for Tanzania's textile sector development

Tanzania's industrial decline in the 1980s has taken place in a world buzzing with dynamic developments, also in the textile industry. The end of these developments is not in sight. Comparatively speaking, Tanzania's lost decade has resulted in a 'double deficit' in industrial development, which is growing in real terms. Halting this trend will require sustained efforts on many fronts. But, what type of interventions will be necessary to salvage the sector and lay the foundation for future, efficient growth?

Detailed performance analysis for Tanzanian firms has shown that despite this overall gloomy picture some firms are quite viable, while others contain elements, such as good overall or technical management, technology, training facilities, and, last but not least, a skilled labour force. All these assets should not be lost in the general current of structural adjustment and rationalization. Thus, first of all, the general conclusion with regard to policy intervention is that a targeted approach is called for, supplementing general macroeconomic policies. The rationale for this is that, although Tanzania's textile sector on average seems to perform roughly in accordance with its position on the 'technology, trade and policy ladders', large upward and downward deviations at firm level have been observed. These deviations occurred along dimensions of ownership and management (but more specific than the public-private dichotomy), foreign and local linkages, technology, financial structure, and export performance. Optimum policy intervention would have to be tuned to these differences, implying a targeted policy approach in addition to general supportive macroeconomic measures. One particular area for targeted policy intervention is credit supply. While general relaxation of credit supply to the productive sector may be inflationary, given the large number of rather inefficient firms supported beyond economic rationality, individual cases exist where credit supply acts as a real constraint to production increases. Targeting credit to such enterprises would have supply multiplier effects which would be deflationary rather than inflationary.

Second, a coordinated set of measures is required in the form of a textile plan, very much like the Belgian Textile Plan, combining micro-, sectoral, and macro-interventions. Government, employers and labour unions should join hands to determine what is required to put the textile sector on a healthy footing. Attention should be given to technical and management training, technological rehabilitation and upgrading, increasing specialization, improving internal and external linkages.

Third, export orientation should be encouraged both in terms of more neutral trade policies as well as on a firm by firm basis. The role of exports must be seen as to overcome the domestic constraints of limited markets and foreign exchange shortages: 'trade as a handmaiden of growth' (Linneman 1992:13) rather than an engine of growth. Only after that, in the long term, will fully-fledged export-oriented development, integrated with local capabilities, become feasible. As yet, the increasingly attractive export market cannot be fully captured because of lack of quality achieved by many firms. To the extent that this problem is overcome, an export orientation is feasible within the margins set by international developments in consumer demand and related technological and trade developments, in trade regulation (Multi-Fibre Arrangement), and competition of other low wage countries in the standardized and (for the time being) lower quality end of the market. In contrast to an import substitution strategy, export oriented development does not automatically run into a macroeconomic foreign exchange constraint. Export retention schemes provide both an export incentive (even if only to earn foreign exchange for production for the domestic market) and a mechanism to ensure that exporting firms will not face foreign exchange constraints. The Open General Licence scheme, when extended to many import categories, may prove to be a step too far towards full deregulation, draining the balance of payments without sufficiently stimulating exports.

Fourth, the analysis has shown that full scale privatization is not only politically infeasible, but also undesirable since this will imply transferring ownership to foreign firms or to the Tanzanian ethnic minority group of Indian descent. While the Indian entrepreneurship can certainly be seen as an asset, which can spearhead Tanzania's textile development, the long run objective of ethnically broader-based industrial development (as was perhaps attempted by state-led industrialization) will be jeopardized by full scale privatization. Ignoring the individually determined opportunistic elements of the argument (public managers' lobby), this may explain the apparent reluctance of the Tanzanian government to privatize. The only politically feasible economic solution would be a rather drastic but phased form of commercialization of public enterprises. Rather than subscribing to the private-public dichotomy, a continuum between the extremes of public and private management forms can be identified. Private sector linkages could be introduced through suppliers' contracts, management assistance, full management contracts, or participation in ownership. Such intermediate forms of management will induce and enable public sector firms to improve commercially, thus delivering the required improvements in efficiency. First priority would be to rationalize government-parastatal governance relationships to allow the parastatals to run like private sector firms. This would have to go hand in hand with increased accountability of the management. Tanzania is in the midst of such policy considerations. For instance, the one and only public sector garment firm has already entered into contractual arrangements with a USA-based firm. It is also exploring the possibility of extending such contracts to other foreign firms (in the EC). Although not without problems, these arrangements present real opportunities for quality improvement, management advice, and market information and could be considered for other firms as well (Egan and Mody 1992).

Fifth, during the decline in the 1980s, there was a tendency towards vertical integration, especially with the high performers, and towards specialization by most firms into those products that were least affected by limited effective consumer demand for domestic products. Rationalization would imply further specialization to avoid the increasing competition on the shrinking domestic market and, after lasting restoration of quality in subsector and mutual trust, intersectoral linkages may once more develop, including the growth of smaller production units. UNIDO's strategic management approach could provide a forum for exploring such developments.

Sixth, the analysis has concluded that large improvements in technological capability are possible. This will lead to higher quality in all parts of the cotton garments chain and to more efficient use of production inputs. Technological capability should be seen in relation to the appropriateness of technology chosen. The long lasting, high performance of Friendship Textile Mill, using relatively simple technology, has been cited as a case in point. While some of the above suggestions may positively affect this aspect, management and skill training should also be addressed separately. It was shown that the public sector plays an important role in skill training, also to the benefit of the private sector. A special textile technology, marketing and training centre would be able to identify suitable technologies, develop technological adaptation capacity, coordinate and initiate training activities related to all aspects of production and management, and supply market information on both inputs an outputs. Coordination of repair services and spare part production facilities for better utilization of available capacity (technicians and workshops) would benefit the whole sector.

Seventh, small-scale production is feasible in spinning, weaving and especially garmenting. In Tanzania this sector is underdeveloped. This is not just a question of technology but of further market improvements, small-scale large-scale linkages, and general policy, none of which are presently conducive to small scale development. Small-scale establishments provide a potential source of indigenous management.

Eighth, some integrated public sector firms are unviable by their location, water supply, or by the state and age of their machinery and buildings. Closure of infeasible activities in those firms, transfer of redundant equipment (if worthwhile) and concentration on feasible activities would allow some of these firms to survive.

Finally, where initial government (or donor) support is required (for rehabilitation, debt management, and working capital) and external relations are established, ranging from supply contracts to joint ventures and foreign investment, controlling these developments will present problems of their own, including dependencies between state and firms assumed to be typical for an import substitution strategy. Lessons from the Asian NICs suggest that any supportive measures should be temporary, regulated by contracts specifying clear performance criteria turning support into incentives to perform. The memorandum of understanding approach can be extended to the private sector when particular government support is supplied. This issue begs the question, to what extent government is strong enough to administer such policies thus posing a major challenge to the Tanzanian administration.

The nature of the state in Tanzania has developed in mutual interaction with economic developments towards more control over its resources and increasing internal softness. The generally low level of productivity in turn leads to further economic problems and changes in the nature of the state. In addition, it has been shown that despite increasing pressures by the World Bank, the Tanzanian government has undertaken no fundamental changes in the size or the control system of the parastatal system. In the more competitive environment it has continued to provide ailing public enterprises with direct financial support. Where government has succumbed to World Bank pressure in virtually every other aspect, it continues to keep its hold on the parastatal sector which thus appears to be a core interest to the ruling elite. How long the government will be able to do so remains to be seen, however.

To the extent that the Tanzanian government will remain with its productive role, it will in the first place have to become more strict with itself in order to perform its tasks within the limits of its own financial and human resources (as discussed with reference to the concepts of 'embeddedness' and 'hardness/softness' of the state developed in Chapter 2). This could go hand in hand with a changing conception of the 'commanding heights' of the economy in the direction of disciplined implementation of consistent economic policies and away from direct control of productive assets. The extent to which this can be achieved by the contending internal forces within the state elite, by imposition of conditionality by IMF, World Bank, and donor countries, or by some mixture of both, will determine the success of the eventual outcome in the medium and long term. The responsibility for industrial development and accumulation in general will have to be carried by the state at large and cannot be imposed exclusively from outside.

General implications for African industrialization

Despite differences between the groups of countries (European, Asian, and African), much of the diverse country experience can be captured under the general headings of the role of the state, the role of the market, foreign linkages, technology and intersectoral linkages. While these issues have been detailed for the textile sector, they equally apply to the industrial sector at large.

The role of the state has taken many forms, ranging from the design and implementation of policies, to provision of supporting services and to participation in production, and may itself be shaped by both external and internal political factors. EC policy towards Belgium and IMF/World Bank policy for African countries have been important external political factors. Conditions internal to the country determine the balance of power, and thus on one hand help to explain the nature of the state and thereby the nature of its action and on the other limit its range of action.

Within this field of forces, the emphasis of state intervention has shifted towards targeted policies and even firm specific measures. For some countries this implied a shift away from direct participation in production, particularly in countries such as Ghana, Kenya, Bangladesh, and Sri Lanka. For most, the general intervention (determining, for instance, the level of effective protection) shifted from import substitution to export promotion.

As corroborated explicitly by the case of Kenya, public corporations with local and politically appointed management are the worst economic performers. But state participation in production can take other forms. Especially where there is little local entrepreneurial capacity, few prospects for foreign investment, and an inability to control and integrate foreign investment, state participation in equity of private enterprises, foreign management of public enterprises (such as the high performer Morogoro Canvas in Tanzania), commercialization of public enterprises, and development of linkages between foreign buyers and local firms have potential gains that should not lightly be thrown away in the general fashionable wave of across-the-board privatization. For the textile/clothing sector the apparent problems of backwards integration (discussed in more detail below) define a field in which government action may be desired. Assessment of feasibility of these options, especially in respect of the degree of state control, requires a thorough analysis of the state in individual countries.

Ironically, the cases of Ghana and Tanzania show that the state, while participating in production, has become incapable of providing supporting services to production – a role for the state that is considered non-controversial and even essential from whichever ideological point of view one takes. Infrastructural services, support for commerce and trade, education and health are all essential, not just for the short term recovery, but equally for long term growth. With regard to the clothing/textile sector and in addition to general services, state involvement in technical training, technological research and commercial support has been part of the textile plans of nearly all countries reviewed.

For economic policies towards industry the issue at stake is not the role of the state as such but the type, extent and time-horizon of such policies. The export cum foreign investment oriented policies pursued in various degrees in all countries reviewed involve direct and indirect transfers to firms which may create dependencies similar to those developed under import substitution regimes when the state is not strong enough to gradually and selectively phase out such measures. Policies targeting industry, including the textile/clothing sector, are those that release the foreign exchange constraint for export production (as applied by Zimbabwe). Full, indiscriminate liberalization of imports (especially second-hand imports) may do more harm than good when industries have become accustomed to a protected environment, but gradual adjustment assumes a determined and capable state able to steer conflicting social forces in the desired direction.

It is thus not the size of the state that determines its effectiveness in economic planning and policy making but rather its strength as expressed by its relative autonomy with respect to major economic actors. Although it may be easy to reduce the size of the state and with that some major inefficiencies, strengthening the state is not a matter of better training or more policy advisors. Rather it is the result of socio-economic and political forces as they have been shaped by the past. A reorientation of such forces towards private enterprise does not affect the strength of the state but enforces its servicing role to the private sector. Especially in that light, overemphasizing direct and indirect measures in favour of private and foreign led export development may prove counter effective in the longer run.

Structural adjustment policies emphasized the role of free markets for their capacity to produce appropriate price signals for efficient resource allocation and production. In addition, increased competition and a better supply of market information may enhance efficiency and quality. The experiences with export oriented policies in the countries reviewed have revealed the important role that information on market requirements for quality and design have had for success in garment exports and that this has penetrated upstream into the textile sector. However, in the less successful countries such as Sri Lanka, Ghana, Kenya and Tanzania, overall structural adjustment policies have tended to dominate the rather underdeveloped export policy packages.

There is no necessary conflict between free markets and a certain degree of state participation as even under state ownership competition can be built into the system by individualizing public firms and making them function as private enterprises – thus leaving aside other objectives that government may want to realize with public enterprises incongruent with short term allocation efficiency. Recent experiences with the management contract system have been positive (Trivedi and Gopal 1990).

A distinction has to be made between domestic markets and export markets, and within each between the different quality requirements demanded by different income categories. The high quality export market in textiles and garments is largely the high income market of Europe and the US, and liberalizing access to these markets would benefit the advanced textile producers amongst the developing countries such as the NICs, Thailand and to some extent Bangladesh. The developing countries of the ACP already enjoy free access, and in fact benefit from investment relocation by more advanced countries in response to the MFA restrictions. The high quality end of the export market is out of reach for countries like Tanzania so that only the more standardized and lower quality segment remains where cost competition is most fierce.

The low quality end of the domestic market faces strong competition from second-hand clothing. The question that arises here is to what extent such imports should be liberalized or restricted. There is an apparent consumer interest in used consumer goods, but the industry is threatened by this competition with possible losses in employment, income and productive skills. The obvious answer would be that local industries should specialize towards higher quality domestic and export markets. However the conditions in the textile/clothing system are such that quick transformation is impossible. An intermediate approach allowing slower adjustment to regulated parameters is called for. But can the state administer such gradual change?

All the countries reviewed have adopted policies for technological upgrading. Depending on the country this served different objectives: entering the race for the fashion market for Belgium, facing the challenge of low wage competition for many firms in Spain, venturing into the low to medium quality export market for firms in Thailand, Bangladesh and Zimbabwe, deepening the value-added component of the final product for firms in Thailand and Mauritius, and at the lowest end of the spectrum revitalizing industries that had reached the end of their life-cycle as in the case of enterprises in Ghana, Kenya and Sri Lanka. The scope as well as the need for technological upgrading was highest in the textile sector, the garment sector being labour intensive, technologically simpler with more limited scope for technological innovation. Thus, the type of technological upgrading depended on market orientation, and reflected the factor endowments, the subsector and the stage of industrialization.

Technological upgrading should not take place in isolation. Factors that have contributed to deterioration of industry's capacity and/or factors that will be crucial for the new role that the sector is envisaged to play should be addressed simultaneously. For instance, physically rehabilitating firms in Ghana without restoring profitability will slowly bring the firm back to point zero and the country will be saddled with higher international debts. Pack's (1987) conclusion for Kenyan firms that management improvements should be given priority over technological improvement also applies to Tanzanian firms. Particularly in the public sector, financial and overall management are in a worse shape than technical management, although even here large improvements are possible.

Within the textile/clothing subsystem the main product (or subsector) linkages are cotton/yarn, polyester/yarn, yarn/fabric and fabric garments. Another type of linkage is between firms within the same subsector and between firms belonging to different parts of the textile/clothing system. There can be a systematic lack of integration between firms such as between large and small scale firms, between firms supplying different type of markets (exports/domestic or high/low quality or different types of consumers in terms of culture), and between firms with different ownership characteristics. These instances may merely reflect a general lack of integration.

Negative implications of lack of integration are the loss of foreign exchange when subsectoral linkages are replaced by imports and lost economies of specialization and flexibility when linkages between firms are underdeveloped. Major instances of areas with linkage problems are discussed below.

Most developing countries experienced problems integrating the garments export sector and the domestic textile sector. The immediate reason given for this is that the domestic textile sector cannot supply fabrics of sufficiently high quality required for exports. But there are more fundamental causes. First of all, there is a great difference in the complexity of technology and management between garments and textiles resulting in more problems in the textile sector. Second, domestic markets are less sensitive to quality differences than are export markets. This in its turn may be influenced by the low average income and lack of competition during past protective policy regimes. Third, the garment sector has often started as an export sector, so export market requirements are automatically incorporated. Fourth, foreign investment flows almost exclusively into garment exports. Finally, the MFA requirements on domestic input content apparently allow the use of non-domestic textiles, so that from the point of view of the foreign producer, merely shifting the location of the garment manufacturing will be sufficient, leaving all other parts of the production and supply network intact.

Instances of lack of integration between small scale and large scale producers were reported for Thailand, Bangladesh, Sri Lanka and Ghana, all with rather substantial handloom sectors.

The availability of local cotton has the immediate advantage of good supply even when foreign exchange shortages are severe. However, local cotton is not always of the right quality, and institutions and policies may develop around the cotton sector that limit the ability of firms to choose their best options with regard to cotton inputs (for example in Kenya and Nigeria). Such policies should be adjusted to reap the benefits of an adequate local cotton supply wherever agricultural conditions make this possible.

Firms often produce a wide range of products to satisfy the demands of a limited number of distributors (Kenya). This can be viewed as a case of horizontal intersectoral linkages. Although this may be a rational response of firms to the prevailing marketing conditions in their countries (transaction costs), limited linkages between firms decrease efficiencies that could have been achieved by more specialization and reduce the overall flexibility of the system. Market development is therefore an important policy area.

Finally, foreign linkages, broadly defined as including all linkages between the country and the outside world, are most easily established by foreign firms but not necessarily so. Most advantages arise from the substance of the linkage such as marketing networks and possibilities, technology transfer, information on markets and technology, capital for inputs and investments through suppliers credit and other forms of finance and access to managerial and technical skills. Most disadvantages flow from the concrete form in which these linkages materialize in terms of foreign control and ownership such as foreign dependency, high financial incentives and outflow of surplus.

These disadvantages can be reduced by different forms of foreign linkages. Inflow of foreign capital can take the form of joint ventures between the foreign investor and local private entrepreneurs or the state. Foreign managerial and technical skills can be acquired through management contracts. Marketing linkages can be organized in different forms leaving a substantial degree of autonomy with the local firms. Countries aiming at export promotion with the help of foreign investment such as Thailand, Bangladesh, Mauritius, Sri Lanka and recently also Kenya show a wide variety of such forms. Zimbabwe's particular ownership structure, although in other respects not desirable from the government's point of view, also allows some of the benefits of foreign linkages to be reaped. The case of Tanzania has shown the advantage of foreign linkages under foreign exchange constraints. But also under more favourable economic conditions, contract arrangements for production with foreign firms offer great advantages.

The above summary and conclusions have provided detailed insights into the problems and possibilities of industrialization in Africa. Indeed, a major contribution of this study has been to show that a differentiated view is required to understand the nature of industrialization in Africa. Successes and failures live side by side. Yet the general outlook for dynamic industrial development in Africa is very bleak. Markets, firms, and states interact to produce non-optimal conditions for reaching internationally competitive levels of efficiency. Policy interventions directed at industrial recovery and renewed growth will have to address inefficiencies in markets, states, and firms simultaneously. Careful introduction of world market forces and opportunities is more desirable than overnight liberalization. Even with optimum policies for each and every aspect African industrialization will be an uphill struggle. But uphill as it may be, it is worth fighting since it is the only long term route to higher productivity and increased welfare.

Appendix

Table A.1 Estimates of installation (1979–88) of spinning equipment and total spinning capacity (1987) by type of equipment in African countries and other regions

Country	(1) Spindles installed (1987)	(2) Spindles installed as % of world total (1987)	(3) Spindles installed as % of continent total (1987)	(4) O-E rotors as % of total spindles	(5) Ring	(6) O-E	(7) O-E rotors as % of 1988 spindle shipments*	(8) Indicators of 1987 installed spindles per mln. inhabitants	(9) Modernity	(10) Tech. change
					New spindles installed in 1979 to 1988 as % of 1987 total				Indicators of modernity and technological change	
Algeria	315 000	0.18	4.03	0.0	28.77	0.00		13.6	29	0.0
Angola	50 000	0.03	0.64	0.0	45.70	0.00		5.4	46	0.0
Benin	40 000	0.02	0.51	0.0	0.00	0.00		9.3	0	0.0
Botswana	16 300	0.01	0.21	8.0	0.00	8.25		13.9	8	6.9
Burkina Faso	7 000	0.00	0.09	0.0	0.00	0.00		0.8	0	0.0
Cameroon	55 464	0.03	0.71	0.0	9.35	0.30		5.1	10	0.3
Chad	8 000	0.00	0.10	0.0	11.80	0.00	0.0	1.5	11	0.0
Congo	11 000	0.01	0.14	0.0	0.00	0.00		6.0	0	0.0
Côte d'Ivoire	129 900	0.07	1.66	0.7	2.57	0.63	100.0	11.7	3	17.3
C. African R.	23 000	0.01	0.29	0.0	0.00	0.00		8.5	0	0.0
Egypt	3 070 500	1.77	39.28	0.9	26.41	0.86	0.0	60.5	27	0.8
Ethiopia	200 000	0.12	2.56	0.0	21.28	0.00	41.2	4.3	21	6.7
Ghana	120 400	0.07	1.54	0.3	13.28	0.14		9.0	13	0.3
Guinea	8 000	0.00	0.10	0.0	100.00	0.00		1.6	100	0.0
Kenya	110 200	0.06	1.41	1.1	24.37	1.08	4.9	4.8	25	1.7

Table A.1 continued

Country	(1) Spindles installed (1987)	(2) Spindles installed as % of world total (1987)	(3) Spindles installed as % of continent total (1987)	(4) O-E rotors as % of total spindles	(5) New spindles installed in 1979 to 1988 as % of 1987 total Ring	(6) O-E	(7) O-E rotors as % of 1988 spindle shipments*	(8) Indicators of 1987 installed spindles per mln. inhabitants	(9) Indicators of modernity and technological change Modern-ity	(10) Tech. change
Libya		0.00	0.00					0.0	0	0.0
Madagascar	72 000	0.04	0.92	2.8	26.38	4.10	0.0	6.6	30	3.4
Malawi	50 000	0.03	0.64	0.0	27.70	0.34		6.6	28	0.3
Mali	40 000	0.02	0.51	0.0	0.00	0.00		4.6	0	0.0
Mauritius	3 840	0.00	0.03	100.0	9.58	100.00		2.1	110	83.3
Morocco	404 000	0.23	5.17	6.9	21.00	3.64	2.3	17.3	25	6.1
Mozambique	50 000	0.03	0.64	0.0	28.08	0.00		3.4	28	0.0
Niger	14 000	0.01	0.18	0.0	0.00	0.00		2.2	0	0.0
Nigeria	716 000	0.41	9.16	2.2	24.91	2.25	17.8	7.0	27	4.8
Senegal	40 000	0.02	0.51	0.0	60.24	0.00		5.8	60	0.0
Somalia	20 000	0.01	0.26	0.0	0.00	0.00		2.9	0	0.0
South Africa	817 000	0.47	10.45	2.3	20.61	1.52	9.2	24.7	22	3.5
Sudan	518 000	0.30	6.63	3.5	7.51	3.47		22.4	11	2.9
Swaziland	18 000	0.01	0.23	0.0	100.00	0.00	0.0	25.3	100	0.0
Togo	26 000	0.01	0.33	0.0	53.65	0.00	8.3		54	0.0

Table A.1 continued

Country	(1) Spindles installed (1987)	(2) Spindles installed as % of world total (1987)	(3) Spindles installed as % of continent total (1987)	(4) O-E rotors as % of total spindles	(5) New spindles installed in 1979 to 1988 as % of 1987 total Ring	(6) O-E	(7) O-E rotors as % of 1988 spindle shipments*	(8) Indicators of 1987 installed spindles per mln. inhabitants	(9) Indicators of modernity and technological change Modern-ity	(10) Tech. change
Tanzania	400 000	0.23	5.12	0.0	39.56	0.08		17.2	40	0.1
Zaire	128 000	0.07	1.64	2.3	0.00	0.15		3.9	0	1.9
Zambia	51 800	0.03	0.66	3.5	45.63	3.44	20.1	6.8	49	6.3
Zimbabwe	124 000	0.07	1.59	3.2	13.55	5.31	20.3	14.4	19	7.8
Total Africa	7 817 304	4.51	100.00	1.7	23.49	1.45	5.8		25	2.4
Total World	173 435 563			4.1	13.85	3.82	17.3		18	6.3

Note: * A blank entry implies no shipment of any kind of spindles, an entry of zero implies that the share of O-E spindles in total spindles shipments is zero.

Source: Calculated from Industry and Development (UNIDO 1990b) and Demographic Yearbook 1988 (United Nations 1990).

Table A.2 Estimates of installation (in 1988) of weaving equipment and total installed weaving capacity (1987/88) by type of equipment in African countries and other regions

Country	(1) Total looms installed (1988)	(2) Shuttle-less as % of total looms installed (1988)	(3) Installed looms per 100 000 inhabitants (1988)	(4) Total looms installed as % of world total (1988)	(5) Total looms installed as % of continent total (1988)	(6) Spending shuttle-less as % total spending on looms* (1988)	(7) New loom installations 1979 to 1988 as % of total looms installed — Shuttle	(8) New loom installations 1979 to 1988 as % of total looms installed — Shuttle-less	(9) Indicators of modernity and technological change — Modernity	(10) Indicators of modernity and technological change — Tech. change
Algeria	10 532	19.3	4.6	0.37	7.23	100	7.58	18.17	26	26.6
Angola	860	7.0	0.9	0.03	0.59		25.70	0.23	26	6.3
Benin	1 500	0.0	3.5	0.05	1.03		0.00	0.00	0	0.0
Botswana	120	100.0	1.0	0.00	0.08		0.00	100.00	100	90.9
Burkina Faso	200	0.0	0.2	0.01	0.14		1.00	0.00	1	0.0
Cameroon	1 200	16.7	1.1	0.04	0.82		6.67	6.67	13	15.2
Chad	280	0.0	0.5	0.01	0.19		0.00	0.00	0	0.0
Congo	190	0.0	1.0	0.01	0.13		0.00	0.00	0	0.0
Côte d'Ivoire	2 630	24.0	2.4	0.09	1.80		15.89	5.55	21	21.9
C. African R.	500	0.0	1.8	0.02	0.34		20.00	0.00	20	0.0
Egypt	58 823	6.2	11.6	2.09	40.36	61	11.95	6.93	19	11.8
Ethiopia	3 312	9.7	0.7	0.12	2.27	91	2.42	7.97	10	17.1
Ghana	3 640	0.8	2.7	0.13	2.50		0.05	0.00	1	0.7
Guinea	130	0.0	0.3	0.00	0.09		100.00	0.00	100	0.0

Table A.2   continued

Country	(1) Total looms installed (1988)	(2) Shuttle-less as % of total looms installed (1988)	(3) Installed looms per 100 000 inhabitants (1988)	(4) Total looms installed as % of world total (1988)	(5) Total looms installed as % of continent total (1988)	(6) Spending shuttle-less as % total spending on looms* (1988)	(7) New loom installations 1979 to 1988 as % of total looms installed — Shuttle	(8) Shuttle-less	(9) Indicators of modernity and technological change — Modernity	(10) Tech. change
Kenya	1 718	12.7	0.7	0.06	1.18	100	5.94	7.28	13	20.7
Libya	3 000	13.3	7.3	0.11	2.06		0.00	14.03	14	13.0
Madagascar	1 930	10.4	1.8	0.07	1.32		12.18	8.34	21	9.4
Malawi	666	9.9	0.9	0.02	0.46	100	0.00	9.91	10	18.1
Mali	1 120	0.0	1.3	0.04	0.77		0.00	0.00	0	0.0
Mauritius	64	100.0	0.3	0.00	0.04	100	53.13	100.00	153	100.0
Morocco	6 056	19.1	12.6	0.21	4.15	100	0.00	26.14	26	32.9
Mozambique	2 450	0.8	1.7	0.09	1.68		0.04	0.82	1	0.7
Niger	280	0.0	0.4	0.01	0.19		2.14	0.00	2	0.0
Nigeria	19 257	11.7	1.9	0.68	13.21	100	3.99	7.52	12	19.7
Senegal	650	100.0	0.9	0.02	0.45		3.08	20.92	24	90.9
Somalia	410	36.6	0.6	0.01	0.28		0.00	0.00	0	33.3
South Africa	5 881	57.5	1.8	0.21	4.03	100	4.07	27.34	31	61.4

Table A.2 continued

Country	(1) Total looms installed (1988)	(2) Shuttle-less as % of total looms installed (1988)	(3) Installed looms per 100 000 inhabitants (1988)	(4) Total looms installed as % of world total (1988)	(5) Total looms installed as % of continent total (1988)	(6) Spending shuttle-less as % total spending on looms* (1988)	New loom installations 1979 to 1988 as % of total looms installed		Indicators of modernity and technological change	
							(7) Shuttle	(8) Shuttle-less	(9) Modernity	(10) Tech. change
Sudan	1 000	0.0	0.4	0.04	0.69		15.06	0.08	15	0.1
Swaziland	42	100.0	0.6	0.00	0.03	100	0.00	100.00	100	100.0
Togo		0.0	0.0	0.00	0.00		0.00	0.00	0	0.0
Tunisia	4 779	22.6	6.3	0.17	3.28	100	1.90	17.10	19	29.7
Uganda	1 400	17.1	0.8	0.05	0.96		23.38	0.00	23	15.5
Tanzania	5 150	2.9	2.2	0.18	3.53		22.29	3.07	25	2.6
Zaire	2 790	3.2	0.9	0.10	1.91		6.38	3.30	10	3.0
Zambia	1 140	12.3	1.5	0.04	0.78		20.61	12.63	33	11.5
Zimbabwe	1 954	18.1	2.3	0.07	1.34	100	1.74	15.82	17	25.5
Total Africa	145 757	12.2		5.17	100.00					
Total World	2 819 684	19.5		100.00		88	9.09	8.74	18	19.1

Note: * A blank entry implies no expenditure on any kind of looms. An entry of zero implies that the share of shuttle-less looms in total loom expenditure is zero.
Source: Calculated from Industry and Development (UNIDO 1990b) and Demographic Yearbook 1988 (United Nations 1990).

Table A.3   Manufacturing in Africa: some summary statistics

Country	Ratio of MVA to GDP 1985	Ratio Manufactured to Total Exports			% Share in MVA (1985)	
		1966	1976	1986	Food	Text. & Cloth.
Algeria						
Angola	2.9					
Benin	6.4				58	16
Botswana	6.0	12	13.2	21.7	52	12
Burkina Faso	13.8	4	5.9	12.6	62	18
Burundi	8.4	5.4	1.2	11.6	75	11
Cameroon	11.0	2.8	9.3	5.9	50	13
Chad	8.5					
Congo	7.3	54.8	12.4	18.6	47	13
Côte d'Ivoire	11.6	4	7.5	9	40	13
C.A.R.	7.4	53.7	17.6	32.7	44	19
Egypt						
Ethiopia	10.2	1.3	2.1	0.7	51	23
Gabon	6.0	9	1.1	12.6		
Ghana	13.6	3.9	3.5	2.6	53	6
Guinea	3.6					
Kenya	12.6	7	20.5	15.8	35	12
Liberia	7.6	3.3	2.5	1.5		
Libya						
Madagascar	11.2	6.2	7.8	12.3	35	47
Malawi	14.8	5.6	7	16.1	49	13
Mali	7.6	1.6	1.4	29.7		
Mauritius	18.3	1	19.8	41.8	37	34
Morocco						
Mozambique	6.4					
Niger	4.0	4	2.5	3		
Nigeria	5.0	2.7	0.6	1.5	29	11
Rwanda	18.0	0.2	1.5	0.8	77	1
Senegal	16.3	5.5	13.2	28.8	48	15
Sierra Leone	4.1	57.5	641	56.4	36	4
Somalia	7.8				46	21
South Africa						
Sudan	9.1	1.1	1.2	6.5	22	25
Togo	4.8	2.8	5.3	20.8		
Tunisia						
Uganda	4.5	0.6	0.4	0.2		
Tanzania	5.2	13.9	11.6	16.9	28	26
Zaire	1.3	6.6	4.1	5.8	40	16
Zambia	20.0	0.7	0.8	3	44	13
Zimbabwe	27.7	10	24.7	36.7	28	16

Source: Manufacturing Africa, Riddell (ed.), 1990a.

Table A.4   Labour cost comparisons in spinning and weaving, 1980–90 (US$/hour)

	1980	1984	1987	1988	1989	1990
Switzerland	9.65	8.65	15.70	17.15	14.58	19.23
Belgium	11.82	8.84	13.66	15.07	14.08	17.85
Netherlands	11.68	9.80	13.75	15.62	14.06	17.84
West Germany	10.16	7.54	12.98	14.67	13.17	16.46
Italy	9.12	6.35	12.67	13.81	13.03	16.13
Japan	4.35	6.28	11.99	14.93	13.98	13.96
France	7.91	6.07	9.99	10.88,	9.82	12.74
UK	5.75	5.46	7.09	8.43	8.18	10.20
USA	6.37	8.60	9.24	9.42	9.71	10.02
East Germany						8.28
Spain	4.90	3.87	4.78	5.69	5.65	7.69
Greece	3.49	4.30	4.00	4.47	4.32	5.65
Taiwan	1.26	1.64	2.09	2.94	3.56	4.65
South Korea	0.78	1.89	1.77	2.29	2.87	3.22
Hong Kong	1.91	1.65	1.93	2.19	2.44	3.05
Singapore	0.94					2.83
Tunisia	1.13	1.21	2.56	2.69	2.37	2.82
Portugal	1.68	1.28	1.83	2.19	2.03	2.75
Mexico	3.10	2.62	0.83	1.84	2.11	2.21
Brazil			1.62	0.89	1.78	1.97
Uruguay	0.89		1.97	1.69	1.78	1.86
Turkey	0.95	1.19	1.28	1.01	1.27	1.82
Colombia		2.81	1.66	1.69	1.71	1.71
South Africa		1.64	0.82	0.86	0.69	1.57
Argentinia	3.33	2.23	1.60	1.24	1.42	1.42
Venezuela		3.27	2.35	1.27	1.26	1.37
Morocco	0.85		0.74	1.10	1.10	1.28
Hungary						1.24
Peru			1.40	1.64	1.13	1.23
Syria	0.96	3.12	4.29	0.67	0.86	0.94
Thailand	0.33	0.56	0.58	0.66	0.68	0.92
Ethiopia		0.27	0.29	0.68	0.78	0.87
Malaysia				0.81	0.82	0.86
India	0.60	0.71	0.65	0.77	0.65	0.72
Philippines	0.57	0.64	0.64	0.67		
Kenya		0.53	0.62	0.60	0.54	0.63
Egypt	0.39	0.90	1.19	0.41	0.45	0.45
Pakistan	0.34	0.49	0.37	0.40	0.37	0.39
China		0.26	0.23	0.27	0.40	0.37
Tanzania						0.32
Nigeria		2.13	0.48	0.39	0.26	0.30
Indonesia		0.23	0.20	0.22	0.23	0.25
Sri Lanka		0.28	0.31	0.30	0.26	0.24

Source: Werner International, reproduced in Finnerty (1991).

Table A.5 GDP at factor cost by industrial origin (m. TShs in constant 1976 prices)

	1976	1977	1978	1979	1980	1981	1982	1983	1984	1985	1986	1987	1988	1989
Agriculture, hunting, forestry and fishing	9 046	9 150	8 998	9 066	9 418	9 511	9 639	9 914	10 312	10 931	11 557	12 066	12 606	13 183
Mining and quarrying	214	231	189	200	189	193	193	174	186	174	154	149	138	139
Manufacturing	2 811	2 641	2 730	2 821	2 683	2 382	2 304	2 103	2 159	2 075	1 991	2 075	2 187	2 299
Water and electricity	219	244	286	318	400	417	420	413	439	461	544	584	574	588
Construction	884	915	783	879	932	890	930	549	660	601	705	736	780	821
Wholesale, retail trade, hotels and restaurants	2 839	2 782	2 797	2 839	2 839	2 725	2 668	2 612	2 640	2 662	2 958	3 112	3 225	3 378
Transport and communications	1 685	1 652	1 699	1 634	1 818	1 652	1 694	1 473	1 482	1 509	1 504	1 551	1 652	1 730
Finance and commercial activities	2 036	2 089	2 208	2 338	2 483	2 529	2 702	2 817	2 984	3 046	3 318	3 395	3 500	3 632
Public administration and other services	2 342	2 497	2 997	3 255	3 188	3 551	3 556	3 543	3 549	3 616	3 225	3 243	3 343	3 442
Less imputed bank charges	424	462	485	501	531	549	667	716	755	797	886	862	920	940
GDP at factor cost	21 652	21 739	22 202	22 849	23 419	23 301	23 439	22 882	23 656	24 278	25 070	26 049	27 085	28 272

Source: United Republic of Tanzania (1990a).

Table A.6 Tanzania – Summary of important statistics, 1980–89

	1980	1981	1982	1983	1984	1985	1986	1987	1988	1989
1. Population (m.)	18.1	18.7	19.2	19.6	20.2	20.7	21.3	21.9	22.5	23.1
2. GDP at 1976 prices (m. T.Shs)	23 419	23 301	23 439	22 882	23 656	24 278	25 070	26 049	27 085	28 272
3. Growth (%)	4.1	−0.5	0.6	−2.4	3.4	2.6	3.3	3.9	4	4.4
4. Per capita GDP (1976 prices)	1 350	1 292	1 255	1 167	1 171	1 172	1 181	1 186	1 203	1 223
5. Exports (F.O.B.)* (m. US$)	571	566	442	406	331	339	348	353	380	395
6. Imports (C.I.F.) (m. US$)	1 240	1 172	1 128	930	836	999	1 047	1 150	1 192	1 230
7. Current A/C Balance**(m. US$)	−565.1	−407.2	−539.3	−308.3	−369.4	−415.0	−312.0	−264.8	−348.5	−401.7
8. Consumer Price Index***	156.7	196.9	253	322.6	439.2	585.4	775.3	1 007.4	1 321.5	1 663.2
9. Average exchange rate (Shs/US$)	8.2	8.3	9.4	11.7	16.3	17.2	38.2	68.6	108.3	154.7
10. Inflation rate (%)	30.4	25.7	28.9	27.1	36.1	28.2	33.2	28.9	28.2	23.8
11. Exports/GDP (%)	10.9	5	5.9	4	7	6.8	9.4	12.4	14.16	17.4
12. Imports/GDP (%)	26.3	20.7	15.2	12.8	15.9	15.6	28.4	40.4	44.4	54.2
13. Exports/Imports (%)	46.8	49.2	39.2	46.6	39.5	33.9	33.2	30.7	31.9	32.1

Notes: *   Excludes re-exports
      **   Includes capital transfers
      ***   For town dwellers, 1977 = 100: Mainland Tanzania average

Sources: Economic Survey 1989 (June 1990), Bank of Tanzania, Bureau of Statistics (for food imports 1980–87)
Tanzania Economic Trends (April 1989).

Table A.7 Efficiency in the manufacturing sector, 1984

Subsector	Net eff. rate of protection (%) (1)	Eff. rate of protection (%) (2)	Actual Short-run DRC (3)	Actual Long-run DRC (4)	Capacity utilization(%)	Attainable Capacity utilization(%)	Attainable Short-run DRC (5)	Attainable Long-run DRC (6)
Food	102	65.1	0.39	1.48	17	43	0.27	0.81
Beverages & tobacco	507	83.8	0.37	0.93	48	63	0.27	0.70
Textiles	268	55.4	0.87	2.01	47	61	0.78	1.74
Leather	inf.	41.3	inf.	inf.	10	31	inf.	inf.
Plastics, pharmac'als	inf.	45.4	inf.	inf.	13	45	inf.	inf.
Chemicals, fertilizers	inf.	1.6	inf.	inf.	27	49	inf.	inf.
Non-metallic mineral products	182	27.9	1.14	2.93	31	63	0.62	1.45
Iron, steel and metal products	6 732	28.1	11.12	32.16	35	61	1.95	5.18
Machinery, transport equipment	1 464	25.0	2.11	7.56	17	37	4.72	13.00
Total	525		0.93	2.45	30	53	0.68	1.69
– public	524		0.92	2.35	35	56	0.68	1.66
– private	532		1.00	3.12	26	51	0.72	1.87
Total (without brewery & tobacco)	502		1.40	3.72	29	53	0.97	2.39
– public	492		1.54	3.93	33	55	1.07	2.61
– private	532		1.00	3.12	26	51	0.72	1.87

Notes: (1) Net effective rate of protection incorporates the effects of quantity restrictions as well.
(2) Actual short-run DRC: labour costs divided by value added at world prices.
Source: Summarized from World Bank (1987c).

Table A.8   Constraints to expansion of production in the textile sector in 1988

	(1)	(2)	(3)	(4)	(5)	(6)	(7)	(8)	(9)	(10)	(11)	(12)
Mwatex	3	3		2	4	5	1					
Ubungo			5						4			
Morogoro Canvas					4	5		1	1	2	3	
Friendship	4	5	1		1	3		2				
Mutex	4	4		3	5							
Sunguratex	3	4	5			2		1				
Taboratex		2	4	1	5			3				
Blanket Man	5	5	4	1	2							
Mbeyatex	1	2	5	3				4				
Polytex	4	4	5		1			2				
A to Z		5										
Tang.Tex			5									
Ellen			5									4
Polyknit	5	5			3			1	2			
Tangamano		3	5	4								
TOTAL	34	30	43	14	25	15	1	13	7	2	3	4
Rank	2	3	1	6	4	5	12	7	8	11	10	9
TOTAL Public	24	23	28	10	22	15	1	11	7	2	3	0
Rank	2	3	1	7	4	5	11	6	8	10	9	12
TOTAL Private	10	7	15	4	3	0	0	2	0	0	0	4
Rank	2	3	1	4	6			7			5	

Key: (1) Lack of foreign exchange for raw materials
　　　　　(2) Lack of foreign exchange for spares
　　　　　(3) Lack of working capital (domestic credit)
　　　　　(4) Transport problems
　　　　　(5) Electricity interruptions
　　　　　(6) Water interruptions
　　　　　(7) Fuel supply problems
　　　　　(8) Shortage and high turnover of skilled labour
　　　　　(9) Labour undiscipline
　　　　　(10) Supply of raw materials
　　　　　(11) Rising input and output prices
　　　　　(12) High taxes, no competitiveness (no entries)

Notes: The weighting was 5 to 0 for priorities 1 to 6.
　　　　　The highest score therefore reflects the most important constraint.
　　　　　Total number of firms is 15 of which 6 are private and 9 public.

Table A.9 Foreign exchange allocation, January–June 1987 (millions of US$)

Applicant	(1)	(2)	(3)	(4)	(5)	(6)	(7)	(8)	(9)
Public									
Ubungo (Sp)		0.33	0.20	0.42			0.20	0.20	
Tabora (Sp)		0.05						0.00	
Friendship	35.0	1.82	1.40	0.16		0.02	1.00	1.02	2.9
Mwatex	46.0	2.62	0.40	0.27			0.30	0.30	0.7
Sunguratex	21.6	0.92	0.40	0.22			0.30	0.30	1.4
Kiltex	21.0	2.26	1.00	1.58			0.50	0.50	2.4
Mutex	22.0	2.24	0.50	0.83		0.02	0.30	0.32	1.5
Mbeyatex	21.5	0.21	0.16				0.16	0.16	0.7
Polytex	16.0	2.22	0.80				0.50	0.50	3.1
Moro. Canvas	4.6	1.20	0.44	0.72			0.40	0.40	8.7
TEXCO					0.40	0.26		0.66	
Private									
Cotex (I)		0.34	0.16			0.06	0.10	0.16	
CIC	8.5	2.88	0.30			0.06	0.30	0.36	4.2
Tang. Text.	4.5	0.53	0.24	0.02			0.15	0.15	3.3
Calico	3.4	0.45	0.24	0.06			0.15	0.15	4.4
Sunflag	15.4	6.12	0.60	0.31		0.19	0.30	0.49	3.2
Moshi Text.	12,1						0.00	0.0	
MB Text.	1.8	0.77	0.32			0.01	0.20	0.21	11.4
A to Z	3.8	4.10	0.50	0.16			0.30	0.30	7.9
JV	10.2	1.31	0.50	0.50	0.27	0.06	0.20	0.53	5.2
Cotex (Z+DSM)	5.0	4.76	0.40	0.24			0.20	0.20	4.0
Total	252.4	35.13	8.56	5.49	0.67	0.67	5.56	6.90	2.7
Total Public	187.7	13.86	5.30	4.19	0.40	0.30	3.66	4.36	2.3
Total Private	64.7	21.27	3.26	1.30	0.27	0.37	1.90	2.54	3.9
Public/Private	2.9	0.7	1.6	3.2	1.5	0.8	1.9	1.7	

Key:
(1) Capacity (m.mts.)
(2) Request
(3) Sector recommendation
(4) L/C pending
(5) Import support
(6) Export retention
(7) Recommended
(8) Total funds
(9) Allocation/capacity

Source: Compiled from internal data from Bank of Tanzania and CBS.

Table A.10   Domestic market supply and textile consumption per caput, 1985–88

	1985	**1986**	**1987**	**1988**
Total fabric exports:				
tons	647	1 058	1 502	1 492
1000 m.	3 109	5 021	7 074.5	7 379.5
Second-hand clothing imports:				
tons	2 363	4 283	5 189	5 846
1000 m.	12 996.5	23 556.5	28 539.5	32 153
Local production:				
tons	14 647	16 419	16 482	13 958
1000 m.	67 617	75 906	76 314	64 783
Production + imports – exports:				
tons	16 363	19 644	20 169	18 312
1000 m.	77 504.5	94 441.5	97 779	89 556.5
Consumption/caput:				
kg per caput	0.71	0.85	0.88	0.80
metres per caput	3.37	4.11	4.25	3.89
Assuming second-hand imports 20 percent above reported level: Consumption/caput:				
kg per caput	0.73	0.89	0.92	0.85
metres per caput	3.48	4.31	4.50	4.17
Other imports:				
tons	4 712	1 225	1 385	16 944
1000 m.	26 609	6 514	8 202	96 097
Consumption of other imports per caput:				
kg per head	0.20	0.05	0.06	0.74
metres per head	1.16	0.28	0.36	4.17
Total consumption per caput				
metres per head	4.53	4.39	4.61	8.06
Consumption per caput estimated by MoI&T:				
kg per caput	1.07	4.7	2.4	3.4
metres per caput	5.3	25	13	18

Notes: Conversion factors used in calculations
      Woven cotton 0.22 kg/m^2 or 4.5 m^2/kg
      Knitted cotton 0.20 kg/m^2 or 5.0 m^2/kg
      Other woven fabric 0.154 kg/m^2 or 6.5 m^2/kg
      Clothing 0.18 kg/m^2 or 5.5 m^2/kg
      Population is taken as 23 million
Source: Table 6.2, Table 6.3, and URT (1990d).

References

Abeyratne, S. (1993) *Anti-Export Bias in the 'Export-Oriented' Economy of Sri Lanka* (VU University Press, Amsterdam).

Adomako, K.N. (1990) 'The Ghana Industrial Holding Corporation (GIHOC)', *Public Enterprise*, Vol. 10, No. 1.

Alavi, H. (1972) 'The State in Post-Colonial Societies: Pakistan and Bangladesh', *New Left Review*, No. 74.

Andrae, G. and B. Beckman (1987) *Industry Goes Farming*, Research Report No. 80 (Scandinavian Institute of African Studies, Uppsala).

Athukorala, P. (1986) 'The Impact of 1977 Policy Reforms on Domestic Industry', *Upanathi*, Vol. 1, No. 1.

Ayub, M.A. and S.O. Hegstad (1986) *Public Industrial Enterprises: Determinants of Performance*, Industry and Finance Series Vol. 17 (World Bank, Washington, DC).

Bagachwa, M.S.D. (1992) 'Choice of Technology in Small and Large Firms: Grain Milling in Tanzania', *World Development*, Vol. 20, No. 1.

Bain, J.S. (1968) *Industrial Organization*, 2nd edn (John Wiley & Sons, New York).

Bank of Tanzania (1989) *Economic and Operations Report* (Bank of Tanzania, Dar es Salaam).

Bank of Thailand (1990) *Annual Report 1989* (Bank of Thailand, Bangkok).

Baran, P.A. (1973) *The Political Economy of Growth* (Penguin Books, New York).

Barro, R.J. and H.I. Grossman (1974) 'Suppressed Inflation and the Supply Multiplier', *Review of Economic Studies*, Vol. 41, No. 1.

Baumol, W.J. (1959) *Business Behaviour, Value and Growth* (Macmillan, New York).

Baumol, W.J., J. Panzar and R.D. Willig (1982) *Contestable Markets and the Theory of Industrial Structure* (Harcourt Brace Jovanovich, New York).

Bhagwati, J. (1991) 'Economics in the Post-Socialist Century', *Economic Journal*, Vol. 101, No. 1.

Bhagwati, J. (1982) 'Directly Unproductive, Profit-Seeking (DUP) Activities', *Journal of Political Economy*, Vol. 90, No. 5.

Bhalla, A., D. James and Y. Stevens (eds) (1984) *Blending of New and Traditional Technologies* (Tycooly International Publishing Ltd. Dublin).

Bhuiyan, Md.M.H. (1991) 'The Textile and Clothing Industry in Bangladesh', *Textile Outlook International*, March 1991.

Bienefeld, M. (1982) 'Evaluating Tanzanian Industrial Development', *Industry and Accumulation in Africa*, M. Fransman (ed.) (Heinemann, London).

Blinder, A.S. (1989) *Macroeconomics Under Debate* (Harvester Wheatsheaf, New York).

Board of External Trade (1988) 'Duty Drawback Scheme in Tanzania', *Trade Currents*, Vol. 2, No. 5 (Board of External Trade, Tanzania, Dar es Salaam).

Bonanno, G. and D. Brandolini (eds) (1990) *Industrial Structure in the New Industrial Economics* (Clarendon Press, Oxford).

Boon, G.K. (1981) *Technology Transfer in Fibres, Textile and Apparel* (Sijthoff & Noordhoff, Alphen aan den Rijn).

348

Bös, D. (1985) *Public Enterprise Economics* (North Holland, Amsterdam).

Bruno, M. (1972) 'Domestic Resource Costs and Effective Protection: Clarification and Synthesis', *Journal of Political Economy*, Vol. 80, No. 1.

Bulmer-Thomas, V. (1982) *Input-Output Analysis in Developing Countries* (John Wiley & Sons, New York).

Burch, D.F. (1987) *Overseas Aid and the Transfer of Technology* (Avebury, Aldershot).

Bureau of Statistics (1988) *1988 Population Census: Preliminary Report* (Ministry of Finance, Economic Affairs and Planning, Dar es Salaam).

Central Bank of Sri Lanka (1989) *Annual Report* (Central Bank of Sri Lanka, Colombo).

Chakravarty, S. (1991) 'Development planning: a reappraisal', *Cambridge Journal of Economics*, Vol. 15, No. 1.

Chowdhury, J.A. (1990) 'Privatization in Bangladesh', *Working Paper Series*, No. 92 (Institute of Social Studies, The Hague).

Clive, H. (1989) 'The Irrelevance of Economic Liberalization of the Third World', *World Development*, Vol. 17, No. 10.

Coase, R.H. (1937) 'The Nature of the Firm', *Economica*, Vol. 4.

Coker, J. (1990) 'World Textile Trade and Consumption: Forecasts to 2000', *Textile Outlook International*, May 1990.

Colander, D.C. (1979) 'Rationality, Expectations and Functional Finance', *Essays in Post-Keynesian Inflation*, J.H. Gapinski and C.E. Rockwood (eds) (Ballinger Publishing Company, Cambridge, MA).

Colclough, C. and J. Manor (eds) (1991) *States or Markets? Neo-liberalism and the Development Policy Debate* (Clarendon Press, Oxford).

Collier, P. (1989) 'Peasant Supply Response and Real Incomes: Theory and Application to Tanzania 1977–88', Working Paper with D. Bevan, J.W. Gunning and P. Horsnell, Unit for the Study of African Economies, University of Oxford.

Collier, P. and J.W. Gunning (1989) 'The Tanzanian Recovery 1983–89', in World Bank (1991) *Tanzania Economic Report: Towards Sustainable Development in the 1990s*, Vol. 2 (World Bank, Washington, DC).

Commons, J.R. (1934) *Institutional Economics* (University of Wisconsin Press, Madison).

Cooper, C. and R. Kaplinsky (1985) 'Second-hand Equipment in Developing Countries: Jute Processing Machinery in Kenya', *Technology and Employment in Industry*, A.S. Bhalla (ed.), 3rd edn (ILO, Geneva).

Copeland, M. (1969) *The Game of Nations: The Amorality of Power Politics* (Simon & Schuster, New York).

Coughlin, P. (1986) 'The Gradual Maturation of an Import-Substituting Industry: the Textile Industry in Kenya', Report for the World Bank, Nairobi (mimeo).

Coughlin, P, and G.K. Ikiara (eds) (1988) *Industrialization in Kenya: In Search of a Strategy* (James Currey, London).

Coulson, A. (1982a) 'The State and Industrialization in Africa', *Industry and Accumulation in Africa*, M. Fransman (ed.) (Heinemann, London).

Coulson, A. (1982b) *Tanzania: A Political Economy* (Oxford University Press, Oxford).

Cranenburgh, O. van (1990) *The Widening Gyre: The Tanzanian One-Party State and Policy towards Rural Cooperatives* (Eburon Publishers, Delft).

Dao, G.C. (1989) 'The Developing World and the Multifibre Arrangement', *Developing Countries and the Global Trading System*, Vol. 2, J. Whalley (ed.) (Macmillan, Basingstoke).

De Alessi, L. (1983) 'Property Rights, Transaction Costs, and X-Efficiency: An Essay in Economic Theory', *American Economic Review*, Vol. 73 (March).

De Bandt, J. (1989) *Etude de Cas par Pays Senegal*, Working Paper no. 6, Regional Workshop on Structural Adjustment and the Industrial Sector in Africa (UNIDO, Vienna).

Donge, J.K. van (1994) 'The Continuing Trial of Development Economics: Policies, Prices and Output in Tazanian Agriculture', *Journal of International Development*, Vol. 6, No. 2, pp. 157–84.

Doornbos, M. (1991) 'Staatsvorming Onder Toezicht: De Zorg Om "Governance"', Paper for NSAV-study seminar on Staatvorming, Utrecht.

Dornbusch, R. and F.L.C.H. Helmers (1988) *The Open Economy: tools for policy-makers in developing countries* (Oxford University Press, Oxford).

EC (1991) *Annual Report on the Textile and Clothing Industry* (Brussels).

EC (1990) *Jaarlijks Verslag over de Toestand in de Textiel – en Kledingindustrie* (Brussels).

EC (1988) *Verslag over de Toestand in de Textiel – en Kledingindustrie* (Brussels).

Eichner, A.S. (ed.) (1978) *A Guide to Post-Keynesian Economics* (Sharpe Inc., New York).

Ellison, C. and G. Gereffi (1990) 'Explaining Strategies and Patterns of Industrial Development', *Manufacturing Miracles*, G. Gereffi and D.L. Wyman (Princeton University Press, Princeton, NJ).

Egan, M.L. and A. Mody (1992) 'Buyer-Seller Links in Export Development', *World Development*, Vol. 20, No. 3.

Evans, H.D. (1990) 'Outward Orientation: An Assessment', *Export Promotion Strategies: Theory and Evidence from Developing Countries*, C. Milner (ed.) (Harvester/Wheatsheaf, New York).

Evans, P.B. (1989) 'Predatory, Developmental, and Other Apparatuses: A Comparative Political Economy Perspective on the Third World State', *Sociological Forum*, Vol. 4, No. 4.

Fama, E. (1980) 'Agency Problems and the Theory of the Firm', *Journal of Political Economy*, Vol. 88, pp. 288–307.

Farrell, M.J. (1957) 'The Measurement of Productive Efficiency', *Journal of the Royal Statistical Society*, Series A, 120, Part 3.

Finnerty, A. (1991a) *Textiles and Clothing in South East Asia* (The Economist Intelligence Unit, London).

Finnerty, A. (1991b) 'Profile of the Belgian Textile and Clothing Industry', *Textile Outlook International*, March 1991.

Fischer, S. (1988) 'Recent Developments in Macroeconomics', *Economic Journal*, Vol. 98, No. 391.

Fitzpatrick, J. and M. Montague (1990) 'Textiles and Clothing in Spain: Facing the EC Challenge', *Textile Outlook International*, September 1990.

Førsund, F.R. and L. Hjalmarson (1979) 'Generalized Farrel Measures of Inefficiencies', *Economic Journal*, Vol. 89, No. 354.

Freyhold, M. von (1980) 'The Post-Colonial State and Its Tanzanian Version: Contribution to a Debate', *The State in Tanzania* (H. Othman, Dar es Salaam University Press, Dar es Salaam).

Gabszewicz, J.J. (1990) 'The Stability of Collusive Agreements: Some Recent Theoretical Developments', *Industrial Structure in the New Industrial Economics*, G. Bonanno and D. Brandolini (eds) (Clarendon Press, Oxford).

Gereffi, G. and D.L. Wyman (1990) *Manufacturing Miracles* (Princeton University Press, Princeton, NJ).

Gerschenkron A. (1962) *Economic Backwardness in Historical Perspective* (Harvard University Press, Cambridge, MA).

Gillis, M., D.H. Perkins, M. Roemer, and D.S. Snodgrass (1987) *Economics of Development*, (W.W. Norton & Co., New York).

Gorp, P.J.M. van and A.J.G.M. Hombergen (1972) *Textielwaren* (Wolters-Noordhoff, Groningen, 24th print).

Green, A. and D. Mayes (1991) 'Technical Inefficiencies in Manufacturing Industries', *The Economic Journal*, Vol. 101, No. 406.

Green, R.H. (1987) *Stabilization and Adjustment Policies and Programmes: Ghana, Country Case Study 1* (WIDER Publications, Helsinki).

Green, R.H. (1982) 'Industrialization in Africa', *Industry and Accumulation in Africa*, M. Fransman (ed.) (Heinemann, London).

Green, R.H., D.G. Rwegasira and B. Van Arkadie (1980) *Economic Shocks and National Policy Making: Tanzania in the 1970s* (Institute of Social Studies, The Hague).

Grosh, B. (1990) 'Public, Quasi-Public and Private Firms in Kenya: The Surprising Case of a Cliché Gone Astray', *Development Policy Review*, Vol. 8, No. 1.

Grosskopf, S. (1986) 'The Role of Reference Technology in Measuring Productive Efficiency', *The Economic Journal*, Vol. 96, No. 382.

Hamilton, C. (1989) 'The Irrelevance of Economic Liberalization in the Third World', *World Development*, Vol. 17, No. 10.

Hargreaves Heap, S. (1989) *Rationality in Economics* (Basil Blackwell, Oxford).

Haynes, J. (1989) 'Ghana: indebtedness, recovery and the IMF 1977–87' *The African Debt crisis*, W.P. Trevor and S.P. Riley (eds) (Routledge, London).

Heald, D. (1990) 'The relevance of privatization to developing countries', *Public Administration and Development*, Vol. 10, No. 1.

Hecox, W.E. (1988) 'Structural Adjustment, Donor Conditionality and Industrialization in Kenya', *Industrialization in Kenya: In Search of a Strategy*, P. Coughlin and G.K. Ikiara (eds) (James Currey, London).

Helleiner, G.K. (1990) 'Trade Strategy in Medium-Term Adjustment', *World Development*, Vol. 18, No. 6.

Herbst, J. (1990) 'The Structural Adjustment of Politics in Africa', *World Development*, Vol. 18, No. 7.

Hoeven, R. van der and J. Vandemoortele (1987) 'Kenya', *Wider Country Study on Stabilization and Adjustment Policies and Programmes* (World Institute for Development Economics Research, Helsinki).

Hoffman, K. (1989) 'Technological and Organizational Change in the Global Textile-Clothing Industry. Implications for Industrial Policy in Developing Countries', Chapter 3, *New Technologies and Global Industrialization* (UNIDO, Vienna, limited distribution).

Holmstrom, B.R. and J. Tirole (1989) 'The Theory of the Firm', *Handbook of Industrial Organization*, Vol. 1 (North Holland, Amsterdam).

Horn, M.J. (1988) 'The Political Economy of Public Administration', unpublished PhD Thesis, Harvard University, Cambridge, MA.

Hutchful, E. (1989) 'From Revolution to Monetarism in Ghana', *Structural Adjustment in Africa*, B.K. Campbell and J. Loxley (eds) (Macmillan, Basingstoke).

Hutti, E.K. (1990) 'Quick Response', *New Challenges for the European Textile Industry*, International Textile Manufacturing, Vol. 13/1990, pp. 38–42 (International Textile Manufacturers Federation, Zurich).

Hyden, G. (1982) *No Shortcuts to Progress* (Heinemann, London).

Ikiara, G.K. (1989) 'Kenya's Participation in Regional and Global Trade Arrangements', *Developing Countries and the Global Trading System*, Vol. 2, J. Whalley (ed.) (Macmillan, Basingstoke).

IMF (1991) *International Financial Statistics*, Vol. 44, No. 1 (International Monetary Fund, Washington, DC).

IMF (1990) *International Financial Statistics*, Vol. 43, No. 1 (International Monetary Fund, Washington, DC).

IMF (1980) *Annual Report 1980* (Washington, DC).

Irvin, G. (1990) *Macro and Industrial Policy: Notes on a Research Agenda*, Report produced for the Institute of Policy Studies, Colombo.

Irvin, G. (1978) *Modern Cost-Benefit Methods* (Macmillan, Basingstoke).

James, J. (ed.) (1989) *The Technological Behaviour of Public Enterprises in Developing Countries* (Routledge, London).

Jenkins, R. (1991) 'The Political Economy of Industrialization: A Comparison of Latin American and East Asian Newly Industrializing Countries', *Development and Change*, Vol. 22, No. 2.

Jones, J.V.S. (1981) *Resources and Industry in Tanzania* (Tanzania Publishing House, Dar es Salaam).

Jones, L.P. (1975) *Public Enterprise and Economic Development: The Korean Case* (University Press of Hawaii, Honolulu, HI).

Kahler, M. and J. Odell (1989) 'Developing Country Coalition-Building and International Trade Negotiations', *Developing Countries and the Global Trading System*, Vol. 1, J. Whalley (ed.) (Macmillan, Basingstoke).

Kapinga, W.B.L. (1985) 'State Control of the Working Class through Labour Legislation', *The State and the Working People in Tanzania*, I.G. Shivji (Codesria, Dakar).

Kaplinsky, R. (1984) *Third World Industrialization in the 1980s: Open Economies in a Closing World* (Frank Cass, London).

Karmiloff, I. (1990) 'Cameroon', *Manufacturing Africa*, R.C. Riddell (ed.) (James Currey, London).

Kenyon, P. (1978) 'Pricing', *A Guide to Post-Keynesian Economics*, A.S. Eichner (ed.) (Sharpe Inc., New York).

Khan, H.A. (1985) 'Technology Choice in the Energy and Textile Sectors in the Republic of Korea', *Technology and Employment in Industry*, A.S. Bhalla (ed.), 3rd edn (ILO, Geneva).

Khan, M.S., P. Montiel, and N.U. Haque (1990) 'Adjustment with Growth: Relating the Analytical Approaches of the IMF and the World Bank', *Journal of Development Economics*, Vol. 32, No. 1.

Khanna, R. (1989) 'Market Sharing Under Multifibre Arrangement: Consequences of Non-Tariff Barriers in the Textiles Trade', paper presented at the Academy of International Business, Singapore.

Khatun, R. and F.S. Begum (1990) 'Garments Industries in Bangladesh: Achievements and Possibilities', *Development Review*, Vol. 2, No. 2.

Kilby, P. (1983) 'An Entrepreneurial Problem', *The American Economic Review*, Vol. 73, No. 2.

Killick, T. (1990) *A Reaction Too Far, Economic Theory and the Role of the State in Developing Countries* (Overseas Development Institute, London).

Killick, T. (1989) 'Industrialization Policies in Ghana', *Industrial Adjustment in Sub-Saharan Africa*, G.M. Meier and W.F. Steel (eds) (Oxford University Press, Oxford).

Killick, T., and S. Commander (1988) 'State Divesture as a Policy Instrument in Developing Countries', *World Development*, Vol. 16, No. 12.

Kirkpatrick, C.H., N. Lee and F.I. Nixson (1984) *Industrial Structure and Policy in Less Developed Countries* (George Allen & Unwin, London).

Kopp, R.J. (1981) 'The Measurement of Productive Efficiency: A Reconsideration', *The Quarterly Journal of Economics*, Vol. 95, No. 3.

Kornai, J. (1979) 'Resource-constrained Versus Demand-constrained Systems', *Econometrica*, Vol. 47, No. 4.

Kregel, J.A. (1978) 'Income Distribution', *A Guide to Post-Keynesian Economics*, A.S. Eichner (ed.) (Sharpe Inc., New York).

Krueger, A.O. (1972) 'Evaluating Restrictionist Trade Regimes: Theory and Measurement', *Journal of Political Economy*, Vol. 80, No. 1.

Kunz, F.A. (1991) 'Liberalization in Africa–Some Preliminary Reflections', *African Affairs*, Vol. 90, No. 359.

Laidlaw, R.G. (1990) 'Quick Response', *New Challenges for the European Textile Industry*, International Textile Manufacturing, Vol. 13/1990, pp. 34–37 (International Textile Manufacturers Federation, Zurich).

Laird, S. and A. Yeats (1990) 'Trends in Nontariff Barriers of Developed Countries', *Weltwirtschaftliches Archiv*, Vol. 126, No. 2.

Laird, S. and J. Nogues (1989) 'Trade Policies and the Highly Indebted Countries', *The World Bank Economic Review*, Vol. 3, No. 2.

Lal, D. (1989a) 'A Simple Framework for Analysing Various Real Aspects of Stabilisation and Structural Adjustment Policies', *Journal of Development Studies*, Vol. 25, No. 3.

Lal, D. (1989b) 'The Political Economy of Industrialization in Primary Product Exporting Economies: Some Cautionary Tales', *The Balance between Industry and Agriculture in Economic Development*, Vol. 5, N. Islam (ed.) (St. Martin's Press, New York).

Lal, D. (1987) 'The Political Economy of Economic Liberalization', *World Bank Economic Review*, Vol. 1, No. 2.

Lall, S. (1992) 'Technological Capabilities and Industrialization', *World Development*, Vol. 20, No. 2.

Lall, S. (1990) *Building Industrial Competitiveness in Developing Countries* (OECD, Paris).

Leff, N.H. (1979) '"Monopoly Capitalism" and Public Policy in Developing Countries', *Kyklos*, Vol. 32, No. 4.

Leff, N.H. (1978) 'Industrial Organization and Entrepreneurship in the Developing Countries: The Economic Groups', *Economic Development and Cultural Change*, Vol. 26, No. 4.

Leibenstein, H. (1987) *Inside the Firm* (Harvard University Press, Cambridge, MA).

Leibenstein, H. (1976) *Beyond Economic Man* (Harvard University Press, Cambridge, MA).

Leijdekkers, P.K.J. (1990) 'The Future of Textile Printing', *New Challenges for the European Textile Industry*, International Textile Manufacturing, Vol. 13/1990, pp. 43–46 (International Textile Manufacturers Federation, Zurich).

Lindblom, C.E. and D. Cohen (1972) *Usable Knowledge* (Yale University Press, New Haven, CN).

Linder, S.B. (1967) *Trade and Trade Policy for Development* (Pall Mall Press, London).

Linnemann, H. (1992) 'Internationale handel en economische groei in de ontwikkelingslanden', *Research Memorandum*, 1992–28 (Vrije Universiteit, Amsterdam).

Lippman, S.A. and J.J. McCall (1984) 'The Economics of Uncertainty: Selected Topics and Probability Methods', *Handbook of Mathematical Economics Vol. 1*, K.J. Arrow and M.D. Intriligator (North Holland, Amsterdam, second print).

Lipumba, N.H.I. (1989) 'Domestic Supply Constraints versus Market Access: International Trade and Economic Development in Tanzania', *Developing Countries and the Global Trading System*, Vol. 2, J. Whalley (ed.) (Macmillan, Basingstoke).

Lipumba, N.H.I. (1984) 'The Economic Crisis in Tanzania', *Economic Stabilization Policies in Tanzania*, N.H.I. Lipumba, L.A. Msambichaka and S.M. Wangwe (eds) (University of Dar es Salaam, Dar es Salaam).

Little, I.M.D. and J.A. Mirrlees (1974) *Project Appraisal and Planning for Developing Countries* (Basic Books, New York).

Maliyamkono, T.L. and M.S.D. Bagachwa (1990) *The Second Economy in Tanzania* (James Currey, London).

March, J.G. (1988) 'The Business Firm as a Political Coalition', *Decisions and Organizations*, J.G. March (Basil Blackwell, Oxford).

March, J.G. (1978) 'Bounded Rationality, Ambiguity, and the Engineering of Choice', *The Bell Journal of Economics*, Vol. 9, No. 2.

March, J.G. (1966) 'The Power of Power', *Varieties of Political Theory* (Prentice Hall, Englewood Cliffs, NJ).

March, J.G. and H.A. Simon (1958) *Organizations* (John Wiley, New York).

Mark, J. and A. Weston (1989) 'The Havana Charter Experience: Lessons for Developing Countries', *Developing Countries and the Global Trading System*, Vol. 1, J. Whalley (ed.) (Macmillan, Basingstoke).

Marris, R. (1964) *The Economic Theory of 'Managerial' Capitalism* (Macmillan, Basingstoke).

Mazzonis, D., U. Colomba and G. Lanzavecchia (1983) 'Cooperative Organization and Constant Modernization of the Textile Industry at Prato, Italy', *New Frontiers in Technology Application*, E.U. Weizsacker, M.S. Swaminatan and A. Lemma (eds) (Tycooly International Publishing Ltd, Dublin).

Mbelle, A. (1989) 'Industrial (Manufacturing) Performance in the ERP Context in Tanzania', *Tanzania Economic Trends*, Vol. 2, No. 1.

Mbelle, A. (1988) 'Foreign Exchange and Industrial Development: A Study of Tanzania', unpublished PhD thesis, University of Goteborg, Sweden.

Mbelle, A. (1982) 'Capacity Utilization under Foreign Exchange Constraint: The Case of Selected Industrial Linkages in Tanzania', unpublished MA Thesis, University of Dar es Salaam.

Mbelle, A. and T. Sterner (1991) 'Foreign Exchange and Industrial Development: A Frontier Production Function Analysis of Two Tanzanian Industries', *World Development*, Vol. 19, No. 4.

McQueen, M. (1990) 'ACP Export Diversification: the Case of Mauritius', ODI Working Paper 41, Overseas Development Institute, London.

McQueen, M. and C. Stevens (1989) 'Trade Preferences and Lomé IV: Non-traditional ACP Exports to the EC', *Development Policy Review*, Vol. 7, No. 3.

Meier, G.M. (1989) *Leading Issues in Economic Development*, 5th edn (Oxford University Press, Oxford).

Meier, G.M. and W.F. Steel (eds) (1989) *Industrial Adjustment in Sub-Saharan Africa* (Published for the World Bank by Oxford University Press, Oxford).

Meijer, F. (1990) 'Structural Adjustment and Diversification in Zambia', *Development and Change*, Vol. 21, No. 4.

Menako, J.K.A. (1987) 'A Brighter Outlook for Textiles', *Indutech Journal*, Vol. 2, No. 1 (Ministry of Industries, Science and Technology, Accra, Ghana).

Mihyo, P.B. (1994) *Non-Market Controls and the Accountability of Public Enterprises in Tanzania* (Macmillan, Basingstoke).

Mihyo, P.B. (1987) 'Control and Regulation of Public Enterprises in Tanzania', unpublished paper.

Milgrom, P. and J. Roberts (1990) 'New Theories of Predatory Pricing', *Industrial Structure in the New Industrial Economics*, G. Bonanno and D. Brandolini (eds) (Clarendon Press, Oxford).

Milner, C. (ed.) (1990) *Export Promotion Strategies: Theory and Evidence from Developing Countries* (Harvester/Wheatsheaf, New York).

Ministry of Policy Planning and Implementation (1989) *National Accounts of Sri Lanka 1989* (Ministry of Policy Planning and Implementation, Colombo).

Mintzberg, H. (1979) *The Structuring of Organizations* (Prentice-Hall, Englewood Cliffs, NJ).

Mody, A. and D. Wheeler (1990) *Automation and World Competition* (Macmillan, Basingstoke).

Mosley, P. and J. Toye (1988) 'The Design of Structural Adjustment Programmes', *Development Policy Review*, Vol. 6, No. 4.

Mushi, S.S. and H. Kjekshus (1982) *Aid and Development: Some Tanzanian Experiences* (Norwegian Institute of International Affairs, Flekkefjord).

Nabli, M.K. and J.B. Nugent (1989) *The New Institutional Economics and Development* (North Holland, Amsterdam).

National Bank of Commerce (1988) 'Financing of Working Capital of TEXCO Group Companies under ERP: Problems and Prospects', Paper presented at the General Managers Conference 1988, Arusha.

Nayar, B.R. (1990) *The Political Economy of India's Public Sector* (Sangam Books Ltd, London).

Ndulu, B.J. (1986) 'Stabilization and Adjustment Programmes in Tanzania 1978–1985', Unpublished paper, University of Dar es Salaam.

Ndulu, B.J., W.M. Lyakurwa, J.J. Semboja and A.E. Chaligha (1987) *Import Tariff Study*, Ministry of Finance, Economic Affairs and Planning, United Republic of Tanzania, Internal Document.

NEI (1987) 'Commodity Import Support of the Netherlands to Tanzania', Unpublished Report, Netherlands Economic Institute, Rotterdam.

Nelson, R.R. and S.G. Winter (1982) *An Evolutionary Theory of Economic Change* (Harvard University Press, Cambridge, MA).

Ngemera, A.R. (1987) 'Export Retention Schemes', *Trade Currents*, Vol. 1, No. 1, (Board of External Trade, Tanzania, Dar es Salaam).

Niehans, J. (1987) 'Transaction Costs', *The New Palgrave, A Dictionary of Economics*, J. Eatwell, M. Milgate and P. Newman (Macmillan, Basingstoke).

Nijhuis, J.J. (1990) 'Quick Response', *New Challenges for the European Textile Industry*, International Textile Manufacturing, Vol. 13/1990, pp. 30–33 (International Textile Manufacturers Federation, Zurich).

Nyalali, F.L. (1975) *Aspects of Industrial Conflict* (East African Literature Bureau, Dar es Salaam).

Ostrom, V. (1988) 'Cryptoimperialism, Predatory States, and Self-Governance', *Rethinking Institutional Analysis and Development*, V. Ostrom, D. Feeny, and H. Picht (eds) (ICS Press, San Francisco).

Ostrom, V., D. Feeny, and H. Picht (eds) (1988) *Rethinking Institutional Analysis and Development* (ICS Press, San Francisco).

Othman, H. (ed.) (1980) *The State in Tanzania* (Dar es Salaam University Press, Dar es Salaam).

Oyejide, T.A. (1989) 'Resource Exports, Adjustment Problems and Liberalization Prospects in Nigeria', *Developing Countries and the Global Trading System*, Vol. 2, J. Whalley (ed.) (Macmillan, Basingstoke).

Pack, H. (1988) 'Industrialization and Trade', *Handbook of Development Economics*, Vol. 1, H. Chenery and T.N. Srinivasan (North Holland, Amsterdam).

Pack, H. (1987) *Productivity, Technology and Industrial Development* (Oxford University Press, Oxford).

Pack, H. (1985) 'The Choice of Technique and Employment in the Textile Industry', in *Technology and Employment in Industry*, A.S. Bhalla (ed.), 3rd edn (ILO, Geneva).

Page, J.M. Jr (1980) 'Technical Efficiency and Economic Performance: Some Evidence from Ghana', *Oxford Economic Papers* (New Series) Vol. 32, No. 2.

Pakkiri, L., P. Robinson, and C. Stoneman (1988) 'Industry and Planning in a Small Country', *Zimbabwe's Prospects*, C. Stoneman (ed.) (Macmillan, Basingstoke).

Perkins, F.C. (1983) 'Technology Choice, Industrialization and Development Experiences in Tanzania', *Journal of Development Studies*, Vol. 19, No. 2.

Perry, M.K. (1989) 'Vertical Integration: Determinants and Effects', *Handbook of Industrial Organization*, Vol. I, R. Schmalensee and R.D. Willig (eds) (Elsevier Science Publishers, Amsterdam).

Picton, J. and J. Mack (1989) *African Textiles* (British Museum Publications Ltd, London), 2nd edn.

Polanyi, M. (1962) *Personal Knowledge: Towards a Post-Critical Philosophy* (Harper Torchbooks, New York).

Porter, M.E. (1990) *The Competitive Advantage of Nations* (Macmillan, Basingstoke).

Ramboer, W. (1985) 'The Restructuring of the Textile Industry in Belgium – A Success Story', UNIDO, Vienna, unpublished report.

Reserve Bank of Zimbabwe (1990) *Quarterly Economic and Statistical Review Mar/Jun 1990* (Reserve Bank of Zimbabwe, Harare).

Riddell, R.C. (1990) 'A Forgotten Dimension? The Manufacturing Sector in Africa Development', *Development Policy Review*, Vol. 8, No. 1, pp. 5–27.

Riddell, R.C. (ed.) (1990a) *Manufacturing Africa* (James Currey, London).

Riddell, R.C. (1990b) 'Zimbabwe', *Manufacturing Africa*, R.C. Riddell (ed.) (James Currey, London).

Riddell R.C. (1990c) 'ACP Export Diversification: the Case of Zimbabwe', ODI Working Paper 38, Overseas Development Institute, London.

Riddell, W. and E. Taylor (1989) 'Country Case Study: Ghana', *Working Paper No. 2*, Paper presented at the Regional Workshop on Strategic Management of the Adjustment Process in the Industrial Sector in Africa, UNIDO, Vienna.

Robinson, B. (1990) 'Collaborative Sector Analysis: A Foreign Assistance Technique for Improving LDC Sector Management', *World Development*, Vol. 18, No. 7.

Rodrik, D. (1990) 'How Should Structural Adjustment Programmes Be Designed?', *World Development*, Vol. 18, No. 7.

Roemer, M., G.M. Tidrick and D. Williams (1975) 'The Range of Strategic Choice in Tanzanian Industry', Development Discussion Paper no.7, Harvard Institute for International Development, Cambridge, MA.

Rogerson, C.M. (1993) 'Export-Processing Industrialisation in Mauritius: The Lessons of Success', *Development Southern Africa*, Vol. 10, No. 2.

Rweyemamu, J. (1973) *Underdevelopment and Industrialization in Tanzania* (Oxford University Press, Oxford).

Sah, R.K. (1991) 'Fallibility in Human Organizations and Political Systems', *Journal of Economic Perspectives*, Vol. 5, No. 2.

Sampson, G.P. (1989) 'NTBs Facing Developing Country Exports', *Developing Countries and the Global Trading System*, Vol. 1, J. Whalley (ed.) (Macmillan, Basingstoke).

Sappington, D.E.M. (1991) 'Incentives in Principal–Agent Relationships', *Journal of Economic Perspectives*, Vol. 5, No. 2.

Saul, J.S. (1980) 'The State in Post-Colonial Societies: Tanzania', *The State in Tanzania*, H. Othman (Dar es Salaam University Press, Dar es Salaam).

Sawyer, M.C. (1985) *The Economics of Industries and Firms* (Croom Helm, London), 2nd edn.

Schaffer, B.B. (1984) 'Towards Responsibility: Public Policy in Concept and Practice', *Room for Manoeuvre* (Fairleigh Dickinson University Press, Rutherford, NJ).

Schmalensee, R. (1990) 'Empirical Studies of Rivalrous Behaviour', *Industrial Structure in the New Industrial Economics*, G. Bonanno and D. Brandolini (eds) (Clarendon Press, Oxford).

Self, P. (1985) *Political Theories of Modern Government* (George Allen & Unwin, London).

Shapiro, H. and L. Taylor (1990) 'The State and Industrial Strategy', *World Development*, Vol. 18, No. 6.

Sharpley, J. and S. Lewis (1990) 'Kenya', *Manufacturing Africa*, R.C. Riddell (ed.) (James Currey, London).

Shaw, T.M. (1991) 'Reformism, Revisionism, and Radicalism in the African Political Economy During the 1990s', *Journal of Modern African Studies*, Vol. 29, No. 2.

Sher, W. and R. Pinola (1981) *Microeconomic Theory* (Elsevier North Holland, New York).

Shivji, I.G. (1982) 'The State in the Dominated Social Formations of Africa: Some Theoretical Issues', *Debate on Class, State & Imperialism*, Y. Tandon (ed.) (Tanzania Publishing House, Dar es Salaam).

Simon, H.A. (1991) 'Organizations and Markets', *Journal of Economic Perspectives*, Vol. 5, No. 2.

Skarstein, R. and S.M. Wangwe (1986) *Industrial Development in Tanzania: Some Critical Issues* (Tanzania Publishing House, Dar es Salaam).

Sobhan, R. (1979) 'Public Enterprises and the Nature of the State', *Development and Change*, Vol. 10, No. 1.

Södersten, B. (1980) *International Economics*, 2nd edn (Macmillan, Basingstoke).

Sri Lanka Government (1990a) *Annual Report 1989 Central Bank of Sri Lanka* (Government of Sri Lanka, Colombo).

Sri Lanka Government (1990b) *National Accounts of Sri Lanka 1989* (Department of Census and Statistics, Ministry of Policy Planning and Implementation, Government of Sri Lanka, Colombo).

Srinivasan, T.N. (1985) 'Neoclassical Political Economy, the State, and Economic Development', *Asian Development Review*, Vol. 3, No. 2.

Srinivasan, T.N. and J.N. Bhagwati (1978) 'Shadow Prices for Project Selection in the Presence of Distortions: Effective Rates of Protection and Domestic Resource Costs', *Journal of Political Economy*, Vol. 86, No. 1.

Stein, H. (1992) 'Deindustrialization, Adjustment, the World Bank and the IMF in Africa', *World Development*, Vol. 20, No. 1.

Stevens, C. (1990) 'ACP Export Diversification: Jamaica, Kenya and Ethiopia', ODI Working Paper 40, Overseas Development Institute, London.

Steward, F., H. Thomas and T. de Wilde (1990) *The Other Policy: The Influence of Policies on Technology Choice and Small Enterprise Development* (Intermediate Technology Publications, London).

Stiglitz, J.E. (1991a) 'Symposium on Organizations and Economics', *Journal of Economic Perspectives*, Vol. 5, No. 2.

Stiglitz, J.E. (1991b) 'Another Century of Economic Science', *Economic Journal*, Vol. 101, No. 404.

Stiles, K.W. (1990) 'IMF Conditionality: Coercion or Compromise?', *World Development*, Vol. 18, No. 7.

Stoneman, C. (1989) 'The World Bank and the IMF in Zimbabwe', *Structural Adjustment in Africa*, B. Campbell and J. Loxley (eds) (Macmillan, Basingstoke).

Streeten, P. (1987) 'Structural Adjustment: A Survey of the Issues and Options', *World Development*, Vol. 15, No. 12.

Sutcliffe, R.B. (1971) *Industry and Underdevelopment* (Addison-Wesley, London).

Sutton, J. (1990) 'Endogenous Sunk Costs and Industrial Structure', *Industrial Structure in the New Industrial Economics*, G. Bonanno and D. Brandolini (eds) (Clarendon Press, Oxford).

Sweezy, P. (1939) 'Demand Under Conditions of Oligopoly', *Journal of Political Economy*, Vol. 47, pp. 568–573.

Tanzanian Economic Trends (TET) (1989), Vol. 2, No. 1. (Economic Research Bureau, University of Dar es Salaam, Dar es Salaam).

Tanzanian Economic Trends (1988), Vol. 1, No. 3. (Economic Research Bureau, University of Dar es Salaam, Dar es Salaam).

TAPO (1989) *Problems of Parastatals and Proposals for Structural Reforms* (Tanzania Association of Parastatal Organizations, Dar es Salaam).

Taylor, L. (1988) *Varieties of Stabilization Experience: Towards Sensible Macroeconomics in the Third World* (Clarendon Press, Oxford).

TEXCO (1988) 'Participation of TEXCO in the Trade Liberalization Policy: a Review of TEXCO Group Companies Performance during the Years 1986/87 and 1987/88', Paper presented at the General Managers Conference 1988, Arusha.

TEXCO (1986) *Corporate Strategic Plan 1986–1990* (TEXCO, Dar es Salaam).

TEXCO (1974–88) *Annual Report and Accounts*, 1974–88.

Torre, J. de la (1984) *Clothing-industry Adjustment in Developed Countries* (Travor Hobbs, London).

Trivedi, P., and V. Gopal (1990) 'Memorandum of Understanding and Other Performance Improvement Systems – A Comparison', *Public Enterprise*, Vol. 10, Nos 3–4.

UNIDO (1990a) *Industry and Development, Global Report 1990/91* (UNIDO, Vienna).

UNIDO (1990b) 'The Regeneration of Kenyan Manufacturing Industry with Emphasis on Selected Industries', *Special Reports on Industrial Rehabilitation*, No. 6 (UNIDO, Vienna).

UNIDO (1989a) *Introductory Report on Strategic Management of the Adjustment Process in the Industrial Sector in Africa* (UNIDO, Vienna).

UNIDO (1989b) *Industry and Development, Global Report 1989/90* (UNIDO, Vienna).

UNIDO (1989c) *New Technologies and Global Industrialization* (UNIDO, Vienna) limited distribution.

UNIDO (1988) *Industrial Restructuring Policies in Developing Asian Countries with Particular Attention to the Textile and Garment Industry* (UNIDO, Vienna) limited distribution.

UNIDO (1987) *Textile Policy Issues for Developing Countries* (UNIDO, Vienna) limited distribution.

United Nations (1990) *Demographic Yearbook 1988* (United Nations, New York).

United Nations (1989) *1987 International Trade Statistics Yearbook*, Vols One and Two (United Nations, New York).

United Republic of Tanzania (URT) *Economic Surveys* (various issues) (Government Printer, Dar es Salaam).

United Republic of Tanzania (1990a) *Economic Survey 1989* (Government Printer, Dar es Salaam).

United Republic of Tanzania (1990b) *Economic Recovery Programme II* (Government Printer, Dar es Salaam).

United Republic of Tanzania (1990c) *National Investment Promotion Policy* (Government Printer, Dar es Salaam).

United Republic of Tanzania (1990d) *Industrial Rehabilitation Study of the Textile Subsector of Tanzania*, Ministry of Industries and Trade (Government Printer, Dar es Salaam).

United Republic of Tanzania (1989) *Task Force Report on Tanzania Leather Associated Industries and its Subsidiaries* (Government Printer, Dar es Salaam).

United Republic of Tanzania (1988) *Economic Survey 1987* (Government Printer, Dar es Salaam).

United Republic of Tanzania (1986) *Economic Recovery Programme* (Government Printer, Dar es Salaam).

United Republic of Tanzania (1982a) *The National Economic Survival Programme* (Government Printer, Dar es Salaam).

United Republic of Tanzania (1982b) *Structural Adjustment Programme for Tanzania* (Government Printer, Dar es Salaam).

United Republic of Tanzania (1982c) *Implementation Schedule for the Structural Adjustment Programme* (Government Printer, Dar es Salaam).

Valk, P. de (1990) 'State, decentralization, and participation', in *Decentralizing for Participatory Planning?*, de Valk and Wekwete (eds) (Gower, Aldershot).

Valk, P. de (1992) 'A General Framework for Evaluating the Performance of Textile Enterprises in LDCs, with an Application to Tanzania under Structural Adjustment', PhD dissertation, – University of Amsterdam.

Valk, P. de and A. Mbelle (1990) *Textile Industry under Structural Adjustment in Tanzania (1980–1988)* (Institute of Social Studies, The Hague) limited distribution.

Valk, P. de and B.M.C. Sibanda (1986) 'About Pigs?: Decisions, Outcomes, and Project Planning', *Public Administration and Development*, Vol. 6, No. 4.

Vernon, R. (1966) 'International Investment and International Trade in the Product Cycle', *Quarterly Journal of Economics*, Vol. 80, pp. 190–207.

Wangwe, S.M. (1984) 'Economic Stabilization Policies in the Industrial Sector', in N.G.H. Libumba, L.A. Msambichaka, and S.M. Wangwe (eds), *Economic Stabilization Policies in Tanzania* (University of Dar es Salaam, Dar es Salaam).

Wangwe, S.M. (1979) 'Capacity Utilization and Capacity Creation in Manufacturing in Tanzania with Special Reference to the Engineering Sector', Unpublished Ph.D. Thesis, University of Dar es Salaam.

Waterson, M. (1989) 'Models of Product Differentiation', *Bulletin of Economic Research*, Vol. 41, No. 1.

Wells, L.T. (1975) 'Economic Man and Engineering Man', *The Choice of Technology in Developing Countries*, C.T. Timmer, J.W. Woodward Thomas, L.T. Wells and D. Morawetz (Centre for International Affairs, Harvard University, Cambridge MA).

Whalley, J. (ed.) (1989) *Developing Countries and the Global Trading System*, Vol. 1 (Macmillan, Basingstoke).

Williamson, O.J. (1989) 'Transaction Cost Economics', *Handbook of Industrial Organization*, Vol. 1 (North Holland, Amsterdam).

Williamson, O.J. (1975) *Markets and Hierarchies* (Free Press, New York).

Williamson, O.J. (1963) 'A Model of Rational Managerial Behavior', *Behavioral Theory of the Firm*, R.M. Cyert and J.G. March (Prentice-Hall, Englewood Cliffs).

Winsemius, P. (1990) 'Quick Response', *New Challenges for the European Textile Industry*, International Textile Manufacturing, Vol. 13/1990, pp. 30–33 (International Textile Manufacturers Federation, Zurich).

Wiseman, J. (1991) 'The Black Box', *Economic Journal*, Vol. 101, No. 1.

Wood, B. (1988) 'Trade Union Organization and the Working Class', *Zimbabwe's Prospects*, C. Stoneman (ed.) (Macmillan, Basingstoke).

World Bank (1991) *Tanzania Economic Report: Towards Sustainable Development in the 1990s* (World Bank, Washington, DC).

World Bank (1989a) *Sub-Saharan Africa: From Crisis to Sustainable Growth* (World Bank, Washington, DC).

World Bank/UNDP (1989b) *Africa's Adjustment and Growth: Trends and Perspectives in the 1980s* (Washington, DC).

World Bank (1988) *Parastatals in Tanzania, Towards a Reform Programme* (World Bank, Washington, DC).

World Bank (1987a) *World Development Report 1987* (Oxford University Press, Oxford).

World Bank (1987b) *Zimbabwe: An Industrial Sector Memorandum* (World Bank, Washington, DC).

World Bank (1987c) *Tanzania: An Agenda for Industrial Recovery*, Vol. I and II (World Bank, Washington, DC).

World Bank (1986) *Report to the Consultative Group for Tanzania on the Government's Economic Recovery Programme* (World Bank, Washington, DC).

World Bank (1984) *Tanzania: Country Economic Memorandum* (World Bank, Washington, DC).

Index